# Cloud Computing and Software Services

## Theory and Techniques

# Cloud Computing and Software Services

## Theory and Techniques

Edited by
Syed A. Ahson • Mohammad Ilyas

CRC Press
Taylor & Francis Group
Boca Raton   London   New York

CRC Press is an imprint of the
Taylor & Francis Group, an **informa** business
AN AUERBACH BOOK

CRC Press
Taylor & Francis Group
6000 Broken Sound Parkway NW, Suite 300
Boca Raton, FL 33487-2742

---

**Library of Congress Cataloging-in-Publication Data**

---

Cloud computing and software services : theory and techniques / editors, Syed A. Ahson, Mohammad Ilyas.
    p. cm.
  Includes bibliographical references and index.
  ISBN 978-1-4398-0315-8 (hardcover : alk. paper)
   1. Web services. 2. Cloud computing. I. Ahson, Syed. II. Ilyas, Mohammad, 1953- III. Title.

TK5105.88813.C58 2011
004.67'8--dc22
                                              2010020562

---

**Visit the Taylor & Francis Web site at**
**http://www.taylorandfrancis.com**

**and the CRC Press Web site at**
**http://www.crcpress.com**

# Contents

# Preface

Cloud computing has gained significant traction in recent years. The proliferation of networked devices, Internet services, and simulations has resulted in large volumes of data being produced. This, in turn, has fueled the need to process and store vast amounts of data. These data volumes cannot be processed by a single computer or a small cluster of computers. Furthermore, in most cases, these data can be processed in a pleasingly parallel fashion. The result has been the aggregation of a large number of commodity hardware components in vast data centers. Among the forces that have driven the need for cloud computing are falling hardware costs and burgeoning data volumes. The ability to procure cheaper, more powerful CPUs coupled with improvements in the quality and capacity of networks have made it possible to assemble clusters at increasingly attractive prices. By facilitating access to an elastic (meaning the available resource pool that can expand or contract over time) set of resources, cloud computing has demonstrable applicability to a wide range of problems in several domains. Among the many applications that benefit from cloud computing and cloud technologies, the data/compute-intensive applications are the most important. The deluge of data and the highly compute-intensive applications found in many domains, such as particle physics, biology, chemistry, finance, and information retrieval, mandate the use of large computing infrastructures and parallel processing to achieve considerable performance gains in analyzing data. The addition of cloud technologies creates new trends in performing parallel computing.

The introduction of commercial cloud infrastructure services has allowed users to provision compute clusters fairly easily and quickly by paying a monetary value for the duration of their usages of the resources. The provisioning of resources happens in minutes, as opposed to hours and days required in the case of traditional queue-based job-scheduling systems. In addition, the use of such virtualized resources allows the user to completely customize the virtual machine images and use them with administrative privileges, another feature that is hard to achieve with traditional infrastructures. Appealing features within cloud computing include access to a vast number of computational resources and inherent resilience to failures. The latter feature arises because in cloud computing the focus of execution is not a specific, well-known resource but rather the best available one. The availability of open-source cloud infrastructure software and open-source virtualization software stacks allows organizations to build private clouds to improve the resource utilization of the available computation facilities. The possibility of dynamically provisioning additional resources by leasing from commercial cloud infrastructures makes the use of private clouds more promising. Another characteristic of a lot of programs that have been written for cloud computing is that they tend to be stateless. Thus, when failures do take place, the appropriate computations are simply relaunched with the corresponding datasets.

This book provides technical information about all aspects of cloud computing, from basic concepts to research grade material including future directions. It captures the current state of cloud computing and serves as a comprehensive source of reference material on this subject. It consists of 17 chapters authored by 50 experts from around the world. The targeted audience include designers and/or planners for cloud computing systems, researchers (faculty members and graduate students), and those who would like to learn about this field.

The book is expected to have the following specific salient features:

■ To serve as a single comprehensive source of information and as reference material on cloud computing
■ To deal with an important and timely topic of emerging technology of today, tomorrow, and beyond
■ To present accurate, up-to-date information on a broad range of topics related to cloud computing
■ To present the material authored by the experts in the field
■ To present the information in an organized and well-structured manner

Although, technically, the book is not a textbook, it can certainly be used as a textbook for graduate courses and research-oriented courses that deal with cloud computing. Any comments from the readers will be highly appreciated.

Many people have contributed to this book in their own unique ways. First and foremost, we would like to express our immense gratitude to the group of highly talented and skilled researchers who have contributed 17 chapters to this book. All of them have been extremely cooperative and professional. It has also been a pleasure to work with Rich O'Hanley and Jessica Vakili of CRC Press; we are extremely grateful to them for their support and professionalism. Special thanks are also due to our families who have extended their unconditional love and support throughout this project.

**Syed Ahson**
*Seattle, Washington*

**Mohammad Ilyas**
*Boca Raton, Florida*

# Editors

**Syed Ahson** is a senior software design engineer at Microsoft. As part of the Mobile Voice and Partner Services group, he is currently engaged in research on new end-to-end mobile services and applications. Before joining Microsoft, Syed was a senior staff software engineer at Motorola, where he contributed significantly in leading roles toward the creation of several iDEN, CDMA, and GSM cellular phones. He has extensive experience with wireless data protocols, wireless data applications, and cellular telephony protocols. Before joining Motorola, Syed worked as a senior software design engineer at NetSpeak Corporation (now part of Net2Phone), a pioneer in VoIP telephony software.

Syed has published more than 10 books on emerging technologies such as *Cloud Computing, Mobile Web 2.0*, and *Service Delivery Platforms*. His recent books include *Cloud Computing and Software Services: Theory and Techniques* and *Mobile Web 2.0: Developing and Delivering Services to Mobile Phones*. He has authored several research articles and teaches computer engineering courses as adjunct faculty at Florida Atlantic University, Boca Raton, where he introduced a course on Smartphone technology and applications. Syed received his MS in computer engineering from Florida Atlantic University in July 1998, and his BSc in electrical engineering from Aligarh University, India, in 1995.

**Dr. Mohammad Ilyas** is an associate dean for research and industry relations and professor of computer science and engineering in the College of Engineering and Computer Science at Florida Atlantic University, Boca Raton, Florida. He is also currently serving as interim chair of the Department of Mechanical and Ocean Engineering. He received his BSc in electrical engineering from the University of Engineering and Technology, Lahore, Pakistan, in 1976. From March 1977 to September 1978, he worked for the Water and Power Development Authority, Lahore, Pakistan. In 1978, he was awarded a scholarship for his graduate studies and he received his MS in electrical and electronic engineering in June 1980 from Shiraz University, Shiraz, Iran. In September 1980, he joined the doctoral program at Queen's University in Kingston, Ontario, Canada. He completed his PhD in 1983. His doctoral research was about switching and flow control techniques in computer communication networks. Since September 1983, he has been with the College of Engineering and Computer Science at Florida Atlantic University. From 1994 to 2000, he was chair of the Department of Computer Science and Engineering. From July 2004 to September 2005, he served as interim associate vice president for research and graduate studies. During the 1993–1994 academic year, he was on sabbatical leave with the Department of Computer Engineering, King Saud University, Riyadh, Saudi Arabia.

Dr. Ilyas has conducted successful research in various areas, including traffic management and congestion control in broadband/high-speed communication networks, traffic characterization, wireless communication networks, performance modeling, and simulation. He has published 1 book, 16 handbooks, and over 160 research articles. He has also supervised 11 PhD dissertations and more than 38 MS theses to completion. He has been a consultant to several national and international organizations. Dr. Ilyas is an active participant in several IEEE technical committees and activities and is a senior member of IEEE and a member of ASEE.

# Contributors

**Jonathan Appavoo**
Department of Computer Science
Boston University
Boston, Massachusetts

and

IBM Thomas J. Watson Research
  Center
Yorktown Heights, New York

**Chaitan Baru**
San Diego Supercomputer Center
University of California at San Diego
La Jolla, California

**Scott Beason**
Community Grids Laboratory
Pervasive Technology Institute
Indiana University
Bloomington, Indiana

**Raphael Bolze**
Information Sciences Institute
University of Southern California
Marina del Rey, California

**Maria Butrico**
IBM Thomas J. Watson Research
  Center
Yorktown Heights, New York

**Jinjun Chen**
Centre for Complex Software Systems
  and Services
Faculty of Information and
  Communication Technologies
Swinburne University of Technology
Melbourne, Victoria, Australia

**Xian Chen**
Department of Computing Science
University of Alberta
Edmonton, Alberta, Canada

**Jong Youl Choi**
School of Informatics and Computing
Indiana University
Bloomington, Indiana

**Ciprian Craciun**
Computer Science Department
West University of Timisoara

and

Research Institute e-Austria Timisoara
Timisoara, Romania

**Dilma M. Da Silva**
IBM Thomas J. Watson Research
  Center
Yorktown Heights, New York

**Ewa Deelman**
Information Sciences Institute
University of Southern California
Marina del Rey, California

**Kemal Delic**
Institut d'Administration des
    Entreprises
Université Pierre-Mendès-France
Grenoble, France

**Jack Dongarra**
Department of Electrical Engineering
    and Computer Science
University of Tennessee
Knoxville, Tennessee

and

Computer Science and Mathematics
    Division
Oak Ridge National Laboratory
Oak Ridge, Tennessee

**Jaliya Ekanayake**
Community Grids Laboratory
Pervasive Technology Institute
Indiana University

and

School of Informatics and Computing
Indiana University
Bloomington, Indiana

**Geoffrey Fox**
Community Grids Laboratory
Pervasive Technology Institute
Indiana University

and

School of Informatics and Computing
Indiana University
Bloomington, Indiana

**Marc Frincu**
Computer Science Department
West University of Timisoara

and

Research Institute e-Austria Timisoara
Timisoara, Romania

**Dennis Gannon**
Date Center Futures
Microsoft Research
Redmond, Washington

**Thilina Gunarathne**
Community Grids Laboratory
Pervasive Technology Institute
Indiana University

and

School of Informatics and Computing
Indiana University
Bloomington, Indiana

**Thomas J. Hacker**
Computer and Information
    Technology
Discovery Park Cyber Center
Purdue University
West Lafayette, Indiana

**Chathura Herath**
School of Informatics and Computing
Indiana University
Bloomington, Indiana

**Jane Hunter**
School of Information Technology &
    Electrical Engineering
The University of Queensland
Brisbane, Queensland, Australia

**Kate Keahey**
Computation Institute
University of Chicago
Chicago, Illinois

and

Argonne National Laboratory
Argonne, Illinois

**Sun Kim**
School of Informatics and Computing
Indiana University
Bloomington, Indiana

**Wen-Syan Li**
SAP Research China
Shanghai, People's Republic of China

**Yuan-Fang Li**
School of Information Technology &
   Electrical Engineering
The University of Queensland
Brisbane, Queensland, Australia

**Hai Liu**
College of Computer
National University of Defense
   Technology
Changsha, People's Republic of China

**Huan Liu**
Accenture Technology Labs
San Jose, California

**Suresh Marru**
School of Informatics and Computing
Indiana University
Bloomington, Indiana

**John McGee**
Renaissance Computing Institute
University of North Carolina
Chapel Hill, North Carolina

**Christopher Moretti**
Department of Computer Science and
   Engineering
University of Notre Dame
Notre Dame, Indiana

**Andrew Newman**
School of Information Technology &
   Electrical Engineering
The University of Queensland
Brisbane, Queensland, Australia

**Shrideep Pallickara**
Department of Computer Science
Colorado State University
Fort Collins, Colorado

**Marlon Pierce**
Community Grids Laboratory
Pervasive Technology Institute
Indiana University
Bloomington, Indiana

**Xiaohong Qiu**
Community Grids Laboratory
Pervasive Technology Institute
Indiana University
Bloomington, Indiana

**Kaijun Ren**
College of Computer
National University of Defense
   Technology
Changsha, People's Republic of China

**Jeff Riley**
School of Computer Science and
   Information Technology
RMIT University
Melbourne, Victoria, Australia

**Keith Seymour**
Department of Electrical Engineering
    and Computer Science
University of Tennessee
Knoxville, Tennessee

**Paul Sorenson**
Department of Computing Science
University of Alberta
Edmonton, Alberta, Canada

**Abhishek Srivastava**
Department of Computing Science
University of Alberta
Edmonton, Alberta, Canada

**Douglas Thain**
Department of Computer Science and
    Engineering
University of Notre Dame
Notre Dame, Indiana

**Nancy Wilkins-Diehr**
San Diego Supercomputer Center
University of California at San Diego
La Jolla, California

**Rich Wolski**
Eucalyptus Systems
University of California at Santa
    Barbara
Santa Barbara, California

**Wenjun Wu**
Computation Institute
University of Chicago
Chicago, Illinois

**Jianfeng Yan**
SAP Research China
Shanghai, People's Republic of China

**Ying Yan**
SAP Research China
Shanghai, People's Republic of China

**Youngik Yang**
School of Informatics and Computing
Indiana University
Bloomington, Indiana

**Asim YarKhan**
Department of Electrical Engineering
    and Computer Science
University of Tennessee
Knoxville, Tennessee

**Lamia Youseff**
Department of Computer Science
University of California, Santa Barbara
Santa Barbara, California

**Jin Zhang**
SAP Research China
Shanghai, People's Republic of China

**Weimin Zhang**
College of Computer
National University of Defense
    Technology
Changsha, People's Republic of China

**Jinzy Zhu**
IBM Cloud Computing Labs &
    HiPODS
IBM Software Group/Enterprise
    Initiatives
Beijing, People's Republic of China

## Chapter 1

# Understanding the Cloud Computing Landscape

Lamia Youseff, Dilma M. Da Silva,
Maria Butrico, and Jonathan Appavoo

## Contents

1

## 1.1 Introduction

The goal of this chapter is to present an overview of three different structured views of the cloud computing landscape. These three views are the *SPI* cloud classification, the *UCSB-IBM* cloud ontology, and *Hoff's* cloud model. Each one of these three cloud models strives to present a comprehension of the interdependency between the different cloud systems as well as to show their potential and limitations. Furthermore, these models vary in the degree of simplicity and comprehensiveness in describing the cloud computing landscape. We find that these models are complementary and that by studying the three structured views, we get a general overview of the landscape of this evolving computing field.

## 1.2 Cloud Systems Classifications

The three cloud classification models present different levels of details of the cloud computing landscape, since they emerged in different times of evolution of this computing field. Although they have different objectives—some are for academic understanding of the novel research area, while others target identifying and analyzing commercial and market opportunities—they collectively expedite comprehending some of the interrelations between cloud computing systems. Although we present them in this chapter in a chronological order of their emergence—which also happens to reflect the degree of details of each model—this order does not reflect the relative importance or acceptance of one model over the other. On the other hand, the three models and their extensions are complementary, reflecting different views of the cloud. We first present the *SPI* model in Section 1.2, which is the oldest of the three models. The second classification is the *UCSB-IBM* ontology, which we detail in Section 1.3. We also present a discussion of a recent extension to this ontology in Section 1.4. The third classification is *Hoff's* cloud model, which we present in Section 1.5. We discuss the importance of these classifications and their potential impact on this emerging computing field in Section 1.6.

## 1.3 SPI Cloud Classification

As the area of cloud computing was emerging, the systems developed for the cloud were quickly stratified into three main subsets of systems: Software as a Service (SaaS), Platform as a Service (PaaS), and Infrastructure as a Service (IaaS). Early on, these three subsets of the cloud were discussed by several cloud computing experts, such as in [24,30,31]. Based on this general classification of cloud systems, the SPI model was formed and denotes the Software, Platform, and Infrastructure systems of the cloud, respectively.

## 1.3.1 Cloud Software Systems

This subset of cloud systems represents applications built for and deployed for the cloud on the Internet, which are commonly referred to as Software as a Service (SaaS). The target user of this subset of systems is the end user. These applications, which we shall refer to as cloud applications, are normally browser based with predefined functionality and scope, and they are accessed, sometimes, for a fee per a particular usage metric predefined by the cloud SaaS provider. Some examples of SaaS are salesforce customer relationships management (CRM) system [33], and Google Apps [20] like Google Docs and Google SpreadSheets.

SaaS is considered by end users to be an attractive alternative to desktop applications for several reasons. For example, having the application deployed at the provider's data center lessens the hardware and maintenance requirements on the users' side. Moreover, it simplifies the software maintenance process, as it enables the software developers to apply subsequent frequent upgrades and fixes to their applications as they retain access to their software service deployed at the provider's data center.

## 1.3.2 Cloud Platform Systems

The second subset of this classification features the cloud platform systems. In this class of systems, denoted as Platform as a Service (PaaS), the provider supplies a platform of software environments and application programming interfaces (APIs) that can be utilized in developing cloud applications. Naturally, the users of this class of systems are developers who use specific APIs to build, test, deploy, and tune their applications on the cloud platform. One example of systems in this category is Google's App Engine [19], which provides Python and Java runtime environments and APIs for applications to interact with Google's runtime environment. Arguably, Microsoft Azure [26] can also be considered a platform service that provides an API and allows developers to run their application in the Microsoft Azure environment.

Developing an application for a cloud platform is analogous to some extent to developing a web application for the old web servers model, in the sense that developers write codes and deploy them in a remote server. For end users, the final result is a browser-based application. However, the PaaS model is different in that it can provide additional services to simplify application development, deployment, and execution, such as automatic scalability, monitoring, and load balancing. Furthermore, the application developers can integrate other services provided by the PaaS system to their application, such as authentication services, e-mail services, and user interface components. All that is provided through a set of APIs is supplied by the platform. As a result, the PaaS class is generally regarded to accelerate the software development and deployment time. In turn, the cloud software built for the cloud platform normally has a shorter time-to-market. Some academic projects have also emerged to support a more thorough understanding of PaaS, such as AppScale [5].

Another feature that typifies PaaS services is the provision of APIs for metering and billing information. Metering and billing permits application developers to more readily develop a consumption-based business model around their application. Such a support helps integrate and enforce the relationships between end users, developers, PaaS, and any lower-level providers, while enabling the economic value of the developers and providers.

### 1.3.3 Cloud Infrastructure Systems

The third class of systems, according to the SPI classification model, provides infrastructure resources, such as compute, storage, and communication services, in a flexible manner. These systems are denoted as Infrastructure as a Service (IaaS). Amazon's Elastic Compute Cloud (EC2 [8]) and Enomalism elastic computing infrastructure [10] are arguably the two most popular examples of commercial systems available in this cloud category.

Recent advances in operating system (OS) Virtualization have facilitated the implementation of IaaS and made it plausible on existing hardware. In this regard, OS Virtualization technology enables a level of indirection with respect to direct hardware usage. It allows direct computer usage to be encapsulated and isolated in the container of a virtual machine (VM) instance. As a result, OS Virtualization enables all software and associated resource usage of an individual hardware user to be treated as a schedulable entity that is agnostic to the underlying physical resources that it is scheduled to use. Therefore, OS Virtualization allows IaaS providers to control and manage efficient utilization of the physical resources by enabling the exploitation of both time division and statistical multiplexing, while maintaining the familiar and flexible interface of individual standard hardware computers and networks for the construction of services using existing practices and software. This approach is particularly attractive to IaaS providers given the underutilization of the energy-hungry, high-speed processors that constitute the infrastructure of data centers. Amazon's infrastructure service, EC2, is one example of IaaS systems, where users can rent computing power on their infrastructure by the hour. In this space, there are also several academic open-source cloud projects, such as Eucalyptus [14] and Virtual Workspaces [38].

## 1.4 UCSB-IBM Cloud Ontology

The UCSB-IBM cloud ontology emerged through a collaboration effort between academia (University of California, Santa Barbara) and industry (IBM T.J. Watson Research Center) in an attempt to understand the cloud computing landscape. The end goal of this effort was to facilitate the exploration of the cloud computing area as well as to advance the educational efforts in teaching and adopting the cloud computing area.

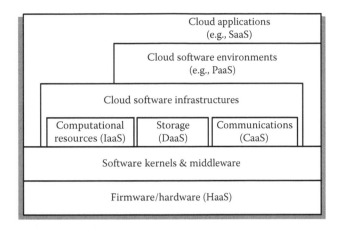

**Figure 1.1 UCSB-IBM Cloud Computing Classification Model depicted as five layers, with three constituents to the cloud infrastructure layer.**

In this classification, the authors used the principle of composability from a Service-Oriented Architecture (SOA) to classify the different layers of the cloud. Composability in SOA is the ability to coordinate and assemble a collection of services to form composite services. In this sense, cloud services can also be composed of one or more of other cloud services.

By the principle of composability, the UCSB-IBM model classified the cloud in five layers. Each layer encompasses one or more cloud services. Cloud services belong to the same layer if they have an equivalent level of abstraction, as evident by their targeted users. For example, all cloud software environments (also known cloud platforms) target programmers, while cloud applications target end users. Therefore, cloud software environments would be classified in a different layer than cloud applications. In the UCSB-IBM model, the five layers compose a cloud stack, where one cloud layer is considered higher in the cloud stack if the services it provides can be composed from the services that belong to the underlying layer. The UCSB-IBM cloud model is depicted in Figure 1.1.

The first three layers of the UCSB-IBM cloud are similar to the SPI classification, except that the authors break the infrastructure layer into three components. The three components that compose the UCSB-IBM infrastructure layer are computational resources, storage, and communications. In the rest of this section, we explain in more detail this ontology's components.

## 1.4.1 Applications (SaaS)

Similar to the SPI model, the first layer is the cloud application layer. The cloud application layer is the most visible layer to the end users of the cloud. Normally, users access the services provided by this layer through the browser via web portals, and are sometimes required to pay fees to use them. This model has been recently proven to be attractive to many users, as it alleviates the burden of software maintenance and the ongoing operation and support costs. Furthermore, it exports the computational work from the users' terminal to the data centers where the cloud applications are deployed. This in turn lessens the hardware requirements needed at the users' end, and allows them to obtain superb performance for some of their CPU-intensive and memory-intensive workloads without necessitating large capital investments in their local machines. Arguably, the cloud application layer has enabled the growth of a new class of end-user devices in the form of "netbook" computers, which are less expensive end-user devices that rely on network connectivity and cloud applications for functionality. Netbook computers often have limited processing capability with little or no disk drive-based storage, relying on cloud applications to meet the needs for both.

As for the providers of cloud applications, this model simplifies their work with respect to upgrading and testing the code, while protecting their intellectual property. Since a cloud application is deployed at the provider's computing infrastructure (rather than at the users' desktop machines), the developers of the application are able to roll smaller patches to the system and add new features without disturbing the users with requests to install updates or service packs. The configuration and testing of the application in this model is arguably less complicated, since the deployment environment, i.e., the provider's data center becomes restricted. Even with respect to the provider's profit margin, this model supplies the software provider with a continuous flow of revenue, which might be even more profitable on the long run. This *SaaS* model conveys several favorable benefits for the users and providers of the cloud application. The body of research on SOA has numerous studies on composable IT services, which have a direct application to providing and composing *SaaS*.

The UCSB-IBM ontology illustrates that the cloud applications can be developed on the cloud software environments or infrastructure components (as discussed in Sections 1.3.2 and 1.3.3). In addition, cloud applications can be composed as a service from other services, using the concepts of SOA. For example, a payroll application might use another accounting system's SaaS to calculate the tax deductibles for each employee in its system without having to implement this service within the payroll software. In this respect, the cloud applications targeted for higher layers in the stack are simpler to develop and have a shorter time-to-market. Furthermore, they become less error prone, since all their interactions with the cloud are through pretested APIs. However, being developed for a higher stack layer limits the flexibility of the application and restricts the developers' ability to optimize its performance.

Despite all the advantageous benefits of this model, several deployment issues hinder its wide adoption. Specifically, the security and availability of the cloud applications are two of the major issues in this model, and they are currently addressed by the use of lenient service-level agreements (SLAs). Furthermore, coping with outages is a realm that users and providers of *SaaS* have to tackle, especially with possible network outage and system failures. Additionally, the integration of legacy applications and the migration of the users' data to the cloud are slowing the adoption of *SaaS*. Before they can persuade users to migrate from desktop applications to cloud applications, cloud applications' providers need to address end-users' concerns about security and safety of storing confidential data on the cloud, users' authentication and authorization, uptime and performance, as well as data backup and disaster recovery.

## 1.4.2 Cloud Software Environment (PaaS)

The second layer in the UCSB-IBM cloud ontology is the cloud software environment layer (also dubbed the software platform layer). The users of this layer are cloud applications' developers, implementing their applications and deploying them on the cloud. The providers of the cloud software environments supply the developers with a programming-language-level environment of well-defined APIs to facilitate the interaction between the environments and the cloud applications, as well as to accelerate the deployment and support the scalability needed by cloud applications. The service provided by cloud systems in this layer is commonly referred to as *Platform as a Service* (*PaaS*). Section 1.2 mentioned Google's App Engine and Microsoft Azure as examples of this category. Another example is SalesForce's Apex language [2] that allows the developers of the cloud applications to design, along with their applications' logic, their page layout, workflow, and customer reports.

Developers reap several benefits from developing their cloud application for a cloud programming environment, including automatic scaling and load balancing, as well as integration with other services (e.g., authentication services, e-mail services, and user interface) supplied to them by the *PaaS* provider. In such a way, much of the overhead of developing cloud applications is alleviated and is handled at the environment level. Furthermore, developers have the ability to integrate other services to their applications on demand. This makes the development of cloud applications a less complicated task, accelerates the deployment time, and minimizes the logic faults in the application. In this respect, a Hadoop [21] deployment on the cloud would be considered a cloud software environment, as it provides its applications' developers with a programming environment, namely, the Map Reduce [7] framework for the cloud. Yahoo Research's Pig [28] project, a high-level language to enable processing of very large files in the Hadoop environment, may be viewed as an open-source implementation of the cloud platform layer. As such, cloud software environments facilitate the development process of cloud applications.

## 1.4.3 Cloud Software Infrastructure

The third layer in the USCB-IBM ontology is the cloud software infrastructure layer. It is here that this ontology more distinctly departs from the SPI ontology. The USCB-IBM ontology takes a finer-grain approach to distinguishing the roles and components that provide the infrastructure to support SPI ontology's PaaS layer. Specifically, it breaks the infrastructure layer down into a software layer that is composed of three distinct parts and places these on top of two additional layers. The three components, *computational resources, storage,* and *communications*, composing the cloud software infrastructure layer are described below.

a. *Computational resources:* VMs are the most common form for providing computational resources to cloud users at this layer. OS Virtualization is the enabler technology for this cloud component, which allows the users unprecedented flexibility in configuring their settings while protecting the physical infrastructure of the provider's data center. The users get a higher degree of flexibility since they normally get super-user access to their VMs that they can use to customize the software stack on their VM for performance and efficiency. Often, such services are dubbed *IaaS*.

b. *Storage:* The second infrastructure resource is data storage, which allows users to store their data at remote disks and access them anytime from any place. This service is commonly known as *Data-Storage as a Service (DaaS)*, and it facilitates cloud applications to scale beyond their limited servers. Examples of commercial cloud *DaaS* systems are Amazon's S3 [32] and EMC Storage Managed Service [9].

c. *Communication:* As the need for guaranteed quality of service (QoS) for network communication grows for cloud systems, communication becomes a vital component of the cloud infrastructure. Consequently, cloud systems are obliged to provide some communication capability that is service oriented, configurable, schedulable, predictable, and reliable. Toward this goal, the concept of Communication as a Service (CaaS) emerged to support such requirements, as well as network security, dynamic provisioning of virtual overlays for traffic isolation or dedicated bandwidth, guaranteed message delay limits, communication encryption, and network monitoring. Although this model is currently the least discussed and adopted cloud service in the commercial cloud systems, several research papers and articles [1,11,13] have investigated the various architectural design decisions, protocols, and solutions needed to provide QoS communication as a service. One recent example of systems that belong to CaaS is the Microsoft Connected Service Framework (CSF) [25]. Voice over IP (VoIP) telephone systems, audio and video conferencing, as well as instant messaging are candidate cloud applications that can be composed of CaaS and can in turn provide composable cloud solutions to other common applications.

In addition to the three main layers of the cloud, the UCSB-IBM model includes two more layers: the software kernel and the firmware/hardware layer.

## 1.4.4 Software Kernel Layer

It provides the basic software management for the physical servers that compose the cloud. Unlike the SPI ontology, the UCSB-IBM ontology explicitly identifies the software used to manage the hardware resources and its existing choices instead of focusing solely on VM instances and how they are used. Here, a software kernel layer is used to identify the systems software that can be used to construct, manage, and schedule the virtual containers onto the hardware resources. At this level, a software kernel can be implemented as an OS kernel, hypervisor, VM monitor, and/ or clustering middleware. Customarily, grid computing applications were deployed and run on this layer on several interconnected clusters of machines. However, due to the absence of a virtualization abstraction in grid computing, jobs were closely tied to the actual hardware infrastructure, and providing migration, check-pointing, and load balancing to the applications at this level was always a complicated task.

The two most successful grid middleware systems that harness the physical resources to provide a successful deployment environment for grid applications are, arguably, Globus [15] and Condor [36]. The body of research in grid computing is large, and several grid-developed concepts are realized today in cloud computing. However, additional grid computing research can potentially be integrated to cloud research efforts. For example, grid computing microeconomics models [12] are possible initial models to study the issues of pricing, metering, and supply–demand equilibrium of the computing resources in the realm of cloud computing. The scientific community has also addressed the quest of building grid portals and gateways for grid environments through several approaches [4,6,16,17,34,35]. Such approaches and portal design experiences may be very useful to the development of usable portals and interfaces for the cloud at different software layers. In this respect, cloud computing can benefit from the different research directions that the grid community has embarked for almost a decade of grid computing research.

## 1.4.5 Cloud Hardware/Firmware

The bottom layer of the cloud stack in the UCSB-IBM ontology is the actual physical hardware and switches that form the backbone of the cloud. In this regard, users of this cloud layer are normally big enterprises with large IT requirements in need of subleasing *H*ardware as a *S*ervice (*HaaS*). For this, the *HaaS* provider operates, manages, and upgrades the hardware on behalf of its consumers for the lifetime of the sublease. This model is advantageous to the enterprise users, since often they do not need to invest in building and managing data centers. Meanwhile, *HaaS* providers have the technical expertise as well as the cost-effective infrastructure to host the systems. One of the early *HaaS* examples is Morgan Stanley's sublease contract with IBM in 2004 [27]. SLAs in this model are stricter, since enterprise users have predefined business workloads with strict performance requirements. The margin benefit for *HaaS* providers materializes from the economy of scale of building data-centers with huge floor space, power, cooling costs, as well as operation and management expertise.

*HaaS* providers have to address a number of technical challenges in operating their services. Some major challenges for such large-scale systems are efficiency, ease, and speed of provisioning. Remote, scriptable boot loaders is one solution to remotely boot and deploy a complete software stack on the data centers. PXE [29] and UBoot [37] are examples of remote bootstrap execution environments that allow the system administrator to stream a binary image to multiple remote machines at boot time. Other examples of challenges that arise at this cloud layer include data center management, scheduling, and power and cooling optimization. IBM Kittyhawk [3] is an example of a research project that targets the hardware cloud layer. This project exploits novel integrated scalable hardware to address the challenges of cloud computing at the hardware level. Furthermore, the project attempts to support many of the software infrastructure features at the hardware layer, thus permitting a more direct service model of the hardware. Specifically, it provides an environment in which external users can obtain exclusive access to raw metered hardware nodes in an on-demand fashion, similar to obtaining VMs from an IaaS provider. The system allows the software to be loaded and network connectivity to be under user control. Additionally, the prototype Kittyhawk system provides users with UBoot access, allowing them to script the boot sequence of the potentially thousands of Blue Gene/P nodes they may have allocated.

# 1.5 Jackson's Expansion on the UCSB-IBM Ontology

The UCSB-IBM model was adapted by several computing experts to facilitate the discussions and conversations about other aspects of the cloud. One of these aspects was the cloud security. With a focus on supporting cloud computing for governmental agencies, Jackson [23] adapted the original UCSB-IBM model and extended on it with the goal of supporting a more detailed view of the security aspects of the cloud computing field. By adding several additional layers to support cloud access management, workflow orchestration, application security, service management, and an explicit connectivity layer, Jackson highlighted several particulars of the security challenges for this emerging computing field. Specifically, he modified the original ontology to add the following three sets of layers:

1. *Access management layer:* This new layer is added above the cloud application layer and is intended to provide access management to the cloud applications implementing SaaS. In the form of different authentication techniques, this layer can provide a simplified and unified, yet efficient, form of protection. In

turn, this can simplify the development and usage of the SaaS applications while addressing the security concerns for these systems. In this way, one of the security risks in the cloud could simply be contained and addressed in one high-level layer, thereby confining one of the main risk factors in the cloud applications.

2. *Explicit SOA-related layers:* This set of layers offers several SOA features in a more explicit form that simplifies their utilization. Jackson added this set of layers between the application (Saas) and platform (Paas) layers in the original UCSB-IBM ontology. For example, one of the layers in this set is the workflow orchestration layer, which provides services for managing and orchestrating business-workflow applications in the cloud. Another layer in this set is the service discovery layer, which also facilitates the discovery of services available to an application and potentially simplifies its operation and composition of other services.

3. *Explicit connectivity Layers:* The third set of layers in this extension was mainly added to support explicit networking capability in the cloud. Realizing that network connectivity in the cloud is an important factor in addressing the security of data, Jackson extended the model by adding extra network security layers. These additional layers were placed between the cloud software infrastructure layers and their components. By analyzing the security of the "*data in motion*" and "*data at rest*," Jackson's model covered the security aspects of the data in the cloud at the network level as well.

# 1.6 Hoff's Cloud Model

Inspired by the SPI model and the UCSB-IBM cloud ontology, Christofer Hoff [22] organized an online collaboration and discussion between several cloud computing experts to build an ontology upon the earlier models. Hoff's Model, as shown in Figure 1.2, presented a new cloud ontology in more detail.

This model focused on analyzing the three main cloud services: IaaS, PaaS, and SaaS. The model dissects the *IaaS* layer to several other components. Data center facilities, which include power and space, is the first component. Hardware is the second component in the IaaS layer, which consists of compute node, data storage, and network subcomponents. Abstraction is the next component, which abridges the hardware through systems like VM monitors, grid, and cluster utilities. The next component is the core connectivity and delivery, which provides the various services supporting the systems utilizing the IaaS layer, such as authentication services and DNS services. In this model, the abstraction component and the connectivity and delivery component are interleaving, since they are closely interdependent on each other's services. The API component presents the management services as well as a simplified interface to the next layer in the cloud. One system, for example, that implements this API sub-layer is the *GoGrid CloudCenter*

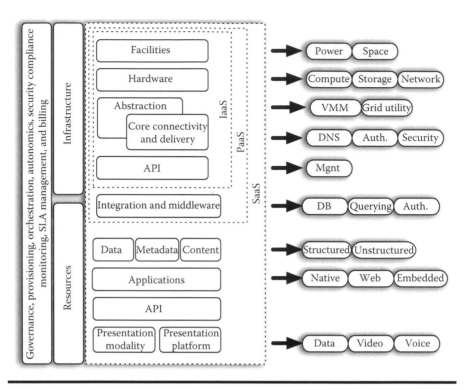

**Figure 1.2  Hoff's cloud ontology, which emerged as an online collaboration and discussion between different cloud computing experts to further analyze the cloud components.**

*API* [18]. This next layer in Hoff's model, which is the *PaaS*, is composed of one sub-layer that provides the integration services in the cloud. This sub-layer provides several services, such as authentication, database, and querying services.

The *SaaS* layer in Hoff's model is also further broken down into several sub-layers and components. The cloud application *data sub-layer* is shown to consist of the actual data, the metadata describing the real data, and its content, which can be in a structured or unstructured form. The application component in the SaaS layer is categorized into three categories: native applications, web applications, and embedded applications. A native application can be a desktop application that uses a cloud service. A web application is a cloud application that is accessed via the web browser. Finally, an embedded application is a cloud application that is embedded into another application. The final two sub-layers in the *SaaS* layer in Hoff's model are the applications' API and the presentation sub-layers. Hoff's model further decomposed the presentation sub-layers into data presentation, video presentation, and voice presentation, recognizing the different forms of cloud data presentations.

As portrayed in Figure 1.2, Hoff's model addresses more details of the composition of the cloud. The increased detail reveals additional aspects and challenges to cloud computing; however, it comes at the cost of simplicity. Nevertheless, the three cloud models presented in this chapter are regarded complementary and represent different viewpoints of the new emerging cloud computing field.

## 1.7 Discussion

As the cloud computing technology continues to emerge, more cloud systems are developed and new concepts are introduced. In this respect, a fundamental understanding of the extent to which cloud computing inherits its concepts from various computing areas and models is important to understand the landscape of this novel computing field and to define its potentials and limitations. Such comprehension will facilitate further maturation of the area by enabling novel systems to be put in context and evaluated in the light of existing systems. Particularly, an ontological, model-based approach encourages new systems to be compared and contrasted with existing ones, thus identifying more effectively their novel aspects. We contend that this approach will lead to more creative and effective cloud systems and novel usage scenarios of the cloud. With this in mind, our approach has been to determine the different layers and components that constitute the cloud, and study their characteristics in light of their dependency on other computing fields and models.

An ontology of cloud computing allows better understanding of the interrelations between the different cloud components, enabling the composition of new systems from existing components and further recomposition of current systems from other cloud components for desirable features like extensibility, flexibility, availability, or merely optimization and better cost efficiency. We as well postulate that understanding the different components of the cloud allows system engineers and researchers to deal with hard technological challenges. For example, comprehending the relationship between different cloud systems can accentuate opportunities to design interoperable systems between different cloud offerings that provide higher-availability guarantees. Although high availability is one of the fundamental design features of every cloud offering, failures are not uncommon. Highly available cloud applications can be constructed, for example, by deploying them on two competitive cloud offerings, e.g., Google's App Engine [19] and Amazon's EC2 [8]. Even in the case that one of the two clouds fails, the other cloud will continue to support the availability of the applications. In brief, understanding the cloud components may enable creative solutions to common cloud system problems, such as availability, application migration between cloud offerings, and system resilience. Furthermore, it will convey the potential of meeting higher-level implementation concepts through interoperability between different systems. For example, the high-availability requirement may be met by formulating an inter-cloud protocol, which enables migration and load balancing between cloud systems. Resilience in the cloud, for example, can also be met through concepts of self-healing and autonomic computing. The broad objective of this classification is to attain a better understanding of cloud computing and define key issues in current systems as well as accentuate some of the research topics that need to be addressed in such systems.

Not only can an ontology impact the research community, but it also can simplify the educational efforts in teaching cloud computing concepts to students and new cloud applications' developers. Understanding the implications of developing cloud applications against one cloud layer versus another will equip developers with the knowledge to make informed decisions about their applications' expected time-to-market, programming productivity, scaling flexibility, as well as performance bottlenecks. In this regard, an ontology can facilitate the adoption of cloud computing and its evolution. Toward the end goal of a thorough comprehension of the field of cloud computing, we have introduced in this chapter three contemporary cloud computing classifications that present cloud systems and their organization at different levels of detail.

# References

1. J. Hofstader. Communications as a service. http://msdn.microsoft.com/en-us/library/bb896003.aspx
2. Apex: Salesforce on-demand programming language and framework. http://developer.force.com/
3. J. Appavoo, V. Uhlig, and A. Waterland. Project kittyhawk: Building a global-scale computer: Blue Gene/P as a generic computing platform. *SIGOPS Oper. Syst. Rev.*, 42(1):77–84, 2008.
4. M. Chau, Z. Huang, J. Qin, Y. Zhou, and H. Chen. Building a scientific knowledge web portal: The nanoport experience. *Decis. Support Syst.*, 42(2):1216–1238, 2006.
5. N. Chohan, C. Bunch, S. Pang, C. Krintz, N. Mostafa, S. Soman, and R. Wolski. AppScale: Scalable and Open AppEngine application development and deployment. Technical Report TR-2009-02, University of California, Santa Barbara, CA, 2009.
6. M. Christie and S. Marru. The LEAD portal: A teragrid gateway and application service architecture: Research articles. *Concurr. Comput. Pract. Exp.*, 19(6):767–781, 2007.
7. J. Dean and S. Ghemawat. MapReduce: Simplified data processing on large clusters. *Proceedings of the Sixth Symposium on Operating System Design and Implementation (OSDI)*, San Francisco, CA, pp. 137–150, 2004.
8. Amazon Elastic Compute Cloud. http://aws.amazon.com/ec2/
9. EMC Managed Storage Service. http://www.emc.com/
10. Enomalism elastic computing infrastructure. http://www.enomaly.com
11. A. Hanemann et al. PerfSONAR: A service oriented architecture for multi-domain network monitoring. In B. Benatallah et al., editors, *ICSOC*, Amsterdam, the Netherlands, *Lecture Notes in Computer Science*, vol. 3826, pp. 241–254. Springer, Berlin, Germany, 2005.

12. R. Wolski et al. Grid resource allocation and control using computational economies. In F. Berman, G. Fox, and A. J. G. Hey, editors, *Grid Computing: Making the Global Infrastructure a Reality*, pp. 747–772. John Wiley & Sons, Chichester, U.K., 2003.

13. W. Johnston et al. Network communication as a service-oriented capability. In L. Grandinetti, editor, *High Performance Computing and Grids in Action, Advances in Parallel Computing*, vol. 16, IOS Press, Amsterdam, the Netherlands, March 2008.

14. Eucalyptus. http://eucalyptus.cs.ucsb.edu/

15. I. Foster and C. Kesselman. Globus: A metacomputing infrastructure toolkit. *Int. J. Supercomput. Appl.*, 11(2):115–128, 1997.

16. D. Gannon et al. Building grid portal applications from a web-service component architecture. *Proc. IEEE* (Special Issue on Grid Computing), 93(3):551–563, March 2005.

17. D. Gannon, B. Plale, M. Christie, Y. Huang, S. Jensen, N. Liu, S. Marru, S. Pallickara, S. Perera, and S. Shirasuna. Building grid portals for e-science: A service oriented architecture. *High Performance Computing and Grids in Action*. IOS Press, Amsterdam, the Netherlands, 2007.

18. GoGrid Cloud Center API. http://www.gogrid.com/how-it-works/gogrid-API.php

19. Google App Engine. http://code.google.com/appengine

20. Google Apps. http://www.google.com/apps/business/index.html

21. Hadoop. http://hadoop.apache.org/

22. C. Hoff. Christofer hoff blog: Rational survivability. http://rationalsecurity.typepad.com/blog/

23. K. L. Jackson. An ontology for tactical cloud computing. http://kevinljackson.blogspot.com/

24. M. Crandell. Defogging cloud computing: A taxonomy, June 16, 2008. http://refresh.gigaom.com/2008/06/16/defogging-cloud-computing-a-taxonomy/

25. Microsoft Connected Service Framework. http://www.microsoft.com/serviceproviders/solutions/connectedservicesframework.mspx

26. Microsoft Azure. http://www.microsoft.com/azure

27. M. Stanley. IBM ink utility computing deal. http://news.cnet.com/2100-7339-5200970.html

28. C. Olston, B. Reed, U. Srivastava, R. Kumar, and A. Tomkins. Pig latin: A not-so-foreign language for data processing. In *SIGMOD '08: Proceedings of the 2008 ACM SIGMOD International Conference on Management of Data*, Vancouver, Canada, pp. 1099–1110, 2008. ACM, New York.

29. Preboot Execution Environment (PXE) Specifications, Intel Technical Report, September 1999.

30. R. W. Anderson. Cloud services continuum, July 3; 2008. http://et.cairenenet/2008/07/03/cloud-services-continuum/

31. R. W. Anderson. The cloud services stack and infrastructure, July 28, 2008. http://et.cairene.net/2008/07/28/the-cloud-services-stack-infrastructure/

32. Amazon Simple Storage Service. http://aws.amazon.com/s3/

33. Salesforce Customer Relationships Management (CRM) system. http://www.salesforce.com/

34. T. Severiens. Physics portals basing on distributed databases. In *IuK*, Trier, Germany, 2001.

35. P. Smr and V. Novek. Ontology acquisition for automatic building of scientific portals. In J. Wiedermann, G. Tel, J. Pokorný, M. Bieliková, and J. Stuller, editors, *SOFSEM 2006: Theory and Practice of Computer Science: 32nd Conference on Current Trends in Theory and Practice of Computer Science*, pp. 493–500. Springer Verlag, Berlin/ Heidelberg, Germany, 2006.

36. D. Thain, T. Tannenbaum, and M. Livny. Distributed Computing in Practice: The Condor Experience. *Concurrency and Computation: Practice and Experience*, 17(2–4):323–356, 2005.

37. Das U-Boot: The universal boot loader. http://www.denx.de/wiki/U-Boot/WebHome

38. Virtual Workspaces Science Clouds. http://workspace.globus.org/clouds/

*Chapter 2*

# Science Gateways: Harnessing Clouds and Software Services for Science

Nancy Wilkins-Diehr, Chaitan Baru,
Dennis Gannon, Kate Keahey, John McGee,
Marlon Pierce, Rich Wolski, and Wenjun Wu

## Contents

## 2.1 Science Gateways—Background and Motivation

*Nancy Wilkins-Diehr*

The pursuit of science has evolved over hundreds of years from the development of the scientific method to the use of empirical methods. This evolution continues today at an increasingly rapid pace. Scientific pursuit has always been marked by advances in technology. Increasingly powerful microscopes and telescopes have led to new discoveries and theories; access to sensor data improves the ability to analyze and monitor events and understand complex phenomena, such as climate change, and advances in sequencing technologies will very soon result in personalized medicine.

The evolution of science with technology continues today as well. The 1970s and 1980s saw the significant development of computational power. Computer simulations were considered a third pillar of science in addition to theory and experiment.

One of the biggest impacts in modern times has been the release of the Mosaic browser in 1992. This ushered in the modern information age and an explosion of knowledge sharing not seen since the invention of the printing press. The impact on science has been tremendous, but we contend that the extent of this impact is just beginning. The availability of digital data continues to grow and access and sharing mechanisms continue to evolve very quickly. Early Web 3.0 ideas are outlining how we move from information sharing on social Web sites and wikis to programmatic data sharing via standards (Resource Description Framework) and database queries (SPARQL query language) [1].

In the 1990s, scientists were beginning to develop and rely heavily on the Internet and communication technologies. The National Center for Biotechnology Information's BLAST server provided scientists with an early sequence alignment tool that made use of remote computing capabilities [2]. Queries and results were exchanged via e-mail. This service was later made available on the Web and continues to operate today.

In 1995, the headline was "International Protein Data Bank Enhanced by Computer Browser" [3]. The Protein Data Bank (PDB), first established in 1971, is the worldwide repository for three-dimensional structure data of biological macro-molecules. Over time, technology developments have changed many aspects of the PDB. Structures are determined by different methods and much more quickly, the number of new structures per year has increased nearly three orders of magnitude from 1976 to 2008. The expectations of the community have changed as well. Text files including structure descriptions were originally available for download via ftp. Today the PDB features sophisticated data mining and visualization capabilities, as well as references to PubMed articles and structure reports [4].

A report from a 1998 workshop entitled *Impact of Advances in Computing and Communications Technologies on Chemical Science and Technology* [5] takes an early look at the impact of computing and communications technology on science. The authors point out that before the advent of the Internet, the practice of chemistry research had remained largely unchanged. They saw the Internet improving access to scarce instruments and removing the constraints of time and distance previously imposed on potential collaborators. They believed these advances would fundamentally change both the types of scientific problems that can be tackled (the best minds can be brought to bear on the most challenging problems) and the very way in which these problems are addressed. They were accurate in their assessment.

Against this backdrop, the TeraGrid Science Gateway program was initiated in 2003. Previously, supercomputers were accessed by a small number of users who were members of elite research groups. TeraGrid architects recognized that the impact of high-end resources could be greatly increased if they could be coupled onto the back end of existing web portals being developed prolifically by scientists.

Today, gateways span disciplines and provide very diverse capabilities to researchers. The Social Informatics Data Grid (SIDGrid) provides access to mul-timodal data (voice, video, images, text, numerical) collected at multiple times-cales. SIDGrid users are able to explore, annotate, share, and mine expensive data sets with specialized analysis tools. Computationally intensive tasks include media transcoding, pitch analysis of audio tracks, and fMRI image analysis. Researchers utilize SIDGrid, but are unaware of the computational power performing these calculations behind the scenes for them. PolarGrid provides access to and analy-sis of ice sheet measurement data collected in Antarctica. Linked Environments for Atmospheric Discovery (LEAD) will allow researchers to launch tornado simulations on demand if incoming radar data display certain characteristics. The Asteroseismic Modeling Portal is ingesting data from NASA's Kepler satellite mis-sion, which was launched in March 2009. The portal allows researchers to deter-mine the size, position, and age of a star by doing intensive simulations using the observed oscillation modes from satellite data as input. In all of these examples, the gateway interfaces allow scientists to focus on their work while providing the required computing power behind the scenes.

Technology continues to evolve with increasing rapidity. In 2009, cloud computing and "Software as a Service" (SaaS) were examples of virtualized access to high-end resources that enable science. This chapter highlights several activities in these areas, with a focus on the scientific application of the technologies. First, an overview of cloud computing and SaaS are presented. Next, two approaches to cloud deployment (Eucalyptus and NIMBUS) are described in some detail. Examples of scientific applications using virtualized services are provided throughout.

Finally, several detailed science examples are featured. Scientists can run sequence alignment codes from an iGoogle web page via gadgets provided by the Open Life Sciences Gateway. They have 120 different bioinformatics packages at their fingertips through the RENCI science portal. In both examples, software is offered truly as a service. The back-end high performance and high throughput computing, which makes the most rigorous computations possible, is completely hidden from the scientist. The final project looks at data subsetting and database distribution using clouds with high resolution topographic data as a driver. Future directions in all areas are summarized at the conclusion of the chapter.

## 2.2 Clouds and Software Services

*Dennis Gannon*

The term "cloud computing" means using a remote data center to manage scalable, reliable, on-demand access to applications. The concept has its origins in the early transformation of the World Wide Web from a loose network of simple web servers into a searchable collection of over 100 million Web sites and 25 billion pages of text. The challenge was to build such a searchable index of the Web and to make it usable and completely reliable for tens of thousands of concurrent users. This required massive parallelism to handle user requests and massive parallelism to sort through all that data. It also required both data and computational redundancy to assure the level of reliability demanded by users. To solve this problem, the web search industry had to build a grid of data centers that today have more computing power than our largest supercomputers. The scientists and engineers who were working on improving search relevance algorithms or mining the Web for critical data needed to use these same massively parallel data centers because that is where the data was stored. The most common algorithms they used often followed the "MapReduce" [6] parallel programming pattern. They shared algorithms and designs for distributed, replicated data structures and developed technology that made it simple for any engineer to define a MapReduce application and "upload it to the cloud" to run. Google was the first to use this expression and publicize the idea. Yahoo later released an open-source version of a similar MapReduce framework called Hadoop [7]. Microsoft has a more general technology based on the same concepts called Dryad/LINQ.

A programming model has evolved that allows a developer to design an application on a desktop and then push it to a data center for deployment and execution. Google had released AppEngine, which allows a programmer to build a Python program that accesses the Google distributed cloud storage when pushed to the cloud. Microsoft has introduced Azure, which allows developers to build highly scalable parallel cloud web services. Together these software frameworks for building applications are referred to as Platform as a Service (PaaS) models for cloud computing.

If we take a closer look at the data center system architecture that lies at the heart of systems like Azure, we see another model of cloud computing based on the use of machine virtualization technology. The most transparent example of this is the Amazon EC2 [8] and S3 [9] clouds. The idea here is very simple. The application developer is given a machine OS image to load with applications and data. The developer hands this loaded image back to EC2 and it is run in a virtual machine (VM) in the Amazon data center. The critical point is that the image may be replicated across multiple VMs so that the application it contains may scale with user demand. The developer is only charged for the resources actually used. In this chapter, we describe several significant variations on this "Infrastructure as a Service" (IaaS) concept.

While IaaS and PaaS form the foundation of the cloud technologies, what the majority of users see is the application on their desktop or phone. The client application may be a web browser or an application that is connected to a set of services running in the cloud. Together, the application and the associated cloud services are often referred to as SaaS. There are many examples. Social networks provide both web and phone clients for their SaaS cloud application. Collaboration and virtual reality is provided in the cloud by second life. Photo sharing tools that allow users to upload, store, and tag images are now common features shipped with new phones and cameras. Microsoft's LifeMesh is a cloud-based software service that allows the files and applications on your PC, laptop, and Mac to be synchronized.

Science gateways are tools that allow scientists to conduct data analysis and simulation studies by using the resources of a remote supercomputer rather than a remote data center. They share many of the same scalability and reliability requirements of SaaS tools but they have the additional requirement that the back-end services need to be able to conduct substantial computational analysis that require the architectural features not supported by large data centers.

Supercomputers and data centers are very similar in many respects: they are both built from large racks of servers connected by a network. The primary difference is that the network of a supercomputer is designed for extremely low latency messaging to support the peak utilization of each central processing unit (CPU). Data centers are designed to maximize application bandwidth to remote users and are seldom run at peak processor utilization so that they can accommodate surges in demand. Data center applications are also designed to be continuously running services that never fail and always deliver the same fast response no matter how large the load. But failure is constant in large systems, so data center applications tend to be as stateless as possible and highly redundant. Supercomputer applications are design for peak performance, but they fail frequently. In these cases, checkpointing and restart is the only failure recovery mechanism.

The challenge for science gateways is to meet the requirements of both SaaS cloud applications for reliability and scalability and the high performance requirements of their scientific analysis components. The ideal architecture for science gateways would be a hybrid of the externally facing, data-rich data center with a supercomputing capability in the back end. An alternative would be a data center architecture where server nodes could be dynamically clustered into small but highly powerful computational clusters that could operate as a small supercomputer for short periods of time. This is an area of research that is currently underway in several locations.

## 2.3 Science Clouds, Public and Private

*Rich Wolski*

Cloud computing [10,11] has emerged as a new paradigm for providing programmatic access to scalable Internet service venues.* While significant debates continue with regard to the "optimal" level of abstraction that such programmatic interfaces should support (cf., SaaS versus PaaS versus IaaS [12–14]), the general goal is to provide users or "clients" with the ability to program resources within a very-large-scale resource "cloud" so that they can take advantage of the potential performance, cost, and reliability benefits that access to scale makes possible.

Notice that from a technology perspective, the way in which users account for their usage is independent of the cloud computing model itself (although it is by no means independent of the usage models employed by those users). That is, users may be able to use a "pay-as-you-go" billing methodology or alternatively one where quota-limited and/or time-limited access is enforced by the cloud system. Thus "billing" (or more properly user accounting) is one way to differentiate between public and private clouds. A public cloud is one in which a fee is charged to each user account by the cloud provider, either for recorded usage or by quota-controlled subscription. In a private cloud, typically, a quota of usage (possibly time limited) is assigned by the administrative organization (to which both the cloud provider and the users belong) to each user account or to groups of user accounts. Technologically however, the systems otherwise present the same interface to their users.

---

* The term "cloud computing" is considered by some to be synonymous with the terms "elastic computing," "utility computing," and occasionally "grid computing." For the purposes of this chapter, we will use the term "cloud computing" to refer to cloud, elastic, or utility computing but not to grid computing.

In a cloud providing IaaS, this interface is as follows:

■ Self-service—Users are granted resources allocations from the cloud (or denied an allocation) automatically without human intervention. In addition, users can choose pre-fabricated configurations that have been previously published within the cloud and can also generate and save their own customized configurations, again without intervention by a human administrator or programmer.

■ Quality-of-service aware—Users are able to specify a quality of service (QoS) to be associated with each allocation request. The QoS level associated with each granted request adjusts the "charge" (either in terms of cost or quota depletion) assigned to the user account.

Perhaps the best known example of an IaaS-style cloud is Amazon.com's AWS [15]. Through either a simple command-line interface or through a "RESTful" programmatic one, users can request rental of computing capacity (EC2) and storage capacity (S3 and EBS [16]). The interface is self-service, and a fixed number of discrete QoS levels are supported.

## 2.3.1 Eucalyptus—Open-Source IaaS

Eucalyptus (Elastic Utility Computing Architecture Linking Your Programs to Useful Systems) [17–19] is an open-source infrastructure developed in the Computer Science Department of the University of California, Santa Barbara that implements IaaS-style cloud computing using local machine and cluster resources. The software components that make up a Eucalyptus cloud are based on web services (SOAP, WSDL, etc.) and are implemented using only freely available software packages, many of which are part of the common Linux distributions.

In addition, while the infrastructure itself is modularized so that a variety of interfaces can be supported, we have included an initial interface module to Eucalyptus that conforms to the Amazon AWS interface specification. Thus, once installed and running, a Eucalyptus cloud supports the same programmatic and user interfaces that AWS does with respect to IaaS provisioning.

We chose AWS as an initial interface for several reasons. First, Eucalyptus is the product of a research effort in which we, the researchers, were interested in the viability of AWS as a scientific computing platform. Thus, as a local cloud infrastructure compatible with AWS, Eucalyptus is designed to function as an instrumentable development platform that provides transparent and controlled experimentation prior to AWS deployment. Second, the AWS compatibility allows scientists to leverage the rich ecosystem of tools and services that is emerging from the AWS community (e.g., the RightScale [20] and CohesiveFT [21] management platforms, rPath [22] compatibility, etc.). Third, Eucalyptus is designed to foster greater usage of cloud computing in general, and AWS (as the de facto standard) in particular, as a way of stimulating and accelerating the development of the paradigm. Open-source projects such as AppScale [23,24] and dotCloud [25] use it as a high-performance cloud platform, both for their own development and for application support. Thus, AWS interface compatibility has proved essential to promoting greater AWS usage and thus greater cloud computing uptake.

## 2.3.2 Engineering Challenge

In designing Eucalyptus, we had to ensure that it would be able to deploy and execute in hardware and software environments specified not by us, but by the installer and/ or maintainer of the cloud. This requirement is distinct from public cloud offerings in which the software can be written only to exploit the specific features engineered into the hardware platform that has been procured. Put another way, the designers of public cloud software need only consider the hardware that they know their organization has procured (or will procure) and not any hardware platform that might become available. In a scientific computing setting, the software platform typically cannot dictate the hardware configuration. Rather, each cluster or machine setting is unique making it necessary for the cloud platform to be able to conform to the local infrastructure. Because IaaS requires fairly low-level control of hardware resources, this need for portability strongly influences the design of Eucalyptus.

To make Eucalyptus available as open-source software with the smallest possible engineering effort, we leverage existing open-source software components to the greatest extent possible. We tried to identify the most commonly used package or system for each constituent functionality Eucalyptus requires as a way of selecting the most robust and reliable "building blocks" to use as a foundation. Nonetheless, there is considerable variation among the non-Eucalyptus software components upon which Eucalyptus depends. Much of the engineering effort has focused on developing a high-quality, reliable, and predictable cloud computing platform that depends, in part, upon community-contributed, freely available software.

In the same vein, we wish to encourage greater adoption of open-source software in production computing settings. While software quality is certainly a factor we took seriously, we have also focused on developing an internal architecture that enables customization and tuning. In particular, we have chosen a modularity and service decomposition that admits the replacement or modification of internal components, the addition of new services and different interfaces, and the possibility for considerable (but potentially nonportable) performance tuning.

## 2.3.3 Eucalyptus Architecture

Eucalyptus is designed to function as a collection of cooperating web services that can be deployed in environments where network connectivity is not necessarily symmetric. Academic research groups (who must be supported by Eucalyptus) have access to small clusters, pools of workstations, and various server/desktop machines. Public IP addresses, however, are usually scarce and the security ramifications of allowing complete access from the public Internet can be daunting so system administrators commonly deploy clusters as pools of "worker" machines on private, unroutable networks with a single "head node" responsible for routing traffic between the worker pool and a public network. Although this configuration provides security while using a minimum of publicly routable addresses, it also means that worker machines can initiate connections to external hosts but external hosts cannot typically connect to worker machines running within each cluster. Thus, Eucalyptus adopts a hierarchical design (Figure 2.1). Logically, there are four service components within a functioning Eucalyptus installation: the client API translator, the cloud controller, one or more cluster controllers, and one or more node controllers. The interfaces between these components are described by individual WSDL specifications so that any functional component may be replaced or modified. Client requests are translated to a canonical Eucalyptus-internal protocol before they are passed to the cloud controller. The cluster controllers act as message proxies between the publically routed networks to which each head node is attached and the internal private networks that worker nodes can access. Cluster controllers

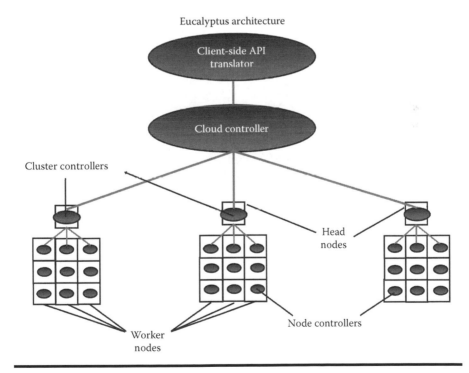

**Figure 2.1** **The service architecture within a Eucalyptus installation is hierarchical to cope with multiple clusters and asymmetric network connectivity.**

also implement a scalable scheduling protocol for VM assignment although this scheduling module can be replaced as a plug in. Finally, each machine within a cloud that is expected to contribute resources (CPU, memory, or disk) to user allocations must run a node controller.

## 2.3.4 User Experience

In addition to making the software available for download, we maintain a small, publically available persistent cloud at the University of California, Santa Barbara called the Eucalyptus Public Cloud (EPC) [26]. The purpose of the EPC is three-fold. First, it permits users to preview the quality of the Eucalyptus software by experimenting with a "live" installation. Second, it provides a test facility for features and/or engineering upgrades that will ultimately be packaged into a future Eucalyptus release. Finally, it permits us to observe the performance and stability of the cloud under a controlled user load.

The EPC is a small system that is vastly under-provisioned for the load it will support: the SLA scheduler installed on the EPC will schedule as many as four VMs per processor. In this way, user load "stresses" the internal Eucalyptus subsystems so that we can observe worst-case performance scenarios. Table 2.1 shows a comparison of the average instance start times in seconds for the same small image in both AWS and the EPC.

In addition to the average start time, we also show the 95% confidence bound on the average. The first column compares a one instance start, and the second column compares the time to start eight instances in a single user request. Notice that on average Eucalyptus is faster, but also experiences more variation (i.e., the confidence bounds are wider). From a user perspective, then, an EPC user experiences similar instance start-up performance to that provided by AWS. It is important to realize, however, that AWS is able to achieve this level of performance at a massive scale, while the EPC is (by design) a small, under-powered system. That is, while Eucalyptus provides a similar user experience to AWS at a much smaller scale, it complements rather than replaces AWS.

## 2.3.5 Notes from the Private Cloud

While a great deal has been written and discussed with respect to public clouds, comparatively little discussion of private clouds and their usage has yet emerged.

**Table 2.1  Small Instance Start Time**

|      | One Instance | Eight Instances |
|------|--------------|-----------------|
| AWS  | 18.6 s (±6.5 s) | 23.4 s (±5.14 s) |
| EPC  | 11.4 s (±7.6 s) | 17.9 s (±10.8 s) |

The Eucalyptus project maintains a public discussion board and a set of e-mail reflectors as a way of engaging community contributions, and from time to time contributors discuss their usage scenarios. While these anecdotes are far from definitive, we believe that they provide insight into how private clouds are being used.

In the science community, one common use for Eucalyptus appears to be as an application development platform in advance of a public cloud deployment. Eucalyptus is transparent in that while it is running a cloud application, that application can be interrogated and monitored both from inside and outside the cloud that implements it. Often, familiarity with local hardware and software configuration characteristics is an invaluable debugging aid. By knowing how the application functions outside the cloud on local hardware, it is possible to isolate problems that arise strictly because of cloud deployment.

A second usage scenario that we have observed is one in which Eucalyptus serves as a locally controllable and protected execution platform for application software that is also executing in a public cloud. Cloud applications, once debugged and tuned, tend to be quite robust and scalable. It is often advantageous to be able to leverage the engineering investment that has gone into a successful public cloud application deployment within the confines of a local data center where physical security permits these applications to access more sensitive data.

Notice that these private cloud scenarios are, in fact, hybrid cloud scenarios in which the private cloud augments the capabilities offered by a public cloud. Eucalyptus makes this hybridization with AWS possible through its interface compatibility. We believe that the trend will be toward greater use of the public clouds, and that this trend is greatly accelerated by the ability to use private and public clouds as a hybrid. In the same vein, it is our view that this hybrid cloud model is how enterprise cloud computing will be implemented in the future. While public clouds make it possible to outsource some aspects of enterprise IT, doing so makes it possible to use local infrastructure more cost effectively and efficiently.

## 2.3.6 Leveraging the Ecosystem

Because Eucalyptus supports the AWS interface, commercial and open-source tools designed for use with the AWS public cloud also work with Eucalyptus in scientific computing settings. This "ecosystem" allows scientists to leverage the considerable investment in public cloud technologies for their own applications on-premise and in the public clouds.

One such example is the free cloud management services offered by RightScale. RightScale is a company that provides cloud users with a management dashboard for developing, deploying, and controlling their applications and machine images. Originally developed for Amazon. AWS, it now supports the RackSpace, GoGrid, and FlexiScale public cloud platforms and Eucalyptus as a private cloud. In an analogy to free software, RightScale offers users a basic management capability as a "free service." When installed, a Eucalyptus cloud administrator can choose to register his or her cloud with the RightScale service venue that is hosted in Amazon's AWS. Users of the Eucalyptus cloud can then use the RightScale dashboard offering to manage their private cloud allocations. Notice that the RightScale dashboard operates as SaaS and not downloadable open-source code. However, combining RightScale's free SaaS with open-source Eucalyptus clouds creates a new and powerful tool combination for science cloud users.

Eucalyptus also enables other open-source cloud platforms to coexist with its interface. AppScale [18,19] implements a scalable, on-premise version of the Google AppEngine [27] PaaS using either AWS or Eucalyptus as a lower-level cloud platform. Thus, by installing AppEngine, a scientist can leverage the AppEngine or AWS APIs on his or her local machines and also execute the applications in both the Amazon and Google public clouds without changing the application code modification. Thus, for science, these open-source platforms provide a new application development environment that allows a single application to combine multiple public clouds using only standard APIs.

### 2.3.7 Future Growth

We anticipate that the open-source cloud ecosystem will continue to grow as new platforms and new free SaaS offerings become available. In our view, the utility computing model implemented by the public clouds will continue to reduce the cost of IT. We also believe that local infrastructure will continue to be necessary, but to amplify the cost savings offered by the public clouds, open-source cloud platforms like Eucalyptus and free SaaS will become critical technologies.

## 2.4 Cloud Computing for Science

*Kate Keahey*

The access to remote resources offers many benefits to scientific applications: it "democratizes" computing for many communities, allowing them to leverage economies of scale as well as use remote resources in times of increased demand. While grid computing pioneered remote resource usage on a large scale, two challenges—(1) the inability to control the configuration of environments provided on remote resources and (2) the inability to negotiate flexible modes of access to those resources—provided a significant barrier to many applications.

The first challenge reflects the fact that many scientific applications are complex and hard to port across different environments. Even minor differences in operating system support, libraries, and tools may cause these applications to fail. More importantly, even if the applications do run, the same minor differences in the environment can cause them to produce results that are inconsistent across runs executed on different sites or even at different times on the same site. Resolving these dependencies on a remote platform can take weeks or months of work. Furthermore, this work has to be repeated for multiple remote sites and over time as systems on these sites are upgraded.

Once obtained, the access to the remote sites is often of limited use. Access to grid resources is typically provided via remote interfaces to batch schedulers (e.g., by using such mechanisms as GRAM [28]) that run jobs according to implicit and often nonnegotiable site priorities. A job may languish in a scheduler queue for many hours or days making this mode of resource provisioning unsuitable for communities where resource need is dynamic e.g., the processing needs of experiments. In addition, in many instances, scientists simply need access to a resource (e.g., to log in and debug an application) rather than just running a job.

Our work on overcoming these challenges gave rise to the development of the Nimbus toolkit and contributed toward a computing paradigm that we call IaaS cloud computing.

## 2.4.1 Nimbus Goals and Architecture

The challenges described above led us to define the abstraction of a "workspace": a user-defined environment that can be dynamically overlaid on remote resources with specific availability constraints. Our first attempts to implement this abstraction focused on the management and configuration of physical resources [29] before we focused on virtualization [30,31] in 2003. The Workspace Service, first released in September 2005, allowed users to deploy and terminate VMs on remote resources, providing functionality similar to Amazon's Elastic Compute Cloud (EC2) [6] released in August 2006. Over the years, our work with the scientific communities motivated many revisions of the Workspace Service as well as the development of additional services such as the Context Broker [32] and an IaaS protocol adapter. In mid-2008, we started using the name "Nimbus Toolkit" to describe the growing collection of cloud services.

Today, Nimbus is an extensible, open-source toolkit built around the following three goals:

1. *Allow providers to build compute clouds.* This functionality continues to be provided by the Workspace Service [33] component of Nimbus, which orchestrates VM deployment on a cluster based on remote requests. The Workspace Service provides two sets of interfaces: one based on the Web Service Resource Framework (WSRF) [34] set of protocols and another based on Amazon's EC2. The deployment request processed by these interfaces can be combined with a choice of two Nimbus back-end implementations: (a) the workspace resource manager, which provides EC2-style VM deployment but requires the "ownership" of a cluster or (b) the "workspace pilot" [35] that extends popular schedulers to deploy VMs as a glidein. The workspace pilot

does not require a special cluster configuration and allows jobs and VMs to coexist, but provides weaker deployment semantics (VMs are deployed batch-style). The Workspace Service has been deployed by several academic institutions forming the Science Clouds test bed [36].

2. *Provide tools allowing users to use clouds.* IaaS providers, such as EC2 or the Science Clouds, allow users to deploy groups of unconnected VMs, whereas scientists typically need a ready-to-use "turnkey" cluster whose nodes share a common configuration and security context. The Nimbus Context Broker [28] bridges this gap by securely orchestrating an exchange of deployment-time information for groups of deployed VMs, potentially among VMs deployed across different clouds. Examples of Context Broker applications are described in Section 2.4.2. Another service geared toward the end-user is the Nimbus gateway, which serves as both a protocol adapter allowing users to move between clouds and provides account management for the use of commercial clouds.

3. *Allow researchers and developers to extend and experiment with Nimbus.* Nimbus is designed as a set of APIs that allow developers to extend it for research and development purposes. For example, a group of scientists at the Vienna University of Technology implemented research extensions to Nimbus to provide functionality that would ensure data privacy for the biomedical communities [37]. An example of production extensions are monitoring components provided by the high-energy physics group at the University of Victoria.

These three goals are reflected in Nimbus production services and implementation, Nimbus documentation, research projects ranging from efficient VM deployment and service levels [38–40] to configuration management [28], and projects with the various application communities. This set of goals allows us to address the full set of challenges from workspace deployment to its eventual use and gives us the flexibility to adapt our infrastructure across the stack as new requirements become understood.

## 2.4.2 Science Clouds Applications

The Science Clouds test bed [32] comprises multiple small clouds in the academic space with access granted to science-related projects on a voluntary basis. All clouds are configured with the EC2-compatible Nimbus, making it possible to easily move or replicate environments between clouds including EC2 resources as needed for large-scale deployments. At the same time, each cloud may provide slightly different service levels to the user. Thus, apart from providing a platform on which scientific applications explore cloud computing, the Science Cloud test bed is a laboratory in which different IaaS providers use compatible technologies to provide different service offerings allowing us to experiment with interoperability.

This section presents three Science Clouds applications that have been selected to illustrate different ways in which cloud resources were provided to the application and different scenarios in which they were used. The first application describes a simple but impactful integration that consists of extending the application test bed by a dynamically provisioned virtual cluster. The second application goes one step further and describes an ecosystem around the provisioned resources that allows the user to leverage them through existing mechanisms. The third application exploits the fact that cloud computing changes our assumptions about remote resources to create a distributed site.

### 2.4.2.1 Nimbus Helps Meet STAR Production Demands

STAR is a nuclear physics experiment associated with the Relativistic Heavy Ion Collider (RHIC) at the Brookhaven National Laboratory that studies nuclear matter under unique conditions of extremely high energy densities and temperature. Such conditions, which existed only shortly after the big bang, allow us to study fundamental properties of nuclear matter.

STAR computations rely on a complex software stack that can take months to configure on remote resources. This motivated STAR scientists to turn to virtualization: VM images can be configured and validated for STAR production runs and then deployed on many different resources. To implement this vision, STAR started collaborating with the Nimbus team contributing requirements for the development of the Workspace as well as the Context Broker Services. The latter allows them to dynamically and repeatably combine deployed VMs into fully configured virtual Open Science Grid (OSG) clusters with one command. Once such an OSG cluster is deployed, the STAR job scheduler can simply submit jobs to it, elastically extending the test bed available to STAR.

The STAR team started out by using a small Nimbus cloud at the University of Chicago. However, since STAR production runs require hundreds of nodes, the collaborating teams soon started moving those clusters to Amazon's EC2, which hosted the first STAR production run in September 2007. In March 2009, the advantages and potential of cloud computing for the community were dramatically illustrated [41] with a late-coming request to produce simulation results needed for Quark Matter, a major physics conference. Normally, this would not have been possible to do: there was roughly 1 week to produce the results and all the available computational resources—both local and distributed—were either committed to other tasks or did not support the environment needed for STAR. However, by this time, the STAR scientists had developed validated VM images and trusted Nimbus to deploy them. The deployed images—300 virtual nodes at a time—were used to elastically extend the resources available to STAR. As the simulation progressed, the images were upgraded to more powerful EC2 instances to speed the calculations and ensure meeting the deadline.

This deployment marks the very first time cloud computing has been used in nuclear physics for significant scientific production work with full confidence in the results. It also illustrates that cloud computing can be used not only to provide a consistent environment for computations to run but also successfully provide an environment for time-critical simulations. At the same time, the experiments demonstrated a need for a wider "ecosystem" needed to support the use of cloud computing: to be efficient and reliable, image development needs to be a part of the application production process to ensure seamless migration from local to resource elastically provisioned in the cloud.

## 2.4.2.2 Building a Cloud Computing Ecosystem with CernVM

A Large Ion Collider Experiment (ALICE) is one of the four experiments associated with the Large Hydron Collider (LHC) device at CERN whose focus is on heavy ion simulations. The scientists wanted to explore dynamically provisioning cloud resources and integrating them into the global pool of resources available to ALICE—managed by ALICE's AliEn scheduler [42]—to provide for the time-varying needs of their applications. The important objectives of this integration were to (1) make the process transparent to the end-user so that they do not need to change the ways in which they use the system and (2) make the integration so that no changes are required to the existing components of the infrastructure (e.g., the AliEn scheduler). This required the development of an ecosystem that not only supplied the images, but estimated the need for additional resources and automated provisioning them without the user's involvement.

Like the STAR scientists, LHC is working with applications requiring complex and consistent environment configurations and investigated virtualization as a potential solution. This resulted in the development of the CernVM project [43], which provides production environments supporting all four LHC experiments in VM images of various formats. The CernVM technology was originally started with the intent of supplying portable environments that scientists could easily deploy on their laptops and desktops for development work. However, flexible technology choices ensured support for a variety of VM formats, including the Xen images used by the Amazon EC2 as well as Science Clouds; the developed production images were also available for cloud computing.

The remaining challenge was to find a way to deploy these images so that they would dynamically and securely register with the AliEn scheduler and thus join the ALICE resource pool. This was achieved using the Nimbus Context Broker, which allows a user to securely provide context-specific information to a VM deployed on remote resources and vice versa. The resulting system [44] first dynamically deploys CernVM virtual machines on the Nimbus cloud at the University of Chicago. The deployed VMs then join the pool of resources available to AliEN as orchestrated by the Context Broker. Finding a new available resource, the AliEn scheduler schedules jobs on it. With the addition of a queue sensor that deploys and terminates VMs based on demand (as evidenced by the presence of jobs in the queue), the researchers can experiment with ways to balance the cost of the additional resources against the need for them.

The integration succeeded in achieving its objective of leveraging cloud resources while retaining a job management interface familiar to the end-user and using unmodified middleware. In this specific integration example, virtual nodes provisioned in the cloud are treated as remote resources requiring a grid scheduler (AlieEN) to manage. But these resources are different from the usual grid resource in that they now have a configuration that can be trusted—a feature that could potentially be leveraged to produce a simpler system.

### 2.4.2.3 CloudBLAST: Creating a Distributed Cloud Platform

To date, users have typically treated resources available in the distributed environment as untrusted and developed special ways of interacting with them. Cloud computing introduces an important innovation in that it allows users to fully configure remote resources (contained in VMs) so that their configuration can now be trusted. If we also manage to secure the network traffic between sites, we can create a platform where a collection of distributed resources can have the same level of trust a site has.

To build such a platform, we combined Nimbus with the ViNE overlay [45], an efficient network overlay implementation developed at the University of Florida. The resulting platform allows the user to select IaaS allocations from a few different cloud providers, potentially offering different service levels. We built a secure environment on top of those allocations using a provider-independent network overlay and the Context Broker for configuration exchange. The advantage of this approach is that it creates an environment with site-level trust, so that applications can be ported to it directly for ease of experimentation and use.

The Distributed Cloud Platform has been used for computer science experiments with latency-sensitive tools such as the Hadoop [6] implementation of MapReduce [6] and the Message Passing Interface [46] conducted across resources provisioned in multiple, widely distributed clouds [47]. They have shown that distributed cloud resources can provide a viable platform for applications using those tools (in the investigated case: the bioinformatics BLAST application).

## 2.5 Gadgets and OpenSocial Containers

### Wenjun Wu and Marlon Pierce

One way science gateways and others are providing SaaS is through the use of portlets or gadgets. Both portlets and gadgets are web components that can be used to aggregate dynamic web contents. But the design concepts of portlets and gadgets are very different. Portlet frameworks achieve web content aggregation on the server side, while gadget frameworks enable client-side aggregation following the Web 2.0 paradigm. A gadget can be regarded as a miniature web application and can define its content and control logic in client-side JavaScript and HTML. In this way, it has less dependence on its container than a portlet. Many science gateways projects have already built their web portals based on the JSR-168 portlet framework. Currently, Google gadgets are becoming an increasingly popular way of delivering customized web content and accessing cloud computing services. This new approach can leverage science gateway portals in terms of rich user interface and social network capability, which will promote the adoption of science gateways for advanced education and the next generation of young scientists.

A standardized gadget framework is necessary for the development and deployment of gadgets. The Google-led OpenSocial [48] consortium defines a framework that standardizes the practices of gadget and social-networking sites, enabling web developers to write gadgets that can run in any OpenSocial compliant container. Many social networking sites have adopted the OpenSocial framework and have opened their containers to developers. For example, an OpenSocial gadget can be easily added into the iGoogle sandbox [49]. Moreover, the Apache Shindig [50] incubator project provides a reference implementation of the OpenSocial container for PHP and Java. It can be used as a platform for gateway developers to understand the internals of the OpenSocial framework and test their gadgets before deploying the gadgets to commercial social networking sites.

The Open Grid Computing Environments (OGCE) project has undertaken a pilot project to test the feasibility of using the Open Social framework for science gateways. We have developed a set of gadgets for both Open Life Science Gateway (OLSG) [51] and the SIDGrid [52]. OLSG is a computational portal that integrates a group of bioinformatics applications and data collections. SIDGrid provides a cyber-infrastructure to help social and behavioral scientists collect and annotate data, collaborate and share data, and analyze and mine large data repositories.

The OLSG includes three gadgets (Figure 2.2): ClustalW, BLAST, and JobHistory, which can be loaded in iGoogle or any compatible container. Both BLAST and ClustalW are very commonly used sequence alignment tools in bioinformatics. Through these two gadgets, users can post DNA or protein sequences and run the OLSG's alignment services. The JobHistory gadget allows users to check the status of their computing tasks and retrieve the result reports from the finished tasks. We also built a SIDGrid Preview Gadget (Figure 2.3) that can visualize social experiment data including video, audio, and annotation in a synchronized way.

OpenSocial gadgets are associated with OAuth [53], an emerging standard for Web security. To support OAuth in our gadgets, we have developed an OAuth provider that consists of a group of Java Servlets. By using OAuth tokens, an OpenSocial container and our science gateway build up their mutual trust so that the science gateway can authorize requests from the container to access the restricted data and services.

**Figure 2.2    Three OLSGW Gadgets running on the iGoogle page.**

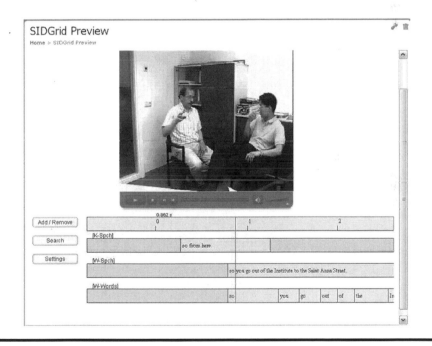

**Figure 2.3    SIDGrid Flash Preview Gadget running on the Orkut social networking site.**

Based on our initial experiments, we conclude that OpenSocial and related standards like OAuth are a suitable platform for building science gateways. Code originally developed for the OLSG and SIDGrid have been contributed back to the OGCE, and we are examining ways to generalize these contributions for new gateways. The current research in OpenSocial gadgets will eventually lead to a "social cloud" that can support collaborative computing and data analysis through world wide OpenSocial platforms and cloud computing infrastructure. In this "social cloud," cross-domain researchers will be able to easily build up their communities based on their existing social connections in the science domains and share their computational workflows, analysis data results, and even cloud computing cycles in a secured and collaborative environment.

## 2.6 Architecture of an SaaS Science Gateway

*John McGee*

The RENCI science gateway [54] is one example of providing scientific SaaS with a supercomputing capability on the back end. The vision for this gateway is to provide multiple means of access to a large and growing number of scientific applications that will run on high performance (HPC) and/or high throughput (HTC) compute systems. To achieve this vision, we have developed a highly scalable process for creating, deploying, and hosting services that are backed by national scale HPC/HTC resources.

A variety of different access mechanisms for the software services is desirable to accommodate different usage models with varying levels of capability and correlated ease of use. The gateway provides synchronous services for simpler scenarios where the service client can be expected to maintain a connection to the gateway for the lifetime of the service interaction. This is a simple way for an SaaS client to test or probe the functions of the scientific software systems on the other side of the service interface. It is not, however, useful in a case where the service invocation results in a large amount of compute activity that will be scheduled on an HPC resource or distributed among a large number of systems in an HTC solution. In this case, an asynchronous service interface will be required to handle the long running job(s) and the programming of the client to interact with the service is slightly more complicated. Having both of these interfaces for each scientific application on the back end enables the gateway to support a broad range of cases, such as calling the service on a range of cells in an Excel spreadsheet or running BLAST against 100,000 DNA sequences.

Providing and maintaining a large number of applications via multiple service interfaces can be challenging from a management and maintenance perspective. The RENCI Science Portal currently has 120 such scientific applications available. In addition to the interfaces themselves, additional components must be maintained for each application, for example documentation, a portlet, information for web service registries, and information needed to launch these applications into the HPC/HTC systems. To achieve the desired scale, we have implemented a process where all of the required information per application is collected in the form of metadata for that application. From the metadata for a given science application, we then generate all of the service interfaces and other components described above. Another benefit to this approach is that we can more easily add entirely new access mechanisms (e.g., Google Gadgets or other Web 2.0 client technologies) across all science applications, simply by adding new modules to the generator.

By definition, the science gateway is a value layer in between the large HPC/HTC national resources and the researchers using the software services. Figure 2.4 shows the architecture of this value layer for the RENCI science gateway. The back-end computational and data analysis capabilities are scalable due to the use of a local Condor pool to cache, manage, and match the jobs with HPC/HTC resources.

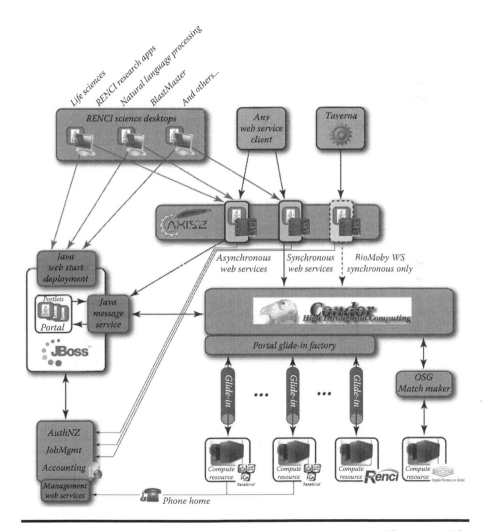

**Figure 2.4  Architecture of the RENCI Science Gateway, providing Scientific SaaS.**

Jobs known to have a short runtime are easily directed to local resources avoiding queue wait time on the in-demand national resources, and a submission of a very large number of jobs can be spread across many back-end HPC/HTC resources. Additional back-end engines such as Amazon EC2 or Microsoft Azure could also be added based on demand.

The hosting infrastructure for this SaaS solution is scalable in terms of supporting high volumes of simultaneous access via the deployment architecture as a result of using enterprise class features and industry standard technologies, such as message queuing (Java Message Service), enterprise middleware (JBoss), web service framework (Apache Axis2), application framework (Spring), and distributed computing (Condor). The core components of this architecture can be deployed on separate dedicated hardware systems or VMs and support clustering for load balancing and failover.

## 2.7 Dynamic Provisioning of Large-Scale Scientific Datasets

*Chaitan Baru*

Scientific data management systems are faced with a deluge of data from a variety of sources, from large-scale simulations to data from various instruments and observing platforms [55]. These systems need to be capable of managing very large data volumes and serving them in useful ways to a community of users. Thus far, resource constraints and assumptions from previous generations of technology have constrained these systems to adopt a relatively static, "one size fits all" approach to managing data, even as they serve communities of users with a wide and varying range of access and processing requirements. New approaches are required to effectively and efficiently serve these data to end users and applications. Given advances in sensor, processor, storage, and networking technologies, the data deluge can only be expected to increase with time.

A number of new factors have now come to the fore and provide opportunities to rethink the approaches to storage, including the following:

- Availability of very large clusters with fault resilient software environments. Systems like Apache Hadoop, which was inspired by Google's MapReduce and the Google File System (GFS) [56], now make it easier to manage and process large data sets using large clusters.
- Increasing awareness of the total cost of acquisition and ownership, with emphasis being placed not only on the acquisition cost, but also on personnel costs for programming applications and for system management, as well as ownership costs, including in terms of power consumption. Data management solutions ought to keep all these costs in mind.

■ Changing software environments. Service-oriented architectures (SOA) provide more opportunities to observe user access patterns and workloads and correspondingly optimize the system for better performance. Traditionally, providers have made data available as files—sized typically according to what may have been convenient for the data acquirer or provider—to be shipped on media or downloaded via ftp. Users download data and work with them on their own systems, thus missing the opportunity for the data center to optimize data management based on the community's use of the data. Common data repositories and portal-based environments not only help amortize costs, but also provide the opportunity for observing and optimizing user access patterns. Furthermore, workflow-based systems also make it possible to more easily provide alternative, or customized, processing strategies.

## 2.7.1 Science Gateways for Data

Science gateways for data provide users with easy, online access to very large data sets with the ability to perform basic queries and subsetting operations on the data as well as invoke processing and visualization operations. An example of such a gateway is the OpenTopography.org portal that provides Web-based access to high-resolution LiDAR topographic data, allowing users to process these data to generate custom digital elevation models (DEMs) or access pre-computed, "derived" data products [57,58]. The OpenTopography portal allows users to subset remote sensing data (stored as "point cloud" data sets), process it using different algorithms, and visualize the output. About 5 TB (~13.5 billion points) of data are hosted by the system using IBM's DB2 database system implemented on an eight-node cluster with extensions to support spatial data. In the LiDAR data collection, different data sets are of different sizes. The smaller datasets are distributed (declustered) across fewer nodes (three nodes) while the larger datasets are declustered across all nodes. Implementing the system using DB2 provides powerful capabilities for spatial indexing of the data as well as for subsetting the data using SQL.

## 2.7.2 Cloud Computing and Data

For very large scientific data archives, there is the opportunity to provision the data differently based on the frequency and nature of access to data. A "provisioning strategy" is a resource allocation strategy that a system employs in order to provide the best possible qualities of service, such as response times, quality of data, and the range of available capabilities. Resources may include the number of nodes, number of processors, number of disks, disk layout, and software used. Cloud computing is predicated on the ability to dynamically allocate resources to a given computational problem. In the case of large data sets, this requires the ability to dynamically and efficiently load data sets into the system and to serve the data to the user or application. Large Hadoop clusters provide one possible solution for serving such data. For example, Amazon has introduced the Elastic MapReduce service, which allows data sets to be dynamically loaded into a system and processed using the MapReduce-style processing [59].

A number of storage abstractions and models are being proposed in the context of cloud computing. Microsoft Azure, for example, provides abstractions such as Table, Blob, and Queue. Amazon provides the Simple Storage Service [7], Elastic Block Storage [15], and a key/blob store [60]. MapReduce itself depends on the Google File System [56] and the corresponding Hadoop implementation uses the Hadoop Distributed File System [61]. Several database abstractions have been developed for MapReduce and Hadoop, such as HIVE [62], CloudBase [63], and BigTable [64]. HIVE is a data warehouse infrastructure built on top of Hadoop that provides tools to enable easy data summarization, ad hoc querying, and analysis of large datasets data stored in Hadoop files. It provides a mechanism to put structure on this data and it also provides a simple query language called QL, which is based on SQL and enables users familiar with SQL to query this data. At the same time, this language also allows traditional map/reduce programmers to be able to plug in their custom mappers and reducers to do more sophisticated analysis, which may not be supported by the built in capabilities of the language. CloudBase is also built on top of the MapReduce architecture and provides the ability to query flat log files using an implementation of ANSI SQL. BigTable is also a distributed storage system built on GFS that is designed to scale to very large databases. The data model is a sparse, distributed, persistent, multidimensional sorted map indexed by row and column keys and a time stamp.

Amazon's Elastic MapReduce supports processing of vast amounts of data utilizing a hosted Hadoop framework running on the web-scale infrastructure of Amazon EC2 and S3. Using Elastic MapReduce, one can provision as much or as little capacity as needed to perform data-intensive tasks. Elastic MapReduce automatically spins up a Hadoop implementation of the MapReduce framework on Amazon EC2 instances, subdividing the data in a job flow into smaller chunks so that they can be processed (the "map" function) in parallel and eventually recombining the processed data into the final solution (the "reduce" function). Amazon S3 serves as the source for the data being analyzed and as the output destination for the end results.

The CloudStor Project [65] at the San Diego Supercomputer Center is studying trade-offs between parallel database systems, such as DB2 and Oracle in a cluster, versus Hadoop and Hadoop-based storage systems, for dynamically provisioning data-intensive applications. Standard database implementations can provide high performance access to the data using spatial indexes and supports rich functionality using SQL and spatial extensions to SQL. To do so, the data must be loaded into a database system and indexed for efficient access. Optimizing data load times is an important consideration since we are interested in dynamic data serving strategies where only a part of the data may be loaded into the database, based either on user request or by observing workload patterns. Load times can be improved by partitioning the set of input data files into distinct table partitions and then loading each partition in parallel across all nodes of the clustered database. In some cases, database systems are also designed to directly access data in external files without going through a load phase. The various alternatives need to be evaluated for performance.

The DB2 architecture is well suited for clusters since it is able to exploit cluster (shared-nothing) parallelism by partitioning databases across the nodes of a cluster. The optimal number of nodes for a database depends on the database size and the specified workload. The speeds of data loading, indexing, and query processing are important considerations in supporting the capability to create databases on-demand. Such databases will have a "residence time" that is determined by the user or by the system, after which time they may be deleted or dropped from the system. The time to create a database should be much shorter than the residence time of the database, e.g., 1 day to create/load a database versus 2 months of residence time. The output of a SQL query in a clustered database can be generated in parallel so that each node of the cluster outputs its part of the result as a separate file. Thus, a particular user request could generate parallel output, represented by a set of files. This is useful in cases where the output is then processed by another parallel program.

The database performance can be compared with the performance of "pure" Hadoop-based solutions where the data are kept in flat files in GFS or HDFS, and the data subset operation is performed using MapReduce. The MapReduce implementations can be tuned in many ways. By default, MapReduce automatically splits the input files into M pieces for the map phase and the intermediate files into R partitions for the reduce phase. Both M and R can be controlled via optional parameters. One can optimize the values of M and R for the data sizes and compute cycles available on the cluster. Furthermore, the default partitioning function may not always be the best option. Custom splitting routines that take the nature of data and the type of applications into account may perform better. For example, a range partitioning scheme based on certain key values may result in better overall performance than a random, hash-based partitioning.

Cloud computing is promising as an approach for the dynamic provisioning of data-intensive applications. However, rigorous performance testing is needed to determine the best implementation for a given application and for tuning of system parameters. The CloudStor Project at SDSC is engaged in such performance studies using a variety of cloud computing platforms, including the Google-IBM CluE cluster and the newly acquired Triton Shared Resource Cluster at UC San Diego.

## 2.8 Future Directions

The pursuit of science will continue to be shaped by technology developments in new and important ways. Our ability to gain insights from the increasingly numerical scientific world of environmental sensors, particle accelerators, individualized DNA sequencing, and the like depends on our ability to intelligently interpret these data. Cloud computing and SaaS provide the type of flexible, demand-driven technologies that can help with such analysis.

Some scientific computing algorithms, traditionally run on tightly coupled supercomputers, require access to thousands of processors simultaneously and depend on low latency network connections and an environment where all processors stay up for the length of a run. These seem less suited to a cloud architecture than applications that require millions of single processor jobs. However, new trends in very high processor count supercomputer systems are driving algorithmic development, which may in fact improve the ability of some scientific algorithms to run effectively in a cloud environment.

Cloud computing can be a time saver for scientists in several regards. Wolski notes that "Cloud applications, once debugged and tuned, tend to be quite robust and scalable." This could significantly reduce the time spent on software maintenance for scientists, though as hardware developments continue, software should still be occasionally tuned so as not to miss significant performance benefits. Reproducible results should be much easier to achieve using clouds as well. Wolski also notes that IT investments can be significantly reduced through the use of clouds. This can make the ability to analyze all that incoming data more realistic for small science teams and can reduce the dependence on graduate students for system administrator duties within a research group.

The Nimbus environment is designed as a set of APIs and as such will be well suited to the many directions scientists may want to explore with this technology. Early extensions to Nimbus include data privacy and monitoring components for the biomedical and high-energy physics communities, respectively. Nimbus has also been used successfully under deadlines to produce results for a major conference. Experiences such as these will continue to increase confidence in the technology and reduce the perception that "I need my own cluster to meet my deadlines." We see tremendous growth in this area.

SaaS also holds great promise for science. The analysis required for the increasingly digital nature of science will be carried out by software on computers. The ability to abstract both the software and the computing will clearly benefit scientists. The ability to fit these capabilities into a young scientist's lifestyle will benefit science even further. Seventy-five percent of 18 to 24 year olds have social networking Web sites [66].

Work with the OLSG and the SIDGrid indicates that some science applications can be adapted to the social networking environment. This exponentially increases the potential for collaboration—both within and between disciplines—on the most challenging science problems. All of today's social networking infrastructures can be leveraged to connect scientists doing similar work. Computational workflows, data, and even cloud computing cycles will be shared in a secured and collaborative environment.

For groups wanting to deploy very large numbers of software packages as a service, an automated approach such as that outlined by the RENCI team is absolutely essential. Coupling this level of organization with the availability of flexible cloud computing resources delivers valuable capabilities to biologists who rely on many different software packages. Through the use of such a framework, software interfaces can easily be adapted to changing technologies—from web services to OpenSocial interfaces.

Finally, in the data-intensive world of today's science, the ability of clouds to effectively handle data provisioning is key to their relevance to the scientific community. Science and engineering applications are often data intensive and the ability to adapt data delivery and analysis methods to this new infrastructure are very promising. Commercial enterprises can dynamically and efficiently load data sets into the system to serve the data to the user or application. A variety of database strategies in particular have been developed. The CloudStor Project at the San Diego Supercomputer Center is studying the trade-offs between parallel database systems, such as DB2 and Oracle in a cluster versus Hadoop and Hadoop-based storage systems, for dynamically provisioning data-intensive applications. Provisioning data via clouds and sharing it programmatically with others via Web 3.0 are some very exciting directions for science.

# References

1. Hendler, J. Web 3.0 emerging. *IEEE Computer*, 42(1): 111–113, January 2009.
2. Tao, T. NCBI Blast, 2006. http://www.ncbi.nlm.nih.gov/staff/tao/URLAPI/blastall/blastall_node2.html [Retrieved: April 22, 2009, from National Center for Technology Information].
3. Azgad, Y. International Protein Data Bank enhanced by computer browser. *Interface*, November 2, 1995.
4. http://www.rcsb.org
5. Dunning, T.R.B. *Impact of Advances in Computing and Communications Technologies on Chemical Science and Technology: Report of a Workshop*. Chemical Sciences Roundtable, Board on Chemical Sciences and Technology, Commission on Physical Sciences, Mathematics, and Applications. Washington, DC: National Academy Press, 1999.
6. Dean, J. and S. Ghemawat. MapReduce: Simplified data processing on large clusters. In *OSDI'04: Sixth Symposium on Operating System Design and Implementation*, San Francisco, CA, 2004.
7. Hadoop. http://hadoop.apache.org/
8. Amazon Elastic Compute Cloud (Amazon EC2). http://www.amazon.com/ec2
9. Amazon Simple Storage Service. Available from: http://aws.amazon.com/s3/ [Accessed: May 12, 2009].
10. Buyya, R., C.S. Yeo, and S. Venugopal. Market-oriented cloud computing: Vision, hype, and reality for delivering IT services as computing utilities. In *10th IEEE International Conference on High Performance Computing and Communications*, Dalian, China, 2008.
11. Skillicorn, D.B. The case for datacentric grids. In *Parallel and Distributed Processing Symposium (IPDPS)*, Fort Lauderdale, FL, 2002.

12. Chang, M., J. He, and E. Castro-Leon. Service-orientation in the computing infrastructure. In *SOSE'06: Second IEEE International Symposium on Service-Oriented System Engineering*, Shanghai, China, 2006.
13. Greschler, D. and T. Mangan. Networking lessons in delivering "software as a service": Part I. *Int. J. Netw. Manag.*, 12(5): 317–321, 2002.
14. Laplante, P.A., J. Zhang, and J. Voas. What's in a name? Distinguishing between SaaS and SOA. *IT Professional*, 10(3): 46–50, 2008.
15. Amazon Web Services home page. http://aws.amazon.com/
16. Amazon Elastic Block Store. Available from: http://aws.amazon.com/ebs/ [Accessed: May 12, 2009].
17. Nurmi, D., R. Wolski, C. Grzegorczyk, G. Obertelli, S. Soman, L. Youseff, and D. Zagorodnov. The eucalyptus open-source cloud-computing system. In *Proceedings of the ACM/IEEE International Symposium on Cluster Computing and the Grid (CCGrid 2009)*, Shanghai, China, 2009.
18. Nurmi, D., R. Wolski, C. Grzegorczyk, G. Obertelli, S. Soman, L. Youseff, and D. Zagorodnov. Eucalyptus: A technical report on an elastic utility computing architecture linking your programs to useful systems. In UCSB Technical Report ID: 2008-10, 2008.
19. The eucalyptus project page. http://eucalyptus.cs.ucsb.edu/
20. RightScale home page. http://www.rightscale.com/
21. CohesiveFT. http://www.cohesiveft.com
22. rPath. http://www.rpath.com
23. Chohan, R., C. Bunch, S. Pang, C. Krintz, N. Mostafa, S. Soman, and R. Wolski. Appscale design and implementation. In UCSB Technical Report ID: 2009-02, 2009.
24. The AppScale project page. http://appscale.cs.ucsb.edu/
25. dotCloud. http://www.dotcloud.org.
26. The Eucalyptus Public Cloud. http://eucalyptus.cs.ucsb.edu/wiki/EucalyptusPublicCloud
27. Google App Engine. http://code.google.com/appengine/
28. Czajkowski, K., I. Foster, N. Karonis, C. Kesselman, S. Martin, W. Smith, and S. Tuecke. A resource management architecture for metacomputing systems. In *Fourth Workshop on Job Scheduling Strategies for Parallel Processing*, Orlando, FL, Springer-Verlag, Heidelberg, Germany, 1998, pp. 62–82.
29. Keahey, K. and K. Doering. From sandbox to playground: Dynamic virtual environments in the grid. ANL/MCS-P1141-0304, 2003.
30. Keahey, K., K. Doering, and I. Foster. From sandbox to playground: Dynamic virtual environments in the grid. In *Fifth International Workshop in Grid Computing*, Pittsburgh, PA, 2004.
31. Keahey, K., I. Foster, T. Freeman, X. Zhang, and D. Galron. Virtual Workspaces in the Grid. In *EuroPar*, Lisbon, Portugal, 2005.
32. Keahey, K. and T. Freeman. Contextualization: Providing one-click virtual clusters. In *eScience*, Indianapolis, IN, 2008.
33. Keahey, K., I. Foster, T. Freeman, and X. Zhang. Virtual workspaces: Achieving quality of service and quality of life in the grid. *Sci. Programming J.*, 13(5):265–275, 2005.
34. Foster, I.C., K. Czajkowski, D.F. Ferguson, J. Frey, S. Graham, T. Maguire, D. Snelling, and S. Tuecke. Modeling and managing state in distributed systems: The role of OGSI and WSRF. *Proc. IEEE*, 93(3): 604–612, 2005.
35. Freeman, T. and K. Keahey. Flying low: Simple leases with workspace pilot. In *EuroPar 2008*, Las Palmas de Gran Canaria, Spain, 2008.
36. Science Clouds. http://workspace.globus.org/clouds/

37. Descher, M., P. Masser, T. Feilhauer, A.M. Tjoa, and D. Huemer. Retaining data control to the client in infrastructure clouds. In *ARES*, Fukuoka, Japan, 2009.

38. Freeman, T., K. Keahey, I. Foster, A. Rana, B. Sotomayor, and F. Wuerthwein. Division of labor: Tools for growth and scalability of the Grids. In *ICSOC 2006*, Chicago, IL, 2006.

39. Sotomayor, B., K. Keahey, and I. Foster. Overhead matters: A model for virtual resource management. In *First International Workshop on Virtualization Technology in Distributed Computing (VTDC)*, Tampa, FL, 2006.

40. Sotomayor, B., K. Keahey, and I. Foster. Combining batch execution and leasing using virtual machines. In *HPDC 2008*, Boston, MA. 2008.

41. Heavey, A. Clouds make way for STAR to shine. http://www.isgtw.org/?pid=1001735

42. AliEn. http://alien.cern.ch/twiki/bin/view/AliEn/Home

43. CernVM. http://cernvm.cern.ch/cernvm/

44. Harutyunyan, A. and P. Buncic. Dynamic virtual clusters for AliEn. In *CHEP09*, Prague, Czech Republic, 2009.

45. Tsugawa, M. and J. Fortes. A virtual network (ViNe) architecture for grid computing. In *IPDPS*, Rhodes Island, Greece, 2006.

46. Snir, M. and W. Gropp. *MPI The Complete Reference*. Cambridge, MA: MIT Press, 1994.

47. Matsunaga, A., M. Tsugawa, and J. Fortes. CloudBLAST: Combining MapReduce and virtualization on distributed resources for bioinformatics applications. *eScience 2008*, Indianapolis, IN, 2008.

48. OpenSocial Specification. http://www.opensocial.org/

49. iGoogle sandbox. http://code.google.com/apis/igoogle/docs/igoogledevguide.html

50. Shindig. http://incubator.apache.org/shindig/

51. Wu, W., R. Edwards, I.R. Judson, M.E. Papka, M. Thomas, and R. Steves. TeraGrid Open Life Science Gateway. In *TeraGrid 2008 Conference*, Las Vegas, NV, June 9–13, 2008. http://archive.teragrid.org/events/teragrid08/Papers/papers/24.pdf

52. Bertenthal, B., R. Grossman, D. Hanley, M. Hereld, S. Kenny, L. Gina-Anne, M.E. Papka et al. Social informatics data grid. In *E-Social Science 2007 Conference*, Ann Arbor, MI, October 7–9, 2007. http://ess.si.umich.edu/papers/paper184.pdf

53. OAuth. http://oauth.net/core/1.0

54. http://portal.renci.org

55. Anderson, C. The end of theory: The data deluge makes the scientific method obsolete. *Wired Magazine*. Available from: http://www.wired.com/science/discoverics/magazine/16-07/pb_theory [Accessed: May 12, 2009].

56. Ghemawat, S., H. Gobioff, and S.T. Leung. The Google file system. In *Proceedings of the 19th ACM Symposium on Operating Systems Principles*, Lake George, NY, pp. 20–43, 2003.

57. Crosby, C.J., J.L. Blair, V. Nandigam, A. Memon, C. Baru, and J.R. Arrowsmith. KML-based access and visualization of high resolution LiDAR topography. *Eos Trans, AGU*, Fall Meet Suppl., Abstract IN41B-1149, 2008

58. Jaeger-Frank, E., C.J. Crosby, A. Memon, V. Nandigam, J.R. Arrowsmith, J. Conner, I. Altintas, and C. Baru. A three tier architecture for LiDAR interpolation and analysis. In *Lecture Notes in Computer Science*, 3993, April 2006, pp. 920–927, DOI:10.1007/11758532_123.

59. Amazon Elastic MapReduce. Available from: http://aws.amazon.com/elasticmapreduce/ [Accessed: May 12, 2009].

60. Amazon SimpleDB. Available from: http://aws.amazon.com/simpledb/ [Accessed: May 12, 2009].

61. HDFS Architecture. Available from: http://hadoop.apache.org/core/docs/current/hdfs_design.html [Accessed: May 12, 2009].
62. HIVE. Available from: http://hadoop.apache.org/hive/ [Accessed: May 12, 2009].
63. CloudBase. Available from: http://sourceforge.net/projects/cloudbase/ [Accessed: May 12, 2009].
64. Chang, F., J. Dean, S. Ghemawat, W. Hsieh, D. Wallach, M. Burrows, T. Chandra, A. Fikes, and R. Gruber. Bigtable. A distributed storage system for structured data. In *OSDI'06: Seventh Symposium on Operating System Design and Implementation*, Seattle, WA, November, 2006.
65. http://cloudstor.sdsc.edu
66. http://pewresearch.org/pubs/1079/social-networks-grow

*Chapter 3*

# Enterprise Knowledge Clouds: Next Generation Knowledge Management Systems?

Jeff Riley and Kemal Delic

## Contents

# 3.1 Introduction

The field of knowledge management (KM) has been through several cycles of hype and disappointment and has created important disputes along the lines of "knowledge" being the philosophical discourse and science and "management" being the empirical and experiential teaching. In reality, it has created a booming business for technologists, consultants, and a wide variety of technology vendors. Seen today, after a few decades, it still seems that the term "knowledge management" remains undefined, fuzzy, and disputed. Indeed, the very definition of "knowledge" and the distinction between data, information, and knowledge is poorly defined and still not well understood by many. Still, we are all aware of the rudimentary elements of "knowledge reuse" in a wide variety of business operations. Some will even hint that the contemporary Internet is a type of "knowledge bazaar" where individuals and corporations can shop for all manner of "knowledge consumables." In this chapter, we discuss the possibility that the treatment of knowledge management systems (KMS), which represent an intricate part of many business enterprises, has yet another chance of reappearing in totally new technological, market, and social circumstances.

In Section 3.2, we sketch the context in which we see the emergence of massive, globally dependable infrastructure(s) used by several hundreds of millions of users across the globe. We position business aims and interest in this subject and narrow those into enterprise needs for knowledge to operate. We then outline a generic knowledge management architecture within contemporary business enterprises, which typically appears in the form of the enterprise stack application, hosted in data centers.

After observing the current deficiencies and projecting future developments, we depict a high-level architecture for the Enterprise Knowledge Cloud (EKC) as a collaborative, cooperating, competing mega-structure providing computing, networking, and storage services to various "knowledge producers and consumers"—such as devices, people, and applications. Some architectural and design landscapes are provided for illustration. We conclude with a no-nonsense list of things we expect to observe happening as a sign of the mega-shift from the industrial to post-industrial world of the twenty-first century. We believe that EKCs are potential breakthrough applications marking an enterprise technology transition all the way from mainframe computers to networked PCs, to grids and emerging computing clouds.

## 3.1.1 Emerging Cloud Computing Infrastructures

The U.S. National Institute of Standards and Technology (NIST) draft definition of cloud computing is as follows:

> Cloud computing is a model for enabling convenient, on-demand network access to a shared pool of configurable computing resources

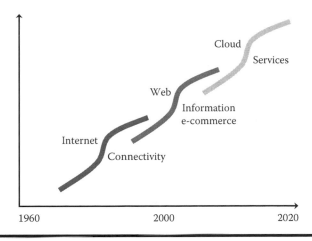

**Figure 3.1   The Internet evolving into the cloud. (Adapted from Delic, K.A. and Walker, M.A., *ACM Ubiquity*, 9, 31, 2009.)**

> (e.g., networks, servers, storage, applications, and services) that can be rapidly provisioned and released with minimal management effort or service provider interaction. (Mell and Grance 2009)

Based on this definition, it can immediately be seen that cloud computing encompasses infrastructure, which to some extent at least already exists today in the form of the World Wide Web ("the Web") providing a wide variety of information technology (IT) services that can be purchased on-demand (computing cycles, storage, and network) in a highly simplified procedure. Over time, just as "the Internet" has evolved into "the Web," the Web will evolve into "the cloud" (Figure 3.1).

We predict future growth in which we will see a huge number of common devices interconnected and totally new applications emerging. It will most likely emerge as a hugely re-scaled version of today's Internet. This growth will likely be stimulated via innovative applications starting to proliferate: a well-known social network has provided a platform for 4,000 applications written by 80,000 developers in just 6 months; the Amazon Elastic Compute Cloud (Amazon EC2) has 330,000 registered application developers.

We observe that the cloud infrastructure is global, highly dependable, and supports innovative business models and new types of social phenomena such as blogs, MySpace, Facebook, YouTube, and Twitter, not to mention the myriad multiplayer, role-playing games and virtual reality sites.

### 3.1.2  Collective Intelligence

Collective intelligence is a phenomenon that emerges from the interaction—either collaboration or competition—of many individuals. By some estimates, today there are 80 million people worldwide writing weblogs ("blogs"). The blogs are typically topic-oriented and some attract important readership. Authors range from large company CEOs to housewives and young children. When taken together, the cloud computing infrastructure that hosts *blogospheres* looks like a big social agglomeration providing a kind of "collective intelligence." But it is not just blogs that form the collective intelligence—the phenomenon of collective intelligence is nurtured and enhanced by the social and participatory culture of the Internet, so all content developed and shared on the Internet becomes part of the collective intelligence. The Internet then, and the content available there, appears as an omnipresent, omniscient, cloud-like giant infrastructure—as a new form of "knowledge management." Today this represents a massive collaboration of mostly people only, but very soon in the future we may envisage intelligent virtual objects and devices collaborating with people—this is already beginning to happen to some extent with Internet-attached devices starting to proliferate. Thus, rescaling from the actual ~1.2 billion users to tens or hundreds of billions of real-world objects having a data representation in the virtual world is probably realistic. A real danger, and a real problem to be solved by knowledge management practitioners, is how to sort the wheat from the chaff—or the knowledge from the data and information—in an environment where the sheer amount of data and information could be overwhelming.

### 3.1.3 Intelligent Enterprise

Business enterprises today use the existing Internet infrastructure to execute various business operations and provide a wide variety of services. As we see the shift of all nonphysical operations versus the Internet, we observe a new type of enterprise emerging: we call it the *Intelligent Enterprise* (Delic and Dayal 2002).

The Intelligent Enterprise is able to interact with its environment and change its behavior, structure, and strategy—behaving actually as an intelligent entity. It is able to adapt to rapid changing market circumstances, gradually change its business model, and survive into the next market cycle. The Intelligent Enterprise as we see it is characterized by its ability to learn from and adapt to changes in its environment and reinvent itself, sometimes with surprising results. In order to keep up with the rapidly changing demands of doing business, most enterprises implement increasingly complex IT solutions. Although implemented to make the enterprise more efficient, coupled with the organizational complexity of such large enterprise business, the technical complexity introduced by the many and varied IT solutions helps create pockets of inefficiencies within the organization. We see future Intelligent Enterprises deriving efficiencies through the automation of their core business processes and the exploitation of knowledge inherent in their organization. Their ability to respond quickly to changes will improve significantly as the knowledge base and "intelligence density" within the enterprise grows and problem-solving capabilities improve dramatically. Intelligent Enterprises will form dynamic partnerships with other enterprises to create dynamic business ecosystems, which will be self-managed, self-configured, and self-optimized. In short, future enterprises will become smarter—more intelligent—and by doing so will evolve automatically into organizations more suited to their changing environment.

We postulate that the emergence of collective intelligence in the cloud computing infrastructure will influence markets and established businesses, allowing—even encouraging—Intelligent Enterprises to emerge and reshape the contemporary approach to enterprise knowledge management (EKM). Next, we describe the current state of EKM.

## 3.2 Enterprise Knowledge Management: Architecture and Technologies

Constantly evolving markets exercise pressure on business enterprises to continually evolve and improve. One of the most widely used business paradigms is about EKM—as a means to capture and express tacit human knowledge into an explicit form (externalized knowledge or content) that could be later (hopefully) reused. Various schools of thought were proposed, several assistive technologies were developed, and an important number of successful EKM stories were reported. From our experience, the best domain for EKM is in the enterprise IT domain (Delic and Dayal 2000, Noël and Delic 2002, Delic and Douillet 2004)—as it is a domain under huge cost pressure, but one which is essential for strategic development.

From a highly abstracted view, the EKM IT domain consists of problem solving, monitoring, tuning and automation, business intelligence reporting, and decision-making tasks (Figure 3.2).

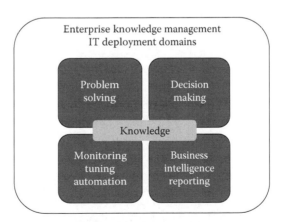

**Figure 3.2 EKM: IT deployment domains. (Adapted from Delic, K.A. and Riley, J.A., Enterprise knowledge clouds: Next generation KM systems?** *Proceedings of the 2009 International Conference on Information, Process, and Knowledge Management (eKnow 2009)***, Cancun, Mexico, February 2009.)**

Problem solving, especially in the EKM IT domain, is the task for which knowledge management techniques and systems are most commonly deployed. The proliferation of knowledge management systems for problem analysis and solving is many and varied, spanning the gamut from knowledge capture, representation, and transformation through to recognition, extraction, and reuse. Knowledge from all sources, including human expertise, in the form of plain text, models, visual artifacts, executable modules, etc. is used by intelligent knowledge management systems to enable users to solve problems without reference to scarce, and often expensive, human experts.

In recent years, a wide variety of artificial intelligence (AI) techniques and heuristics have been deployed in knowledge management systems in an effort to make the systems smarter and more responsive. These smarter knowledge management systems are particularly well suited to automation and self-management tasks, where the goal is to provide automated monitoring of system use and predictive tuning of system parameters to achieve automatic system scale out.

Business intelligence (BI) refers to a range of methodologies, technologies, skills, competencies, and applications businesses implement and utilize in order to better understand their commercial context. Typically business intelligence systems are knowledge management systems that provide current and predictive views of the business based on historical and current data relating to the business itself and the commercial environment in which it exists. Business intelligence reporting is more than the simple reporting of data gathered—it uses a wide range of AI techniques to extract relevant knowledge from incoming data streams and repositories and provides observations, hints, and suggestions about trends and possible futures.

Decision making is most often done by humans after understanding the results of the business intelligence reporting, but with the volume of business intelligence available to analysts increasing almost exponentially, it is becoming more and more difficult for humans to make sensible, rational, and timely decisions, so this task is increasingly becoming the responsibility of AI systems tuned to the environment of their deployment.

The tasks of problem solving, monitoring, tuning and automation, business intelligence reporting, and decision making are the most promising areas for the future deployment of EKCs. These areas will have a special flavor for the development of a slew of new technologies addressing the problems that previous computing facilities could not resolve.

Currently, the majority of the indicated IT tasks include people, while we suggest that this balance will be changed in the future through automation, ultimately leading to self-managing enterprise IT systems (Delic et al. 2007). When mapped into a more precise form, this conceptual drawing (Figure 3.2) will evolve into the enterprise-scale knowledge management application stack (Figure 3.3).

All knowledge management applications today can be layered into three essential subsystems:

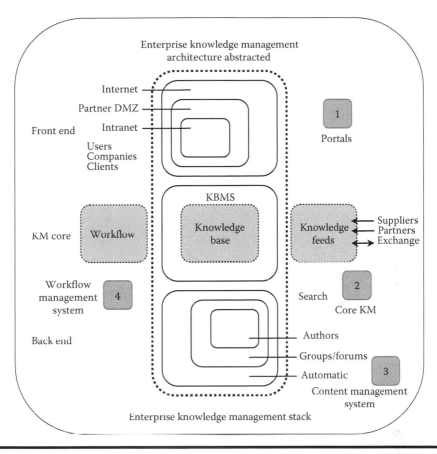

**Figure 3.3 EKM: Architectural view. (Adapted from Delic, K.A. and Riley, J.A., Enterprise knowledge clouds: Next generation KM systems?** *Proceedings of the 2009 International Conference on Information, Process, and Knowledge Management* **(e***Know 2009***), Cancun, Mexico, February 2009.)**

- Front-end portals that manage interactions with internal users, partner's agents, and external users while rendering various "knowledge services." Different classes of users—e.g., internal vs. external—are often presented with slightly different portals allowing access to different types of knowledge and services.

- A core layer that provides the knowledge base and access/navigation/guidance/management services to knowledge portals and other enterprise applications. The core layer provides the Knowledge Base Management System (KBMS), the knowledge feeds—the means by which knowledge is added to the knowledge base or exchanged with other knowledge management systems or users—as well as the mechanism to distribute and inject appropriate knowledge into business processes throughout the enterprise.

■ The back-end that supplies "knowledge content" and the content management system from various sources, authors, and communities that enables a refresh of the knowledge base.

The Enterprise Workflow System captures interactions with users and provides necessary context for the EKM system. Various feeds enable the flow and exchange of knowledge with partners and suppliers. Today these feeds are mainly proprietary, while we expect that they will evolve into standards-based solutions for large-scale content flows (RESTful services, RSS, ATOM, SFTP, JSON, etc.). To indicate the scale and size of the typical corporate knowledge management system, we presume that the knowledge base contains several million knowledge items, and users number in the hundreds of thousands. EKM is considered a high-end, mission-critical corporate application, which resides in the corporate data center. High availability and dependability are necessary engineering features for such global, always-on, always-available systems.

Thus, EKM is typically a three-tier enterprise application probably spread over several geographically dispersed data centers and typically interconnected or integrated with enterprise portals, content, and workflow management systems. In essence, EKM consists of the enterprise knowledge base (KB) with appropriate knowledge management routines (add/remove/modify KB), whose content is usually accessed via search access routines.

The ultimate result is that we are witnessing emerging social phenomena (writing blogs, participating in social networks, collaborating in wikis) enabled by an always-available, globally accessible, and secure infrastructure that can be used for free, or at a very low-cost, and running a mushrooming number of user-created applications. Some major companies are already announcing their intention to enter, drive, and dominate this field (*The Economist* 2008).

### 3.2.1 Enterprise Knowledge Management Infrastructure

Enterprise data centers are the key computational, storage, and network resources arranged around an efficient corporate network as the backbone of the enterprise IT infrastructure. Consequently, they are designed in such a way that the enterprise applications are categorized according to their criticality and provided with adequate infrastructural support. Thus, if many millions of users are critically dependent on an application, it would be categorized as a mission-critical, nonstop application and would be supported $24 \times 7$ and be always available. Some less critical applications will have yet another label, be supported $24 \times 5$, will not be considered nonstop, and would be something less than always available.

Thus, for EKM, if the risk of monetary and/or reputation loss is high, we will provide the infrastructure (clusters or high-end servers with some distinctive disaster recovery capabilities) and support, which will fulfill expectations and fit into dependability requirements—with appropriate trade-offs between cost and features.

### 3.2.2 *Enterprise Knowledge Management Applications*

Once we have categorized our EKM needs and provided the appropriate infrastructure, we should architect, design, and engineer EKM applications so that they fit into the entire EKM criticality. Thus, if the infrastructure is mission-critical, then EKM should have all the necessary features of a mission-critical application. It is out of the scope of this chapter to discuss this in more depth, but one should be well aware of this requirement as it will have implications for the software architecture, choice of operating system, platform, and programming environment: they should all respect the criticality label of the EKM system.

### 3.2.3 *Enterprise Knowledge Management Content*

Having briefly described the EKM infrastructure and applications, we should consider how enterprise knowledge will be represented, captured, processed, and delivered. Problem solving documents (Problem Description-Problem Solution) are the most simple and widely used way of capturing problem solving tasks. Some early EKM systems used a rule-based representation of knowledge; executable models (decision trees, case-based reasoning systems, neural networks) are more recent knowledge capturing paradigms. We believe that multimedia content will become dominant in the future and that new methods for knowledge capture and rendering will be devised.

### 3.2.4 *Enterprise Knowledge Management Users*

The evolution of technology in consumer and corporate domains has created a new type of user who will be very different from contemporary users. While sketching the architecture of future EKM systems, one should seriously analyze and consider several aspects and dimensions of future users. The best way would be to look at our children: they seem to have developed a way to quickly exchange information snippets, being either very short text messages or particular multimedia content. Also, it seems that they have a much better ability to multitask naturally while not losing or intermixing communication threads. This is the natural consequence of their exposure to gaming and new work and living styles. The so-called Millennium Generation will be the model for future users of EKM systems.

## 3.3 Enterprise Knowledge Cloud

Following social developments in the Internet world, it will be in the interest of business enterprises to deploy some of these new paradigms (social networks, blogging, open source) within their environments and with business intentions. Extrapolating what's going on in the open Internet, we project that enterprises will create several clouds for various purposes.

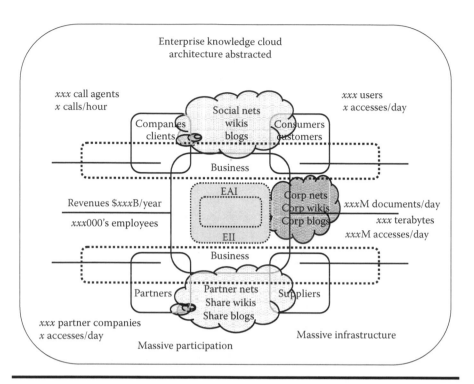

**Figure 3.4 EKC: Architectural view. (Adapted from Delic, K.A. and Riley, J.A., Enterprise knowledge clouds: Next generation KM systems?** *Proceedings of the 2009 International Conference on Information, Process, and Knowledge Management* **(eKnow 2009), Cancun, Mexico, February 2009.)**

An abstracted business enterprise architecture is shown in Figure 3.4. This architecture interconnects business partners and suppliers to company customers and consumers and uses future cloud technologies to harvest, process, and use internal knowledge (corporate nets, wikis, blogs). Furthermore, similar partner/supplier clouds will be developed to harvest, enrich, and deploy yet another knowledge cloud. Finally, the largest enterprise cloud will cover clients and consumers, which could be used for a wide variety of purposes.

Each of the clouds shown in Figure 3.4 is an autonomous entity, existing for its own purpose and capable of collecting, warehousing, managing, and serving knowledge to its own group of users. However, while the clouds discussed are independent, they should be capable of interconnection, overlap, and knowledge-sharing with appropriate rules and safeguards, so that, for example, customers and consumers might have access to appropriate internal enterprise knowledge or even partner/supplier knowledge through the cloud.

The emergence of these clouds (Private, Partner, Public) and their coalescence into the EKC allows, indeed encourages, the collective intelligences formed within each cloud to emerge and cooperate with each other, thus becoming the driving force for the true Intelligent Enterprise. As an example, internal IT operations will use Private Clouds, Sales, and Marketing and would operate on Public Clouds, while the Outsourcing business may reside on the Partner Clouds—each having different types of users and customers. The interaction and cooperation of the user groups, their knowledge, and the collective intelligences across the three clouds shown in Figure 3.4 provides the infrastructure for behavioral, structural, and strategic adaptation in response to changes in the respective (business) environment.

To see this happening in the future, we would expect to see the development of some major cloud computing technologies and adoption of common standards. This will enable yet another type of mega-application—Knowledge Exchange, for example, enabling the trade, exchange, and monetizing of knowledge assets. However, one should not underestimate the huge obstacles in the security, privacy, performance, and dependability of those clouds as the clear precondition for real-world deployments. One intricate problem to address will be the interoperability of clouds, leading to enabling technical standards but also aiming to establish monetary/value ground (accounting and billing systems) for the exchange of various cloud contents. All this is in a very early stage, but one should sense that developments may go in this direction.

## 3.4 The Next 5 to 15 Years

Today's enterprise applications are developed by IT departments, but for the future we predict a shift towards user-developed applications: mash-ups written in high-level mash-up languages. Content today is mainly text-based, but for the future we see an evolution towards multimedia context and active content (later).

Users today are either fixed or mobile—tomorrow we expect they will be virtual and later will take personalities of "avatars" to protect privacy and integrity.

Standards will evolve with the current Web 2.0 and will eventually evolve into something like Web 3.0—which we assume to be cloud computing.

Current EKM systems are enterprise applications in data centers, while we expect them to evolve into "enterprise grids" on which others envisage the development of "KM grids" (Cannataro and Talia 2003). Once the technology is stable and markets grow, we predict the development of clouds as the super-structure of enterprise grids, interconnecting enterprise data centers providing various functionalities.

Thus, while the architecture of today's EKM systems is built around the enterprise stack, tomorrow's EKM architecture will be distributed and loosely coupled and later will move to decoupled, completely pluggable, intelligent knowledge management appliances capable of adapting to interface with EKCs as required (Table 3.1).

We are in the midst of important social, technological, and market changes where we see some major companies announcing their intention to enter, drive,

**Table 3.1 Evolution of EKM Systems**

| EKM Systems | Today | Tomorrow | Beyond |
|---|---|---|---|
| Architecture | Enterprise stack | Distributed | Decoupled/pluggable |
| Infrastructure | Datacenter | Grid | Cloud |
| Application | IT controlled | User produced | On demand |
| Content | Mainly text | Multimedia | Active |
| Users | Fixed/mobile | Virtual | Avatars |
| Standards | 3W.org | Web 2.0 | Web 3.0 |

and dominate the field of cloud computing (Weiss 2007, Forrester Research 2008, Hayes 2008). We see this as a precondition for the emergence of the intelligent, adaptive enterprise that was announced in the previous century, but can be created only in the right technological circumstances.

We believe that enterprise intelligence will draw its capacities from the EKCs embedded in the global, dependable fabrics consisting of subjects, objects, and devices. Cloud computing will enable massive and rapid rescaling of the content production, consumption, and participation of the various groups of cloud users at an unprecedented scale. This may yet evolve into a "social computing" paradigm as the likely advanced form of future society.

Massive collaboration (on content tagging, for example) followed by the emergence of ontologies based on the Semantic Web, and adjusted by the *folksonomies* developed as user-oriented Web 2.0 applications, will embody "collective intelligence" as the new source of knowledge. To see this happen, we postulate the necessity of massive, global, mega-scale infrastructure in the form of "cloud computing" (interconnected grids and data centers). We are at the very beginning of important new developments where we expect that the field of EKM will be rescaled by an order of magnitude and will spawn the creation of "a new kind of EKM system." We expect that the monetary value of the enterprise knowledge exchanges will largely surpass the cost of the use of the cloud infrastructure based on commodity components. This will fulfill an old predicament of the "content as the king" of commerce.

# References

Cannataro, M. and Talia, D. 2003. The knowledge grid. *Communications of the ACM* 46(1): 89–93, January 2003.

Delic, K.A. and Dayal, U. 2000. Knowledge-based support services: Monitoring and adaptation. *DEXA Workshops 2000*, London, U.K., pp. 1097–1101.

Delic, K.A. and Dayal, U. 2002. The rise of the intelligent enterprise. *ACM Ubiquity*, 2002(45) (December 1–31, 2002) (accessed August 1, 2009).

Delic, K.A. and Douillet, L. 2004. Corporate IT knowledge workbench: Case study. *DEXA Workshops 2004*, Zaragoza, Spain, pp. 494–497.

Delic, K.A. and Riley, J.A. 2009. Enterprise knowledge clouds: Next generation KM systems? *Proceedings of the 2009 International Conference on Information, Process, and Knowledge Management (eKnow 2009)*, Cancun, Mexico, February 2009.

Delic, K.A. and Walker, M.A. 2009. Emergence of the academic computing cloud. *ACM Ubiquity*, 9(31) (August 5–11, 2008) (accessed August 1, 2009).

Delic, K.A., Riley, J., and Faihe, Y. 2007. Architecting principles for self-managing enterprise IT systems. *Proceedings of the Third International Conference on Autonomic and Autonomous Systems*, Athens, Greece, August 2007.

Forrester Research. 2008. Is cloud computing ready for the enterprise? *Forrester Research*, March 7, 2008.

Hayes, B. 2008. Cloud computing. *Communications of the ACM*, 51(7): 9–11, July 2008.

Mell, P. and Grance, T. 2009. Draft NIST working definition of cloud computing. http://csrc.nist.gov/groups/SNS/cloud-computing/index.html (accessed August 1, 2009).

Noël, F. and Delic, K.A. 2002. Knowledge-based self-support system for corporate users. *DEXA Workshops 2002*, Aix-en-Provence, France, pp 149–156.

*The Economist*. 2008. When clouds collide, February 7, 2008.

Weiss, A. 2007. Computing in the clouds. *netWorker*, 11(4): 16–25, December 2007.

## Chapter 4

# Real Cases and Applications of Cloud Computing

Jinzy Zhu

## Contents

# 4.1 Cloud Computing: IT as a Service

As an evolutionary computing model, cloud computing has been in the making for a long time—it embodies the development and aggregation of existing computing styles such as grid computing and utility computing. Some traces of grid computing and utility computing can be found in cloud computing use cases. However, cloud computing distinguishes itself from previous technology with its combination of the latest in technical developments and emerging business models, creating remarkable commercial value in new use scenarios.

In a nutshell, the existing Internet provides us with content in the form of videos, e-mails, and information served on web pages. With cloud computing, the next generation of the Internet will allow us to "buy" IT services from a web portal, drastically expanding the types of merchandise available beyond those on e-commerce sites such as eBay and Taobao. We would be able to rent from a virtual storefront the basic necessities needed to build a virtual data center, such as a CPU, memory, and storage and add on top of that the middleware necessary, such as web application servers, databases, enterprise server bus, etc., as the platform(s) to support the applications we would like to either rent from an Independent Software Vendor (ISV) or develop ourselves. Together this is what we call IT as a Service (ITaaS) bundled to us the end users as a virtual data center.

Within ITaaS, there are three layers starting with Infrastructure as a Service (IaaS) comprised of the physical assets we can see and touch: servers, storage, and networking switches. At the IaaS level, what cloud computing service providers can offer is basic computing and storage capability, such as the cloud computing center founded by IBM in Wuxi Software Park and Amazon EC2. Taking computing power provision as an example, the basic unit provided is the server, including the CPU, memory, storage, operating system, and system monitoring software.

In order to allow users to customize their own server environment, server template technology is used, which means binding certain server configurations and the operating system and software together and providing customized functions as required at the same time.

Using virtualization technology, we could provide as little as 0.1 CPU in a virtual machine to the end user, therefore drastically increasing the utilization potential of a physical server to multiple users.

With virtualization increasing the number of machines to manage, service provision becomes crucial since it directly affects service management and the IaaS maintenance and operation efficiency. Automation, the next core technology, can make resources available for users through self-service without getting the service providers involved. A stable and powerful automation management program can reduce the marginal cost to zero, which in turn can promote the scale effect of cloud computing.

On the basis of automation, dynamic orchestration of resources can be realized. The dynamic orchestration of resources aims to meet the requirements of service levels. For example, the IaaS platform will add new servers or storage spaces for users automatically according to the CPU utilization of the server, so as to fulfill the terms of service levels made with users beforehand. The intelligence and reliability of the dynamic orchestration of resource technology is a key point here. Additionally, virtualization is another key technology. It can maximize resource utilization efficiency and reduce the cost of an IaaS platform and user usage by promoting physical resource sharing. The dynamic migration function of virtualization technology can dramatically improve the service availability and this is attractive for many users.

The next layer within ITaaS is Platform as a Service (PaaS). At the PaaS level, what the service providers offer is packaged IT capability, or some logical resources, such as databases, file systems, and application operating environment. Currently, actual cases in the industry include Rational Developer Cloud of IBM, Azure of Microsoft, and AppEngine of Google. At this level, two core technologies are involved. The first is software development, testing, and running based on cloud. The PaaS service is software developer–oriented. It used to be a huge difficulty for developers to write programs via networks in a distributed computing environment, and now due to the improvement of network bandwidth, two technologies can solve this problem. The first type of technology is online development tools. Developers can directly complete remote development and application through browser and remote console (development tools run in the console) technologies without the local installation of development tools. The second type of technology is the integration technology of local development tools and cloud computing, which means deploying the developed application directly into the cloud computing environment through local development tools. The second core technology is the large-scale distributed application operating environment. It refers to scalable application middleware, databases, and file systems built with a large amount of servers. This application operating environment enables the application to make full use of abundant computing and storage resources in the cloud computing center to achieve full extension, go beyond the resource limitation of single physical hardware, and meet the access requirements of millions of Internet users.

The top of the ITaaS is what most non-IT users will see and consume: Software as a Service (SaaS). At the SaaS level, service providers offer consumer or industrial applications directly to individual users and enterprise users. At this level, the following technologies are involved: Web 2.0, Mashup, service-oriented architectures (SOA), and multi-tenancy.

The development of the AJAX technology of Web 2.0 makes web applications easier to use and brings the user experience of desktop applications to web users, which in turn makes people adapt to the transfer from desktop applications to web applications easily. The Mashup technology provides the capability of assembling contents on the Web, which can allow users to customize Web sites freely and aggregate contents from different Web sites, and enables developers to build applications quickly.

Similarly, SOA provides combination and integration function as well, but it provides the function in the background of the Web. Multi-tenancy is a technology that supports multi-tenancies and customers in the same operating environment. It can significantly reduce resource consumptions and cost for every customer.

Table 4.1 shows the different technologies used in different cloud computing service types.

Transforming any IT capability into a service may be an appealing idea, but to realize it, integration of the IT stack needs to happen. To sum up, key technologies used in cloud computing are: automation, virtualization, dynamic orchestration, online development, large-scale distributed application operating environment, Web 2.0, Mashup, SOA, multi-tenancy, etc. Most of these technologies have matured in recent years to enable the emergence of cloud computing in real applications.

## 4.2 Cloud Computing Security

One of the biggest user concerns about cloud computing is its security, as is natural with any emerging Internet technology. In the enterprise data centers and Internet Data Centers (IDC), service providers offer racks and networks only, and the remaining devices have to be prepared by users themselves, including servers,

**Table 4.1  IaaS, PaaS, and SaaS**

| Service Type | IaaS | PaaS | SaaS |
|---|---|---|---|
| Service category | VM rental, Online storage | Online operating Environment, Online database, Online message Queue | Application and software rental |
| Service customization | Server template | Logic resource template | Application template |
| Service provisioning | Automation | Automation | Automation |
| Service accessing and using | Remote Console, Web 2.0 | Online development and debugging, Integration of offline Development tools and cloud | Web 2.0 |
| Service monitoring | Physical resource monitoring | Logic resource monitoring | Application monitoring |
| hService level management | Dynamic orchestration of physical resources | Dynamic orchestration of logic resources | Dynamic orchestration of application |
| Service resource optimization | Network virtualization, Server virtualization, Storage virtualization | Large-scale distributed file system, Database, middleware, etc. | Multi-tenancy |
| Service measurement | Physical resource metering | Logic resource usage metering | Business resource usage metering |
| Service integration and combination | Load balance | SOA | SOA, Mashu |
| Service security | Storage encryption and isolation, VM isolation, VLAN, SSL/SSH | Data isolation, Operating environment isolation, SSL | Data isolation, Operating environment isolation, SSL, Web authentication and authorization |

firewalls, software, storage devices, etc. While a complex task for the end user, he does have a clear overview of the architecture and the system, thus placing the design of data security under his control. Some users use physical isolation (such as iron cages) to protect their servers. Under cloud computing, the backend resource and management architecture of the service is invisible for users (thus the word "cloud" to describe an entity far removed from our physical reach). Without physical control and access, the users would naturally question the security of the system.

A comparable analogy to data security in a cloud is in financial institutions where a customer deposits his cash bills into an account with a bank and thus no longer has a physical asset in his possession. He will rely on the technology and financial integrity of the bank to protect his now virtual asset. Similarly, we will expect to see a progression in the acceptance of placing data in physical locations out of our reach but with a trusted provider.

To establish that trust with the end users of clouds, the architects of cloud computing solutions do indeed design rationally to protect data security among end users and between end users and service providers.

From the point of view of the technology, the security of user data can be reflected in the following **rules of implementation**:

1. The privacy of user storage data. User storage data cannot be viewed or changed by other people (including the operator).
2. The user data privacy at runtime. User data cannot be viewed or changed by other people at runtime (loaded to system memory).

**Table 4.2 Recommendations to Operators and Users on Cloud Security**

| | *To Other Users* | *To Operators* |
|---|---|---|
| The privacy of user storage data | SAN network zoning, Mapping Clean up disks after callback<br><br>File system authentication | Bare device encryption, File system encryption |
| The privacy of user data at runtime | VM isolation, OS isolation | OS isolation |
| The privacy when transferring user data through network | SSL, VLAN, VPN | SSL, VPN |
| Authentication and authorization needed for users to access their data | Firewall, VPN authentication, OS authentication | VPN authentication, OS authentication |

3. Privacy when transferring user data through the network. It includes the security of transferring data in cloud computing center Intranet and Internet. It cannot be viewed or changed by other people.
4. Authentication and authorization needed for users to access their data. Users can access their data through the right way and can authorize other users to access.

To ensure security, the cloud computing services can use the corresponding technologies shown in Table 4.2.

In addition to the technology solutions, business and legal guidelines can be employed to enforce data security, with terms and conditions to ensure user rights to financial compensation in case of breached security.

# 4.3 Cloud Computing Model Application Methodology

Cloud computing is a new model for providing business and IT services. The service delivery model is based on future development considerations while meeting current development requirements. The three levels of cloud computing service (IaaS, PaaS, and SaaS) cover a huge range of services. Besides computing and the service delivery model of storage infrastructure, various models such as data, software application, programming model, etc. can also be applicable to cloud computing. More importantly, the cloud computing model involves all aspects of enterprise transformation in its evolution, so technology architecture is only a part of it and multi-aspect development, such as organization, processes, and different business models should also be under consideration. Based on standard architecture methodology with best practices of cloud computing, a Cloud Model Application Methodology can be used to guide industry customer analysis and solve potential problems and risks that emerge during the evolution from current computing model to cloud computing model. This methodology can also be used to instruct the investment and decision making analysis of the cloud computing model and determine the process, standard, interface, and public service of IT assets deployment and management to promote business development. Figure 4.1 shows the overall status of this methodology.

## 4.3.1 Cloud Computing Strategy Planning Phase

Cloud strategy contains two steps to ensure a comprehensive analysis of the strategy problems that customers might face when applying cloud computing mode. Based on the Cloud Computing Value Analysis, these two steps will analyze the model condition needed to achieve the customers' target and then will establish a strategy to function as the guideline.

IBM cloud computing blueprint model

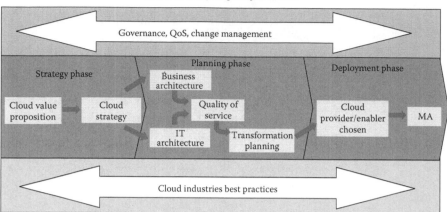

**Figure 4.1   Cloud computing methodology overview.**

1. *Cloud computing value proposition*

   The target of this step is to analyze the specific business value and possible combination point between the cloud computing mode and specific
   users by leveraging the analysis of the cloud computing users' requirement
   model and considering the best practices of the cloud computing industry.
   Analyze the key factors that might influence customers to apply the cloud
   computing mode and make suggestions on the best customer application
   methods. In this analysis, we need to identify the main target for customers to apply the cloud computing mode and the key problems they
   wish to solve. Take some common targets as examples: IT management
   simplification, operation, and maintenance cost reduction; business mode
   innovation; low-cost outsourcing hosting; high service quality outsourcing
   hosting, etc.

   The analysis results will be provided to support decision-making levels to
   make condition assessments and strategy for future development and to prepare for the strategy establishment and organization of the following cloud
   computing.

2. *Cloud computing strategy planning*

   This step is the most important part of the strategy phase. Strategy establishment is based on the analysis result of the value step and aims to establish
   the strategy documentation according to a good understanding of various
   conditions that customers might face when applying the cloud computing
   mode to plan for future vision and perspective. A professional analysis made
   by the method above typically involves broad customer business model
   research, organization structure analysis, and operation process identification; also, there are some non-functional requirements and limitations in

the plan, such as the concern for security standards, reliability requirements, and rules and regulations.

## *4.3.2 Cloud Computing Tactics Planning Phase*

At the phase of cloud planning, it is necessary to make a detailed investigation on the customer's position and to analyze the problems and risks in the cloud application both at present and in the future. After that, concrete approaches and plans can be drawn to ensure that customers can use cloud computing successfully to reach their business goals. This phase includes some practicable planning steps in multiple orders listed as follows:

1. *Business architecture development*: While capturing the organizational structures of enterprises, the business models also get information on business process support. As various business processes and relative networks in enterprise architecture are being set down one after another, gains and losses brought by relative paths in the business development process will also come into people's understanding. We categorize these as business interests and possible risks brought on by the cloud computing application from a business perspective.

2. *IT architecture development*: It is necessary to identify the major applications needed to support enterprises business processes and the key technologies needed to support enterprise applications and data systems. Besides, cloud computing maturity models should be introduced and the analysis of technological reference models should be made, so as to provide help, advice, and a strategy guide for the design and realization of the cloud computing mode in the enterprise architecture.

3. *Requirements on quality of service development*: Compared with other computing modes, the most distinguishing feature of the cloud computing mode is that the requirements on quality of service (also called non-functional needs) should be rigorously defined beforehand, for example, the performance, reliability, security, disaster recovery, etc. This requirement is a key factor in deciding whether a cloud computing mode application is successful or not and whether the business goal is reached; it is also an important standard in measuring the quality of cloud computing service or the competence in establishing a cloud computing center.

4. *Transformation plan development*: It is necessary to formulate all kinds of plans needed in the transformation from current business systems to the cloud computing modes, including the general steps, scheduling, quality guarantee, etc. Usually, an infrastructure service cloud covers different items, such as an infrastructure consolidation plan report, operation and maintenance management system plan, management process plan, application system transformation plan, etc.

### 4.3.3 Cloud Computing Deployment Phase

The deployment phase focuses mainly on the programming of both the strategy realization phase and the planning phases. Two steps are emphasized in this phase:

1. *Cloud computing provider or enabler chosen*: According to the past analysis and programming, customers may have to choose a cloud computing provider or an enabler. It is most important to know that the requirement for a service level agreement (SLA) is still a deciding factor for providers in winning a project.
2. *Maintenance and technical service*: As for maintenance and technical service, different levels of standards are adopted; these standards are defined by the requirements on quality of services made beforehand. Cloud computing providers or builders have to ensure the quality of services, for example, the security of customers in service operation and the reliability of services.

## 4.4 Cloud Computing in Development/Test

Economic crises can bring with it enterprise unprecedented business challenges and more competitions for the same markets. To address these challenges, enterprises have to optimize and update their business operations. At this critical moment, only by offering agile operating systems to end users can enterprises turn the crises into opportunities and promote better development.

Years of IT development has closely linked IT with the business systems, operation systems, and maintenance systems of enterprises. To a large extent, the optimization and updating of business is indeed that of the IT system, which requires enterprises to keep innovating in the business system. As a result, developing new IT systems quickly while doing rigorous tests to provide stable and trustworthy services for customers has become the key to enterprise development. Thus, the development testing centers have become the engines of enterprises growth and keeping the engines operating in a quick and effective way has become a major concern for enterprise Chief Information Officers (CIOs).

As the importance of development centers in companies grows, there will be more and more projects, equipment, and staff in these centers. Establishing a smart development center has become many people's concern. As the latest IT breakthrough, how will cloud computing help to transform development test centers and bring competitive advantages to enterprises? We want to illustrate this problem through the following case.

Director A is the manager of an information center and he is now in charge of all development projects. Recently, he has been thinking about how to best optimize his development and testing environment. After investigation, he concludes that the requirements of the new test center are as follows:

1. Reducing the investment on hardware
2. Providing an environment quickly for new development testing projects
3. Reusing equipment
4. Ensuring project information security

Based on A's requirement analysis, he can use cloud computing solutions to establish a cloud computing–based test development center for his company.

## 4.4.1 Reducing the Cost

In traditional test development systems, companies would set up an environment for each test and development project. Different test systems may have different functions, performances, or stabilities and thus software and hardware configurations will vary accordingly. However, in a cloud test development platform, all the servers, memories, and networks needed in test development are pooling-managed; and through the technology of virtualization, each test or development project is provided with a logical hardware platform.

The virtual hardware platforms of multiple projects can share the same set of hardware resources, thus through integrating the development test project, the hardware investment will be greatly reduced.

## 4.4.2 Providing an Environment for New Projects

A cloud can automatically provide end users with IT resources, which include computing resources, operating system platforms, and application software. All of these are realized through the automation module of the cloud.

Automation of computing resources: In the cloud service interface, when end users input the computing resources (processor, storage, and memory) needed according to the requirements of the application system, the cloud platform will dynamically pick out the resources in the corresponding resource pool and prepare for the installation of the system platform.

Automation of system platforms: When the computing resources allocation is finished, the automation of system platforms will help you to install the system with the computing resources on the base of the chosen system platform (Windows, Linux, AIX, etc.) dynamically and automatically. It can concurrently install operation system platforms for all computers in need and it can customize an operation system with customization parameters and system service for customers. Moreover, the users, networks, and systems can all be set automatically.

Automation of application software: The software of enterprises would be controlled completely. The software distribution module can help you to deploy complex mission-critical applications from one center spot to multiple places quickly and effectively.

Through automation, clouds can provide environments for new development test projects and can accelerate the process of development tests.

### 4.4.3 Reusing Equipment

Cloud has provided a resource management process based on a development lifecycles test. The process covers many operations such as computing resource establishment, modification, release, and reservation. When the test development projects are suspended or completed, the cloud platform can make a back-up of the existing test environment and release the computing resources, thereby realizing the reuse of computing resources.

### 4.4.4 Ensuring Project Information Security

The cloud computing platform has provided a perfect means of ensuring the security and isolation of each project. There are two ways for users to access the system: accessing the web management interface or accessing the project virtual machine. To access a web interface, one needs a user ID and a password. To control virtual machine access, the following methods can be adopted:

1. User authentication is conducted through the VPN equipment in the external interface of the system.
2. Each project has only one virtual local area network (VLAN), and the virtual machine of each project is located inside the VLAN. The switches and the hypervisors in the hosts can guarantee the isolation of the VLAN.
3. The isolation of the virtual machine is guaranteed by the virtual engine.
4. Besides, user authentication of the operation systems can also protect user information.

A VLAN is created dynamically along with the establishment of the project. Unicast or broadcast messages can be sent among project virtual machines or between the virtual machine and the workstation of the project members. Virtual machines of different projects are isolated from each other, thereby guaranteeing the security of project data. A user can get involved in several projects and meanwhile visit several virtual machines of different projects.

The new generation of intelligent development test platforms needs the support of intelligent IT infrastructure platforms. By establishing intelligent development test platforms through cloud computing, a new IT resource supply mode can be formed. Under this mode, the test development center can automatically manage and dynamically distribute, deploy, configure, reconfigure, and recycle IT resources based on the requirements of different projects; besides, it can also install software and application systems automatically. When projects are over, the test development center can recycle the resources automatically, thereby making the best use of the computing capabilities.

## 4.5 Cloud-Based High Performance Computing Clusters

In the development history of information science from the last half a century, high performance computing (HPC) has always been a leading technology. It has become a major tool for future innovations of both theoretical and research science. As new cross-disciplines combining traditional subjects and HPC emerge in the areas of computational chemistry, computational physics, and bioinformatics, computing technology needs to take a leap forward as well to meet the demands of these new research topics.

With the current financial crisis, providing higher computing performance with less resource input has become a big challenge for the HPC centers. In the construction of a new generation of computing centers with high performance, we should not only pay attention to the choice of software and hardware, but also take a full account of the center operation, utilization efficiency, technological innovation cooperation, and other factors. The rationality of the general framework and the effectiveness of resource management should also be fully considered. Only by doing this can the center gain long-term high-performance capacity in computing research and supply.

In other words, the new generation of a high-performance computing center does not provide traditional high-performance computing, nor is it only a high-performance equipment solution. The management of resources, users, and virtualization and the dynamic resource generation and recycling should also be taken into account. In this way, the high-performance computing based on cloud computing technology was born.

The cloud computing-based high-performance computing center aims to solve the following problems:

1. A high-performance computing platform generated dynamically
2. Virtualized computing resources
3. High-performance computer management technology combined with traditional ones
4. High-performance computing platform generated dynamically

In traditional high-performance computing environments, physical equipment is configured to meet the demands of customers; for example, Beowulf Linux and WCCS Architecture are chosen to satisfy the customers' requirements on computing resources. All of the operation systems and parallel environments are set beforehand, and cluster management software is used to manage the computing environment. However, as high-performance computing develops, there are more and more end users and application software; thus, the requirements on the computing platform become more diverse. Different end users and application software may require different operation systems and parallel environments. High-performance computing requires a new way of resource supply in which the platform should be dynamically generated according to the needs of every end user and application software; the platform can be open, including Linux, Windows, or UNIX.

### 4.5.1 Virtualized Computing Resources

Since few virtualized architectures are used in traditional high-performance computing, this kind of platform cannot manage virtualized resources. However, as high-performance computing develops, in many cases we need to attain more virtualized resources through virtualization, for example, the development and debugging of parallel software and the support for more customer applications, etc.

In the cloud computing–based high-performance computing center, the virtualization of physical resources can be realized through the cloud platform; moreover, virtualized resources can be used to establish high-performance computing platforms and generate high-performance computing environments whose scale is larger than that of the actual physical resource so as to meet the requirements of customers.

### 4.5.2 Combination with Traditional Management Technology

The cloud computing–based high-performance computing platform can not only manage computers through virtualization and dynamic generation technology, but can also work together with traditional cluster and operation management software to enable users to manage the virtualized high-performance computers in a traditional way and submit their own work.

A new IT resources provision model can be attained by the adoption of cloud computing infrastructure and high-performance computing center construction. In this model, the computing center can automatically manage and dynamically distribute, deploy, configure, reconfigure, and recycle the resources. The automatic installation of software and application can be realized, too. By the use of the model, the high-performance computing resources can be distributed efficiently and dynamically. When the project is finished, the computing center can automatically recycle the resources to make full use of the computing power. Taking advantage of cloud computing, the high-performance computing center can not only provide high calculating power for scientific research institutions, but can also expand the service content of the computing center. In other words, it can serve as a data center to support other applications and promote higher utilization efficiency of entire resources.

# 4.6 Use Cases of Cloud Computing

## 4.6.1 Case Study: Cloud as Infrastructure for an Internet Data Center

In the 1990s, Internet portals made huge amounts of investment to attract eyeballs. Rather than profits and losses, their market valuation was based on the number of unique "hits" or visitors. This strategy proved to work out well as these portals begin to offer advertisement opportunities targeting their installed user base, as well as new paid services to the end user, thereby increasing revenue per capita in a theoretically infinite growth curve.

Similarly, IDCs have become a strategic initiative for cloud service providers to attract users. With a critical mass of users consuming computing resources and applications, an IDC would become a portal attracting more applications and more users in a positive cycle.

The development of the next generation of IDC hinges on two key factors. The first factor is the growth of the Internet. By the end of June 2008, for example, Internet users in China totaled 253 million and the annual growth rate was as high as 56.2%.* As a result, the requirement on Internet storage and traffic capacity grows, which means Internet operators have to provide more storage and servers to meet users' needs. The second factor is the development of mobile communication. By the end of 2008, the number of mobile phone users in China has amounted to 4 billion. The development of mobile communication drives server-based computing and storage, which enables users to access the data and computing services needed via the Internet through lightweight clients.

In the time of dramatic Internet and mobile communication expansion, how can we build new IDCs with core competency? Cloud computing provides an innovative business model for data centers, and thereby can help telecom operators to promote business innovation and higher service capabilities against the backdrop of the whole business integration of fixed and mobile networks.

### 4.6.1.1 Bottleneck on IDC Development

Products and services offered by a traditional IDC are highly homogenized. In almost all of the IDCs, basic co-location services account for a majority of the revenue, while value-added services add only a small part of it. For example, in one of the IDCs of a telecom operator, the hosting service claims 90% of its revenue, while

---

* *Source*: *CCIDConsulting*, 2008–2009 China IDC *market research annual report.*

value-added service takes only 10%. This makes it impossible to meet customers' requirements on load balance, disaster recovery, data flow analysis, resource utilization analysis, etc.

The energy utilization is low, but the operation costs are very high. According to CCID research statistics, the energy costs of IDC enterprises make up about 50% of their operating costs and more servers will lead to an exponential increase in the corresponding power consumption (see footnote on page 75). With the increase of the number of Internet users and enterprise IT transformation, IDC enterprises will have to face a sharp increase in power consumption as their businesses grow. If effective solutions are not taken immediately, the high costs will undermine the sustained development of these enterprises.

Besides, as online games and Web 2.0 sites become increasingly popular, all types of content including audio, videos, images, and games will need massive storage and relevant servers to support transmission. This will result in a steady increase in enterprise requirements for IDC services and higher standards on the utilization efficiency of resources in data centers as well as the service level.

Under the full service operation model that emerged after the restructuring of telecom operators, the market competition became more and more fierce. The consolidation of fixed network and mobile services imposes higher requirements on telecom IDC operators as they have to introduce new services to meet market demands in time.

### 4.6.1.2 Cloud Computing Provides IDC with a New Infrastructure Solution

Cloud computing provides IDCs with a solution that takes into consideration both future development strategies and the current requirements for development. Cloud computing builds up a resource service management system in which physical resources are on the input and the output is the virtual resources at the right time with the right volume and the right quality. Thanks to the virtualization technology, the resources of IDCs including servers, storage, and networks are put into a huge resource pool by cloud computing. With cloud computing management platforms, administrators are able to dynamically monitor, schedule, and deploy all the resources in the pool and provide them for the users via a network. A unified resource management platform can lead to higher efficiency of IDC operation and schedule the efficiency and utilization of the resources in the center and lower management complexity. The automatic resource deployment and software installation help to guarantee the timely introduction of new services and can lower the time-to-market. Customers can use the resources in data centers by renting based on their business needs. Besides, as required by business development needs, they are allowed to adjust the resources that they rent and pay fees according to resource usage. This kind of flexible charging mode makes IDCs more appealing. The management through a unified platform is also helpful to IDC expansion. When an IDC operator needs to add resources, new resources can be added to the existing cloud computing management platform to be managed and deployed uniformly.

Cloud computing will make it an unceasing process to upgrade software and add new functions and services, which can be done through intelligent monitoring and automatic installation programs instead of manual operation.

According to the Long Tail theory, cloud computing builds infrastructures based on the scale of market head and provides marginal management costs that are nearly zero in market tail as well as a plug-and-play technological infrastructure. It manages to meet diversified requirements with variable costs. In this way, the effect of the Long Tail theory is realized to keep a small-volume production of various items and by the use of innovative IT technology, and it sets up a market economy model, which is open to competition and favorable to the survival of the fittest.

## 4.6.1.3 Value of Cloud Computing for IDC Service Providers

First of all, based on cloud computing technology, IDC is flexible and scalable and can realize the effect of the Long Tail theory at a relatively low cost. The cloud computing platform is able to develop and launch new products at a low marginal cost of management. Therefore, startup costs of new businesses can be reduced to nearly zero, and the resources would not be limited to a single kind of product or service. So under a specified investment scope, the operators can greatly expand product lines and meet the needs of different services through the automatic scheduling of resources, thereby making the best use of the Long Tail theory.

Secondly, the cloud computing dynamic infrastructure is able to deploy resources in a flexible way to meet business needs at peak times. For example, during the Olympics, the Web sites related to the competitions are flooded with visitors. To address this problem, the cloud computing technology would deploy other idle resources provisionally to support the requirements of resources at peak hours. The United States Olympic Committee has applied the cloud computing technologies provided by AT&T to support competition viewing during the Olympics. Besides, SMS and telephone calls on holidays, as well as the application and inquiry days for examinations also witness the requirements for resources at the peak.

Thirdly, cloud computing improves the return on investment for IDC service providers. By improving the utilization and management efficiency of resources, cloud computing technologies can reduce computing resources, power consumption, and human resource costs. Additionally, it can lead to shorter time-to-market for a new service, thereby helping IDC service providers to occupy the market.

**Table 4.3   Value Comparison on Co-Location, Physical Server Renting, and IaaS for Providers**

|  | Co-Location | Physical Server Renting | IaaS with Cloud Computing |
|---|---|---|---|
| Profit margin | Low. Intense competition | Low. Intense competition | High. Cost saving by resource sharing |
| Value add service | Very few | Few | Rich, such as IT service management, Software renting, etc. |
| Operation | Manual operation. Complex | Manual operation. Complex | Automatic and integrated operation. End-to-end request management |
| Response to customer request | Manual action. Slow | Manual action. Slow | Automatic process. Fast |
| Power consumption | Normal | Normal | Reduce power by server consolidation and sharing. Scheduled power off |

Cloud computing also provides an innovative charging mode. IDC service providers charge users based on the resource renting conditions and users only have to pay for what they use. This makes the payment charging more transparent and can attract more customers (Table 4.3).

### 4.6.1.4 Value Brought by Cloud Computing for IDC Users

First, initial investments and operating costs can be lowered and risks can be reduced. There is no need for IDC users to make initial investments in hardware and expensive software licenses. Instead, users only have to rent necessary hardware and software resources based on their actual needs and pay according to usage conditions. In the era of enterprise informatization, more and more subject matter experts have begun to establish their own Web sites and information systems. Cloud computing can help these enterprises to realize informatization with relatively less investment and fewer IT professionals.

Secondly, an automatic, streamlined, and unified service management platform can rapidly meet customers' increased requirements for resources and can enable them to acquire the resources in time. In this way, customers can become more responsive to market requirements and enhance business innovation.

Thirdly, IDC users are able to access more value-added services and achieve faster requirement responses. Through the IDC cloud computing unified service

**Table 4.4    Value Comparison on Co-Location, Physical Server Renting, and IaaS for Users**

|  | Co-Location | Physical Server Renting | IAAS Using Cloud |
|---|---|---|---|
| Performance | Depend on hardware | Depend on hardware | Guaranteed performance |
| Price | Server investment plus bandwidth and space fee | Bandwidth and server renting fee | CPU, memory, storage, bandwidth fee. Pay per use |
| Availability | Depend on single hardware | Depend on single hardware | High available by hardware failover |
| Scalability | Manual scale out | Manual scale out | Automated scale out |
| System management | Manual hardware setup and configuration. Complex | Manual hardware setup and configuration. Complex | Automated OS and software installation. Remote monitoring and control. Simple |
| Staff | High labor cost and skill requirement | High labor cost and skill requirement | Low labor cost and skill requirement |
| Usability | Need on site operation | Need on site operation | All work is done through Web UI. Quick action |

delivery platform, the customers are allowed to put forward personalized requirements and enjoy various kinds of value-added services. And their requirements would get a quick response, too (Table 4.4).

### 4.6.1.5 Cloud Computing Can Make Fixed Costs Variable

An IDC can provide 24 × 7 hosting services for individuals and businesses. Besides traditional hosting services, these clients also need the cloud to provide more applications and services. In so doing, enterprises are able to gain absolute control on their own computing environment. Furthermore, when necessary, they can also purchase online the applications and services that are needed quickly at any time, as well as adjust the rental scale in a timely way.

### 4.6.1.6 IDC Cloud Example

In one example, an IDC in Europe serves industry customers in four neighboring countries, which cover sports, government, finance, automobiles, and healthcare.

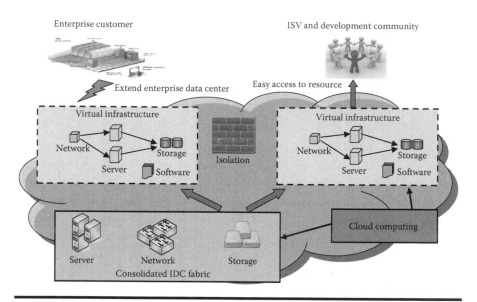

**Figure 4.2  IDC cloud.**

This IDC attaches great importance to cloud computing technology in the hope of establishing a data center that is flexible, demand-driven, and responsive. It has decided to work with cloud computing technology to establish several cross-Europe cloud centers. The first five data centers are connected by virtual SAN and the latest MPLS technology. Moreover, the center complies with the ISO27001 security standards and other security functions that are needed by the banks and government organizations, including auditing functions provided by certified partners, are also realized (Figure 4.2).

The IDC uses the main data center to serve customers at its sister sites. The new cloud computing center will enable this IDC to pay for fixed or usage-based changeable services according to a credit card bill. In the future, the management scope of this hosting center can expand to even more data centers in Europe.

## 4.6.1.7 Influence of Cloud Computing in 3G Era

Ever since the 3G services were launched by the major communication operators, the simple voice and information service can no longer meet the growing requirements of users. The 3G data services have become the focus of competition among operators. Many operators have introduced some specialized services. And with the growth of 3G clients and the expansion and improvement of 3G networks, operators have to provide more diversified 3G services to survive in the fierce market competition. Cloud can be used as a platform to provide such value added services.

In this 3G era, mobile TV, mobile securities, and data backup will all become critical businesses. Huge amounts of videos, images, and documents are to be stored in data centers so that users can download and view them at any time, and they can promote interaction. Cloud computing can effectively support these kinds of business requirements and can get maximal storage with limited resources. Besides, it can also search and promptly provide the resources that are needed for users to meet their needs.

After the restructuring of operators, the businesses of leading service providers will all cover fixed network and mobile services, and they may have to face up to fierce competition in the 3G market. Cloud computing can support unified monitoring and dynamic deployment of resources. So, during the business consolidation of the operators, the cloud computing platform can deploy the necessary resources in time to support business development, and can respond quickly to market requirements to help operators gain a larger market share.

The 3G-enabled high bandwidth makes it easier and quicker to surf the Internet through mobile phones and it has become a critical application of 3G technologies. Cloud computing makes it compatible among different equipment, software, and networks, so that the customers can access the resources in the cloud through any kind of clients.

## 4.6.2 Case Study—Cloud Computing for Software Parks

The traditional manufacturing industry has helped to maintain economic growth in previous generations, but it has also brought along a host of problems such as labor market deterioration, huge consumption of energy resources, environmental pollution, and a higher drive toward lower cost. As emerging economies begin their social transformation, software outsourcing has gained an edge compared with the traditional manufacturing industry: on one hand, it can attract and develop top-level talent to enhance the technical level and competitive power of a nation; on the other hand, it can also prompt the smooth structural transformation to a sustainable and green service industry, thereby ensuring continuous prosperity and endurance even in difficult times.

As such, software outsourcing has become a main business line for many emerging economies to ramp up their service economy, based on economies of scale and affordable costs. To reach this goal, software firms in these emerging economies need to conform their products and services to international standards and absorb experiences from developed nations to enhance the quality of their outsourcing services. More importantly, good policy support from the government and necessary infrastructures are critical components in the durability of these software outsourcing firms.

The IT infrastructure is surely indispensable for software outsourcing and software businesses. To ensure the success of software outsourcing, there are two prerequisites: a certification standard of software management, which is of an international level (such as CMM Level 5), and an advanced software designing, programming, and testing pipeline, namely the software development platform of a data center. The traditional data center only puts together all the hardware devices of the enterprise, leading to the monopolization of some devices by a certain project or business unit. This would create a huge disparity within the system and can't guarantee the quality of applications and development. Besides, it would result in an increase in cost and unnecessary spending and in the long term will undermine the enterprise's competitive power in the international market of software outsourcing. Furthermore, when a new project is put on the agenda, it would take a long time to prepare for and address the bottleneck of the project caused by traditional IT equipment.

To pull the software enterprises out of this dilemma, IBM first developed a brand-new management mode for the software developing environment: the management and development platform of cloud computing. The platform was constructed with the aid of the accumulated experience of IBM itself in the field of software outsourcing service and data center management. The valuable experience from the long-term cooperation with other software outsourcing powers is also taken into consideration. This platform is a new generation of data center management. Compared with traditional data centers, it has outstanding technical advantages.

Figure 4.3 is the schematic diagram of the relationship between the cloud computing platform and software outsourcing ecosystems.

First, the platform can directly serve as a data service center for software outsourcing companies in the Software Park and neighboring enterprises. As soon as a software outsourcing order is accepted, the company can turn to the management and development platform of cloud computing to look for IT resources suitable for use, the process of which is as simple and convenient as booking a hotel via the Internet. Besides, by relying on IBM's advanced technology, the cloud computing platform is able to promote unified administrative standards to ensure the confidentiality, security, stability, and expandability of the platform. That is to say, thanks to its brand effect, the platform developed by the software demonstration plot is up to international advanced levels and could thereby

**Figure 4.3   Cloud computing platform and software outsourcing ecosystems.**

enhance the service level of software outsourcing in the entire park. The final aim is to measure up to international standards and meet the needs of international and Chinese enterprises. Meanwhile, a platform of unified standards can lower IT maintenance costs and raise the response speed for requirements, making possible the sustainable development of the Software Park. Lastly, the management and development platform of cloud computing can directly support all kinds of applications and provide enterprise users with various services including outsourcing and commercial services as well as services related to academic and scientific researches.

The following are the benefits brought to the outsourcing services companies and outsourcing demonstration plot of the Wuxi government by the management and development platform of cloud computing:

1. For outsourcing service companies that apply a cloud computing platform:
   a. An advanced platform with unified standards is provided and the quality is guaranteed.
   b. IT management becomes easier and the costs of developing products is greatly lowered.
   c. Response speed for business demand is enhanced and expandability is ensured.
   d. Existing applications and newly emerging data-intensive applications are supported.
   e. Miscellaneous functions for expediting the speed of innovation are also provided for outsourcing service companies, colleges and universities, and research institutes.
2. Below are the advantages brought to the outsourcing demonstration plot of the Wuxi government through the application of a cloud computing platform:
   a. The government can transform from a supervision mode to a service mode, which is in favor of attracting investments
   b. It is conducive to environmental protection and the build-up of a harmonious society
   c. It can support the development of innovative enterprises and venture companies

Detailed information about the major functions and technical architectures of the management and development platform of cloud computing is introduced below.

## 4.6.2.1 Cloud Computing Architecture

The management and development platform of cloud computing is mainly composed of two functional sub-platforms: the outsourcing software research and development platform and the operation management platform.

1. Outsourcing software research and development platform: an end-to-end software development platform is provided for the outsourcing service companies in the park. In terms of functions, the platform generally covers the entire software developing lifecycle including requirement, designing, developing, and testing of the software. It helps the outsourcing service companies in establishing a software developing procedure that is effective and operable.

2. Operation management platform: according to the outsourcing service company's actual demand in building the research and development platform, as well as the practical situation of the software and hardware resource distribution in the data center, the platform provides automatic provisioning services on demand for software and hardware resources. Also, management on resources distribution is based on different processes, posts, and roles and resource utilization reports will also be provided.

Through the cooperative effect of the two platforms mentioned above, the management and development platform of cloud computing could fully exert its advantage. The construction of outsourcing software research and development platform can be customized according to different project needs (e.g., games development platform, e-business development platform, etc.), which can show the best practices of IBM's outsourcing software development services. And the operation management platform can provide supporting functions such as management on the prior platform, as well as operation and maintenance, and rapid configuration. It is also significant in that it can reduce the workload and costs of operation and management. Unlike the handmade software research and development platform, it is both time-saving and labor-saving, and it is not that easy to make mistakes in it.

## 4.6.2.2 Outsourcing Software Research and Development Platform

The outsourcing software research and development at the enterprise level have to put an emphasis on the cooperation and speed of software development. It manages to combine software implantation with verification, so as to ensure the high quality of the software and shorten the period of development. The program is targeted at and suitable for different types of outsourcing research and development companies with a demand for code development cooperation and document management. The detailed designing of the program varies according to different enterprise needs (Figure 4.4).

As can be seen in the chart, the primary construction of the outsourcing software research and development platform consists of the construction of four sub-platforms:

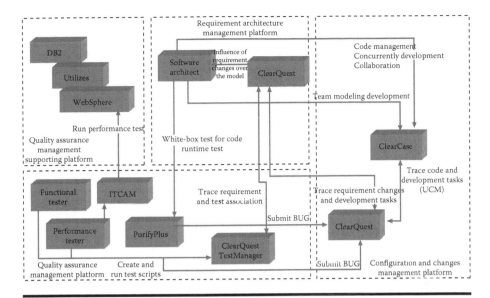

**Figure 4.4  Software outsourcing services platform.**

1. Requirement architecture management platform
2. Quality assurance management platform
3. Quality assurance management supporting platform
4. Configuration and changes management platform

The integrated construction and operation of these four sub-platforms covers the entire developing lifecycle of the requirements, designing, developing, and testing of the software. They are customer-oriented and are featured by high quality and good awareness of quality prevention. With the help of these four sub-platforms, the outsourcing service companies can manage to establish a software development process with high efficiency and operability.

## 4.6.3 Case Study—An Enterprise with Multiple Data Centers

Along with China's rapid economic growth, the business of one state-owned enterprise is also gearing up for fast expansion. Correspondingly, the group has an increasingly higher demand for the supporting IT environment. How can the group achieve maximum return on its IT investment? For the IT department, on one hand is the repetitive and time-consuming work of system operation and management; while there is an increasingly higher demand from the managers to support the company's business, raise its competitive power, and promote business transformation. Faced with this problem, this enterprise is now searching for solutions in cloud computing.

The Enterprise Resources Plan (ERP) plays an important role in supporting the entire business in the company. The existing EAR system is not able to apply automatic technology. Repeated, manual work accounts for a majority of the system maintenance operation, which leads to lower efficiency and higher pressure on the IT system maintenance operation. Meanwhile, on the technical level, it lacks a technology platform to perform the distribution, deployment, as well as state control and recycle of system resources. As a result, the corresponding information resources management is performed through traditional manual work, which is in contradiction with the entire information strategy of the company. The specifics are listed below:

1. The contradiction between the increasing IT resources and limited human resources
2. The contradiction between automatic technology and traditional manual work
3. The effectiveness and persistence of resources information (including configuration information)

The company has invested a lot in information technology. It has not only constructed the ERP system for the management and control of enterprise production, but it has also upgraded the platform, updated the host computer, and improved IT management in infrastructure. In a word, the SAP system is of great significance in the IT system of the Sinochem Group.

The implementation of the cloud computing platform has helped to solve the problems faced by the IT department in this company.

### 4.6.3.1  Overall Design of the Cloud Computing Platform in an Enterprise

The cloud computing platform is mainly related to three discrete environments of the company's data centers: the training, development/test, and the disaster recovery environment. These systems involved in cloud computing are respectively located in data center A, data center B, and the disaster center in data center C. It shows the benefits of cloud computing virtualization crossing physical sites (See Figure 4.5).

Combined with the technical characteristics of the cloud computing platform and the application characteristics of the ERP system in the company, the construction project has provided the following functions:

1. The installation and deployment of the five production systems of ERP
2. The automatic deployment of hardware: logical partition and distribution of hardware resources

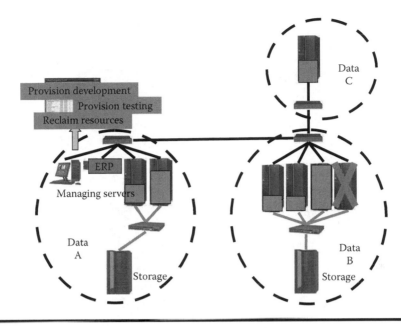

**Figure 4.5  Coverage of cloud computing in Sinochem Group.**

3. The installation and recovery of the centralized AIX operating system
4. The display of system resource usage: CPU/memory/disk usage

### 4.6.4 Case Study: Cloud Computing Supporting SaaS

By adopting cloud computing solutions, a telco can address the IT challenges faced by SMEs. Thanks to the services provided by the Blue Cloud system, VNTT has provided the customers with IBM Lotus Foundation and WebSphere Portal Express business OA service based on Redhat, CentOS, and Windows platforms. Besides, VNTT also provides customers with e-mail services, file sharing, and web servers that are always ready for use. For better internal and external communication, these enterprises need only one portal to rent the portal server based on IBM WebSphere Portal (Figure 4.6).

By applying cloud computing as the underlying infrastructure, a telecommunications company can provide its customers with a larger scale of IT services, including infrastructure hosting, collaborative platform, applications, process and information service; meanwhile, it can also ensure data security, convenience of access and the easy management of the environment. In this instance, clouds will provide strong technical infrastructure support as well as an effective combination with business model innovation.

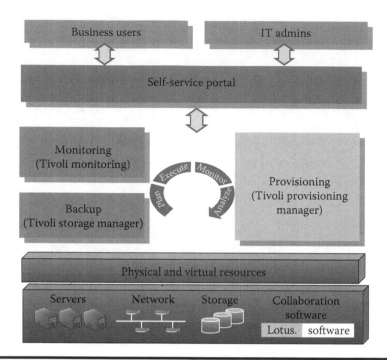

**Figure 4.6  SaaS cloud.**

## 4.7 Conclusion

With cloud computing as a new way to consume IT services, we can be much more flexible and productive in utilizing dynamically allocated resources to create and to operate.

Clouds will continue to evolve as the foundation for the future Internet where we will be interconnected in a web of content and services.

# Chapter 5

# Large-Scale Data Processing

Huan Liu

## Contents

# 5.1 Introduction

An infrastructure cloud, such as Amazon's Web Services offerings, is posed to fundamentally change the IT infrastructure. It provides infrastructure capacity, such as server and storage, on demand from remote locations on the network, fully realizing the vision of utility computing. In addition to Amazon's Web Services, several other commercial cloud providers, such as FlexiScale, Rackspace, GoGrid, and 3Tera, also have similar offerings.

An infrastructure cloud is innovative in several regards. First, it is on demand. In the past, IT had to purchase new hardware for a new or upgraded system. It not only requires high capital investment up front, but the procurement could also take months in an enterprise, significantly slowing down projects. Although hosting providers provide capabilities to rent hardware, they typically require an up-front contract and long-term commitments. In contrast, anyone with a credit card can sign up for Amazon's Elastic Computing Cloud (EC2) offerings and start provisioning virtual servers right away.

Second, it is pay-per-use. For example, Amazon EC2 meter's usage on an hourly basis, and the users pay $10 per hour for the actual hours used. This is in sharp contrast to the traditional hosting model, where the users are billed monthly at best.

Third, an infrastructure cloud provides a virtualized container interface that is easy to use. In particular, Amazon provides a virtual machine (VM) interface that fully emulates an ×86 server. From the customers' standpoint, they cannot tell the difference from a real physical ×86 server. Such a familiar interface not only encourages wide adoption, but also enables easy application migration.

Because of its on-demand and pay-per-use nature, an infrastructure cloud, such as Amazon EC2, is ideal for applications with widely varying computation demand. Primary examples are large-scale data analysis jobs, such as monthly reporting of large data warehouse applications, nightly reconciliation of bank transactions, or end-of-day access log analysis. Their computation profile is as shown in Figure 5.1. Because of business constraints, these jobs have to finish before a deadline. In the past, we typically provisioned dedicated server capacity up front; hence, the server capacity would be idle most of the time when the jobs were not run, wasting valuable computation resources.

Although these large-scale data analysis jobs could benefit greatly from an infrastructure cloud, it is not straightforward to port these applications over. There are challenges both in the programming model and in the underlying infrastructure to analyze the data in the cloud.

From the programming model perspective, parallel programming is both time consuming and error prone. The large-scale analytics applications, as well as a large class of batch applications have obvious parallelism at the data level. It is

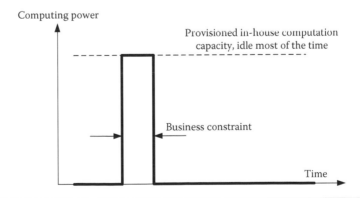

**Figure 5.1  Computation profile of large-scale data analysis jobs. Large computation capacity is required for a short period of time. If dedicated computing power is provisioned, it will be idle most of the time.**

straightforward to partition the job into many independent parts and process them in parallel. However, it is in general not straightforward to implement a parallel application for several reasons. First, some forms of communication, coordination, and synchronization are required between the machines, but they are not trivial to implement correctly. Second, the inherent asynchronous nature of parallel programs makes it hard for the programmers to reason about the interactions between all machines. Compared to sequential programs, there are many more scenarios that need to be examined, making it hard to guarantee program correctness in all cases. Last, there is still not an effective debugging tool. Because of the complex interactions, many bugs are transient in nature, which are hard to reproduce. In addition, it is hard to step through some code when there are many threads running on many machines. The difficulty in implementation translates into higher development cost and longer development cycle. Worse yet, the same programming effort often has to be repeated for each new project.

From the infrastructure perspective, a cloud presents additional challenges. Because of the business model, a cloud is based on commodity hardware in order to lower the cost of computing. First, commodity hardware only has limited computing power per machine. For example, Amazon only offers ×86 servers, and the largest one is equivalent to a 4 core 2 GHz opteron processor with 16 GB memory. Second, commodity hardware is less reliable. Even though a cloud provider's data centers are unlikely to fail because of the various backup mechanisms, individual commodity hardware does fail often due to component failures. This is part of the reason why Amazon only has a 99.9% SLA on S3 (Simple Storage Service) data storage and none yet on the EC2 servers (although it has one on EC2 regions). In comparison, a traditional infrastructure employs high-end servers and they rely on hardware to achieve both scaling and high reliability. For example, the SUN E25K server, a widely used platform in enterprises, has up to 72 processors and 1 TB memory.

To take advantage of a cloud infrastructure, an application must employs horizontal scaling. To overcome the hardware reliability problem, applications should be architected to tolerate hardware failures, i.e., treat hardware failures as a normal event and recover gracefully instead of treating them as a catastrophe. This not only means that data should be replicated, but also means that the applications should be able to restart computations when the underlying hardware fails.

To overcome these challenges, novel programming models, languages, and paradigms have emerged in recent years. This chapter describes some key work around Google's MapReduce programming model. We also point out related works in this space, give a high-level overview of them, and provide references so that interested readers can learn more. A common theme of these works is that they do not attempt to help the programmers find parallelism in their applications. Instead, they assume that the programmers understand their applications well and are fully aware of the parallelization potentials. Further, the programmers have thought through on how to break down the application into smaller tasks and how to partition the data in order to achieve the highest performance. But, instead of asking the programmers to implement the plan in detail, they provide a high-level construct. Their associated implementation not only hides the details of parallel programming, but also alleviates the programmers from much of the pain, such as implementing the synchronization and communication mechanisms or debugging transient behaviors of distributed programs.

# 5.2 MapReduce

Google is one of the first few companies who encountered an explosion in the amount of data. Because they have to index and process billions of web pages, they have to find a scalable way to process the data efficiently. The solution is the MapReduce [6,7] system. MapReduce is a programming model and an associated implementation. Four years after its introduction, more than ten thousand distinct MapReduce programs have been implemented at Google, and on an average, one hundred thousand MapReduce jobs are executed on Google's clusters, processing more than 20 PB of data every day.

## 5.2.1 *Programming Model*

The MapReduce programming model takes a set of key-value pairs as inputs and produces a set of key-value pairs as outputs. A MapReduce programmer expresses his or her computation as two user-defined functions: map and reduce. The user-defined map function takes an input key-value pair and produces a set of intermediate key-value pairs. The MapReduce framework groups together all values associated with the same intermediate key and passes them to the user-defined reduce function. The user-defined reduce function takes an intermediate key and a set of values associated with the key, and it merges these values together to form a potentially smaller set of values. The user-defined reduce function may just output zero or one output value for each key. The intermediate values are supplied to the user-defined reduce function through an iterator.

Let us consider a simple example—the word count application—to illustrate how MapReduce works. The work count application counts the number of occurrences of each word in a large collection of documents. A user would write the user-defined map function similar to the following.

```
mapFunc(String key, String value):
  key: document name
  value: document contents
  for each word w in value:
    EmitIntermediate (w, 1);
```

A user would write the corresponding user-defined reduce function similar to the following.

```
reduceFunc(String key, Iterator values):
  key: a word
  values: a list of counts
  int result=0;
  for each v in values:
    result += ParseInt(v);
  EmitResult (key, result);
```

This map function emits each word and an associated count of occurrences (i.e., 1). The reduce function simply sums up all counts and then outputs the final value.

In a typical implementation, the user-defined map and reduce functions are linked with the MapReduce library. To launch a MapReduce job, the users specify a set of parameters, such as the input and output files, and tuning parameters, and then invoke the MapReduce function.

## 5.2.2 Implementation Sketch

Besides the Google implementation, there are many other different implementations of MapReduce. Hadoop [16] is an open-source implementation written in Java that is designed for the shared-nothing cluster environment, the kind of environment the original Google implementation is designed for. Phoenix [29] is an implementation for the shared-memory multicore processor environment.

In this section, we describe the Hadoop implementation, which is based on the master/slave architecture. Since the Hadoop is modeled closely after the Google implementation, the description below applies equally to the Google implementation. In Section 5.4, we will describe an alternative implementation, which is based on a cloud Operating System (OS). By utilizing a cloud OS, we show that it could be implemented in a fully distributed fashion, and it can be faster, more scalable, and simpler.

The Hadoop implementation consists of two pieces of related software components: the distributed file system (DFS) and the job scheduler.

DFS is closely modeled after the Google File System (GFS) [10]. DFS is responsible for managing files and storing them across all nodes in the system. A large file is typically broken down into many smaller chunks, and each chunk may be stored on a separate node. Among all nodes in the system, one node serves as the name node, and all other nodes serve as data nodes.

The name node holds the name space for the file system. It maintains the mapping from a DFS file to the list of chunks, including which data node a chunk resides on and the location on the data node. It also responds to queries from DFS clients asking to create a new DFS file, as well as allocates new chunks for existing files or returns chunk locations when DFS clients ask to open an existing DFS file. A data node holds chunks of a large file. It responds to DFS client requests for reading from and writing to the chunks that it is responsible for. A DFS client first contacts the name node to obtain a list of chunk locations for a file; then it contacts the data nodes directly to read/write the data.

The job scheduling system includes a master node and many slave nodes. The slave node is responsible for running a task assigned by the master node. The master node is responsible for breaking down a job into many smaller tasks as expressed in the user program. It distributes the tasks across all slave nodes in the system, and it monitors the tasks to make sure all of them complete successfully.

In general, a slave node is often a data node. Thus, when the master schedules a task, it could schedule the task on the node that holds the chunk of data to be processed. By processing data on the local node, we save on precious network bandwidth.

A MapReduce job consists of a map phase and a reduce phase. The map phase is distributed across multiple nodes by automatically partitioning the input data into a set of $M$ splits. Each input split is processed by a separate map task. The map tasks can be processed in parallel by different machines. The reduce phase his distributed by partitioning the intermediate key space into $R$ pieces using a partitioning function. Each partition is processed by a separate reduce task. The number of partitions, $R$, and the partitioning function are specified by the user.

The master node is responsible for coordinating the job. It assigns map tasks and reduce tasks to the slave nodes. A map task reads the contents of the corresponding input split. It parses key-value pairs out of the input data and passes each pair to the user-defined map function. The intermediate key-value pairs produced by the map function are first buffered in memory, and then periodically written to local files on the local disk, partitioned into $R$ regions by the partition function. The locations of these files are passed to the master, who will in turn inform the reduce tasks.

When a reduce task starts, it copies the map tasks' buffered data to the local disk. It sorts the data by the intermediate keys so that all occurrences of the same key are grouped together. The reduce task iterates over the sorted intermediate data, and for each unique intermediate key encountered, it passes the key and the corresponding set of values to the user-defined reduce function. The final key-value outputs produced by the reduce functions are then appended to the final output file.

## 5.2.3 Failure Handling

One of the contributions of MapReduce is its ability to handle failure automatically, alleviating the users from having to handle it themselves.

The master pings the workers periodically. If no response is received from a worker for a certain time, the master marks the worker as failed. Any map tasks either completed by or being processed by the failed node are rescheduled to other slave nodes. Completed map tasks are re-executed because their outputs are still stored on the failed node. However, completed reduce tasks do not need to be re-executed because their outputs are stored in the DFS.

MapReduce relies on re-execution as the primary mechanism to handle failure. When the user-defined map and reduce functions are deterministic functions of their inputs, the re-execution would produce the same output as would have been produced by a sequential execution of the entire program. When the map or the reduce function is nondeterministic, MapReduce provides weaker semantics and the programmer has to handle the potential inconsistency in the application.

MapReduce relies on atomic commits for the map and reduce tasks to guarantee that failures are handled properly. The map task sends a message to the master node with the locations of the $R$ temporary files when it completes. This message serves as the atomic commit mechanism. The reduce task writes outputs to a temporary file first, and then relies on the atomic rename capability provided by DFS as the commit mechanism.

## 5.2.4 Optimizations

A MapReduce implementation employs several optimizations to make the system robust.

One optimization is to conserve network bandwidth usage through locality optimization. Locality optimization takes advantage of the fact that DFS stores the input data on the local disks of the machines in the cluster. DFS breaks up each file into 64 MB chunks and stores several copies of each chunk on different nodes. The master takes the input files locality information into account when it schedules the tasks on the different nodes, and it tries to place tasks on the nodes that hold one replica of the input data.

Another optimization is running backup tasks. One of the common problems is that a straggler takes a significantly longer time, thus slowing down the overall process. Stragglers could arise for a variety of reasons, e.g., a machine may have a bad disk, or other jobs on the same machine may be taking up a significant amount of CPU cycle. To combat this problem, the master may speculatively schedule a task to run on a different node, and takes the result if either the primary or the backup finishes. The MapReduce paper [6] shows that a 44% reduction in the computation time is possible with speculation. Recent improvements in the scheduling algorithm [34] can cut down the processing time further.

Combiner is another optimization that can reduce the amount of data transferred between map and reduce. Some applications have a significant repetition in the intermediate keys produced by each map task, and the user-defined function is commutative and associative. For example, the word count application would produce a lot of "the, 1" key-value pairs, since the key "the" appears frequently in English documents. All these key-value pairs have to be transferred to the reduce task, where it is combined into a single number. A combiner can perform a partial merging on the map node before the data is sent. Typically, the combiner function is the same as the reduce function. The only difference is in how the MapReduce framework handles the output of the function.

### 5.2.5 Related Work

MapReduce is only one of the many new programming models that have emerged in recent years.

Dryad [18] is another programming model, which is developed by Microsoft Research. Dryad takes a much more generic approach, where it models a computation as a set of vertices and a Direct Acyclic Graph (DAG), which describes the communications among the vertices. Each vertex is a separate program that runs on a single computing node. However, different vertices may run on different computing nodes, and communications between them could go through TCP. Dryad could be used as a building block to build other programming models. For example, MapReduce is just a special case that can be easily expressed in Dryad.

MapReduce-Merge [4] is another programming model, which extends MapReduce with a third stage of merging, which could merge results from two different MapReduce jobs.

## 5.3 GridBatch

GridBatch [21,22] is a system we developed at Accenture Technology Labs. It extends the MapReduce programming model and allows programmers to easily convert a high-level design into the actual parallel implementation. The design goal is not to help the programmers find parallelism in their applications. Instead, we assume that the programmers understand their applications well and are fully aware of their parallelization potentials. Further, the programmers have thought through on how to break down the application into smaller tasks and how to partition the data in order to achieve the highest performance. But, instead of asking the programmers to implement the plan in detail, we provide a library of commonly used "operators" (a primitive for data set manipulation) as the building blocks. All the complexity associated with parallel programming is hidden within the library, and the programmers only need to think about how to apply the operators in sequence to correctly implement the application. GridBatch is specifically targeted at analytics applications, whose unique characteristics require special operators. Analytics applications are often interested in collecting statistics from the large data set, such as how often a particular event happens. They often involve correlating data from two or more different data sets (i.e., table joins in database terms).

## 5.3.1 DFS Extension

To facilitate locality optimization for the various operators, we introduce new DFS capabilities.

There are two fundamental data types in GridBatch: a table and an indexed table (borrowed from database terminology). A table contains a set of records (rows) that are independent of each other. All records in a table follow the same schema, and each record may contain several fields (columns). An indexed table is similar to a table except that each record also has an associated index, where the index could simply be one of the fields or other data provided by the user.

A table is analogous to the vector concept in a vector or SIMD (Single Instruction Multiple Data) machine or the stream concept in stream processors [19] in Computer Architecture. A table (or a vector/stream) implies that all records within it are independent of each other, and hence, they can be processed in parallel. A vector/stream allows a computer architect to design specialized hardware that takes one instruction, but applies it to all records in a vector/stream. Similarly, a table allows us to design a software system that can process the records in parallel across many machines in the cloud.

For an indexed table, we introduce another type of files: fixed-num-of-chunk files, where each file has a fixed number of chunks (denoted as $C$, defined by the user) and each chunk could have an arbitrarily large size. When a DFS client asks for a new file to be created, the name node allocates all $C$ chunks at the same time and returns them all to the DFS client. Although the user can choose $C$ to be any value, we recommend a $C$ should be chosen such that the expected chunk size (expected file size divided by $C$) is small enough for efficient processing, e.g., less than 64 MB each.

Each fixed-num-of-chunk file has an associated partition function, which defines how data should be partitioned across chunks. The DFS client submits the user-defined partition function (along with the parameter $C$) when it creates the file, which is then stored by the name node. When another DFS client asks to open the file later, the partition function is returned to the DFS client, along with the chunk locations.

When a new data record needs to be written, the DFS client calls the partition function to determine the chunk number(s); then it appends the record to the end of the chunk(s).

The user-defined partition function takes the form

```
int [] partitionFunc(Index x)
```

where $x$ is the index for the record to be written. The partition function applies a hash function to convert the index into one or more integers in the range of 1 to $C$, which indicates which particular chunk(s) the record should be stored at. In most cases, one integer is returned. However, if the user desires to make the data locally available to more nodes, the partitionFunc could return an array of integers. For example, the user may desire to have a local copy of the data on all $C$ chunks; then the user can design the partition function to return a list of all integers from 1 to $C$.

Typically, $C$ is set to be much larger than $N$, the number of machines in the system. The mapping from $C$ to $N$ is fixed (i.e., data corresponding to a particular chunk number for all indexed tables are on the same machine), and it is prescribed by a system-level lookup table, which is maintained at the name node. Such translation is necessary in order to support dynamic change of the cluster size. When old machines leave (possibly because of failures) and when new machines join, GridBatch can automatically rebalance the storage and workload.

We introduce the fixed-num-of-chunk file type because analytics applications that we are targeting are different from web applications. Web applications (word count, reverse web link, etc.) have a large amount of unstructured data, which work well with fixed-chunk-size files. In contrast, large analytics applications, such as data warehousing, have a large amount of structured data. For efficient processing, data partitioning is commonly used to segment data into smaller pieces (e.g., database partitioning in any modern database systems). If fixed-chunk-size files are used for analytics applications, constant data shuffling is required whenever a new analytics application starts.

Similar to GFS, all data chunks are replicated several times across the nodes in the system. When a machine fails, no data is lost and the system will adjust itself to rebalance the storage and workload. In GFS, the backup chunk is stored on a randomly chosen node, and the same backup chunk for the same chunk (e.g., the first backup chunk for chunk 1) for two different files could be stored on two different nodes. For fixed-chunk-size files, we maintain the same backup scheme. However, for fixed-num-of-chunk files, we fix the mapping from backup chunks to nodes, e.g., the first backup chunks for chunk $i$ for two different files are always stored on the same node. When a node fails, we can simply change the system-wide mapping table so that chunk $i$ is pointing to the backup node and locality will be preserved.

## 5.3.2 GridBatch Operators

GridBatch does not attempt to help a programmer reason the best approach to program an application. Instead, it aims to provide a set of commonly used primitives, called operators, which the programmer can use to save on programming effort. The operators handle the details of distributing the work to multiple machines; hence, the user should not need to worry about parallel programming. Instead, the user just needs to apply a set of operators sequentially, just as if writing a traditional sequential program.

GridBatch extends the capabilities of Google's MapReduce system. MapReduce could be considered as two separate operators: Map and Reduce. The Map operator is applied to all records in a file independent of each other; hence, it can be easily parallelized. The operator produces a set of key-value pairs to be used in the Reduce operator. The Reduce operator takes all values associated with a particular key and applies a user-defined reduce function. Since all values associated with a particular key have to be moved to a single location where the Reduce operator is applied, the Reduce operator is inherently sequential.

GridBatch breaks down MapReduce into elementary operators, and, in addition, introduces additional operators. GridBatch currently consists of the following operators: Map, Distribute, Recurse, Join, Cartesian, and Neighbor.

### 5.3.2.1 Map Operator

The Map operator applies a user-defined function over all records of a table. A sample pseudo-code for the user-defined function is as follows:

```
mapFunc(Record x):
  // Apply necessary processing on Record
  // x to generate Record y
  ......
  EmitResult (Table Y, record y)
```

Record $x$ is one of the records in Table $X$ to which the Map operator is applied. Within the user-defined map function, the user can do any custom processing over record $x$. At the end, the user-defined function could generate one or more records for one or more tables. In the example, we generated one new record $y$ for Table $Y$.

The user would invoke the Map operator as follows:

```
Map(Table X, Func mapFunc)
```

The first argument specifies to which table this Map operator is applied, and the second argument specifies the user-defined function.

Many applications need to process records independently. Using MapReduce, even with an identity reduce function, one would incur unnecessary sorting between the map and the reduce stage. Instead, one can use the Map operator to process these records in parallel.

### 5.3.2.2 Distribute Operator

The Distribute operator converts a table or an indexed table to another indexed table with a different index. The resulting indexed table is stored as a single fixed-num-of-chunk DFS file. This involves shuffling data from whichever chunk the data was on previously to a new chunk as indicated by the partition function for the new index.

The user invokes the Distribute operator as follows:

```
Table Y = Distribute(Table X, Field i, Func newPartitionFunc)
```

*Y* is the resulting table after applying the Distribute operator on *X*. *i* indicates which field of Table *X* should be used as the new index. newPartitionFunc is the new partition function for the newly generated table. It takes the following form:

```
int [] newPartitionFunc(Index x)
```

The function newPartitionFunc returns one or more integers to indicate which chunk(s) one record should be written to. If more than one integer is returned, the same record will be duplicated over all indicated chunks.

When the Distribute operator is invoked, the master node spawns *C* separate slave tasks on the slave nodes, one for each chunk. We refer to the task responsible for the *i*th chunk, "task *i*." For efficient local processing, task *i* is spawned on the same node that holds chunk *i* of Table *X*. The slave tasks run parallel to each other. Each slave task generates *C* output files locally, one for each chunk of Table *Y*. Task *i* goes through each record in chunk *i* of Table *X*, and for each record, it applies the newPartitionFunc to determine the chunk number *j* (or a list of chunk numbers) for Table *Y*, to which the record will be distributed. It then writes the record to the output corresponding to chunk *j* (or to outputs corresponding to the list of chunks).

When a slave task completes, it notifies the master node about the task completion and the location of the *C* local output files. When the master node notes that all slave tasks have been completed, it will spawn another set of tasks, one for each chunk, again on the nodes that will hold the corresponding chunk for Table *Y*. Again, each slave task runs in parallel. Task *j* receives a list of file locations (including the host name), one for each slave task in step 2 indicating the location of Task *i*'s output for chunk *j* of Table *Y*. Task *j* remote copies all files to the local node and merges them into chunk *j* for Table *Y*. The Distribute operator finishes when the master node is notified that all slave tasks have finished.

The actions performed by Map and Distribute operators are similar to part of the actions performed by MapReduce. We extract them out as separate operators because we feel they are fundamental operations that are needed by many applications. Extracting them out as separate operators gives the users greater flexibility when they implement their applications through operator compositions.

Both the fixed-num-of-chunk file and the Distribute operator give users direct control on how data is placed on the nodes. This capability allows users to optimize local processing, thus saving precious network bandwidth. This is especially important in a cloud or a grid consisting of geographically distributed servers across Wide Area Networks (WANs), where the network bandwidth is much smaller than that in a traditional enterprise infrastructure.

### 5.3.2.3 Join Operator

The Join operator takes two indexed tables and merges the corresponding records if the index fields match. The GridBatch system finds the corresponding records that have a matching index, and then invokes a custom function defined by the user. The user-defined function can simply merge the two records, like in a traditional database join, or it can perform any special action as it desires.

The users invoke the Join operator as follows:

```
Join(Table X, Table Y, Func joinFunc)
```

where

$X$ and $Y$ are the two input indexed tables
joinFunc is the custom function provided by the user

A sample pseudo-code for one implementation of the joinFunc is as follows:

```
joinFunc(Record x, Record y)
  // Apply necessary processing on Record
  // x and y to generate Record z
  ......
  EmitResult(Table Z, record z)
```

where $x$ and $y$ are a record of Tables $X$ and $Y$, respectively. When joinFunc is invoked, it is guaranteed that the indices for record $x$ and $y$ match. joinFunc could emit zero or more records for zero or more tables. The example shown only emits one record for one table.

Before the Join operator is called, it is the user's responsibility to make sure that Tables $X$ and $Y$ are partitioned already using the same partition function (e.g., by using the Distribute operator) on the index field that the join is based on. The Join operator simply performs the join locally without worrying about fetching data from other chunks. This is consistent with our philosophy that the user is the most knowledgeable about how to distribute data in order to achieve the best performance.

When the Join operator is invoked, the master node spawns $C$ tasks, one for each chunk, on the slave node holding the corresponding chunks for Table $X$ and $Y$. Task $i$ first sorts chunk $i$ of Tables $X$ and $Y$ individually in increasing order of their indices. Then, task $i$ walks through Tables $X$ and $Y$ with the help of two pointers. Initially, one points at the beginning of $X$ and the other points at the beginning of $Y$. Let $i(x)$ and $i(y)$ denote the index value of the records pointed to by the pointers for Tables $X$ and $Y$, respectively. If $i(x) = i(y)$, joinFunc is invoked with $x$ and $y$ as parameters. Otherwise, if $i(x) < i(y)$, advance the pointer for Table $X$, and if $i(x) > i(y)$, advance the pointer for Table $Y$. This process continues until all records are scanned. The Join operator finishes when the master node is notified that all slave tasks have finished.

In our client application of finding items generated by a set of sources, we first apply the Distribute operator on the barcode table based on the source field, and then simply perform a Join operator between the resulting barcode table and the table holding the list of sources.

### 5.3.2.4 Cartesian Operator

Unlike the Join operator, which only matches records when their index fields match, the Cartesian operator will match every record of Table *X* with every record of Table *Y*, and apply a user-defined function.

In our client's business-rule-checking application, all barcode records are stored as one table and all business rules are stored as another table. The client wants to check all records against all rules to make sure there is no business rule violation. This can be accomplished by simply calling the Cartesian operator. The user-defined function only needs to check if a record violates a particular rule, and the GridBatch system takes care of the dirty plumbing work of matching corresponding records from the two tables.

A Cartesian operator can be used to implement a join. The Join operator only works when both tables are indexed and when we desire an exact match on the index field. When a non-exact match is desired, we have to check every record *x* against every record *y*. The user-defined function can then determine whether *x* and *y* should be joined together.

The users invoke the Cartesian operator as follows:

```
Cartesian(Table X, Table Y, Func cartesianFunc)
```

where *X* and *Y* are the two input tables, and cartesianFunc is the custom function provided by the user.

A sample pseudo-code for one implementation of cartesianFunc is as follows:

```
cartesianFunc(Record x, Record y)
  // Apply necessary processing on Record
  // x and y to generate Record z
  ......
  EmitResult(Table Z, record z)
```

where *x* and *y* are records of Tables *X* and *Y*, respectively. cartesianFunc could emit zero or more records for zero or more tables. The example shown only emits one record for one table.

Like the Join operator, it is the user's responsibility to first distribute the data. The Cartesian operator simply performs the operation locally without worrying about fetching data from other chunks. The user should duplicate one of the tables over all chunks (e.g., using the Distribute operator) to guarantee that every record *x* is matched against every record *y*.

The implementation of the Cartesian operator is similar to that of the Join operator. The only difference is that no matching of indices is needed.

### 5.3.2.5 Recurse Operator

The Reduce part of MapReduce is inherently not parallelizable. But, if there are many reduce operations, an application can still benefit from parallelization by spreading the reduce operations across many nodes. For web applications, it is generally true that there are many reduce operations (e.g., word count). However, this is not necessarily true for analytics applications, where the users are only using a few reduce operations. For example, the user may just want to sort the output for reporting or collect a few statistics. In this case, the Reduce operator becomes a bottleneck, limiting the scalability of the application.

Many reduce operations are commutative and associative, and hence, order independent. For example, counting the number of occurrences of an event involves addition, which is commutative and associative. The order of how addition happens does not affect the end result. Similarly, sorting is order independent.

For these order-independent reduce operations, we introduce the Recurse operator. Users invoke Recurse as follows:

```
Recurse(Table X, Func recurseFunc)
```

where $X$ is the input table, and recurseFunc is the custom function provided by the user. The Recurse operator merges the table into a single record.

A sample pseudo-code for one implementation of recurseFunc is as follows. For conciseness, this example shows the addition operation, but it is equally easy to implement the merge sort algorithm:

```
Record recurseFunc(Record x₁, Record x₂)
  // Apply processing on x₁ and x₂
  return x = x₁ + x₂
```

where $x_1$ and $x_2$ are partial results from merging two subparts of Table $X$. recurseFunc specifies how to merge the two partial results further, and GridBatch applies the function recursively over all records of Table $X$ to eventually produce the overall sum.

Compared to the reduce operation in MapReduce, the recurse operation is more efficient because it can parallelize the reduce operation over many nodes. In addition, the recurse operation can minimize network traffic by merging results from close-by nodes. Since bandwidth is only consumed on local network segments, bandwidth on other links is preserved for other tasks. Network bandwidth consumption can be cut down further if only partial results are desired. For example, if we are only interested in the top 10 records, each node would only compute the local top 10, and send them to the neighboring node, who in turn will merge them with the local result to produce the top 10. Since only 10 records are passed from node to node, the traffic is much smaller than that used by MapReduce, which would require every node sending every record to a single node where the reduce operation is carried out.

When the Recurse operator is invoked, the master node spawns many tasks, one for each chunk, and it is spawned on the slave node that holds that chunk for Table $X$. Task $i$ first merges all records in chunk $i$ using recurseFunc. First, it takes the first two records $x_1$ and $x_2$, and applies recurseFunc. The result is saved in record $s$. Task $i$ then takes the third record, $x_3$, and applies recurseFunc on $s$ and $x_3$. This process continues for all the remaining records.

We now need to merge the results from each chunk together. Half of the tasks will send their results $s$ to another task in the other half, where $s$ is merged with the local result. At the end, only half of the tasks have partial results. This process repeats, i.e., one quarter of the tasks will send their partial results to another task in the other quarter tasks, where results are merged. The process ends when the final result is derived. The master node is responsible for coordinating the merging sequence (who sends results to who else), and it will take the network topology into account so that, most of the time, a task only sends its result to a nearby task.

### 5.3.2.6 *Neighbor Operator*

Unlike database tables, tables in GridBatch could have an implicit order semantic. For example, the barcode table in our client application preserves the scanning order. Some analytics functions, such as our client's interlacing detection problem, need to analyze the sequence to derive meaningful results.

The Neighbor operator groups neighboring records and invokes a user-defined function to analyze the subsequence. The users invoke the Neighbor operator as follows:

```
Neighbor(int k, Table X, Func neighborFunc)
```

where

$k$ is a small constant that indicates how many neighboring records to group together

$X$ is the input table

neighborFunc is the custom function provided by the user

neighborFunc takes $k$ records as arguments. The $k$ arguments follow the order in the table, i.e., the record in argument $j$ immediately follows the record in argument $j - 1$ in the table. A sample neighborFunc pseudo-code for our client's interlacing detection is as follows:

```
neighborFunc(Record x₁, Record x₂)
  // report discontinuity
  if ( x₁.containerID ≠ x₂. containerID )
    EmitResult(Table Z, record x₁)
```

where $x_1$ and $x_2$ are neighboring records of Table $X$.

This function adds the first record to a new Table $Z$ if the two records belong to different containers. To detect whether there is any interlacing, it is sufficient to count the number of occurrences of each container ID in Table $Z$. If any container appears more than once in Table $Z$, then some items from that container have been misplaced (note that the container ID is globally unique). Counting the number of appearances can be accomplished by the Recurse operator.

Interlacing detection using SQL is very hard to do, since databases do not preserve the sequence semantic. Furthermore, it is not possible to perform interlacing detection with MapReduce either for the same reason. Until now, the only alternative is to write a sequential program to scan the whole barcode table and detect any discontinuity. However, this naive solution is very time consuming, since the barcode table is many terabytes long. By using the Neighbor and Recurse operators, we implemented the same logic with only a few lines of code, and yet we were able to achieve very high performance. This demonstrates the power and capabilities of the GridBatch system.

### 5.3.2.7 Block-Level Operator

In addition to exploiting parallelism at the record level (Map operator) and at the neighbor level (Neighbor operator), the BLO operator allows us to exploit parallelism at the chunk level. As an example, we will show how it can be used efficiently to compute medians from a large data set.

The BLO operator applies a user-defined function on a chunk at a time, where a chunk is a set of records, which are stored logically and physically in the same location in the cluster.

The users invoke the BLO operator as follows:

```
BLO(Table X, Func bloFunc)
```

where $X$ is the input table, and bloFunc is the custom function provided by the user.

bloFunc takes an iterator of records as an argument. When iterating through the iterator, the records are returned in the same order as when they were written to the chunk. A sample bloFunc pseudocode for counting the number of records in a chunk is as follows:

```
bloFunc(Iterator records)
  int count=0;
  for each record x in records
    count ++
  EmitResult(Table Z, count)
```

This user-defined function counts the number of records in the input iterator, and at the end, it adds the count value to a new Table $Z$. At the end of this BLO, each chunk will produce a count value. To get the overall count, a MapReduce or a Recurse operator has to be applied to sum up all values in Table $Z$.

Figure 5.2 shows a comparison between the Map, Neighbor, and BLO operators. The Map operator is designed to exploit parallelism among independent records. The user-defined map function is applied to all records at the same time. The Neighbor operator is designed to exploit parallelism among subsequences when analyzing a sequence of records. The user-defined Neighbor function is applied to all subsequences at the same time. The BLO operator implements another pattern

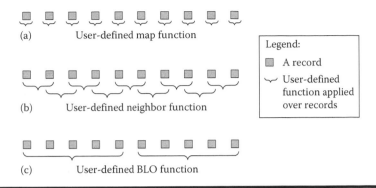

**Figure 5.2    Comparison between (a) Map, (b) Neighbor, and (c) BLO operators.**

of parallel processing. The user-defined BLO function is applied to all chunks at the same time; however, the processing within the chunk could be sequential.

The BLO operator works in conjunction with the FC files, where all data that have to be processed sequentially are arranged in the same chunk already. A chunk is guaranteed to be stored physically on the same node, and hence, it can be efficiently processed locally without consuming network bandwidth. There are a couple of ways to shuffle data into the correct chunks. When data are written into DFS, the user could choose to write to an FC file with a user-defined partition function. The user-defined partition function makes sure that the correct data are loaded to the correct chunks. Alternatively, if the data are already stored in an FS file, the user could invoke the Distribute operator. Again, the user would supply a partition function, which makes sure that data are loaded correctly.

The BLO operator can be considered as the Reduce portion of the MapReduce operator, except that it is a stand-alone operator and involves no sorting and grouping by key. It is implemented as a child class of the Task class, the base class for both the MapTask and ReduceTask classes in the Hadoop implementation. We inherit from Task instead of ReduceTask because BLO does not need the data shuffling and sorting operations in the ReduceTask class.

Similar to the Join operator, the functionality of the BLO operator could be implemented with MapReduce. However, as we will see in our application of computing medians, using MapReduce would be very inefficient, since it would have to invoke the identity mapper, shuffle all data around, and sort the data unnecessarily. This is especially bad when multiple passes of MapReduce are involved, where the work done in one MapReduce pass would have to be repeated in the next pass, since there is no mechanism to save the intermediate data in the MapReduce framework.

## 5.3.3 Sample Application: Computing Median

To illustrate MapReduce and GridBatch in a real application scenario, we consider a real enterprise application—a data warehouse application for a large financial services firm. The company has tens of millions of customers, and they are interested in collecting and reporting high-level statistics, such as average and median, about their customers' account balances. They want to collect these statistics across many different dimensions of their customer base. For example, across age groups, what is the balance for 20–30 years old, 30–40 years old, etc.; or across industries, what is the balance for customers in retail or hightech industries. They are also interested in a combination of many dimensions, such as across age groups within different industries or across job tenure length within different geographies.

We use the term "segmentation" to refer to a particular combination of the dimensions. For example, computing medians across age group is one segmentation and computing medians across both age group and industry is another segmentation. We use the term "bracket" to refer to a range within a segmentation. For example, users that are 20–30 years old and are in the retail industry form one bracket. We need to compute one median for each bracket, and many medians for each segmentation, where each median corresponds to one bracket within the segmentation. We denote the number of dimensions by $D$ and the number of segmentations by $S$. In the worst case, $S$ could be as large as $D!$

The input to the problem is a large fact table with tens of millions of rows. Each row holds all relevant information specific to a customer including the customer's account balance, birthday, industry, geography, job tenure length, education, etc.

Computing the average is relatively easy because one can simply sum up the total and divide it by the count, where both the total and the count are easy to compute in parallel with MapReduce. However, computing a median is quite awkward with MapReduce, because it requires sequential processing. A straightforward implementation would first sort all data and then find the middle point. Both steps are sequential in nature, and hence, they take a long time to complete for a large data set. The problem gets worse in our case when there are a large number of median computations.

We present two efficient approaches, one using MapReduce, and the other using the BLO operator of GridBatch, to compare the two systems. In the following, we first describe the traditional approach to compute the median and point out the deficiencies, and then we describe our approaches using MapReduce and BLO. As we will see, the new programming models, such as MapReduce and GridBatch, can solve these problems much more efficiently.

### 5.3.3.1 Traditional Enterprise Approach

The most common solution in enterprises today for large-scale data warehousing applications is to use a database. Once the fact table is loaded into the database, one can simply write SQL queries to compute the 50 percentile value, or call the median function directly if available from the SQL platform.

When computing medians for a segmentation, it is more efficient to write one SQL query to compute medians for all brackets within the segmentation. This can be achieved by a combination of the group by and case clauses. An example for the age group segmentation is as follows:

```
select
  age_group,
median(balance)
from
(select
  balance,
  age_group=(case 20 < age <30: 0
             case 31 < age < 40: 1
             ...)
from account)
group by age_group
```

The inner `select` statement builds an intermediary table from the original `account` table. It has a `balance` column directly from the `account` table and an intermediary `age _ group` column derived from the age column. All records in the same bracket have the same value in the `age _ group` column. For example, all records whose age is between 20 and 30 have 0 in the `age _ group` column. Once the intermediary table is built, the outer `select` statement uses the `group by` clause to group all records in a bracket together and then computes the median value.

This approach suffers from several problems. First, the case statement is lengthy and hard to maintain, especially when multiple dimensions are involved. Second, a separate SQL query has to be written for each segmentation, which could be an exponential function of $D$, the number of dimensions. Third, each SQL query has to scan the complete data set twice, once to build the intermediary table and once to compute the medians. Since there are $S$ (the number of segmentations) SQL queries, this approach would scan the data set $2S$ times.

An alternative approach is to use an ETL (Extract, Transform, Load) tool to add the intermediary columns (e.g., `age _ group`) first. The ETL tool reads from the fact table one record at a time, applies the necessary logic to build the intermediary column, then writes the result back into a staging table. Because of the higher expressibility of ETL, the column building logic is simpler to write and maintain. Further, this approach cuts down the number of passes needed to build the intermediary columns from $S$ to $D$. However, each SQL query still has to scan the data set separately once to compute the medians. Since there are $S$ SQL queries, we have to scan the data set $S + D$ times.

For a large data set, it is crucial to minimize the number of passes as reading and writing consume most of the time. This is especially important in the traditional enterprise architecture, since all data are stored in a network attached storage and each pass has to consume the limited network bandwidth.

### 5.3.3.2 Algorithm for Finding Medians

In this and the next two sections, we show our approach on how to process the data distributedly in two passes using either MapReduce or the BLO of GridBatch.

Our approach partitions the data set based on the account balance to facilitate parallel processing. Partitions are determined by a set of split-points, where all records whose balance falls in between two neighboring split-points are grouped into the same chunk. The split-points are picked to ensure that the chunk sizes are roughly evenly distributed to maximize parallelism. If the account balance distribution is known, the split-points can be easily determined; otherwise, a preprocessing MapReduce job could be run to collect a sample distribution of account balances (sorting using MapReduce used the same sampling approach to determine distribution [6]).

The split-points should also be picked to ensure that each chunk is small enough to fit into the memory. The BLO operator and the reducer in MapReduce supply the input data as an iterator to the user-defined function so that they can deal with smaller memory by storing large data on disk. However, if the user-defined reduce or BLO function needs to access all data, e.g., during a sort, it is highly desirable to store them all in memory in order to avoid the complexity in the user code to swap data to disk. Having the chunk size small enough will ensure that the reduce or the BLO user-defined function could simply cache all data in memory.

For simplicity of description, we first explain how to compute a single median, the overall median, and then we generalize to multiple medians. We describe the algorithm in terms of the general approach, and in Sections 5.3.3.3 and 5.3.3.4, we describe in more detail how to implement it using MapReduce and BLO. The algorithm has three main steps as follows.

- *Step 1:* We partition the records into chunks such that all records whose balance falls between two split-points are in the same chunk. We then iterate through all data in a chunk to count the number of records in the chunk.
- *Step 2:* The counts for all chunks are aggregated. Since we can easily determine the total by summing up all counts, we know the rank of the median. Since we also know the split-points and the chunk corresponding to two neighboring split-points, we know which chunk the median is in and its rank within that chunk. Let us assume it is chunk $p$ and rank $r$.
- *Step 3:* We sort all data in chunk $p$ and then find the $r$th number, which will be the median.

The above algorithm is for finding one median in a large distributed data set; however, it is easy to extend the algorithm to find many medians, one for each bracket of each segmentation. We keep track of one counter for each bracket. In steps 1 and 3, the counter for a bracket is only incremented if the record belongs to the bracket. Note that we still scan through the data only once in both step 1 and step 3, and we also only sort the data once in step 3.

### 5.3.3.3 MapReduce Approach

In MapReduce, the data set is stored in an FS file and it is not partitioned. Hence, in step 1, we have to count the individual records in the Map and aggregate the count in the reduce phase.

The user-defined map function takes one record as the input, and emits one key-value pair for each bracket to which the record belongs to, where the key is a concatenation of the bracket name and the chunk number and the value is 1. The bracket name uniquely identifies the segmentation and value range, and the chunk number is specified by the partition function, which maps from the account balance into the chunk number based on the set of split-points. For example, the key "Age20-30IndustryRetail_5" refers to the age and industry segmentation, which includes all records that are in age range 20–30 and in the retail industry, and specifies that the balance in the record falls in chunk 5.

```
mapFunc(Key=null, Value=Record x):
  for ( each bracket b )
    if ( x in b )
      p = partition(x.balance)
      EmitResult(b;p, 1)
```

The user-defined combine and reduce functions simply sum up all 1's associated with one key. At the end, they emit one key-value pair, where the key is $b;p$, and the value is $c_{b,p}$—the total count for bracket $b$ and chunk $p$.

In step 2, another MapReduce is used to determine the chunk and rank where the median resides. The map function simply aggregates all counts, $c_{b,p}$, for a bracket, $b$, into the same reduce function. It returns the bracket name as the key, and encodes both the chunk and the count as the value.

```
mapFunc(Key=b;p, Value=c_{b,p}):
  EmitResult(b, p;c_{b,p})
```

The reduce function receives a list of chunk and count pairs for a particular bracket $b$. Based on the ordering of the chunks, it computes the chunk $p_b$ where the median is and its rank $r_b$ within chunk $p_b$.

```
reduceFunc(Key=b, Value=list of p;c_{b,p}):
  Compute p_b and r_b
  EmitResult(b, p_b;r_b)
```

In step 3, we use the $p_b$ and $r_b$ numbers returned to find the actual median value. It involves sorting records in chunk $p_b$ based on their balance, and then returning the $r_b$th number in the chunk. The map function returns the record as its value and the chunk it is in as the key, so that all records in the same chunk are aggregated for the same reduce function.

```
mapFunc(Key=null, Value=Record x):
  p = partition(x.balance)
  EmitResult(p, x)
```

The reduce function first sorts all records based on the account balance; then for each bracket $b$, if the current chunk is $p_b$, it finds the $r_b$th number. Note that we could have sorted only records associated with a bracket. However, there could be multiple brackets in the same chunk, so it is more efficient to sort only once.

```
reduceFunc(Key=p, Value=list of Records X):
  sort X based on x.balance
  for each bracket b
    if ( p == p_b )
      find r_b th record in bracket b
      EmitResult(b, r_b th record's balance)
```

Note that the reduce function reads directly from the output file from step 2, which contains a list of $p_b$;$r_b$ value pairs.

### 5.3.3.4 GridBatch Approach

The GridBatch approach leverages a combination of the BLO operator and the FC files. The data are first stored as FC files to facilitate local processing in the following steps. This can be achieved in two ways: either upload the data to DFS directly as an FC file or, if the data are already stored as an FS file, use the Distribute operator to partition the data. In either case, we simply supply the same `partition` function either to the DFS or to the Distribute operator. Once the data are stored as an FC file, we can proceed to process the same three steps. However, both step 1 and step 3 not only become simpler but are also able to run more efficiently.

In step 1, the BLO user-defined function simply counts how many records are in each bracket for the current chunk. It first computes which chunk $p$ the records are in. Since we know all records are in the same chunk, this computation only needs to take place once.

```
bloFunc(list of records X):
  p=partition(X)
  for each x in X
    for each bracket b
      if (x in b)
        c_{b,p} ++
  for each bracket b
    EmitResult(b;p, c_{b,p})
```

Step 2 is exactly the same as that in the MapReduce approach; hence, we omit the description. In step 3, we invoke another BLO operator to find the actual median value.

```
bloFunc(list of records X):
  p = partition(X)
  sort X based on x.balance
  for each bracket b
    if ( p == p_b )
      find r_bth record in bracket b
      EmitResult(b, r_bth record's balance)
```

Again, we first compute the current chunk number $p$, which only needs to be done once. Then the rest of the processing is identical to the reduce function in step 3 of the MapReduce approach.

## 5.3.3.5 Comparing MapReduce and GridBatch Approaches

Although the MapReduce approach and the GridBatch approach are quite similar, there are two key differences. First, the GridBatch approach takes advantage of the partitioned data structure. Through a combination of moving related data to the same node and processing data on the node where they reside, GridBatch is able to minimize network bandwidth consumption and fully utilize the local disk bandwidth. In comparison, MapReduce, at least the open-source Hadoop [16] implementation, could create splits (a split is Hadoop's terminology for a set of data to be processed by one Map task) that span multiple chunks. Even though Hadoop attempts to localize processing, the spanning means some data will have to traverse the network. In addition, Hadoop has no mechanism to move related data together. Although the users can create many HFS files with one for each partition (a poor man's FC file), the users have no control over where these files are placed; so they could all be stored on a few data nodes. As a result, we either incur a significant communication overhead or an imbalance of load among workers during processing. As the cluster size increases, the total disk bandwidth increases; however, the network bandwidth does not (it is limited by the bottleneck link). Thus, the GridBatch approach is more scalable.

Second, GridBatch has many operators, and each implements a parallel processing pattern. The user not only has the flexibility to choose the operator that is most appropriate for the target problem, but also has the freedom to arbitrarily combine them. In comparison, there is only one choice in MapReduce. Compared to using the BLO operator, using MapReduce introduces the following inefficiencies.

1. The MapReduce pattern forces the intermediary data to be verbose. For example, in step 1, in order to count, each record has to generate $S$ key-value pairs in the form of $(b;p, 1)$, one for each segmentation. Even with the help of the combine function, only the network bandwidth consumed is reduced; the map function still has to write a large amount of data to the disk. Furthermore, the combine function introduces additional overhead since it has to read the data from the disk, sort the data, and combine the output.

2. The intermediary data between map and reduce are not saved. MapReduce has no mechanism for saving the intermediary data and reusing it for later processing. In step 3, we are distributing the records based on their chunk already. Unfortunately, because we cannot save the result, we have to redistribute the data or their derivatives (e.g., the count in step 1) over and over again. This is especially inefficient when many MapReduce steps are involved.

3. MapReduce contains processing that may not be needed for some applications. For example, MapReduce always sorts the key-value pairs based on the keys. In our case, the BLO avoids unnecessary sorting on keys in both step 1 and step 3.

By giving the users a family of operators, GridBatch allows the users to optimize the processing by choosing the right operator for the right job. Experimentally, we have shown that GridBatch is much more efficient than MapReduce, which is in turn much more efficient than the traditional enterprise approach. We omit the experimental results for brevity. We refer interested readers to the GridBatch paper [22] for more details.

# 5.4 MapReduce Implementation on a Cloud OS

In Section 5.2.2, we described a MapReduce implementation on top of a server OS. In this section, we describe how to leverage a cloud OS to implement MapReduce much more efficiently. We describe Cloud MapReduce, a system we have developed at Accenture Technology Labs. The lessons we learned from using the cloud OS should be generic enough to be applicable to a wide range of system projects.

Like a server OS, a cloud OS is responsible for managing resources. In a server (e.g., a PC), the OS is responsible for managing the various hardware resources, such as CPU, memory, disks, network interfaces-everything inside a server's chassis. It hides the hardware operation details and allows these scarce resources to be efficiently shared. A cloud OS serves the same purpose. Instead of managing a single machine's resources, a cloud OS is responsible for managing the cloud infrastructure, hiding the cloud infrastructure details from the application programmers and coordinating the sharing of the limited resources.

But unlike a traditional OS, a cloud OS has to do everything at scale. IBM CEO Thomas J. Watson is well known for his 1943 statement (although only scant evidence exists): "I think there is a world market for maybe five computers." Although it is often laughed at since the advent of Personal Computers, it is becoming a reality again. The only difference is that we refer to these computers as clouds. Today, only a handful of companies, such as Google, Microsoft, Amazon, and Yahoo, need and are capable of building a cloud—a large server farm with hundreds of thousands of servers. For example, it is reported that Google has well over 1 million servers. Managing such big an infrastructure requires the OS to be extremely scalable. It is precisely the scalability that we are leveraging for the Cloud MapReduce implementation.

## 5.4.1 What Is a Cloud OS?

Even though the underlying resources it manages are different, a cloud OS is similar to a traditional server OS in terms of the services it provides. Since our MapReduce implementation is built on top of Amazon web services, we describe the Amazon cloud OS in detail to illustrate what services a cloud OS could provide.

Amazon's EC2 service manages the compute resources just like a traditional OS would. A traditional OS provides a set of process interfaces, such as the POSIX interface, for applications to call to instantiate new processes or terminate existing ones. When processes are running, the OS manages the fair allocation of CPU cycles among the various processes. Similarly, EC2 provides a set of web services API for applications to call to instantiate new or terminate existing VMs. When VMs are running, EC2 manages the fair allocation of compute resources among VMs. The hypervisor schedules the various VMs on the same physical machine to ensure that each gets its promised share of the CPU resource. Although there is no evidence that EC2 is doing dynamic adjustments, it can potentially even change the resource allocation by adjusting the scheduling weight in the hypervisor, or if the underlying physical machine is overcommitted, it can move VMs to a different physical host [5,17,25]. EC2's web services API is designed to be scalable so that many requests could be served at the same time. For example, the service end point is mapped to many IP addresses at the DNS (Domain Name System) level and each IP address can be further hardware-load-balanced to many physical servers.

Another service, Amazon's S3, manages the storage resources just like a traditional OS would. A traditional OS provides a file interface, where an application could call the interface functions to open, read, write, and close a file. Similarly, S3 exposes a set of web services API, to which applications could call to put and get objects. Like EC2, the web services API is designed to be scalable. In addition to the API, object storage is also implemented in a scalable fashion, i.e., objects are distributed among many servers and each object is replicated several times. As of July 2008, S3 stores 22 billion objects—a clear demonstration of its scalability.

Amazon's Simple Queue Service (SQS) is similar to a UNIX pipe. In a UNIX pipe, a process can write messages at one end and another process could consume the messages at the other end. Unlike a UNIX pipe, which is limited to processes running on the same hardware, anyone on the Internet could write to or read from an SQS queue.

Amazon's SimpleDB service is most similar to the registry service in a Windows OS. As its name suggests, it could also be thought of as a simplified database. An application could write some data into SimpleDB, which will be persistently stored. SimpleDB also offers the ability to run simple queries against the stored data.

Similar to EC2 and S3, both SQS and SimpleDB are designed to be highly scalable. Since all Amazon services are exposed as web services APIs, standard techniques to design scalable web applications, such as DNS load balancing and IP load balancing using hardware load balancers, could help make these services scalable.

The Microsoft cloud OS also offers similar services. Microsoft Azure workers provide compute services. It differs from Amazon EC2 in that it provides computation capacity inside a .NET container instead of an ×86 VM. Similar to S3, Microsoft Azure blob provides storage service. Similar to SQS and Unix pipe, Microsoft Azure queue provides messaging service. Lastly, similar to SimpleDB and Windows registry, Microsoft Azure table provides persistent state storage service.

### 5.4.1.1 Advantages Offered by a Cloud OS

A cloud OS is complex to implement. There are two reasons for this complexity. First, the shear scale of the cloud infrastructure pushes technology limit. Few companies have had the experience of managing such a big infrastructure, and the cloud providers are forced to build new solutions from the ground up. For example, Google designed their own GFS [10] to manage files and BigTable [3] to store a large amount of semi-structured data, and Amazon designed Dynamo [8] to manage storage and their own management infrastructure to support their web services API.

Second, a cloud has to be robust and scalable because it is designed to be shared by hundreds or thousands of people instead of just a few users on a PC. Just like the computers in the 1940s, clouds are expensive to build. Both Google and Microsoft are aggressively building out their cloud infrastructure. According to their annual 10K reports, both companies are spending close to a billion dollars a year on capital investment. Only a handful of companies could afford such a big investment. Yet, many companies or individuals require access to a large computation capacity once in a while; thus, a large number of users could potentially time-share the cloud infrastructure at the same time. It is not trivial to support such a large number of users at the same time. As an evidence of the complexity of building a cloud OS, even after 4 years of its introduction, we still found a bug in Amazon's SQS through the course of this research.

Even though a cloud OS is complex to implement, out of necessity, cloud providers have already spent a large amount of engineering effort on building a highly scalable cloud OS that can manage a large infrastructure shared by many people. If we leverage the existing cloud OS, we can potentially lower the application complexity, yet achieve high scalability.

### 5.4.1.2 Challenges Posed by a Cloud OS

A cloud OS' scalability comes at a price. It has to be traded off with other desirable system properties. Eric Brewer, in a keynote address to the PODC (Principles of Distributed Computing) 2000 conference [2], presented the CAP theorem. The theorem states that, of the three properties of shared-data systems—data consistency, system availability, and tolerance to network partition—only two can be achieved at any given time. A more formal confirmation of the CAP theorem can be found in [11]. Because a cloud is used by thousands of people, it has to be highly scalable and always available; thus, the only property it can give up is data consistency.

Indeed, the Amazon cloud OS has embraced a weaker consistency model called "eventual consistency" [32]. Under the eventual consistency model, the system guarantees that if no new updates are made to an object, eventually all accesses will return the last updated value. However, during a small time window, clients may observe inconsistent states. The inconsistency window size cannot be determined a priori because it depends on communication delays, the load on the system, the number of replicas involved in the replication scheme, and the extent of components failure (both the number of and the length of) if any. The most popular system that implements eventual consistency is the DNS. Updates to a domain name are distributed according to a configured pattern and in combination with time-controlled caches; eventually, all clients will see the update.

In addition to eventual consistency, a cloud also employs horizontal scaling. For example, SimpleDB can only sustain a small write throughput per domain; but, a user can write to multiple domains at the same time to increase the aggregate write throughput. Although each Amazon account has 100 domains by default, one can simply send an e-mail to request more domains. This is similar to EC2, which by default has a 20 instances (Amazon's term for VMs) limit, but it can be lifted by a simple e-mail request.

Building applications on top of a cloud OS must overcome its limitations. We describe the manifestations of the eventual consistency model that we are able to observe, and how we architect and implement Cloud MapReduce to overcome the eventual-consistency and horizontal-scaling limitations.

## 5.4.2  Advantages of Cloud MapReduce

We will show that we can greatly simplify the design and implementation of MapReduce by leveraging what a cloud OS has implemented already. We compare with Hadoop [16], an open-source implementation of MapReduce on top of a traditional server OS. The current version (0.20.0) has a total of 285,387 lines of Java code alone. There are also 46,325 lines of Unix shell scripts, which facilitate setting up a cluster, propagating configurations, and launching new MapReduce jobs. In contrast, our implementation has 3000 lines of Java code. Although some of the differences could be attributed to additional features in Hadoop (such as Streaming), we believe that we can maintain at least an order of magnitude of advantage. We discuss the detailed reasons in Section 5.4.5 after we have described our architecture and implementation.

The simplicity means that it is easy to extend the framework beyond simply MapReduce. Many applications do not conform to the MapReduce model. If implemented in the MapReduce framework, the application could experience slow performance. For example, many problems require a map stage only, i.e., these applications only need to spread out the work to as many workers as possible. Using MapReduce, the map output has to go through the reduce phase, which consumes unnecessary compute resources. Using a simple implementation like ours, we can easily change our framework to not only refine the MapReduce model, but also implement a totally different model such as Dryad [18].

Beyond simplicity, we demonstrate that, by leveraging the cloud's scalability, our implementation is both faster and more scalable than Hadoop. Even though a great deal of engineering effort has gone into making Hadoop as scalable as possible, the single master node architecture still reportedly limits its scalability to around 2000 nodes. In Section 5.4.6, we show that Hadoop further has a scalability limit on the number of files it can handle. We observe slow performance when there are a large number of input files. In comparison, Cloud MapReduce has no single point of scalability bottleneck.

Beyond the advantages, Cloud MapReduce also has several highly desirable properties, which seem to be shared by other highly scalable systems (such as Dynamo [8]).

*Incremental scalability:* Cloud MapReduce can scale incrementally in the number of computing nodes. A user not only can launch a number of servers at the beginning, but also can launch additional servers in the middle of a computation if the user thinks the progress is too slow. The new servers can automatically figure out the current job progress and poll the queues for work to process.

*Symmetry and decentralization:* Every computing node in Cloud MapReduce has the same set of responsibilities as its peers. There are no master or slave nodes. Symmetry simplifies system provisioning, configuration, and failure recovery. As implied by symmetry, there is no single central agent (master), which makes the system more available.

*Heterogeneity:* The computing nodes could have varying computation capacity. The faster nodes would do more work than the slower nodes. In addition, the computing nodes could be distributed geographically. In the extreme, a user can even harvest idle computing capacity from servers/desktops distributed on the Internet.

## 5.4.3 Cloud MapReduce Architecture and Implementation

In this section, we describe how we implement Cloud MapReduce using the Amazon cloud OS. We start with the high-level architecture, and then delve into detailed implementation issues we have encountered. We use the word count application as an example to describe our implementation.

We use four infrastructure services that Amazon provides today. We use EC2 APIs to spawn up new VMs (also called instances) to process new MapReduce jobs. We store our input and possibly output data in S3. By leveraging the distributed nature of S3, we can achieve higher data throughput, since data comes from multiple servers and communications with the servers potentially all traverse different network paths. We also use SQS, which is a critical component that allows us to design MapReduce in a simple way. A queue serves two purposes. First, it is a synchronization point where workers (a process running on an instance) can coordinate job assignments. Second, queue serves as a decoupling mechanism to coordinate data flow between different stages. Lastly, we use SimpleDB, which serves as the central job coordination point in our fully distributed implementation. We keep all workers' status here.

### 5.4.3.1 Architecture

Cloud MapReduce architecture is shown in Figure 5.3. There are several SQS queues: one input queue, one master reduce queue, one output queue, and many reduce queues.

As its name implies, the input queue holds the inputs to the MapReduce computation. At the start of the computation, the user provides an input queue, which contains a list of S input key-value pairs. Each key-value pair corresponds to a split

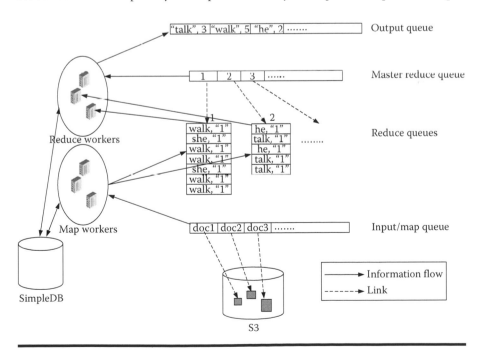

**Figure 5.3   Cloud MapReduce architecture.**

of the input data that will be processed by one map task. To facilitate tracking, each key-value pair also has a unique map ID. In the word count application, this queue contains the document collections where the key is the document name and the value is a pointer into S3 storage. SQS is designed for message communication; hence, it has an 8 kB message size limitation. Because it could be too small to fit a large document, we store a pointer to S3 instead of the data directly in SQS. In addition to pointing to the location in S3, the pointer could also contain a range specification, specifying a chunk of the file. Using ranges, the user could split up a bigger file into pieces and process them separately. Similar to the input queue, the output queue holds the results of the MapReduce computation. In the word count application, the output holds the resulting key-value pairs.

There is only one master reduce queue, and it holds many pointers, one for each reduce queue. As we will see, the master reduce queue is used to assign reduce tasks. There are a large number of reduce queues. The number of them, denoted by $Q$, is a configurable parameter that is set by the user. The reduce queues and the master reduce queue, as well as the entries in the master reduce queue, are created distributedly before the start of the MapReduce job.

A set of map workers, each running as a separate thread on an EC2 instance, poll the input queue for work. When a map worker dequeues one key-value pair, it invokes the user-defined map function to process it. Just like in other MapReduce implementations, the user-defined function processes the input key-value pair and emits a set of output key-value pairs. In the word count example, the input value is a pointer to a document stored in S3. The map function first downloads the document from S3 to the local machine. It then parses the document, and for each word (e.g., "talk") it sees, it emits a key-value pair, where the key is the word (e.g., "talk") and the value is simply "1" to indicate that it has seen this word once.

The MapReduce framework collects the output key-value pairs from the map function, and then writes them to the reduce queues. A reduce key maps to one of the reduce queues through a hash function. A default hash function is provided, but the users can also supply their own. Since the number of reduce keys could be much bigger than $Q$, several keys may map to the same queue. As we will see, each reduce queue is processed by a separate reduce worker; thus, $Q$ should be set to at least as large as the number of reduce workers. Preferably, $Q$ should be much bigger in order to maximize load balancing.

Once the map workers finish their jobs, the reduce workers start to poll work from the master reduce queue. Once a reduce worker dequeues a message, it is responsible for processing all data in the reduce queue indicated by the message. It dequeues messages from the reduce queue and feeds them into the user-defined reduce function as an iterator. After the reduce function finishes processing all data in the reduce queue, the worker goes back to the master reduce queue to fetch the next message to process.

Just like in other MapReduce implementations, the user-defined reduce function writes a set of key-value pairs as the outputs. The reduce workers collect the outputs and write them to the output queue. The name of the output queue has been specified before the start of the MapReduce job. It can be used either as the final output or as the input to the next MapReduce job.

Even though we have shown two sets of workers (map workers and reduce workers) in Figure 5.3, both run on the same set of EC2 instances. Cloud MapReduce initially runs only the map workers on the EC2 instances. When the map phase has finished (discussed below), it stops all map workers and launches new reduce workers to continue in the reduce phase.

Besides reading from and writing to the various queues, the workers also read from and write to SimpleDB to update their status. By communicating status with a central scalable SimpleDB service, we not only avoid a single point bottleneck in our architecture, but we also make our implementation fully distributable. Workers work independent of all other workers, and they do not care how many other workers are there. In addition, workers can be heterogeneous. They can be located anywhere in the world and can have a vastly different computing capacity.

In our architecture, it is easy for the job owner to get a rough sense of the job progress. The input queue length as a percentage of $S$—the original input queue length—is a good approximation of the map progress. Similarly, the master reduce queue length as a percentage of $Q$—the original master reduce queue length—is a good approximation of the reduce progress. Obtaining the approximate queue length is a simple call to the SQS GetQueueAttributes API.

Our current implementation is written in Java. Since the interface functions are in Java, all user-defined map and reduce functions (at least their interface part) have to be written in Java. This limitation could be easily removed by using a mechanism similar to the Streaming mechanism used in the Hadoop [16] implementation.

Because the nodes are symmetric, it is easy to launch a MapReduce job. Users simply launch a certain number of VMs from our custom Amazon Machine Image (AMI), and pass a few job-specific parameters to the VMs as the user data. There is no complicated cluster setup and configuration, and there is no need for selecting a master. Our AMI contains a simple script that parses the user data passed in during launch to determine what application to run and which data set to use, and then the script automatically starts the MapReduce job.

## 5.4.3.2 Cloud Challenges and Our General Solution Approaches

Even though the architecture presented above is simple, we have to get around several limitations posed by the cloud. We list the key challenges we encountered and the general techniques we used to get around them. In the subsequent sections, we get into more details on the implementation.

*Long latency:* Since Amazon services are accessed through the network, the latency could be significant. In our measurement, SQS latency ranges from 20 to 100 ms even from within EC2. Hence, a significant portion of the time will be spent waiting for SQS to respond if we access it synchronously. For example, a simple word count application on 10 MB of documents takes roughly 2 h to complete on 10 nodes; whereas, the same application on a single node would have taken only a few minutes if processed locally. We get around this limitation through two techniques: message aggregation and multi-threading (described in Section 5.4.3.5).

*Horizontal scaling:* Although all Amazon cloud services are based on horizontal scaling, we are only able to observe one concrete manifestation: when using SimpleDB, each SimpleDB domain is only able to sustain a small write throughput. In our experiments, the threshold is roughly 30–40 items per second. To get around this problem, we spread the write workload across many domains, and we aggregate the results from all domains when reading the status. Unlike SimpleDB, other services, such as S3 and SQS, hide the horizontal-scaling details from the end users.

*Do not know when a queue is created for the first time:* According to Amazon documentation, to know whether a worker is the first to create a queue, the worker can call the CreateQueue SQS API with a unique visibility timeout (time for a message to reappear after read) setting. If a queue already exists but has a different visibility timeout, Amazon returns an error message; otherwise, it returns success. In practice, due to eventual consistency, if two workers create the queue at the same time, both may return success. We do not encounter this problem in our current architecture; however, it did limit our architecture design to avoid dynamic queue creation.

*Duplicate message:* According to Amazon documentation, when a worker reads a message from an SQS queue, the message disappears from the queue for a certain amount of time (the visibility timeout). In practice, two workers (or two threads) may read the same message twice if they read at the same time. This is another manifestation of eventual consistency, because each read modifies the message state—hiding it for a visibility timeout. Our solution approach depends on the queue purpose. We use filtering for input and reduce queues, but we use conflict resolution for the master reduce queue. Note that a duplicate message happens rarely; so even if the recovery mechanism is expensive, it will not impact the performance much.

*Potential node failure:* A worker may fail in the middle of processing a map or a reduce task. We use a status update to a central place (SimpleDB) as a commit mechanism, and we use filtering to remove uncommitted results.

*Indeterministic eventual consistency windows:* This problem has a different manifestation in SQS and SimpleDB. In SQS, we find that it frequently reports the queue to be empty even when there are still messages in the queue, especially when there are only a few messages left. Amazon documentation attributes this to the distributed nature of the SQS implementation, where messages for the same queue are stored on different servers. The Amazon documentation states that one can call the dequeue API a few times and the queue would return all messages. Unfortunately, there is neither a bound on the number of API calls nor a bound on the time to wait. Similarly, in SimpleDB, when we read an item right after it is written, we may not get the latest value. One solution is to wait for an arbitrarily long time; unfortunately, it not only does not provide a guarantee, but it will also result in a much slower performance since workers are frequently waiting idle.

Our solution strategy is to set an expectation before reading. For example, we record the number of key-value pairs generated by each map task for each reduce queue. Then, in the reduce phase, we know exactly how many key-value pairs to expect, and we poll from the reduce queue until all are read. As another example, when tallying the total key-value pairs generated for a reduce queue, we make sure that we get $S$ counts from SimpleDB, one reported by each map task.

## 5.4.3.3 Status Tracking

Due to eventual consistency, we have no reliable way of knowing whether or not a queue is empty. To facilitate tracking, each worker updates its progress to SimpleDB. The worker then uses the progress reports from all nodes, including his or her own progress report, to determine whether there are more to get from a queue.

When a map worker finishes a map task, it writes two pieces of information to SimpleDB: the worker ID and map ID $i$ pair, and the number of reduce key-value pairs the worker generated for each reduce queue $j$ while processing map ID $i$ (denoted by $R_{ij}$). Updating the status to SimpleDB serves as the commit mechanism to signify that the input split corresponding to the map ID has been processed successfully.

The worker ID and map ID pair information is used to determine when the input queue is empty. When SQS indicates that there are no more key-value pairs to process in the input queue, the map worker queries SimpleDB to get the list of all worker ID and map ID pairs. It first removes duplicate map IDs by randomly picking a winner. Some map IDs may have been processed by more than one map worker, either because two map workers received the same map ID due to the eventual consistency problem, or because a node failed and a new map worker processed the same map ID again. After duplicate removal, the map worker counts how many map IDs have been processed. If it is the same as $S$, Cloud MapReduce proceeds to the reduce phase; otherwise, the worker goes back to query the input queue again for more work.

The reduce key-value pairs count ($R_{ij}$) is used to determine when a reduce queue has been processed. When a reduce worker is assigned reduce queue $j$ (by querying the master reduce queue), it first queries SimpleDB to sum up $R_{ij}$ for all $i$ to see how many key-value pairs are in reduce queue $j$. It then queries reduce queue $j$ until all $\sum_i R_{ij}$ key-value pairs have been read.

In the reduce phase, we use a simpler status-tracking mechanism. Each reduce worker updates to SimpleDB $C_k$—the number of reduce queues it has processed—after successfully processing a reduce queue. When SQS reports that the master reduce queue is empty, the reduce worker queries SimpleDB to sum up $C_k$. If $\sum_k C_k < Q$, the worker goes back to query the master reduce queue again for more work; otherwise, it declares that the MapReduce job has finished.

To overcome the write throughput limitation of a single SimpleDB domain, each worker randomly picks one of several domains to write the status. When querying SimpleDB for results, each worker launches multiple threads to read from all domains at the same time, and then aggregates the overall result. Even though statuses are maintained centrally, SimpleDB would not be a bottleneck, since it itself is implemented in a distributed fashion.

### 5.4.3.4 Failure Detection/Recovery and Conflict Resolution

We use SQS's visibility timeout mechanism for failure detection and recovery. After a worker reads a message from a queue, the message disappears from the queue for a certain period of time (the visibility timeout). Unless deleted explicitly, a message will reappear after the visibility timeout passes.

The input queue has a visibility timeout that is longer than the time it takes to process a map task. After a map worker has successfully processed a map task, it removes the corresponding message from the queue to prevent other workers from repeating the same work. Similarly, the master reduce queue has a timeout that is longer than the time it takes to process a reduce queue, and a reduce worker only removes the message after it has successfully processed the reduce queue.

If a worker fails while processing a map or a reduce task, the message will reappear in the input or the master reduce queue, so that other workers can take over. All status updates to SimpleDB are done before removing the message from the queue to make sure that the result is committed fully first.

Two map workers may work on the same map task due to either node failure or message duplication as a result of eventual consistency. In the MapReduce programming model, it is acceptable to process the same map task twice, and so we do not take extra steps. In Section 5.4.3.5, we discuss how to filter out duplicate map outputs.

However, two reduce workers processing the same reduce queue could pose a problem. If it happens, we use SimpleDB for conflict resolution. When SQS reports that a reduce queue $j$ is empty, but the reduce worker has not processed all key-value pairs (fewer than $\sum_i R_{ij}$), the reduce worker suspects that there may be a conflict, and so it enters the conflict resolution mode. It first writes the reduce queue ID $j$ and worker ID pair into SimpleDB, and then it queries to see if other workers have claimed the same reduce queue ID. If so, it invokes a deterministic resolution algorithm (same for all nodes) to determine who should be in charge of processing this reduce queue. If the worker loses, it abandons what it has processed and moves on.

However, if the worker wins, it goes back to query the reduce queue again. Even if other workers have read some messages from the reduce queue, the messages will reappear after the visibility timeout for the winning worker to finish its processing.

## 5.4.3.5 Working with SQS

### 5.4.3.5.1 Hide Access Latency

We use two techniques—message aggregation and multi-threading—to hide SQS latency when accessing reduce queues. Message aggregation takes advantage of the 8K SQS message limit, which is typically much bigger than a key-value pair. By aggregating, we turn multiple round trips into one, which not only saves the number of queue write requests, but also saves the number of read requests during the reduce phase.

Note that message aggregation is different from the combiner in the MapReduce framework. A combiner is an application-specific function that reduces the intermediate result size by applying application-specific logic. In contrast, our message aggregation is a framework implementation optimization. The optimization works regardless of the application.

To hide latency further, we use a thread pool of multiple threads for both writing to and reading from the reduce queues. When a worker has a message to write, it hands over the message to one of the idle threads, which in turn talks to SQS directly. For reading from the reduce queues, we allocate a read buffer and set a read buffer threshold. When the number of messages in the buffer falls below the threshold, we ask idle threads to download additional messages. Each idle thread performs one bulk read of 10 messages (10 is the maximum allowed by SQS API). The reduce workers read directly from the read buffer, instead of interfacing with SQS.

Figure 5.4 shows the time for the word count application as a function of the number of threads in the thread pool. The word count application runs on a single

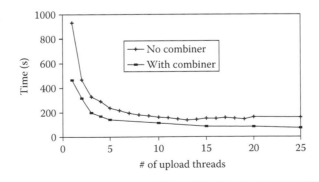

**Figure 5.4  Computation time as a function of the number of threads in the thread pool. Word count on 25 MB data on a single node.**

small EC2 instance and processes a 25 MB data set. We show both the case with the combiner enabled and disabled. When the combiner is disabled, more data is shuffled between the map and reduce stages. As shown, the time quickly decreases as we add more threads, suggesting that the threads are effective at hiding the latency. Since having more threads in the thread pool has little impact on the performance, we initialize 100 threads in the thread pool by default in case some applications require a large amount of data transfer.

The message aggregation and multi-threading techniques are only used on the reduce queues, since the input queue and the master reduce queue serve a very different purpose. The reduce queues are intermediary staging points between the map and reduce phases; thus, they require high throughput. In contrast, the input queue and the master reduce queue are used for job assignments. It is better to read one at a time to ensure a more even workload distribution.

### 5.4.3.5.2 Duplicate Detection

Due to eventual consistency, we may read a message twice from a queue. We use tagging to overcome this problem for the reduce queues. When a map worker writes an SQS message, it tags the message with three pieces of information: the worker ID, the map ID, and a unique number. The tag is simply prepended to the message. When a reduce worker reads an SQS message, it checks the tag to see if it has seen the message before. If so, the reduce worker ignores the message; otherwise, it stores the tag in its database to facilitate future duplicate detection, and then processes the message.

If two map workers read a duplicate message from the input queue (or if a worker failed in the middle of processing a map task), there will be redundant map outputs in the reduce queues. The reduce workers filter out these redundant messages by checking the worker ID and the map ID in the message tag against the list of committed map results (see Section 5.4.3.4 on how we get the list of committed map results from SimpleDB). The reduce workers simply ignore the messages if they are not generated by a committed map.

Two workers may also read a duplicate message from the master reduce queue. As discussed in Section 5.4.3.4, we use a conflict resolution mechanism to get around the problem.

## *5.4.4 Map and Reduce Interfaces*

The user-defined map function must implement the following interface:

```
void map(String key, String value, OutputCollector output)
```

Just as described in [6], both the key and the value are passed to the user-defined map function as strings. The OutputCollector is provided to the map function so that it can emit the output key-value pairs.

The user-defined reduce function in the MapReduce programming model requires an iterator interface for the list of values for each reduce key. In our architecture, we have $Q$ fixed reduce queues; thus, it is possible to have multiple reduce keys in the same reduce queue. Since values for different reduce keys may be mingled in the same reduce queue, we cannot simply feed the queue outputs to the reduce function.

Cloud MapReduce uses a push iterator interface for the reduce function. In the push iterator implementation, we pass to the reduce function one value at a time as we dequeue from the reduce queue, instead of passing to it an explicit iterator. The reduce function is called once for each new value. The push iterator interface consists of three interface functions.

The first is the start interface:

```
T start(String key, OutputCollector output)
```

The start interface is called when we see a key for the first time while dequeuing from the reduce queue. It is called before passing the first value to the reduce function. T is a user-defined class that holds the states that the reduce function needs to keep track of. The key associated with this reduce function is also passed in. For example, for the word count example, the start function initializes a count variable in object T and sets its value to 0.

The second is the actual reduce function:

```
void next(String key, String value, T state, OutputCollector output)
```

A new value for the reduce key is passed in every time this interface is called. As in the Google implementation, both the key and the value are generic strings. The reduce function parses the string to derive the correct data. T is the object that holds the current state. The reduce function processes the current value and updates the state as necessary. For example, in the word count example, the reduce function converts the string to a numerical value, and then adds the value to the count variable stored in T.

The last interface is the end interface:

```
void complete(String key, T state, OutputCollector output)
```

This interface is called when there are no more values associated with the reduce key. In the word count example, the reduce function emits a key-value pair, where the key is the reduce key and the value is the count stored in T.

In our implementation, a reduce worker first dequeues a message from the master reduce queue to know which reduce queue it is responsible for. Then the worker dequeues messages from the reduce queue one by one. If it sees a reduce key for the first time, it invokes the start interface function and keeps the state object T in a collection. For every new key-value pair, it finds the state object T associated with the key, and then calls the `next` interface function. When there are no more messages in the reduce queue, it calls the `complete` interface function for each reduce key it has seen. Even though we have to keep a reduce key collection and search the key collection for each new key-value pair, this could be efficiently implemented because the number of reduce keys in each reduce queue is expected to be small.

One drawback of the push iterator implementation is that we need to maintain a set of states. This is not a problem for a reduce worker, since we can bound the number of reduce keys in each reduce queue by increasing $Q$. However, this may be a problem for a combiner, since a map worker may generate key-value pairs for a large number of keys. Fortunately, a combiner does not need to combine all values for a particular key. Cloud MapReduce currently sets a 64 MB memory limit on the total amount of combiner state a map worker can keep. If the limit is reached, we flush the buffer by invoking the `complete` interface for all reduce keys in the combiner buffer.

## 5.4.5 Why Cloud MapReduce Is Better?

It is obvious why Cloud MapReduce is more scalable. Unlike other MapReduce implementations, we have adopted a fully distributed architecture and we do not have a single master node as a bottleneck. All cloud services we use are implemented in a distributed fashion; so they are not a bottleneck in our system. In our independent tests, we have confirmed that EC2/SQS/S3 are all highly scalable: EC2 is able to launch a large number of instances, and S3 and SQS are able to scale to high throughput. In addition, SimpleDB can sustain a high read throughput, and through our implementation, we have demonstrated that we can use horizontal scaling to scale SimpleDB write throughput.

However, it is not immediately obvious why Cloud MapReduce is simpler and faster than other implementations. The key advantages of Cloud MapReduce are enabled by several specific aspects of the scalability offered by a cloud OS. First, S3 presents an infinite and reliable file storage abstraction, which alleviates us from having to design our own file system. Second, SQS presents an infinite message store, both in terms of the number of queues one can create and the number of messages one can hold in each queue. Such an abstraction allows us to bypass both sorting and using the local storage as a staging area. Third, SimpleDB presents a high-bandwidth status vault, which can sustain a high read and write (through striping) throughput. The high read throughput, in particular, enables our distributed architecture. Instead of relying on the master to instruct the slave nodes (to alleviate the stress on the master), we allow all workers to query the central store for a global knowledge first, and then derive the local actions on their own. Last, both S3 and SQS present a single point of contact that is capable of sustaining a high throughput. We no longer need to worry about spreading the communication among the slave nodes in order to achieve a high system throughput.

We discuss the fundamental reasons in more detail in the following.

## 5.4.5.1 Why Cloud MapReduce Is Simpler?

Cloud MapReduce currently has around 3,000 lines of Java code (including generous comments, three MapReduce applications, and our profiling code to collect statistics), two orders of magnitude smaller than Hadoop (285,387 lines in version 0.20.0). Although some could be attributed to additional features in Hadoop, such as Streaming, we believe a large portion could be attributed to the complexity introduced when interfacing with a traditional server OS. We examine two components in more detail: the file system and the MapReduce framework.

### 5.4.5.1.1 File System Comparison

A server OS presents a limited storage space constrained by the hard disk capacity on a single machine. In order to host a large number of big files, we must design an overlay file system on top of a server OS. GFS [10], HDFS (Hadoop File System), and Dynamo [8] are all examples of this overlay file system.

Specifically, HDFS has to implement the following logic. First, it has to store the name space of the file system. HDFS has a separate name node that keeps track of locations of all file chunks, interfaces with clients, and hands out chunk handles when requested. Second, it has to present a large file abstraction. Because of a single node's capacity constraint and because of efficiency reasons, a large file has to be chopped up into chunks and distributed across many nodes. Third, it has to implement file replication logic to provide reliability. Each chunk has to be replicated on several nodes in order to protect against a single node failure. Fourth, it has to implement load-balancing logic to rebalance the chunk to server assignment, especially when the cluster's membership fluctuates over time.

All these functions have to be implemented by a cloud OS already. For example, S3 transparently replicates each object in order to provide high reliability guarantees. We should note that S3 currently has a 5 GB object size limitation, and so its interface is simplified compared to what HDFS presents. However, other cloud OS, such as Microsoft Azure Blob, can store infinitely large files.

Because of these complexities, the current HDFS in 0.20.0 has 37,196 lines of Java code (package org.apache.hadoop.hdfs under the src/hdfs directory in the Hadoop source distribution). In contrast, Cloud MapReduce has 172 lines of code to interface with S3.

### 5.4.5.1.2 MapReduce Framework Comparison

Compared with Cloud MapReduce, Hadoop, as well as other MapReduce implementations, has to do a lot more in the MapReduce framework, including the following.

*Sorting:* Sorting is required in order to group by keys. This is because a reduce partition could be large, since we cannot bound the number of keys in each reduce partition. Although Hadoop could avoid sorting by using a large number of reducers (like we do using the push iterator), the overhead of scheduling and coordinating data copying on the master node will diminish, if not eliminate, the performance gain.

We should note that there are MapReduce jobs today that rely on the MapReduce framework to perform sorting. Although not part of the MapReduce programming model, both the Google implementation and Hadoop have implicitly promised that the key-value pairs will be sorted. We believe a large fraction of MapReduce jobs do not need the sorting overhead. For those that do, they can simply implement sorting in their own user-defined functions.

*Master/slave communication:* The master is the central coordination point. Hadoop must define and implement a common communication protocol such as a remote procedure call (RPC), to facilitate task assignment, status reporting, and configuration propagation. In comparison, we simply leverage the existing cloud API.

*Configuration:* The asymmetric nature requires the master and slaves to be configured differently. The master must know about all slaves to coordinate job assignments.

*Dealing with slow nodes:* Because the task size (in terms of the input data size or processing time) has to be large in order not to overwhelm the master, a slow node has a much bigger impact on the overall progress. Slow node detection and speculative execution are required to alleviate the impact of stragglers [34]. In comparison, Cloud MapReduce can have a much smaller task size, which is neither constrained by the chunk size (to optimize for local processing) nor constrained by the master node limit. A slow node can at most slow down the overall computation by the time required to process one task, which is small in Cloud MapReduce; thus, there is no need to explicitly detect slow nodes.

*Locality optimization:* Hadoop tries to place computation tasks on the node that hosts the corresponding data chunks so that data access goes through the local hard disk. Extra logic is needed to figure out where a data chunk is stored and how to match it against computation tasks.

*Failure handling:* Hadoop must proactively detect node failures in order to reschedule tasks. In contrast, a cloud OS is designed with frequent failures in mind. We simply leverage SQS' visibility timeout mechanism to automatically handle failure detection and task re-execution.

The current MapReduce framework in 0.20.0 has 60,367 lines of Java code (package org.apache.hadoop.mapred and org.apache.hadoop.mapreduce under the src/mapred directory in the Hadoop source distribution). In contrast, we have 593 lines of MapReduce framework code, 582 lines of SQS interface code, and 797 lines of SimpleDB interface code.

In addition, Hadoop also has 63,128 lines of Java code under src/core directory, which deals with file caching, merge sorting, configuration, file system clients, file system checksums, etc. Additional features that Cloud MapReduce does not have, such as Streaming, are in a separate directory under src/contrib, which is not counted above.

## 5.4.5.2 Why Cloud MapReduce Is Faster?

There are several reasons why Cloud MapReduce is fundamentally faster.

*No sorting:* As described above, the infinite size abstraction presented by SQS (both in terms of the number of queues and the size of each queue) allows us to bypass sorting. Since sorting takes $O(n \log(n))$, we expect Cloud MapReduce to perform even better when the data set is large.

*Parallelize processing and copying:* Cloud MapReduce starts uploading reduce results as soon as they are produced in the map phase even before a map task finishes. This parallelizes the network transfer with CPU-intensive processing.

*No disk paging:* Since the number of key-value pairs in a reduce task is unbounded, Hadoop may have to spill partial sorting results to disk multiple times in order to fit within the main memory.

*No staging:* Hadoop always stores the intermediate results on disks, and then copies over the results to the hard disks on the destination node when instructed by the master. As a result, the data not only transits through the network once, but it also transits twice through the local disk. In comparison, Cloud MapReduce uses SQS as a staging area so that it can do everything in memory; therefore, the data only transits once through the network.

*Finer grain job assignment:* Because a task can be small, job assignments happen at a much finer granularity. Nodes of different capacity are automatically assigned work proportional to their capacity. A straggler is unlikely to drag on the overall computation for too long.

*Incast problem:* Hadoop and other MapReduce implementations start to shuffle data from mappers to reducers at the end of the map stage. The simultaneous transfers of a large amount of data could overflow the switch buffer, resulting in packet losses, which in turn causes TCP to backoff. Current TCP implementations require a 200 ms wait time before they retry, which significantly lowers the overall throughput. This problem is referred to as the incast problem, and it has been observed in data centers [13,27,31]. In contrast, Cloud MapReduce starts to transfer data as soon as it is generated. Because traffic is smoothed out, it is unlikely to trigger the incast problem. Due to the lack of visibility into Amazon's networking infrastructure, we unfortunately do not know whether the incast problem is a contributing factor in our tests.

Figure 5.5 shows the CPU, memory, and network usage during one run of the word count application on a single EC2 instance processing 200 MB of data. We disable combiner in order to stress the network. The CPU remains mostly at peak utilization throughout the job ( 40% is the highest utilization on a small EC2 instance). In Figure 5.5a, at around 21:42, the map phase finishes and the worker waits to flush out all SQS messages before starting the reduce phase. While waiting for the SQS writes to finish, there is a slight drop in the CPU utilization. Unlike

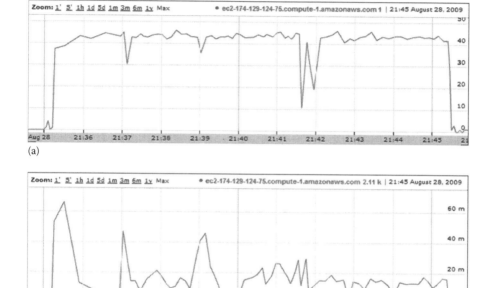

(a)

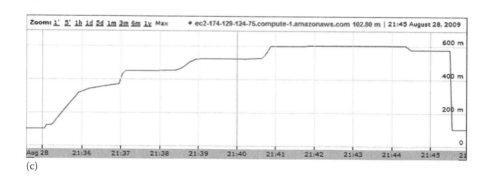

(b)

(c)

**Figure 5.5  Word count on a 200 MB data set on a small instance. (a) CPU usage, (b) network usage, and (c) memory usage.**

other MapReduce implementations, there is not a distinct shuffling stage between map and reduce because we transfer data in parallel with the map stage. Figure 5.5b includes both downloading files from S3 and accessing SQS. The network bandwidth demand is small, staying under 60 Mbps, even with the combiner disabled. In our independent tests, an EC2 instance is able to sustain roughly an 800 Mbps throughput; so the network interface is far from being the bottleneck. Figure 5.5c shows the memory usage, which stays under 600 MB, much less than the 1.7 GB available. Even for large jobs with many gigabytes to process per node, the memory usage typically stays under 1 GB.

The Cloud MapReduce architecture uses the network exclusively for I/O, bypassing all local storage. This is against the conventional wisdom adopted by other MapReduce implementations, where heavy emphasis has been placed to optimize data locality. Locality optimization is not necessarily beneficial in a cloud environment for two reasons. First, due to EC2 instances' ephemeral nature, most users store their data in S3. When they need to analyze the data, they first launch a Hadoop cluster in EC2 and then copy the data from S3 to HDFS. Locality optimization in MapReduce does not bring additional benefits, since the network transfer cost is already incurred in the copying stage. Second, local disks do not have a bandwidth advantage. As it has been shown through independent tests [34], a small EC2 instance can at most sustain a 496 Mbps (62 MBps) throughput, smaller than the network interface speed. Furthermore, a small EC2 instance has only a limited amount of storage at 160 GB. Although one can mount an EBS (Elastic Block Storage) drive as a bigger storage, access to EBS also goes through the network.

We focus only on small EC2 instances. Although the large and extra-large instances have more virtual disks (two and four, respectively), so that one can use striping to improve disk I/O performance, it is more cost effective to use more small instances, where each comes with an 800 Mbps network I/O potential.

Beyond the network interface, the network bisection bandwidth in a cloud data center could be a bottleneck. Typical data center network employs a tree topology. Due to both the root router's switching capacity limit and the high cost of a high-end router, the network bandwidth in a cloud is typically highly oversubscribed. The oversubscription could greatly limit the overall throughput. However, such a problem does not occur often due to two reasons. First, EC2's VM assignment algorithm takes into account the traffic condition in order to launch new VMs in less populated areas. Second, most VMs do not send traffic at their maximum interface speed; hence, the network is not saturated most of the time.

Even though today's data centers are oversubscribed, the next generation data centers are likely to have a much higher bisection bandwidth. Many innovative solutions are proposed to build a high-bisection-bandwidth cloud data center in a cost-effective manner, including fat tree [1], Portland [24], Bcube [14], Dcell [15], and VL2 [12].

Although the above discussion only applies to the Amazon environment, we note that the network interface on enterprise servers is getting faster. It is common to have multiple Gigabit Ethernet interfaces on a server, and the aggregate network interface bandwidth could be higher than the aggregate local disk bandwidth. Furthermore, TCP offloading [9,20,23,30] can cheaply offload network processing to dedicated hardware, alleviating the load on the host CPU.

### 5.4.6 Experimental Evaluation

We have implemented three different common MapReduce applications to evaluate Cloud MapReduce's performance: word count, reverse index, and string matching (distributed grep).

#### 5.4.6.1 Scalability Evaluation

To test out whether Cloud MapReduce will scale in practice, we run the word count application on a 100 GB input data. The combiner is enabled by default. We vary the cluster size up to 1000 nodes, our maximum limit in EC2. All tests reported here were run at night to minimize disruptions to other cloud users. Figure 5.6 shows the inverse of the total computation time, which corresponds to the amount of work completed per unit time. As shown, Cloud MapReduce scales roughly linearly as we increase the cluster size.

#### 5.4.6.2 Performance Evaluation

We compare the performance between Hadoop 0.20.0 and Cloud MapReduce on a small cluster of five small EC2 instances. To make sure that the master node is not interfering with the slave node tasks, we put the master on a separate node (so six nodes in total for Hadoop versus five for Cloud MapReduce).

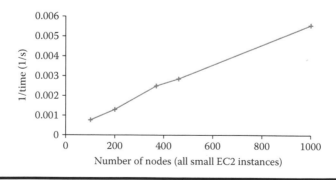

**Figure 5.6  Work completed per second for different size clusters. Word count on 100 GB data.**

For word count and grep, we use the examples provided by the Hadoop distribution. However, for reverse index, we have to implement our own, since it is not included in the Hadoop distribution.

We run the word count application on a text file of roughly 1 GB size. To see the effects of larger data, we run the test with and without the combiner enabled. To enable side-by-side comparison, we also run a version of Cloud MapReduce with the pull iterator interface implemented with in-memory sorting. Table 5.1 shows the time it takes to run the MapReduce job. In both cases, Cloud MapReduce is roughly twice as fast as Hadoop. Even with sorting, Cloud MapReduce still has a large advantage, which suggests that other factors (e.g., parallelizing data transfer and removing scheduling bottleneck) contribute significantly to Cloud MapReduce's advantage.

For the grep application, we use the same 1 GB data as used in the word count example, and we grep for the keyword "which." Cloud MapReduce takes 1001 s, whereas Hadoop takes 1211 s. Adding sorting or combiner makes little difference, since the amount of data in the reduce stage is small. The time difference is not as much because this job is dominated by string matching in the map phase, which is CPU intensive. Also, the map output data is small for the reduce stage; thus, the effects of data shuffling and staging are not as pronounced.

For the reverse index application, we use the same 1.2 GB data that is used in Phoenix evaluation [29]. We are not able to compare our performance with that from Phoenix directly because Phoenix only reported performance numbers in terms of speedup, and not in terms of absolute time.

The data set contains 92,367 HTML files. Hadoop takes 10 h to process all data. In comparison, it took Cloud MapReduce only 569 s, more than 60 times faster. To make sure it is not a problem with our reverse index implementation, we run the word count application on the same data set, and it takes roughly 13 h to complete.

Although we do not know for sure, we believe this is a limitation of the single master node architecture. Since each access to a file requires a contact with the master node, simply requesting the metadata for these files could be overwhelming. In addition, Hadoop creates at least one map for each input file. For this data set, there are 92,367 maps in the MapReduce computation. Such a large number of

**Table 5.1  Time (s) to Run the Word Count Application**

|  | Combiner | No Combiner |
|---|---|---|
| Hadoop | 459 | 907 |
| Cloud MapReduce | 169 | 581 |
| Cloud MapReduce w/sort | 329 | 704 |

*Note:* 1 GB data on 5 nodes.

maps place a strain on the master node to schedule and coordinate computation. In 0.20.0, there is no way to specify the number of maps manually. We also use version 0.19.0, and try to set the number of maps to a much smaller number manually, but the setting is simply ignored.

## 5.5 Higher-Level Programming Languages

The programming models that we have discussed in this chapter are important tools for large-scale analysis. However, they are built for programmers in general, and they may be unnatural for business analysts or for quick ad hoc data analysis.

There are a number of important works on high-level languages for large-scale data processing. Even though we are not able to get into much detail, we highlight the important work in this area so that interested readers can learn more.

Pig Latin [26] is a language developed at Yahoo Research. It is similar to SQL in terms of its ease of use, but it made many design decisions that are radically different from SQL. It uses a procedural method of conveying the analysis task and also uses user-defined functions extensively to support custom analysis. It is implemented on top of Hadoop [16]—the open-source implementation of MapReduce.

Google Sawzall [28] is also built on top of MapReduce. It is another system that dramatically simplifies certain analytical jobs, such as statistical counting.

DryadLINQ [33] is a system developed at Microsoft Research. It is built on top of Dryad [18], and it supports a simple set of LINQ queries, which makes it easy to express a parallel processing job in Dryad.

## References

1. Al-Fares, M., Loukissas, A., and Vahdat, A. A scalable, commodity data center network architecture. In *Proceedings of the SIGCOMM*, Seattle, WA, 2008.
2. Brewer, E. A. Towards robust distributed systems (abstract). In *PODC '00: Proceedings of the Nineteenth Annual ACM Symposium on Principles of Distributed Computing*, Portland, OR, 2000, ACM, New York, p. 7.
3. Chang, F., Dean, J., Ghemawat, S., Hsieh, W. C., and Wallach, D. A. Bigtable: A distributed storage system for structured data. In *Proceedings of the OSDI*, Seattle, WA, 2006, pp. 205–218.
4. Yang, H.-C., Dasdan, A., Hsiao, R.-L., and Parker, D. S. Map-reduce-merge: Simplified relational data processing on large clusters. In *Proceedings of the SIGMOD*, Beijing, China, 2007.
5. Clark, C., Fraser, K., Hand, S., Hansen, J. G., Jul, E., Limpach, C., Pratt, I., and Warfield, A. Live migration of virtual machines. In *Proceedings of the Second Symposium on Networked Systems Design and Implementation* (*NSDI*), Boston, MA, 2005, pp. 273–286.

6. Dean, J. and Ghemawat, S. Mapreduce: Simplified data processing on large clusters. In *OSDI'04: Sixth Symposium on Operating System Design and Implementation*, San Francisco, CA, December 2004.

7. Dean, J. and Ghemawat, S. Mapreduce: Simplified data processing on large clusters. *Commun. ACM 51*(1) (January 2008), 107–113.

8. DeCandia, G., Hastorun, D., Jampani, M., Kakulapati, G., Lakshman, A., Pilchin, A., Sivasubramanian, S., Vosshall, P., and Vogels, W. Dynamo: Amazon's highly available key-value store. *SIGOPS Oper. Syst. Rev. 41*(6) (2007), 205–220.

9. Freimuth, D., Hu, E., LaVoie, J., Mraz, R., Nahum, E., Pradhan, P., and Tracey, J. Server network scalability and TCP offload. In *Proceedings of the USENIX*, Anaheim, CA, April 2005, pp. 209–222.

10. Ghemawat, S., Gobioff, H., and Leung, S.-T. The Google file system. In *19th ACM Symposium on Operating Systems Principles*, New York, October 2003.

11. Gilbert, S. and Lynch, N. Brewer's conjecture and the feasibility of consistent, available, partition-tolerant web services. *SIGACT News 33*(2) (2002), 51–59.

12. Greenberg, A., Jain, N., Kandula, S., Kim, C., Lahiri, P., Maltz, D. A., Patel, P., and Sengupta, S. Vl2: A scalable and flexible data center network. In *Proceedings of the SIGCOMM*, Barcelona, Spain, 2009.

13. Griffith, R., Chen, Y., Liu, J., Joseph, A., and Katz, R. Understanding TCP incast throughput collapse in data-center networks. In *Proceedings of the SIGCOMM WREN Workshop*, Barcelona, Spain, 2009.

14. Guo, C., Lu, G., Li, D., Wu, H., Zhang, X., Shi, Y., Tian, C., Zhang, Y., and Lu, S. Bcube: A high performance, server-centric network architecture for modular data centers. In *Proceedings of the SIGCOMM*, Barcelona, Spain, 2009.

15. Guo, C., Wu, H., Tan, K., Shiy, L., Zhang, Y., and Luz, S. Dcell: A scalable and fault-tolerant network structure for data centers. In *Proceedings of the SIGCOMM*, Seattle, WA, 2008.

16. Hadoop. http://lucene.apache.org/hadoop

17. Hansen, J. G. and Jul, E. Self-migration of operating systems. In *Proceedings of the ACM SIGOPS European Workshop*, Leuven, Belgium, 2004.

18. Isard, M., Budiu, M., Yu, Y., Birrell, A., and Fetterly, D. Dryad: Distributed data-parallel programs from sequential building blocks. In *European Conference on Computer Systems (EuroSys)*, Lisbon, Portugal, March 2007.

19. Kapasi, U., Dally, W., Rixner, S., Owens, J., and Khailany, B. The imagine stream processor. In *Proceedings of International Conference on Computer Design*, Freiburg, Germany, September 2002.

20. Kim, H. and Rixner, S. TCP offload through connection handoff. In *Proceedings of the EuroSys*, Leuven, Belgium, April 2006, pp. 279–290.

21. Liu, H. and Orban, D. Gridbatch: Cloud computing for large-scale data-intensive batch applications. In *IEEE CCGRID*, Lyon, France, 2008.

22. Liu, H. and Orban, D. Computing median values in a cloud environment using gridbatch and mapreduce. In *IEEE Cluster*, New Orleans, LA, 2009.

23. Mogul, J. TCP offload is a dumb idea whose time has come. In *Proceedings of the HotOS IX: The Ninth Workshop on Hot Topics in Operating Systems*, Lihue, HI, 2003, pp. 25–30.

24. Mysore, R. N., Pamboris, A., Farrington, N., Huang, N., Miri, P., Radhakrishnan, S., Subramanya, V., and Vahdat, A. Portland: A scalable fault-tolerant layer 2 data center network fabric. In *Proceedings of the SIGCOMM*, Barcelona, Spain, 2009.

25. Nelson, M., hong Lim, B., and Hutchins, G. Fast transparent migration for virtual machines. In *Proceedings of the USENIX*, Anaheim, CA, 2005, pp. 391–394.

26. Olston, C., Reed, B., Srivastava, U., Kumar, R., and Tomkins, A. Pig latin: A not-so-foreign language for data processing. In *Proceedings of the SIGMOD*, Vancouver, Canada, 2008.

27. Phanishayee, A., Krevat, E., Vasudevan, V., Andersen, D., Ganger, G., Gibson, G., and Seshan, S. Measurement and analysis of TCP throughput collapse in cluster-based storage systems. In *Proceedings of the File and Storage Technologies (FAST)*, San Jose, CA, February 2008.

28. Pike, R., Dorward, S., Griesemer, R., and Quinlan, S. Interpreting the data: Parallel analysis with sawzall. *Sci. Program. J.* Special Issue on Grids and Worldwide Computing Programming Models and Infrastructure *13*(4) (2005), 227–298.

29. Ranger, C., Raghuraman, R., Penmetsa, A., Bradski, G., and Kozyrakis, C. Evaluating MapReduce for multi-core and multiprocessor systems. In *Proceedings of the 13th International Symposium on High-Performance Computer Architecture (HPCA)*, Phoenix, AZ, February 2007.

30. Shivam, P., and Chase, J. S. On the elusive benefits of protocol offload. In *Proceedings of the ACM SIGCOMM Workshop on Network-I/O Convergence*, Karlsruhe, Germany, 2003, pp. 179–184.

31. Vasudevan, V., Phanishayee, A., Shah, H., Krevat, E., Andersen, D., Ganger, G., Gibson, G., and Mueller, B. Safe and effective fine-grained TCP retransmissions for datacenter communication. In *Proceedings of the SIGCOMM*, Barcelona, Spain, 2009.

32. Vogels, W. Eventually consistent. *Commun. ACM 52*(1) (2009), 40–44.

33. Yu, Y., Isard, M., Fetterly, D., Budiu, M., Erlingsson, U., Gunda, P. K., and Currey, J. DryadLINQ: A system for general-purpose distributed data-parallel computing using a high-level language. In *Proceedings of the Symposium on Operating System Design and Implementation (OSDI)*, San Diego, CA, December 2008.

34. Zaharia, M., Konwinski, A., Joseph, A. D., Katz, R., and Stoica, I. Improving mapreduce performance in heterogeneous environments. In *Proceedings of the USENIX OSDI* San Diego, CA, 2008.

## Chapter 6

# Toward a Reliable Cloud Computing Service

Thomas J. Hacker

## Contents

## 6.1 Introduction

Cloud computing services rely on the on-demand provision of a set of resources. As cloud computing becomes more widely adopted, the size and scale of cloud computing systems will necessarily increase to meet a growing demand—both in terms

**139**

of the number of individual requests as well as the amount of resources required per request. In contrast to approaches used in Grid and high-performance computing, in which requests that cannot be immediately serviced are added to a queue for later service, requests for cloud computing resources must be immediately fulfilled, or denied due to a lack of available resources. The challenge facing cloud computing service providers is to provision and have available for immediate allocation sufficient resources ready to be deployed for service requests. The costs of maintaining a pool of spare resources, however, are tremendous. A modern data center, supplied with adequate power and cooling resources to house high-density computer equipment, is expensive to build and operate. With current power utility rates, the cumulative costs of powering computer equipment now exceed hardware costs after only a few short years—well before the end of the useful lifetime of the equipment. Commercial cloud computing organizations seeking to operate a profitable cloud computing service face a serious dilemma. If there are not sufficient idle resources available during the busiest service times, requests that could generate revenue will need to be turned away. On the other hand, if the organization maintains a large pool of idle resources awaiting these requests, the operational costs of running these systems will erode profit margins, making it more difficult to successfully run a service. An additional problem that arises is reliability. If an application requests a large number of resources, or requests resources for a considerable length of time, there is a measurable probability that one or more of the resources dedicated by the cloud computing service for the application will fail during the lifetime of the request, which denies access to resources. The expectation of an organization paying for these resources is that the service will be reliable over the lifetime of the request. One possible option available for a cloud service provider is to provide a number of hot-spare nodes added to the user allocation to ensure the availability of the requested number of resources for the duration of the request. One problem, however, is to estimate the number of additional resources required to provide some level of guarantee of service.

In this chapter, we address these two problems, and present a model for determining the probability of blocking service requests and determining the number of hot-spare nodes needed to provide a reliable cloud computing service. Specifically, given a historic pattern of resource requests along with the total number of computing nodes available in the system, we present a model that can be used to predict the probability of an $N$ node cloud computing service blocking access due to insufficient capacity during a busy service period.

## 6.2 Modeling the Service Load of a Cloud Computing System

At the time of writing this chapter (March 2009), there are two well-known cloud computing services. The best-known commercial one, the Amazon Elastic

Compute Cloud EC2 [1], provides a number of virtual machines based on a Xen hypervisor that provides a selection of virtual machine types: small, consisting of one virtual CPU core; large, containing two CPU cores: and extra large, with four cores. Amazon charges for the use of the virtual machine instances based on an EC2 Compute Unit, which is equivalent to a single CPU. An example of a noncommercial cloud computing effort is the Eucalyptus [13] project, led by Rich Wolski at the University of California, Santa Barbara.

The use of virtual machine technology for cloud computing decouples the number of virtual and physical CPUs. There is a practical upper bound on the number of virtual machines and virtual processors that can be deployed on a server system. If a cloud computing service is oversubscribed, the system will become slow and unreliable, and new requests for service will be denied. Conversely, if the system is undersubscribed, the costs of maintaining unutilized capacity will be unrecoverable over time, and reduce profits. The challenge facing cloud computing service providers is how many resources should be provisioned to reliably service a workload, and what is the probability of blocking new requests at a specific resource-provisioning level?

In this section, we address this question. First, we describe a synthetic workload based on the measured job characteristics of a large grid computing system. Based on this workload, we propose a negotiation process between a user and a cloud computing system to bid for and acquire cloud computing resources. Based on this framework, we derive a model that predicts the probability of blocking a cloud computing service request based on the offered workload during busy periods. Following this, we derive a model of cloud computing node reliability, and propose an approach to improve reliability.

## 6.2.1 Measuring the Workload

There are few cloud computing systems today for which detailed and extensive workload traces are available. The closest analogue to a cloud computing system is a grid computing system, which in many ways is similar to a cloud computing system with one important difference. While grid computing systems have the capability to queue requests for resources into a service queue to wait for available capacity, cloud computing services must either provide *immediate* access to requested resources or *deny* or *block* requests for these resources. Since there are few large-scale cloud computing systems in use today, we developed an offered workload based on the observed workload characteristics of a large grid computing system.

The Parallel Workloads Archive [4,9] maintains an extensive collection of workloads submitted to a variety of high-performance and grid computing systems. To model the offered workload submitted to a cloud computing system, we used logs of computational jobs submitted to the fs0 system, which was part of the grid computing system of the Distributed Advanced School for Computing and Imaging in the Netherlands (DAS2). The grid computing system we analyzed consisted of five distributed Linux clusters with a total of 400 processors, and the workload logs we analyzed contain 432,987 job submissions from January 2003 through December 2003. To understand the stochastic characteristics of the workload, we assessed the time between job submission events, the distribution of the number of processors requested, and the runtime of each job. As found in related work [4,16] the time between job submission events did not follow an exponential distribution, and the workload intensity varied over the lifetime of the logs, with periods of intense and quiescent computational and job submission activities.

## 6.2.2 Framework for Requesting and Allocation Resources

*Step 1: Request for services*
To characterize the workload of a cloud computing system, we first describe a framework for resource requests, allocation, and deployment. Consider the following multistep process from service request to service delivery and final completion. In the first step, a user or application wishes to utilize resources provided by a cloud computing system. A request is formed that consists of (1) a number of required nodes; (2) specific resource requirements, such as operating system, amount of memory, or processor type; (3) estimated maximum length of time for which the cloud resource will be needed; and (4) expectation of desired grade of service and reliability of service over the required time period.

*Step 2: Response of the cloud computing system*
In response to the resource request, the cloud computing system will immediately communicate an offer, which consists of four different types of responses. The first type is an offer to immediately allocate all of the requested resources (just in time) at the time of request with a grade of service/reliability at levels required by the user at a billing rate $X$. The second type of response is to provide an immediate allocation of all resources requested at a reduced grade of service or reliability at a reduced billing rate $Y < X$. This type of response provides an option to the application or user to be able to choose to utilize a degraded cloud computing service at a reduced rate. The third type of response is to offer a subset of the requested resources—either at a full reliability rate or with a degraded grade of service and reliability at a fraction of the full rate. The fourth possible request is a decline response, in which the cloud computing service provider lacks adequate resources to provide service or cannot meet the required grade of service or reliability requirements.

*Step 3: Response to the cloud computing system offer*
In response to a positive offer from the cloud computing service to provide services, the application can either accept or reject the offer. The expectation of the application (or user driving the requesting application) is that the cloud computing system is ready to immediately provide services, without queuing the user request or forcing the user to wait for more than a brief period for access to services.

*Step 4: Cloud computing system service provision*

When an application accepts the cloud computing system's offer, several questions must be addressed. First, can sufficient resources be found within the cloud computing system to provide all of the resources offered by the cloud computing system? Second, what will be the operational reliability of the set of resources committed to the user, and how can the cloud computing system ensure that this level of reliability will be maintained?

*Step 5: Application granted access to resources*

Once the cloud computing system determines that it can provide the offered resources at the required level of reliability, the application is granted access to the resource for use. If, during the time period of use, one (or more) of the resource elements provided by the cloud computing service fails, the application and cloud computing service will face several problems. First, how can the user application detect failure and respond to the failure in a manner that allows it to tolerate failure? Second, what can the cloud computing system do to ensure the continued reliability and grade of service that it agreed to provide during the resource and pricing negotiation phase? Third, at what point will the user and the system determine that the agreed-on grade of service and reliability cannot be met, and how will a resulting reduced billing rate be negotiated? Finally, if there is a minimum grade of service and reliability agreed on during the negotiation process, does the user have the right to terminate the agreement and receive a full or partial refund?

*Step 6: Completion of computation and exit from the system*

When the application terminates and releases resources, or if the application exceeds the wall clock limit and is terminated, the job is completed. Resources released are freed for use by new requests for resources.

## 6.2.3 Modeling the Availability and Reliability of a Cloud Computing Service

Given the resource request process described in the previous section, two questions emerge. First, given a historic workload offered to a cloud computing service, how many free and available resources will the cloud computing system need to keep available to be able to service application requests during the peak period of use? What will be the probability of rejecting those requests due to a lack of available resources? Second, given the mean time to failure (MTTF) of the underlying nodes, what is the reliability of the nodes allocated by the cloud computing system during the application execution time? Additionally, how many hot-spare nodes will the cloud computing system need to allocate in reserve to serve as hot-spares in case of node failure?

To predict the number of resources that must be available in a cloud computing system to service a load of requests, there are several factors that must be considered. First, the number of computational nodes in a cloud computing system is limited, and a request will require the simultaneous allocation of a number of nodes—some may only request one node, but many will request a number of nodes up to the total number of nodes available in the cloud computing system. Second, based on the number of nodes requested, the arrival rate of requests for these resources during the busy periods is a critical factor in driving the overall utilization of the cloud computing system.

To model the workload, we partitioned the fs0 workload (described earlier) into bins based on the number of processors requested: 1, 2, 4, 8, 16, 32, 64, and 128 processors; determined the most active periods of job submission activity over the period of the logs; and calculated the average arrival rate (jobs per hour) and average job runtime for the set of jobs submitted during the busy period.

Table 6.1 shows the number of submission events, average arrival rate, average execution time, and job intensity for each workload class. During the busy periods, the cloud computing system must immediately service requests by allocating the number of requested resources from a pool of free resources, or block and deny access due to a lack of available resources.

## 6.2.3.1 Modeling the Probability of Blocking a Request

To estimate the probability of blocking a request to the cloud computing system during a busy period, we can use a generalized Erlang loss station model [2,7,8].

Consider a cloud computing service that features a total of $C$ computational nodes, each of which can be independently assigned to service a request. A workload

**Table 6.1 Workload Model Partitioned into Resource Classes**

| Resource Class | Node Count | Events | $\lambda$ (jobs/h) | $1/\mu$ (h) | $\alpha = \lambda/\mu$ Erlangs |
|---|---|---|---|---|---|
| 1 | 1 | 6,158 | 3.25 | 0.0913 | 0.297 |
| 2 | 2 | 130,431 | 8.24 | 0.0941 | 0.776 |
| 3 | 4 | 27,156 | 5.01 | 0.1336 | 0.669 |
| 4 | 8 | 15,585 | 4.94 | 0.1012 | 0.503 |
| 5 | 16 | 21,359 | 4.14 | 0.1012 | 0.421 |
| 6 | 32 | 7,918 | 2.08 | 0.0987 | 0.205 |
| 7 | 64 | 9,722 | 4.33 | 0.0676 | 0.293 |
| 8 | 128 | 1,295 | 0.18 | 0.1738 | 0.0313 |

consisting of a mixture of requests is offered to the cloud computing system from a community of users and applications. The service offered by the cloud computing system is partitioned into resource classes of service, distinguished by the number of computational nodes provided by the system in eight categories, each of which contain 1, 2, 4, 8, 16, 32, 64, and 128 node partitions.

Each individual workload request describes the resource class requested (which communicates the number of nodes selected from the set of partitions) and the maximum time for which these resources will be needed. There are 8 classes of service, and the number of nodes in resource class $i$ is $k_i = 2^{(i-1)}$ nodes. The arrival rate of requests from the offered workload for resource class $i$ is denoted by $\lambda_i$, the average requested computational occupancy time by $1/\mu_i$, and the corresponding class intensity (in Erlangs) by $\alpha_i = \lambda_i/u_i$.

To utilize the multiclass Erlang loss model, a common assumption is that the elapsed time between job requests must fit an exponential distribution. In assessing the workload trace, we found that the time between events did not fit an exponential distribution, as was found in [4]. Recent work by Bonald [2] determined that the blocking probability computed from an Erlang or Engset model does not depend on the holding time distribution beyond the mean, and that it is not necessary to assume that resource requests arrive as a Poisson process. It is sufficient to assume that the sequence of resource requests generated by the same user arrives as a Poisson process. For the model presented in this chapter, we assume that user requests generated by the same user or application arrive as a Poisson process.

At any given time, the state of resource use of the cloud computing system is described by the row vector $\mathbf{x} = [x_1, x_2, \ldots, x_k]$, which represents that concurrent number of jobs using resource class $i$. For example, if $x_3 = 2$, then there are two active jobs in resource class 3, each using 4 nodes in the cloud computing system (8 nodes in total). The number of computational nodes that make up each resource class is designated by $\mathbf{r} = [r_1, r_2, \ldots, r_k]$, where resource class $r_i$ describes a partition of $2^{(i-1)}$ nodes. If there are $C$ total computational nodes in the cloud computing system, the maximum number of concurrent jobs occupying the cloud computing system cannot exceed $C$ at any time, specifically,

$$\mathbf{x} \cdot \mathbf{r} = \sum_{i=1}^{k} x_i r_i \leq C. \tag{6.1}$$

Since the number of computational nodes for each request and the number of nodes for each class are integers, the stationary distribution of resource occupancy for each resource class can be computed using the Kaufman–Roberts [7,15] algorithm. Following the derivation of Bonald [2], the probability that the cloud computing system node occupancy is $n$ is

$$p(n) = \sum_{x:xr=n} \frac{\alpha_1^{x_1}}{x_1!} \cdots \frac{\alpha_1^{x_k}}{x_k!}, \quad n = 0, 1, \ldots, C. \tag{6.2}$$

The probability that resource requests of type $i$ will be blocked is then

$$B_i = \frac{\sum_{(n=C-r_i+1)}^{C} p(n)}{\sum_{n=0}^{C} p(n)}. \tag{6.3}$$

For $n = 1, \ldots, C, p(n)$ is

$$p(n) = \sum_{i=1}^{k} \frac{\alpha_i r_i}{n} p(n - r_i), \tag{6.4}$$

with $p(0) = 1$ and $p(n) = 0$ for all $n < 0$. This computation, which is linear in the number of resource classes $k$, is much more feasible than the direct calculation of the stationary distribution based on all combinations of $\mathbf{r}$ and $\mathbf{x}$ that are equal to $n$ in Equation 6.3, which is exponential in the number of resource classes $k$.

Using the recurrence relation described by Equation 6.3, we can compute the probability of the cloud computing system blocking requests for resources in class $i$ using Equation 6.4.

Using the arrival rate $\lambda$, execution time $1/\mu$, and workload intensity $\alpha$ from the workload model, we computed a set of dimensioning curves for a cloud computing system containing a number of nodes ranging from $C = 16$ to $C = 256$ nodes. Figure 6.1 shows the resulting dimensioning curves that describe the probability of blocking requests for each resource class as a function of the number of nodes, $C$, in the cloud computing system.

## 6.2.4 Availability Discussion

From the results shown in Figure 6.1, we make several observations. First, small resource classes with a limited number of nodes have a low probability of blocking. This makes sense, since it is simple to pack a system with a collection of small node partitions. For a given resource class partition of $i$ nodes, as the number of nodes $C$ in the cloud computing system is reduced to $2i$, the blocking probability for the $i$-node resource class rises dramatically. Second, providing reasonable availability for large resource classes (64 and 128 nodes) with a limited system size of 128 nodes will be difficult, due to the high probability of blocking 128 node requests (blocking probability 0.96) and 64 node requests (blocking probability 0.28). Third, for

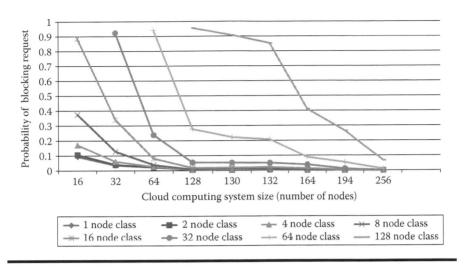

**Figure 6.1   Cloud computing system dimensioning curve for multiple resource classes.**

modest size resource classes (e.g., 32 nodes or less), the marginal benefit in significantly increasing the number of nodes in the cloud computing system is limited. For example, in the 32-node resource class, increasing the number of nodes in the cloud computing system from $C = 128$ nodes to $C = 256$ nodes reduces the blocking probability from 0.055 to 0.002. This is a change of 5%, but at the cost of doubling the size of the cloud computing system. It may not be worth improving the blocking probability by only 5% at the expense of increasing the cost and size of the system by a factor of 2.

Based on the availability results from this section, several conclusions can be drawn. It is possible to provide a high degree of on-demand availability for a cloud computing system for a realistic workload by limiting the resource class size, and by making available at least twice the number of nodes in the largest resource class in the cloud computing system during a busy period based on a historic workload. Second, resource classes containing $\leq C/4$ nodes, where $C$ is the number of nodes available in the cloud computing system, have a low probability of blocking, and there is limited improvement in the probability of blocking as $C$ increases.

# 6.3 Modeling the Reliability of a Cloud Computing Service

The results in the previous section address the question of modeling the availability of a cloud computing service offered a workload. Once an application or user is granted access to a cloud computing service, the next problem that arises is the inherent reliability of the service provided. If one of the nodes fails during the allocated time, the application will lose service, and may potentially terminate. The problem addressed in this section is as follows: given a cloud computing partition of size $M$ available over a time period $[0,T]$, what is the probability of a failure over that time? Additionally, if a failure occurs, what strategies could be used to recover from the failure and provide the required number of functional nodes for the entire allocation time?

## 6.3.1 Node Reliability

The resources provided by a cloud computing system for an individual user or application consist of a partition of size $M$ of a $C$ node cloud computing system. The nodes provided could be a hardware node, as is commonly done for high-performance computing applications, or a virtual machine "slice" of a hardware node. If the MTTF of the underlying hardware platform is known, it is possible to compute the MTTF of a node in a partition of size $M$ of a cloud computing system.

If there are $v$ virtual machines allocated to each hardware node of a cloud computing system, the reliability of the virtual machine is directly linked to hardware reliability. Thus, when the hardware fails, all $v$ virtual machines running on this hardware will also fail. For simplicity, we assume that $v = 1$ for this analysis.

The MTTF of the underlying hardware platform can be obtained from the vendor or estimated from failure logs. Following the derivation of Hacker [6], the MTTF for a partition of a cloud computing system can be computed. As described in Hacker [6], and Nurmi, Brevik, and Wolski [3,11,12], the time between failures for computer systems follows a Weibull distribution with scale parameter $\tau$ and shape parameter $\beta$. The probability of a system failure *during* the time interval $[0,\Delta t]$ for the Weibull distribution of *scale* $\tau$ and *shape* $\beta$ is [10]

$$F(\Delta t, \beta, \tau) = \int_0^{\Delta t} \frac{\beta}{\tau}\left(\frac{t}{\tau}\right)^{\beta-1} e^{-(t/\tau)^\beta}\,dt$$

$$= 1 - e^{-(\Delta t/\tau)^\beta}. \tag{6.5}$$

The probability that a node in the system will *not* fail in this time is

$$R(\Delta t, \beta, \tau) = 1 - F(\Delta t, \beta, \tau)$$

$$= e^{-(\Delta t/\tau)^\beta}. \tag{6.6}$$

The *mean* of the Weibull distribution is given by $\tau\Gamma(1 + 1/\beta)$, where $\Gamma$ is the Euler Gamma function. Assuming that the vendor MTTF corresponds to the *mean* $\tau$,

$$\tau = \frac{\text{MTTF}}{\Gamma\left(1 + \left(1/\beta\right)\right)}. \tag{6.7}$$

We can determine the Weibull reliability function for an $M$ node partition of a cloud computing system similarly—by treating the nodes as individual components. Assuming that all nodes are identical, i.e., characterized by the same $\tau_{\text{node}}$ and $\beta_{\text{node}}$ [14], we find

$$R_{\text{partition}}(\Delta t) = \prod_{i=1}^{M} R_{\text{node}}(\Delta t)$$

$$= \prod_{i=1}^{M} e^{-(\Delta t/\tau_{\text{node}})^{\beta_{\text{node}}}}$$

$$= \exp\left(-M\left(\frac{\Delta t}{\tau_{\text{node}}}\right)^{\beta_{\text{node}}}\right). \tag{6.8}$$

We assume that the partition's reliability function is also governed by the Weibull distribution with the cluster scale parameter, $\tau_{\text{partition}}$, and the cluster shape parameter, $\beta_{\text{partition}}$.

We assume that the node MTTF is identical for all nodes, and that the same Weibull shape parameter applies to the nodes and to the cloud computing partition as a whole; and using $\beta_{\text{node}} = \beta_{\text{partition}} = \beta$, we obtain

$$\tau_{\text{partition}} = \frac{1}{N^{1/\beta}} \tau_{\text{node}} \tag{6.9}$$

and the partitions's MTTF:

$$\text{MTTF}_{\text{partition}} = \frac{1}{N^{1/\beta}} \tau_{\text{node}} \Gamma\left(1 + \frac{1}{\beta}\right)$$

$$= \frac{1}{N^{1/\beta}} \text{MTTF}_{\text{node}}. \tag{6.10}$$

**Table 6.2  Reliability of Cloud Computing Partitions**

| Resource Class | Node Count | $1/\mu$ (h) | Reliability | $100/\mu$ (h) | Reliability |
|---|---|---|---|---|---|
| 1 | 1 | 0.0913 | 0.999 | 9.13 | 0.998 |
| 2 | 2 | 0.0941 | 0.999 | 9.41 | 0.996 |
| 3 | 4 | 0.1336 | 0.999 | 13.36 | 0.992 |
| 4 | 8 | 0.1012 | 0.999 | 10.12 | 0.987 |
| 5 | 16 | 0.1012 | 0.999 | 10.12 | 0.974 |
| 6 | 32 | 0.0987 | 0.998 | 9.87 | 0.951 |
| 7 | 64 | 0.0676 | 0.998 | 6.76 | 0.928 |
| 8 | 128 | 0.1738 | 0.992 | 17.38 | 0.730 |

## 6.3.1.1  Cloud Computing Partition Reliability

Using Equation 6.8 with an estimated shape parameter, $\beta = 0.8$, and an $MTTF_{node} = 36,000\,h$, we can compute the probability of node failure for each partition (which corresponds to resource classes described in the previous section) over a time $[0,T]$. Table 6.2 shows the computed reliability for the resource classes described above, which consist of partitions of the cloud computing system. The computed reliability for the short runtimes derived from the workload is very high—over 99% in all cases. To assess the effects of a longer runtime on reliability, we scaled the runtime by a factor of 100; and as shown in the last two columns of Table 6.2, reliability decreases as the number of nodes in the partition increases—down to 0.73 for the 128-node partition.

While a 99% reliability is reasonably good, as runtime and the number of nodes in a partition increases, reliability will fall. To provide a higher reliability for long-running and large-partition jobs, the cloud computing system could reserve a pool of hot-spare nodes to be used as failover nodes by the cloud computing system or application in the event of node failure. The reliability model for this scenario is a $k$-out-of-$N$ system [5]. In this system, at least $k$ out of $N$ nodes must remain functional during the time $[0,T]$ in order for the entire system to be reliable. If the partition size is $k$, and $(N-k)$ hot-spares are available for use when one of the $k$ nodes fails, the resulting reliability of the $N$ node partition can be computed. The resulting reliability function is then

$$R(\Delta t)_{k/N} = \sum_{i=0}^{N-k} \binom{N}{i} R^{N-i}(\Delta t)(1 - R(\Delta t))^i. \qquad (6.11)$$

**Table 6.3  Reliability Using Spares**

| # Spares | Reliability |
|----------|-------------|
| 0 | 0.703 |
| 1 | 0.951 |
| 2 | 0.994 |
| 3 | 0.999 |
| 4 | 1.0 |
| 5 | 1.0 |

Using Equation 6.11, we can compute the probability of a node failure within a $k$-node cloud computing partition if $(N-k)$ spare nodes are available to take the place of a failed node. Table 6.3 shows the computed failure rate with a maximum runtime of 20 h for a 128-node partition, which includes potentially up to five spares.

From this table, it is clear that adding a few spares has a significant effect on improving reliability. Thus, to provide a good reliability level for a cloud computing system, a cloud computing system should provision a number of spares that can be quickly deployed to replace failed nodes.

## 6.4 Conclusions

In this chapter, we addressed two issues: given a workload, how many nodes are required for a cloud computing system to provide immediate service with a limited probability of blocking service requests; and once a set of resources are allocated, what is the probability of failure of a node in use, and what are the reliability effects of providing a set of hot-spare nodes. Combining a Generalized Erlang Loss Model with a historic workload, it is possible to compute dimensioning curves that can be used by a cloud computing provider to estimate the number of resources needed to satisfy requests during the busy period. By taking into account the inherent Weibull failure characteristics of a cloud computing system, as well as the number of nodes in a cloud computing partition, it is possible to calculate the reliability of the set of nodes over the lifetime of the task. By adding just a few hot-spare nodes, the reliability of long-running and large partitions can be increased significantly.

## References

1. Amazon elastic compute cloud (amazon ec2), 2009.
2. T. Bonald. Insensitive traffic models for communication networks. *Discrete Event Dynamic Systems*, 17(3):405–421, 2007.
3. J. Brevik, D. Nurmi, and R. Wolski. Automatic methods for predicting machine availability in desktop grid and peer-to-peer systems. In *IEEE International Symposium on Cluster Computing and the Grid (CCGRID)*, April 19–22, 2004, Chicago, IL, pp. 190–199. IEEE Computer Society, 2004.
4. D. G. Feitelson and D. Tsafrir. Workload sanitation for performance evaluation. In *IEEE International Symposium on Performance Analysis of Systems and Software (ISPASS)*, March 19–21, 2006, Austin, TX, pp. 221–230.
5. D. L. Grosh. *Primer of Reliability Theory*. John Wiley & Sons, New York, 1989.

6. T. J. Hacker and Z. Meglicki. Using queue structures to improve job reliability. In *Proceedings of the 16th International Symposium on High-Performance Distributed Computing (HPDC-16 2007)*, June 25–29, 2007, Monterey, CA, pp. 43–54. ACM, 2007.

7. J. S. Kaufman. Blocking in a shared resource environment. *IEEE Transactions on Communications*, COM-29, 10:1474–1481, 1981.

8. H. Kobayashi and B. Mark. *System Modeling and Analysis: Foundations of System Performance Evaluation*. Pearson Education, Upper Saddle River, NJ, 2009.

9. H. Li, D. Groep, and L. Walters. Workload characteristics of a multi-cluster supercomputer. In D. G. Feitelson, L. Rudolph, and U. Schwiegelshohn, eds., *Job Scheduling Strategies for Parallel Processing, Lecture Notes in Computer Science*, vol. 3277. Springer-Verlag, New York, 2004, pp. 176–193.

10. D. N. Prabhakar Murthy, M. Xie, and R. Jiang. *Weibull Models*. Wiley Series in Probability and Statistics. John Wiley & Sons, Hoboken, NJ, 2004.

11. D. Nurmi, J. Brevik, and R. Wolski. Quantifying machine availability in networked and desktop grid systems. Technical Report ucsb_cs:TR-2003-37, Department of Computer Science, University of California, Santa Barbara, CA, November 2003.

12. D. Nurmi, J. Brevik, and R. Wolski. Modeling machine availability in enterprise and wide-area distributed computing environments. In *Proceedings of 11th International Euro-Par Conference (Euro-Par 2005)*, August 30 – September 2, 2005, Lisbon, Portugal, *Lecture Notes in Computer Science*, vol. 3648. Springer, Berlin, 2005, pp. 432–441.

13. D. Nurmi, R. Wolski, C. Grzegorczyk, G. Obertelli, S. Soman, L. Youseff, and D. Zagorodnov. The eucalyptus open-source cloud-computing system. In *Proceedings of Cloud Computing and Its Applications*, October 22–23, 2008, Chicago, IL.

14. M. Rausand and A. Høyland. *System Reliability Theory: Models, Statistical Methods and Applications*, 2nd edn. John Wiley & Sons, Hoboken, NJ, 2004.

15. J. W. Roberts. A service system with heterogeneous user requirement. In: Pujolle G. ed., *Performance of Data Communications Systems and Their Applications*. North-Holland, Amsterdam, the Netherlands, 1981.

16. D. Tsafrir and D. G. Feitelson. Instability in parallel job scheduling simulation. The role of workload flurries. In *20th International Parallel and Distributed Processing Symposium (IPDPS)*, April 25–29, 2006, Rhodes Island, Greece.

# Chapter 7

# Abstractions for Cloud Computing with Condor

Douglas Thain and Christopher Moretti

## Contents

## 7.1 Introduction

A *cloud computer* provides a simple interface that allows end users to allocate large amounts of computing power and storage space at the touch of a button. However, many potential users of cloud computers have needs much more complex than simply the ability to allocate resources. In scientific domains, it is easy to find examples

153

of workloads that consist of hundreds or thousands of interacting processes. A user who wishes to run such a workload on a cloud computer faces the daunting task of deciding how many resources to allocate, where to dispatch each process, when and where to move data, and how to deal with the inevitable failures. For this reason, many users with large workloads are reluctant to move away from the predictable environment of a single workstation or multicore server.

Abstractions are an effective way of harnessing large cloud computers while insulating the user from technical complexities. An *abstraction* is a structure that allows one to specify a workload in a way that is natural to the end user. It is then up to the system to determine how best to realize the workload given the available resources. This also allows the user to move a workload from one machine to another without rewriting it from scratch. The concept of abstraction is fundamental to computer science, and examples can be found in many software systems, such as compilers, databases, and filesystems.

*Map-Reduce* [9] is a well-known abstraction for cloud computing. The Map-Reduce abstraction allows the user to specify two functions that transform and summarize data, respectively. If the desired computation can be expressed in this form, then the computation can be scaled up to thousands of nodes. The Map-Reduce abstraction is well suited for analyzing and summarizing large amounts of data, and has a number of implementations of which the open-source *Hadoop* [6] is the most widely deployed.

But are there other useful abstractions? In our work with several scientific communities at the University of Notre Dame, we have encountered a number of large workloads that are regularly structured, but do not fit the Map-Reduce paradigm. In each case, we found workloads that were easy to write on the chalkboard, possible to run on one machine, but very challenging to scale up to hundreds or thousands of nodes. In each case, our research group worked to design an abstraction that could represent a large class of applications, and could execute reliably on a cloud computer.

In this chapter, we will describe the following set of abstractions, in a roughly increasing order of complexity:

- *Map*—Applies a single program to a large set of data
- *All-Pairs*—Computes a Cartesian product on two large sets of data
- *Sparse-Pairs*—Computes a function on selected pairs of two large sets of data
- *Wavefront*—Carries out a large dynamic programming problem
- *Directed Graph*—Runs a large graph of processes with multiple dependencies

We have implemented these abstractions on the Condor distributed processing system. We will begin with a short overview of Condor as a cloud computer, and then explain each abstraction in turn. For each, we will present a formal model, describe how the abstraction is implemented, and give an example of a community that has used the abstraction to scale up an application to hundreds of CPUs. We conclude the chapter by discussing the relative power of each abstraction.

## 7.2 Condor as a Cloud Computer

Our foundation for this work is the *Condor* distributed processing system. Condor was first created in 1987 at the University of Wisconsin, and has remained in continuous development and deployment ever since [15,26]. At the time of writing, it was deployed at several thousand institutions around the world, managing several hundred thousand CPU cores [5,24]. At a typical university, the Condor software is deployed to all available machines, including desktop workstations, classroom machines, and server clusters, all of which are typically idle 90% of the day. Users queue jobs to run in the system, and Condor matches the jobs to run on machines that would otherwise go unused.

A large Condor pool can be considered a *cloud computer*. Like other cloud computing systems, users request service from Condor, but do not care (and cannot control) exactly which resources are used to service that request. A job submitted to Condor could run on a desktop machine down the hall, or in a machine room at another institution. However, Condor is unlike other cloud computing systems in that it employs *preemption* [21]. A job running on a machine may be preempted if the machine's owner returns to type on the keyboard or otherwise uses the CPU.

Figure 7.1 shows the natural variations found in our campus Condor pool over the course of July 2009. The dark "Owner" curve shows the number of CPUs currently in use by their owners, who are either typing at the keyboard or making extensive use of the CPU. The lighter "Condor" curve shows the number of CPUs currently harnessed by Condor. The lightest "Total" curve shows the total number of CPUs in the pool, which varies between 500 and 600. As can be seen, all of these values fluctuate considerable as machines are powered on and off, used during the work day, and harvested for batch workloads.

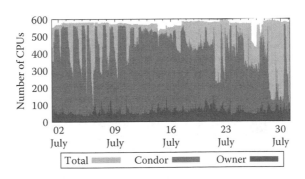

**Figure 7.1   Time variations in a Condor pool.**

Condor has been widely used to run large numbers of long-running computations, typically scientific simulations. However, it is not as well suited to large numbers of tasks that are short running, data intensive, or both. Even in an unloaded system, it takes about 30 s from the time a job is submitted until it actually begins running on a machine. This is because Condor must mediate the needs of many different stakeholders, including the machine owner, the job owner, and the pool manager. (Other cloud computing systems have similar latencies for resource allocation.) Because Condor is careful to clean up thoroughly after a job completes, there is no easy way to maintain state on a machine across multiple jobs.

To compensate for these properties, we have built an intermediate layer of software called *Work Queue* that provides fast execution and data persistence on top of Condor. Work Queue consists of two pieces: a *Master* and a *Worker*. A Worker is a simple process that is submitted to the Condor pool like an ordinary batch job. Once running, it makes a network connection back to a Master process. The Master can send files to the Worker, execute programs, and retrieve outputs.

In this way, the Master can start a new program in milliseconds rather than 30 s. Further, it can take advantage of a semi-persistent filesystem: if two consecutive tasks require the same input data, it only needs to be sent to the Worker once. Of course, if Condor decides to evict the Worker process, it will kill any running processes and delete the local storage. The Master is able to detect these evictions, and reassign tasks to other Workers as needed.

Figure 7.2 shows how all of these pieces fit together. The end user is not exposed to any details of the cloud. Instead, he or she runs a command such as `All-Pairs` or `Wavefront` corresponding to the desired abstraction. The abstraction examines the workload, decides how many Workers it can use, and submits them

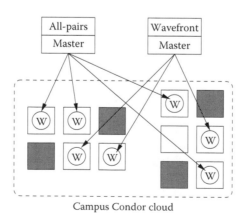

**Figure 7.2  Multiple abstractions sharing a Condor pool.**

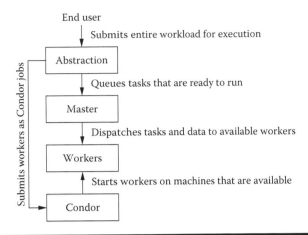

**Figure 7.3  A layered system for cloud computing.**

as jobs to Condor. Condor decides what resources to allocate to each user, and each abstraction schedules tasks on whatever Workers become available. The result is a layered system, where each component has a distinct responsibility, as shown in Figure 7.3.

# 7.3  Map Abstraction

We will begin by describing the simplest abstraction—Map—and then work our way up to more complex abstractions. For each, we will give a formal definition, describe an example, and then explain a significant result achieved using the abstraction.

> *Map( data D[i], function F(data x))*
> *returns array R such that R[i] = F(D[i])*

*Map* applies a function *F* to all elements of a dataset *D*, yielding a result dataset R. Of course, Map and similar operations have been available in functional programming languages, such as LISP [23], for many years, and have long been recognized as a suitable primitive for parallel programming [7,13]. Map is a natural starting point for exploring parallelism.

In practice, our users invoke a stand-alone program called Map that accepts two arguments: the function is the name of a conventional program that transforms one file, and the array is a file listing the names of files to be mapped. In contrast to Map-Reduce [9], which interfaces with C++, and Hadoop [6], which interfaces

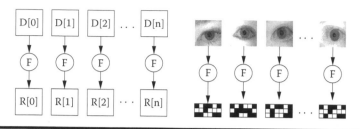

**Figure 7.4   Map abstraction applied to biometrics.**

with Java, Map and the rest of our abstractions use ordinary executable programs as "functions." This allows end users to use whatever language they are most comfortable with, and often are able to plug in existing tools without recoding.

Figure 7.4 shows an application of Map used extensively in biometrics. A common task is to convert a large set of iris images of about 300 kB each into iris codes of about 20 KB each. (An *iris code* is a compressed binary representation of an iris actually used for archival and comparison [8].) A program named ConvertIrisToCode can carry out one conversion in about 19 s.

To execute this workload, the user runs

```
Map IrisListing ConvertIrisToCode
```

Logically, this means to run ConvertIrisToCode once for each entry in IrisListing:

```
ConvertIrisToCode iris001.jpg iris001.code
ConvertIrisToCode iris005.jpg iris005.code
ConvertIrisToCode iris008.jpg iris008.code
...
```

Although one could accomplish a Map by simply submitting batch jobs, our implementation of the abstractions solves a number of technical challenges that would otherwise make using the system very challenging. It caches the executable and other required libraries on the execution nodes, detects failed or evicted Workers, detects compatibility failures with various machines, aborts straggling Workers, preferentially assigns tasks to faster nodes, and deals with network outages and other failures. In this way, the user can focus on their desired work instead of on the details of distributed computing.

A typical example of an unoptimized production run of Map on our cloud converted 58,639 iris images to codes in 2.4 h, using anywhere between 100 and 400 Workers at any given time. The same workload would have taken 309 h on a single CPU, for an effective speedup of 125×. By making use of the Map abstraction on the cloud, the end user can accomplish in a few hours what previously took over a week.

## 7.4 All-Pairs Abstraction

Building on the idea of applying a function to a one-dimensional array of single inputs, we move on to All-Pairs, an abstraction in which each function call is applied onto a pair of inputs.

> *All-Pairs( data A, data B, function F( data x, data y))*
> *returns matrix R such that R[i, j] = F(A[i], B[j])*

The *All-Pairs* abstraction applies a function $F$ to each pair of elements in datasets $A$ and $B$, yielding a result matrix $R$, where each cell is the result of comparing two items. A common variant of All-Pairs is to let $A = B$, in which case it is often only necessary to compute half of the result matrix. Previous researchers have studied All-Pairs theoretically [27] and on small clusters [4]. Our contribution is to scale the problem up to hundreds of nodes in the cloud [16].

As with the previous abstraction, the user provides a "function" in the form of a program that compares two input files. The datasets $A$ and $B$ are text files listing the remaining files to be compared. For small problems, the result matrix is emitted as a plain text file; for large problems, it is stored as a distributed data structure.

All-Pairs problems occur in several fields, such as biometrics, bioinformatics, and data mining. We will focus on biometrics here. A common problem in the field is evaluation of new algorithms developed to improve the state of the art in personal identification. One way to do this is to assemble a large corpus of images and compare all of them to each other using the new algorithm. Results obtained with different algorithms on the same set of images are directly comparable for overall effectiveness.

Figure 7.5 continues with the application from the previous example. Using Map, the user has already reduced 58,639 iris images into an equal number of compact

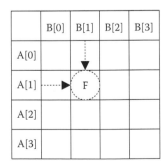
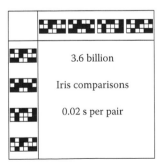

**Figure 7.5  All-Pairs abstraction applied to biometrics.**

iris codes. He or she has written a program `CalculateIrisSimilarity` that computes the masked Hamming distance between two iris codes. The program can complete approximately 50 such comparisons per second. An All-Pairs comparison of these images against each other would consist of 3.4 billion function executions, 795 days of serial computation, and 6.8 TB of aggregate input requirements.

Such a workload is impractical to complete serially, so scaling up to the cloud is required. To invoke the All-Pairs abstraction, the user specifies the input sets and the comparison function:

```
AllPairs SetA SetB CalculateIrisSimilarity
```

The abstraction handles all of the computation and data management. Using a model that takes into account function computation time and data element sizes it calculates how many resources should be used for the workload and how much work they should be given at a time to balance queuing overhead and job runtime. It then distributes data to chosen resources and assigns computation to these resources. If the node has multiple cores, the access pattern is carefully chosen to maximize the cache hit rate. The final results are stored in a large distributed array, which may be accessed directly or downloaded to a local file.

Developing a model for the All-Pairs problem is a critical component for several reasons. First, it relieves the user of the responsibility of determining the number of resources. As problems scale up in size, the number of resources required do not necessarily scale up in kind, and thus users may make poor decisions—underprovisioning the system hurting performance, or overprovisioning the system increasing overhead and wasting resources. Second, the ability to predict very general approximate runtimes based on simple diagnostic benchmarks for work allows the system to manage running processes and detect jobs that are not making progress within a reasonable time (whether due to bugs, hardware misconfigurations, etc.) automatically instead of requiring a user to aggressively monitor his job.

Our largest production run of All-Pairs compared 58,639 iris codes generated from the Iris Challenge Evaluation 2006 [2] dataset all to each other. To our knowledge, this is the largest such result ever computed on a publicly available dataset. The abstraction ran in 10 days on a varying set of 100–200 nodes in the cloud, for an effective speedup of about 80× [16].

## 7.5 Sparse-Pairs Abstraction

There are many workloads that involve the comparison of large sets of objects, but do not require *all possible* comparisons. These workloads require the Sparse-Pairs abstraction.

*Sparse-Pairs( data A, data B, function F( data x, data y), pairs P)*
*returns array R such that F(A[P[i].x], B[P[i].y])*

The *Sparse-Pairs* abstraction applies a function *F* to pairs of elements in sets *A* and *B* given by the set *P*, yielding a result set *R*. Sparse-Pairs fits between the one-dimensional array abstraction of Map, and the two-dimensional array abstraction of All-Pairs. In this way, it is a bit like superimposing the Bag-of-Tasks [3,22] on top of the one-dimensional structure of Map.

Sparse-Pairs problems occur frequently in the field of bioinformatics, particularly in the problem of *genome assembly*. Very briefly, genome assembly is the problem of assembling many small fragments of DNA (hundreds of bytes each) into one long string (billions of bytes) that represents the entire genomic code of an organism. This is much like putting together a jigsaw puzzle: one must compare many pieces to each other in order to determine which should be adjacent.

In principle, one could run an All-Pairs abstraction to compare all fragments to each other, and then match up the pieces with the best scores. However, for a sufficiently large problem, this is computationally infeasible. Fortunately, there exist various heuristics that can be used to filter out the vast majority of these comparisons [19], leaving only a list of "candidate" sequences to compare. This candidate list becomes the *P* set for a Sparse-Pairs workload, as shown in Figure 7.6.

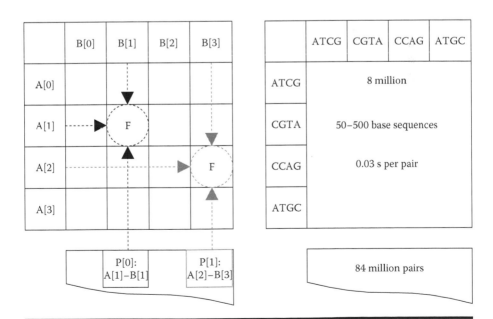

**Figure 7.6** **Sparse-Pairs abstraction applied to bioinformatics.**

The principal complication for Sparse-Pairs is that it is not generally feasible to optimize a bulk transfer of data files to many nodes, because while each data item is used multiple times, the number of repetitive uses may be far less than the number of nodes. Thus, the Master must be active in transferring data, which potentially creates a single bottleneck at the Master's outgoing network link. Additionally, for fast-finishing functions, even if the Master has sufficient bandwidth, the network latency may be too great to keep a sufficient number of Workers satiated.

The first issue can be alleviated with compressed data—in bioinformatics, the language {ACGT} can easily be compressed to two bits per base pair—or multiple Masters. The second can be improved by grouping together many functions into a single "task" sent to the Worker in order to prevent numerous high-latency round-trips in sending data for potentially thousands of functions.

Two data-related factors differentiate Sparse-Pairs from both Map and All-Pairs. First, although the pairs are sparse, each sequence is still used many times throughout the workload. Thus, while the pairs to be computed could be written in full to files in which every pair was a single element, and Map could then be run using that input, this is inefficient. Instead, if the set of sequences is not too large for the main memory, the sequences can be stored only once in their datafile and are read into the Master's memory to construct the tasks for the Workers on the fly as the workload advances.

A Sparse-Pairs result is a subset of a corresponding All-Pairs result. All-Pairs can be optimized to take advantage (via data transfer and assignment of computation to resources) of the fact that every single computation pair will be completed. However, it is unnecessary to complete an entire All-Pairs problem for every case of Sparse-Pairs; and for particularly sparse sets of pairs, it may be very inefficient to do so even if the All-Pairs abstraction is highly optimized. The regular structure of All-Pairs also allows the interface to the abstraction to require only the function and the names of the full sets. Sparse-Pairs only transmits the designated pairs needed for each computation.

Our Sparse-Pairs implementation is in regular use with a bioinformatics research group at Notre Dame. Our largest assembly so far used 8 million sequences extracted from a completed *Sorghum bicolor* genome and completed alignments for 84 million candidate pairs. (The equivalent All-Pairs would have required 64 *trillion* comparisons.) Using 512 CPUs, the assembly is completed in just under 2 h, with an effective speedup of 425× [17].

# 7.6 Wavefront Abstraction

So far, each of the abstractions discussed has allowed computation to be completed in an arbitrary order. However, more complex abstractions, such as Wavefront, have dependencies, requiring one stage of the computation to complete before another can proceed.

$$
\textit{Wavefront}(\textit{data } X, \textit{data } Y, \textit{function } F(\textit{data } x, \textit{data } y, \textit{data } d))
$$

$$
\textit{returns matrix } R[i,j] = \begin{cases} X[i] & \textit{if } j = 0 \\ Y[j] & \textit{if } i = 0 \\ F(R[i-1,j], R[i,j-1], R[i-1,j-1]) & \textit{otherwise} \end{cases}
$$

Figure 7.7 shows the *Wavefront* abstraction, which is a recurrence relation in two dimensions. Given two datasets as original input, and a function that takes three inputs and returns a single output, calculate the function at each of $n^2$ possible states of the system, where each state is defined by the results of its predecessor states. A state's predecessors are its neighbors in a matrix, whose values have been computed by previous function executions. The problem can be generalized to multiple dimensions. Wavefront has previously been studied in the context of multicore processors [1], which our work has extended to clusters and clouds of multicore machines [28].

In practice, the user invokes Wavefront by specifying the input datasets and the recurrence function. As before, the "function" is an arbitrary program that accepts files on the command line

```
Wavefront XData YData RecurrenceFunction
```

Examples of Wavefront problems occur in game theory, economics, bioinformatics, and any problem that involves dynamic programming. In game theory, a recurrence table can be constructed to enumerate all possible states of a simulation with given inputs. Each cell in the table is dependent on its previous neighbor

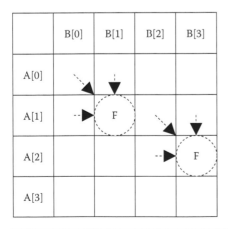

**Figure 7.7** **Wavefront problem applied to bioinformatics.**

states. With a completed table, economists can see the start states, all possible final states, and all possible paths within the simulated context.

A common use of Wavefront in bioinformatics is the alignment of two very large DNA strings. This is done by constructing a dynamic programming table, where each cell gives the "score" of the alignment with each string offset by the coordinates of that cell. The alignment of two complete genomes (billions of bytes) is intractable serially. However, the entire problem can be broken up into a number of smaller sub-alignment problems. Each subproblem computes the dynamic programming table for a fragment of the genome, and then passes the boundary value to its neighbor.

In previous abstractions, the ability to predict runtimes of work units was used primarily to provision resources. Determining which processes have run too long is useful for detecting misconfigured nodes, but a slow node at the beginning or middle of the workload does relatively little damage to the overall performance because there is still a high degree of concurrency. In Wavefront, however, predicting runtimes takes on extra importance. A slow-finishing work unit in Wavefront propagates its delay through to all of its dependents. This is especially harmful early in a workload, when most or all of the remaining computations are dependents, and there is already limited concurrency available in the problem. To combat this, Wavefront makes use of the Work Queue's ability to remove, reschedule, and restart tasks that have run significantly beyond their predicted completion time.

Using the Wavefront abstraction, we were able to complete the alignment of two variants of the Anthrax genome measuring 5.4 million bytes. Each genome was split into 100 fragments of about 54,000 bytes, yielding a 100 × 100 Wavefront problem. Using the cloud, the problem completed in 8.3 h instead of 13 days, achieving an effective speedup of 38×.

## 7.7 Directed Graph Abstraction

The abstractions that we have presented so far have a highly regular structure. However, many users have applications that can only be described as a *directed graph* of programs. There exist a number of *workflow languages* that are capable of expressing arbitrary graphs of tasks, such as Dagman [25], Pegasus [10], Taverna [18], Swift [29], BPEL [14], and Dryad [12], to name a few. Each of these languages has its own syntax and is capable of connecting to a number of remote systems.

However, we often find that end users are reluctant to learn an entirely new language simply to run some programs in a particular distributed system. Fortunately, many are already using a coordination language that easily expresses parallelism. The traditional *Make* [11] tool is typically used to drive the compilation and linking of complex programs, but it can be used to drive any arrangement of programs and files.

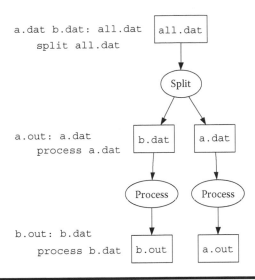

```
a.dat b.dat: all.dat
       split all.dat
```

```
a.out: a.dat
       process a.dat
```

```
b.out: b.dat
       process b.dat
```

**Figure 7.8   Small example of the Makeflow language.**

To this end, we designed a tool called *Makeflow* that implements the Directed Graph abstraction using the same basic language as Make. In many cases, users can take their existing Makefiles and use them unmodified with Makeflow. The Makeflow program reads in a directed graph, and then submits jobs individually to be executed. By changing command-line options, the same directed graph can be run on a single multicore computer, on a Condor pool, or on the Work Queue system. Makeflow keeps a transaction log, so that in the event of failure, the entire workload can be picked up where it was left off, without losing or duplicating jobs.

Figure 7.8 shows a very small example of a Makeflow. The user gives a set of rules, each one stating a program to run, along with the files that it requires and the files that it uses. In the example, the program `split` accepts the file `all.dat` as input and produces the files `a.dat` and `b.dat` as output. Each of these is then consumed by the `process` program.

Figure 7.9 shows a larger example of a real Makeflow written to support a bioinformatics application. In the figure, circles represent programs and squares represent the files that they read and write. In this particular example, the topmost program reads a large input file and splits it into many pieces. Each piece is then processed by a genomic search tool, which creates three different outputs per piece. The results must be joined together and analyzed in order to produce a final result. The system is capable of running workloads consisting of hundreds of thousands of nodes.

Makeflow is currently used as the primary execution engine for a bioinformatics research portal at the University of Notre Dame. A typical Makeflow job executed via the portal consisted of 704 tasks dispatched to the Condor pool and ran on

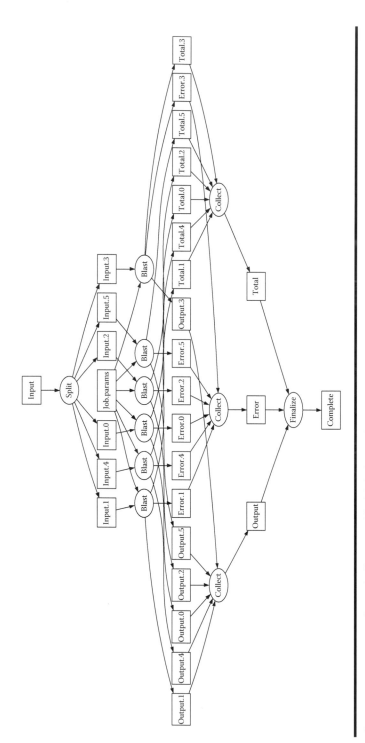

**Figure 7.9  An example Makeflow used in bioinformatics.**

between 25–56 cores on a designated cluster. The overall workflow consumed 686 CPU-hours in 17 h of wall clock time, reducing the runtime from nearly a month down to less than a day.

## 7.8 Choosing the Right Abstraction

As we have mentioned above, some abstractions can be interchanged with each other, with some loss of efficiency. The formal relationship between different abstractions, and how to choose among them, remains an open problem in our field. How, then, can a user choose which one to use for a given problem? So far, we have worked closely with our potential users to choose the appropriate abstraction for their needs. With the growing suite of abstractions, though, it is becoming important that users in various fields can select the right abstraction from the suite based on their knowledge of their own problem.

The intent of providing abstractions is for the user to define a large workload in a simple manner. The user should be able to use codes that are very similar or identical to their serial implementations. The user should be able to garner good performance without having to separately implement complicated resource management, data management, and fault tolerance mechanisms into each application.

Abstractions on the whole shield the user from difficult details about executing a workload in a distributed environment. However, it is often the case that the abstraction that fits the problem best—either due to the design of the abstraction or the way a user has defined the problem—will be more efficient due to less transformation required to scale up to the cloud and because of greater possibilities for problem-specific solution optimizations.

It is our general suggestion that a user should choose the abstraction that fits the way he or she already thinks about his problem. This most easily fulfills the intent of running a workload as is, and simply scaling up to a cloud while abstracting away the messier details of the larger scale. This also usually requires the least amount of user overhead to handle the details of transforming his serial application into an entirely different problem before scaling it up.

An example of additional work required to transform the problem is seen when comparing Wavefront to a general directed acyclic graph (DAG). A particular piece of a Wavefront computation can be referenced simply by coordinates in the results table. This ordered pair, when combined with the problem definition, is sufficient to enumerate all incoming and outgoing edges in the DAG. The more general DAG abstraction would need to define the problem in a less efficient manner, costing execution time to complete the transcription into the more general definition and also the disk/memory resources to store it. Even then, when executing, a general DAG abstraction would still not have the advantages of automatically being able to optimize disk and memory management to the rigid patterns of a Wavefront problem. Thus, it only makes sense for a user who is already looking at his workload as

**Table 7.1  Summary of Typical Workloads**

|  | Application | Problem Size | Runtime on One CPU | Runtime in Cloud |
|---|---|---|---|---|
| Map | Transform to iris code | 58,639 irises | 12.8 days | 2.4 h |
| All-Pairs | Compare iris codes | 58,639 irises | 2 years | 10 days |
| Sparse-Pairs | Sequence overlapping | 84 million pairs | 35 days | 2 h |
| Wavefront | Long-sequence alignment | 5.3 million bytes | 13 days | 8 h |
| Directed Graph | Parallel genome search | 704 nodes | 686 h | 17 h |

a Wavefront problem to use the abstraction that is most specific for that problem—because it fits with how he or she has already designed his approach.

This is, however, only a general suggestion, and must be reevaluated even when scaling up the same workload. An example of a case in which this is important was shown above when discussing the Sparse-Pairs problem. A scientist may start with a fairly dense set of pairs to compute between two sets, and decide to use the All-Pairs problem. However, as the problem is scaled up and the set of pairs becomes sparser, even though the All-Pairs abstraction is still available and will still solve the problem, it no longer is the appropriate choice. Generalizing an arbitrary set of computation pairs into the superset of computation pairs will increase the amount of work he or she requires significantly. Not only will it require much more time to compute all the extraneous pairs that he is not interested in, but the abstraction solving that problem will provision more remote resources (data and worker nodes, for instance) to solve the larger version (Table 7.1).

## 7.9  Conclusion

In this chapter, we have demonstrated several abstractions for cloud computing. An abstraction allows an end user to express a very large workload in a compact form, allowing the underlying system to handle the complexity of allocating resources, dispatching tasks, managing data, and dealing with failures. For each abstraction, we have shown a scientific application that gains significant benefit from the cloud.

Our suite of abstractions is not necessarily complete. Our experience so far suggests that a given community of researchers is likely to engage in the same kinds of computations, albeit with different underlying functions and different scales of data. This is only natural, because both collaborating and competing researchers may use the same underlying techniques and must compare their work to one another. For this reason, one or two abstractions may be sufficient to serve a very large community of people in a given field of study. At our institution, Map and All-Pairs are common tasks in biometrics research, while Sparse-Pairs and Wavefront are useful for bioinformatics. We have found that Makeflow has broad applications.

We have implemented these abstractions in the Condor distributed system because it is widely used to share computing power in academic settings. However, the same concepts can be applied to other systems. For example, the Work Queue system can be deployed on any kind of cloud computer in order to run the same set of abstractions. Further, abstractions need not be implemented with plain programs and files as we have done, but could also be implemented in dynamic languages, such as Java or C#, using formal functions and datatypes. Such implementations would be more strongly typed and have less invocation overhead, but would of course be restricted to the given language.

For more information about these abstractions, the reader may consult our research publications [16,17,20,28]. The code implementing these abstractions can be downloaded from the Cooperative Computing Lab at the University of Notre Dame at http://ccl.cse.nd.edu. The Condor distributed computing software is available from the University of Wisconsin at http://www.cs.wisc.edu/condor

## Acknowledgments

This work was supported in part by the National Science Foundation grants CCF-0621434 and CNS-0643229. We thank Professor Patrick Flynn, Karen Hollingsworth, Robert Mckeon, and Tanya Peters for their collaboration on biometrics applications. We thank Professor Scott Emrich, Michael Olson, Ben Drda, and Rory Carmichael for their collaboration on bioinformatics applications. We thank Ryan Jansen, Joey Rich, Kameron Srimoungchanh, and Rachel Witty for testing early versions of our software.

## References

1. J. Anvik, S. MacDonald, D. Szafron, J. Schaeffer, S. Bromling, and K. Tan. Generating parallel programs from the wavefront design pattern. In *IEEE International Parallel and Distributed Processing Symposium* (*IPDPS*), Fort Eanderdale, FL, p. 165, 2002.
2. Iris Challenge Evaluation 2006, National Institute of Standards and Technology http://iris.nist.gov/ice/ice2006.htm, July 2009.
3. D. Bakken and R. Schlichting. Tolerating failures in the bag-of-tasks programming paradigm. In *IEEE International Symposium on Fault Tolerant Computing*, Montreal, Canada, 1991.

4. A. Radenski, B. Norris, and W. Chen. A generic all-pairs cluster-computing pipeline and its applications. In *Proceeding of the International Conference on Parallel Computing*, Delft, the Netherlands, 1999.

5. Condor World Map. http://www.cs.wisc.edu/condor/map, July 2009.

6. The Hadoop Project. http://hadoop.apache.org, July 2009.

7. G. E. Blelloch. Scans as primitive parallel operations. *IEEE Transactions on Computers*, C-38(11):1526–1538, November 1989.

8. J. Daugman. How iris recognition works. *IEEE Transactions on Circuits and Systems for Video Technology*, 14(1):21–30, 2004.

9. J. Dean and S. Ghemawat. Mapreduce: Simplified data processing on large cluster. In *Operating Systems Design and Implementation (OSDI)*, San Francisco, CA, 2004.

10. E. Deelman, G. Singh, M.-H. Su, J. Blythe, Y. Gil, C. Kesselman, G. Mehta et al. Pegasus: A framework for mapping complex scientific workflows onto distributed systems. *Scientific Programming Journal*, 13(3):219–237, 2005.

11. S. Feldman. Make—A program for maintaining computer programs. *Software: Practice and Experience*, 9:255–265, November 1978.

12. M. Isard, M. Budiu, Y. Yu, A. Birrell, and D. Fetterly. Dryad: Distributed data parallel programs from sequential building blocks. In *Proceedings of EuroSys*, Lisbon, Portugal, March 2007.

13. S. L. P. Jones. Parallel implementations of functional programming languages. *The Computer Journal*, 32:175–186, April 1989.

14. D. Jordan and J. Evdemon. Web services business process execution language version 2.0. OASIS Standard, April 2007.

15. M. Litzkow, M. Livny, and M. Mutka. Condor—A hunter of idle workstations. In *International Conference on Distributed Computing Systems (ICDCS)*, San Jose, CA, June 1988.

16. C. Moretti, H. Bui, K. Hollingsworth, B. Rich, P. Flynn, and D. Thain, All-Pairs: An abstraction for data intensive computing on campus grids. *IEEE Transactions on Parallel and Distributed Systems*, accepted for publication in 2009.

17. C. Moretti, M. Olson, S. Emrich, and D. Thain. Scalable Module Genome Assembly on Campus Grids. Technical Report 2009-04, Computer Science and Engineering Department, University of Notre Dame, Notre Dame, IN, 2009.

18. T. Oinn et al. Taverna: A tool for the composition and enactment of bioinformatics workflows. *Bioinformatics*, 20(17):3045–3054, 2004.

19. M. Pop, S. L. Salzberg, and M. Shumway. Genome sequence assembly: Algorithms and issues. *Computer*, 35(7):47–54, 2002.

20. B. Rich and D. Thain. DataLab: Transactional data parallel computing on an active storage cloud. In *IEEE/ACM High Performance Distributed Computing*, Boston, MA, pp. 233–234, 2008.

21. A. Roy and M. Livny. Condor and Preemptive Resume Scheduling. Kluwer Academic Publishers, Norwell, MA, 2004.

22. D. da Silva, W. Cirne, and F. Brasilero. Trading cycles for information: Using replication to schedule bag-of-tasks applications on computational grids. In *Euro-Par*, Klagenfort, Austria, 2003.

23. G. Steele. *Common LISP: The Language*. Digital Press, Woburn, MA, 1990.

24. D. Thain and M. Livny. How to measure a large open source distributed system. *Concurrency and Computation: Practice and Experience*, 18(15):1989–2019, 2006.

25. D. Thain, T. Tannenbaum, and M. Livny. Condor and the grid. In F. Berman, A. Hey, and G. Fox, eds., *Grid Computing: Making the Global Infrastructure a Reality*. Wiley, New York, 2003.

26. D. Thain, T. Tannenbaum, and M. Livny. Distributed computing in practice: The condor experience. *Concurrency and Computation: Practice and Experience*, 17(2–4):323–356, 2005.

27. K. Theobald, and G. Gao. An efficient parallel algorithm for all pairs examination. In *ACM/IEEE Conference on Supercomputing*, Albuquerque, NM, pp. 742–753, 1991.

28. L. Yu, C. Moretti, S. Emrich, K. Judd, and D. Thain. Harnessing parallelism in multicore clusters with the all-pairs and wavefront abstractions. In *IEEE High Performance Distributed Computing*, Munich, Germany, pp. 1–10, 2009.

29. Y. Zhao, J. Dobson, L. Moreau, I. Foster, and M. Wilde. A notation and system for expressing and executing cleanly typed workflows on messy scientific data. In *SIGMOD*, Baltimore, MD, 2005.

# Chapter 8

# Exploiting the Cloud of Computing Environments: An Application's Perspective

Raphael Bolze and Ewa Deelman

## Contents

## 8.1 Introduction

Traditionally, scientists have been using individual workstations, in-house computational clusters, or campus high-performance resources to conduct their scientific computations. When necessary, they applied for cycles on the top national resources hosted by supercomputing centers and national laboratories. In the past two decades, with the advancement of broad resource sharing technologies such as Condor [1] and Globus [2], efforts such as SETI@home [3], and more recently Cloud technologies [4], scientists are faced with an ever-expanding choice of computing platforms each with its own benefits and drawbacks related to performance, cost, ease of use, and other characteristics. Having this significant number of computational options is a great opportunity for computational sciences providing resources that can scale up with the ever-expanding data collections and ever-increasing computational needs of today's applications.

In this chapter, we examine different types of computing environments, focusing on their characteristics and providing example deployments. We also describe different classes of scientific applications that are being used across the domains of science today and illustrate them with examples (Section 8.2). We focus on three main classes of applications including loosely coupled "bag of tasks" computational paradigms, tightly coupled parallel codes, and computational workflows (Section 8.3). Finally, we provide an analysis of what computational environments suit particular types of applications. The hope is that the analysis will provide domain scientists with the necessary information to make decisions regarding their choice of computing environments.

## 8.2 Computing Environments

This section presents the "cloud" of computing environments available to scientists. Today, we can identify three main types of cyberinfrastructures that can be considered by scientists when reaching for external resources to support computations.

First, we consider *Institutional Grids*. Those distributed platforms have received considerable amount of attention for more than a decade and today several deployments exist in production. These grids can have a national or even worldwide reach. Among them are EGEE [5], PRAGMA [6], TeraGrid [7], Open Science Grid (OSG) [8], DutchGrid [9], and others. These grids rely on the funding from major institutions (the National Science Foundation, the Department of Energy, the European Commission, etc.). These institutions provide the infrastructure and/or the funds to build and maintain these distributed grid deployments.

More recently, *cloud computing* has become a buzzword for on-demand computing provided mainly by industry. Among the main cloud providers are Amazon [10], Google [11], IBM [12], Microsoft [13], and others. These types of platforms are often referred to as *Utility grids* [14] and tend to push the vision of everything as a service (*aaS). Of course, these platforms also come with a business model and provide a variety of services at a specified price and quality of service.

Finally, there is *public computing* or *volunteer computing* such as the World Community Grid [15] or other *Desktop Grids* [16] that use the processing and storage resources provided by volunteers from the general public to help scientists. The idea is to enroll volunteers and use their spare computing time and storage space to perform scientific computations.

In Sections 8.2.1 through 8.2.3, we present the main characteristics of three infrastructures that rely on institutions, industry, and the public to provide computational capabilities. We point out their respective strengths and weakness and we highlight the use requirements from the point of view of a scientific user.

## 8.2.1 Institutional Grid

Institutional Grid Computing is designed to address large-scale computational problems using a network of shared resources. The major motivation is to use aggregated resources that can include computing, storage, and network, and are provided by multiple geographically distributed institutions. These grids are mainly focused on integrating existing resources with their hardware, operating systems (OSs), local resource management, and security infrastructure in order to form a virtual organization (VO) [2]. For example, in the OSG [8] or EGEE [5], when a project joins a VO, it contributes some of its own resources to the overall collaboration while being able to take advantage of the other resources shared within the organization. However, the resource provider maintains control over their own resources and may decide how and when to share them with others. This system works on the principle that not all the resources are needed at the same time, and when a project does not need its own resources, these unutilized computing cycles are made available to others in the broader collaboration/VO.

Other examples of Institutional Grids are the TeraGrid [7] and DEISA [17], which provide a large-scale computational platform for a number of different sciences.

Instead of funding individual clusters or high-performance servers for individual projects, grids pool together financial resources to deliver high-performance computing (HPC) to a broad range of applications. As an example, Figure 8.1 shows the variety of scientific applications running on EGEE today. Initiatives such as the TeraGrid and DEISA are building a cooperative HPC ecosystem, and research projects can apply for allocations of compute cycles that allow them to execute jobs on particular HPC centers or across a number of these centers.

Most grid deployments adopt a layered architecture [2] for the infrastructure. Figure 8.2 presents one possible high-level view of these layers. The hardware layer reflects the physical component of the infrastructure, this includes the characteristics of the processor or cluster, its architecture, and all the specific physical machine attributes that fully describe the platform. The network layer covers the connectivity of the distributed resources orchestrated in the platform, it provides information

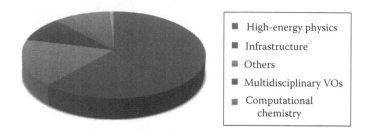

**Figure 8.1 Number of users per application domain. (From EGEE: CIC Operations Portal, http://cic.gridops.org/index.php?section=home&page=volist. With permission.)**

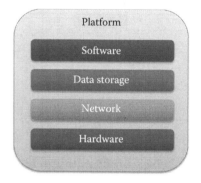

**Figure 8.2 Grid layers and services.**

about the latency and bandwidth of the links, the network protocol, etc. The data storage layer illustrates all the storage and file system space available and also the protocol to access the data across the different resources. Finally, the software layer covers a large spectrum of logical components from the middleware that manages the infrastructure to the scientific application running on the platform.

The Institutional Grid provides several benefits as follows:

- *Support* for the scientific community and resource providers. As the Institutional Grids are designed to serve multiple projects and are hosted in several sites, there exists a community of experienced users and providers who can offer help and advice. As an example, there are the EGEE User forums [19] and many training events are organized [20]. The OSG maintains a *Grid Operation Center,* and the TeraGrid maintains a help desk and other means of providing support and outreach [7].
- There is almost *no restriction* regarding the type of application that can be run on the infrastructure. In the most part, batch execution through queue systems is supported, but there are also solutions to support more interactive applications with interactive execution [21–23].

- *Resources are dedicated* when available. It means that when a job is submitted into the queue management system, it will execute on dedicated resources when released from the queue.
- *Diversity and large scale* are also two strengths of Institutional Grids. There are many sites participating in the grid and so there is potentially a large number of resources that can meet user requirements in terms of characteristics and availability.
- Institutional Grids are *collaboration-oriented* and provide a secure model to share data [2]. The model has been built on the idea that giving access to shared space and distributed computing resources helps researchers from different teams conduct joint scientific projects [24].

Despite all the benefits listed above, Institutional Grids also suffer from some drawbacks as follows:

- The Institutional Grid is a shared environment, in the sense that resources are made available to many users belonging to various collaborations. Thus, *users compete* for resources. When a user's job is submitted to the system, it is placed in a batch queue where it is prioritized based on the site policies. The start time of the job will depend on the load and the scheduling policy of the system [25].
- The environment and the middleware are in a way rigid and constrained. Institutional Grids are designed to serve many domain scientists, including those studying archeology, astronomy, earth sciences, finance, life sciences, etc. [5] As a result, grids provide a *generic software execution environment* and tools. This leaves users to interface their applications to the existing middleware, which can be difficult and usually requires a significant amount of learning. To help alleviate this problem, high-level tools are being developed to assist users. Among them are workflow management systems [26–28] and application-level interfaces [29,30]. Institutional Grids also spend a significant amount of effort on user outreach and education helping new users take advantage of the distributed resources. Finally, scientific communities often come together to provide community-based infrastructure such as science portals [31] to make it easier for a large number of users to run common applications easily [32].
- *Variability, evolution, and changeability* of the grid middleware and the computing environment. Grid software has been evolving over time to match the needs of the community and the understanding of the computational platform. For example, the latest Globus Toolkit, which is widely used on today's infrastructure, has been released in various versions over the years (in sometimes incompatible ways) providing at times custom interfaces (GT 2.0), relying on a standard that was not supported in the long-term (OGSI—and the GT3.0) release. This is the same case with EGEE and its middleware gLite [33]. Users are thus left struggling to adapt their applications to the new middleware as the older software releases are no longer supported.

## 8.2.2 *Cloud Computing*

Recently, cloud computing has emerged as a new alternative for scientists to acquire the computing and storage resources they need. There is still no widely accepted definition for cloud computing but several common points of view are shared: (1) it is scalable and elastic, a user can have as much or as little of a service as he or she wants at any given time; and (2) it has a built-in pricing model, it lets users pay as they go for the services they are asking for. In contrast to the Institutional Grid, cloud computing brings its own stack of components and does not try to integrate and glue the existing infrastructure provided by several sites. Clouds use vitualization, which homogenizes differences in the underlying hardware and software. As a result, they present a configurable environment in terms of the OS and software stack with the virtual machine (VM) as the foundation.

It is clear that cloud computing inherits from the previous decade of research and development in: grid computing, service-oriented architecture, and virtualization. Cloud computing is often depicted as three layers (Figure 8.3) [14]: Platform-as-a-Service (PaaS), Software-as-a-Service (SaaS), and Infrastructure-as-a-Service (IaaS), but many definitions also include some other semantic considerations and everything as a sService (*aaS). The PaaS layer points out the ability to build a computing platform with storage capacity and applications as a service. It includes tools and APIs to quickly build up service-based applications; examples of PaaS are the Google App Engine [11], SalesForce Apex Language [34], and others. The SaaS layer refers to any kind of application available to the user and deployed as a service reusable by any user of the cloud. Google Apps [35] and SalesForce CRMs [36] are examples of such services. In the case of scientific computing, it could be a call to a scientific application or the stack of software needed to deploy the application. The IaaS designates the ability to construct a complete infrastructure with a computing server and storage space. GoGrid [37] or Amazon with Amazon EC2 [10] and

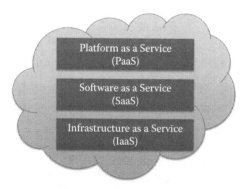

**Figure 8.3    Cloud layer, everything as a service. (From Youseff, L. et al., Toward a unified ontology of cloud computing, in *Grid Computing Environments Workshop* (*GCE '08*), Austin, TX, 2008. With permission.)**

Amazon S3 [38] services are an implementation of such services and provide computing resources and storage space, respectively. In addition to cloud computing services provided by private companies, there exists several tools such as Eucalyptus [39], OpenNEbula [40], and Nimbus [41] that mimic commercial services using clusters to deploy a test-bed cloud environment. With these tools, freely accessible science clouds are being deployed [42].

Already, many scientific projects [43–45] have considered the use of cloud computing services such Amazon EC2 for running their scientific applications.

The main benefits of cloud computing are as follows:

- Through the use of *virtualization*, cloud computing opens the infrastructure to a large number of applications. Indeed, VMs and specialized OSs provide an ideal environment to run legacy applications. These applications are often very sensitive to the execution environment and no one wants to modify these working and validated codes just to adapt it to a specific execution platform.
- Virtualization used by clouds also provides a *customized and reproducible environment* to target a specific application, so that the user can use it immediately and/or reuse it at a later date. This can be an important consideration in favor of cloud computing for a user who wants to be able to reproduce the analysis over time or who deals with legacy applications that are hard to port to new environments.
- The cloud promises scalable and *dynamic resource allocations* to fit user needs. However, it is not clear how well this will be employed in practice when the technologies are being leveraged by a large number of users.

Although clouds can provide a number of benefits, they also have some disadvantages:

- Even though the hardware manufacturers and OSs have made a huge effort to improve virtualization [46,47], the performance still depends on how the underlying hardware, network, and VM have been configured. Although virtual processor performance is close to physical processor performance, *virtual network performance* still lags behind that of the physical interconnect capabilities.
- There exist several actors and providers in the cloud market, but there is *no adopted standard* and, even worse, some technologies rely on proprietary interfaces. As a consequence, there is no compatibility between different vendors. Once a user develops an application for a given cloud, it may take some effort to port that application to a different cloud.
- The pricing model dictates the need to *evaluate and quantify* the computational, storage, and networking needs of an application or application set. This is often hard to predict and can result in unanticipated costs.

The distinction between cloud computing and Institutional Grid is small. For example, we can refer to the early days of the Grid'5000 project [48] (now renamed ALADDIN-G5K), which is a large scale experimental tool with deep reconfiguration capabilities allowing researchers to deploy, install, boot, and run their specific software images and possibly including all the layers of the software stack [49]. Up and running since 2004, this Institutional Grid has almost all the benefits of cloud computing, and the only difference is that this environment was allocated to computer scientists' experiments in grid computing rather than to the broader community.

### 8.2.3 Volunteer Computing

*Volunteer computing* is often named *Desktop computing* [50–52] as it uses desktop computers as the underlying computational resources. Most of the volunteer computing platforms have the same structure: a client program runs on the volunteer's computer. It periodically contacts project servers over the Internet, asking for jobs and sending back the results of completed jobs (see Figure 8.4). This "pull" model provides a mechanism to pass through the user's firewalls that don't allow incoming connections.

There exist a number of frameworks for desktop computing such as Grid MP [53], XtremWeb [54], or OurGrid [16], but certainly the most known and widely used is the BOINC [50] middleware. Today, at least 29 projects [55] are using the open source middleware to support their computations. The applications cover a large spectrum of science: astronomy, physics, chemistry, earth science, mathematics, biology, and medicine. Compared with other types of HPC or cloud

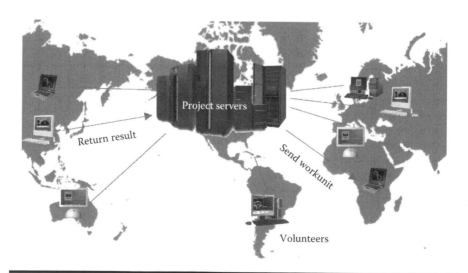

**Figure 8.4   Public volunteer computing platform.**

computing, volunteer computing has by nature a high degree of diversity. The public computers vary widely in terms of hardware, OS, speed, availability, reliability, and network connectivity. The World Community Grid [51] has reported on the diversity of resources: 29 different processor types, from 1 to 64 cores; 14 different OSs; and a huge diversity in the quantity of memory and available disk space. In addition to the heterogeneity in computing and storage resources, the network connectivity of the volunteers can vary greatly as well from a few kB/s to 4 MB/s.

In addition to this mosaic of resources, the application results returned to the master are subject to errors. These errors can occur because of hardware malfunction (particularly on over-clocked computers) or malicious volunteers attempting to get credit for computing not actually performed. To deal with erroneous results, "redundant computing" is employed. Basically, the result is considered valid when it reaches a consensus (a set of similair results) by running the same computations on a number of resources.

From the point of view of the scientist who wants to consider this kind of platform, he or she has to provide an application source code that can run on the biggest set of volunteer resources that have subscribed to the platform. As an example, the World Community Grid asks for the following requirements to technically qualify a scientific project: (1) projects should have a need for millions of CPU hours of computation to proceed; (2) the computer software algorithms required to accomplish the computations should be such that they can be subdivided into many smaller independent computations; and finally (3) if very large amounts of data are required, there should also be a way to partition the data into sufficiently small units corresponding to the computations. Furthermore, the application should be able to make some checkpoints in order to handle the potential interruption of the computation as the volunteer keeps control of their desktop computer and can decide to stop participating in the computation at any time.

The benefits provided by public computing are mainly as follows:

- There are potentially *many resources*. According to Forrester Research [56], there will be 2.2 billion Internet users in the world by 2013.
- The use of public computing resources promotes the project to a high degree of *visibility* to the public. Even if the scientist does not necessarily consider publicity as personally beneficial, it can help motivate the public to actively support the project.

Nevertheless, volunteer computing also has its disatvantages:

- There is *no communication between computing resources*. Thus, the resources need to be treated as totally separate entities and can be suitable only for independent tasks that do not require any inter-task communications.

- There are several technical limitations. The *task data footprint* and data transfers must be small (~MB) and the task runtime has to be short (~10 h).
- The resources are *volatile* and the whole platform depends on the willingness of the public to share their computational power.

## 8.2.4 Comparison of the Different Platforms

The distinction between the three platforms previously presented is not very clearly defined, as they can all be seen as distributed resources. We have chosen to highlight these three computing environments because they can meet the requirements of scientific applications, they are (or promise to be) widely used to produce scientific results in a large range of scientific fields, and they are able to support computations at a large scale. Finally, we want to differentiate between them by the type of resource provider: an institution, a private company, or public volunteers.

Cloud computing brings with it a different cost model. As opposed to grids that are funded by national research agencies or volunteer computing, which is essentially free, business-based cloud computing brings with it a monetary cost, where users pay for the resources they utilize in their work. Several studies have investigated the comparison of the three platforms described above. Most of the studies consider both the performance and the cost-benefits of cloud-based services and compare them to the two other plaforms. In our previous work [43], we studied the cost of running a scientific workflow over a cloud. We estimated the cost of running a given scientific application on such platforms and showed that for data-intensive astronomy applications such as Montage [57] with a large number of short duration tasks, the storage costs were insignificant as compared with the CPU costs. In [58], experiments indicated that the cloud (or Amazon's EC2, at least) is not yet mature enough for HPC computations. The authors observed that the giga-floating point operations per second (GFLOPs) obtained per dollar spent decrease exponentially with increasing computing cores and correspondingly, the cost for solving a linear system increases exponentially with the problem size, very much in contrast to existing scalable HPC systems.

One clear advantage of cloud platforms is the indefinite availability of the resources. The user is not restricted by the wall clock time on a grid cluster or by the sudden unavailability of a volunteer resource. Thus, service-based applications can be easily deployed on the cloud and can be available for long durations of time.

Kondo et al. [59] compared the cloud [10] to volunteer computing [50] from the perspective of an embarrsingly parallel and compute-intensive application (SETI@ home). The authors find that the ratio of volunteer nodes needed to achieve the compute power of a small EC2 instance is about 2.83 active volunteer hosts to 1. In addition, they find that at least 1400 volunteer computers are needed before volunteer computing becomes more cost effective in terms of cents per floating point operations per second (FLOP) (even if the volunteer resources are free, someone has to take care of the infrastructure).

Another study [60] developed formulas to find the real cost of CPU time. With an assumption of 440 million CPU hours annually, the author finds that the purchase mode of ressources is still a good investment compared to leasing resources from a cloud.

These comparisons point out that applications can run within the three environments, even though the cost/benefits vary. In order to choose the appropriate execution environment, the behavior of the application needs to be characterized from the point of view of performance, scalability, or other user-relevant metrics. The associated execution costs of the application in a particular environment can be quantified [43].

# 8.3 Application Perspectives

So far we have examined the computational environments available to the scientists. This section identifies different points of view of scientists who need to rely on distributed resources to conduct their scientific computations. It also describes three commonly used programming models and characterizes the most appropriate execution environments for these models.

There are many reasons that can make a scientist consider the use of external computing resources to achieve his or her work. Some of these reasons are as follows:

- Scaling up the application, running the computation on more data, thus tackling bigger problems that could not be solved unless external resources are used.
- Achieving a scientific goal. Some users do not have enough resources in their own laboratory and therefore need to look for extra computing power or storage. This situation is different from the need to scale up the application. In this case, the user is not even able to run any instance of his or her problem on the internal resources.
- Sharing applications and data with colleagues. If the user is producing data or applications that other partners want to access, he or she needs to have a convenient way to share it.
- Needing to use applications and data already provided by other scientists.
- Decreasing the completion time of the application; when the user has reached a point where the completion time of his or her application is too long to be useful, the user needs to improve the turnaround time of the application by reaching out to external resources.

Beyond the need of the scientists to use external resources to help them reach science goals, there are also some typical use cases or programming paradigms. Programming paradigms are designed to express algorithms elegantly and efficiently. There are many programming models, each suited to a certain class of problems. Through various examples, we identify three basic computing models, which are widely exploited in distributed environments:

■ Highly parallel applications (bag of tags)
■ Tightly coupled applications
■ Scientific workflows

There exist other models but we believe that these three models reflect the most commonly encountered applications deployed in scientific production platforms.

## 8.3.1 Highly Parallel Applications

*Highly parallel computing* is used to denote parallel computations in which each individual (often identical) task can execute without any communication with other tasks. It can also refer to a parameter sweep application where a set of experiments is executed independently from each other. Many scientific applications fall into this category. For example, scientists may want to iterate over a number of parameters to validate their assumptions or they may want to explore a space of parameters to find the suitable case or repetitively process a large amount of data with the same application. Obviously, this case is one of the most convenient from the point of view of the distribution of execution as it deals with independent tasks, which only differ with respect to the input parameters. Nevertheless, this application model still raises a lot of challenges, such as how to use resources efficiently or how to load balance the workload.

An example of a highly parallel application is molecular docking [52], which consists of techniques aiming to predict the interaction between biological molecules. The goal is to find the best way to associate two molecules in order to form a multiprotein complex. Interactions could be between proteins, proteins and DNAs (or RNAs), or proteins and small chemical compounds (ligands). The quality of the interaction can be evaluated through an interaction energy that is calculated according to the space configuration of the complex and the electric charges all over the proteins. Docking methods are based on purely physical principles and are perfectly suited to computer simulation *in silico*. Due to the small amount of data needed to perform a docking computation (molecular structures and parameters are on the order of megabytes), this type of project is particularly well adapted to volunteer computing. However, the Institutional Grid can also handle such applications [61,62].

Another example of highly parallel applications is climate modeling, which simulates the interaction of the atmosphere, ocean, land surface, and ice. The climate varies on the timescales ranging from seasonal to centennial. There exist several computer models of the coupled atmosphere-land surface-ocean-ice systems and there exist scientific tools for understanding and predicting natural and human-caused changes in the Earth's climate. State-of-the-art climate models now include interactive representations of the ocean, the atmosphere, the land, hydrologic and cryospheric processes, terrestrial and oceanic carbon cycles, and atmospheric chemistry. This field of science illustrates how highly parallel applications can take advantage of different kinds of distributed environments. In one case [63], the project carried out a large number of model runs in which parameters were varied within their current range of uncertainty. Then it rejected those that failed to model past climate successfully and used the remainder to study future climate. Such computations required a small amount of input data, produced around 1 GB of temporary files, and the final output was less than 20 MB so it could fit on a desktop computer. In another case [64], even though the computation model fit the parameter sweep paradigm, it was necessary to transfer or access large amounts of data to be able to run climate analysis, and thus the use of a high-performance computer and distributed data storage was necessary.

When a user has a highly parallel application, theoretically, they have the freedom to choose the three remote execution environments previously presented. Nevertheless, practically, the user needs to know whether the application is robust to failures and whether the source code is portable and able to be compiled and executed on any type of environment. The data volume is also an issue; thus, the user needs to know how much input is required and how much output is produced. The task execution time also affects what environment is most suitable for a particular application.

## 8.3.2 Tightly Coupled Application

Tightly coupled applications refer to parallel applications with multiple interdependent processes. These processes exchange data during their execution and have to be synchronized. Typically, these applications are written with parallel libraries such as a message-passing interface (MPI) [65] or parallel virtual machine (PVM) [66] that enable communication between processes. Inter-processes communication is the key feature of these types of applications. It means that running one instance of this application may involve the use of several processes allocated to different processors across the network and the processors will need to be able to exchange data during the execution (see Figure 8.5). The main concern of this type of application is the ability to communicate efficiently and therefore the performance of the network layer that connects the computing resources is of critical importance.

There exist a large number of tightly coupled applications and over the past decades they have motivated the construction of ever larger (in terms of the number of processors and storage) and faster (in terms of network speed and FLOPS) systems.

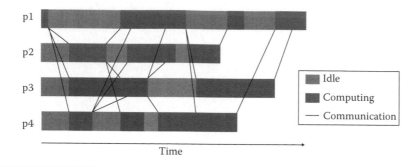

**Figure 8.5** **Gantt chart representation of process activity.**

A typical example of such an application is calculating the solution of a linear system such as $Ax = b$, a matrix solving computation. Matrix-based computations are a key computational kernel in many scientific applications, where physics laws are applied to solve the underlying problem. Typically, parallel implementations of matrix computation work well in multi-processor environments because the input matrices can be sliced horizontally and vertically into small blocks that are mapped onto the available processors. The communications can take place in parallel, and thanks to asynchronous communication libraries, most of these communications can be overlapped with the actual computations. All these characteristics render the matrix product kernel suitable to an efficient parallel implementation on high-performance clusters. In fact, most powerful machines in the world are ranked on the Top 500 [67] list using the highly parallel LINPACK benchmark [68], which solves a dense linear system in double precision.

Another example of a tightly coupled application is wave simulation [69,70], where one strategy is to divide the area of interest into multiple regions and let each processor/process simulate the movements within one region. The movement within a region is not independent of the movement within the other regions, but rather depends on the movement in its neighbor regions, and as a result each process needs to communicate with its neighbors. MPI is employed to exchange data between neighboring nodes at each time step in order to pass the wave-field between neighboring sub-regions.

Because of frequent communications between application tasks, the volunteer computing platform does not offer a feasible solution for tightly coupled applications.

## 8.3.3 Scientific Workflows

In the general case, a workflow is defined as the organization and the formalization of several operations in order to describe a broader application. Adapted to scientific domains, a scientific workflow is the orchestration of programs involving several computing tasks where the output of one task is an input to another task. It may also be called a loosely coupled application as opposed to a tightly coupled application. These loosely coupled applications are composed of many tasks that can be individually scheduled on different computing resources to achieve a greater level of performance.

Workflows constitute the current trend in the composition of large-scale scientific applications. However, unlike the highly parallel applications, data and control dependencies exist between tasks. Workflow tasks can be either standalone applications or service invocations. Scientific workflows are used in many domains such as bioinformatics, climate modeling, image analysis, astrophysics, etc. [71–75].

In addition, scientific workflows can often be depicted as directed graphs, which often helps to visualize the data or control dependencies that exist in the overall application. There are many examples of workflow-based applications [74]. Here, we only describe some of them.

The bioinformatics project at Harvard University is conducting a wide search for small untranslated RNAs (sRNAs) that regulate several processes, such as secretion or virulence in bacteria. The sRNA identification protocol using high-throughput technology (SIPHT) program [76] uses a workflow to automate the search for sRNA encoding-genes for all of the bacterial replicons in the National Center for Biotechnology Information (NCBI) database. The kingdom-wide prediction and annotation of sRNA encoding genes involves a variety of individual programs. These involve the prediction of Rho-independent transcriptional terminators, Basic Local Alignment Search Tools (BLAST) comparisons of inter-genetic regions of different replicons, and the annotations of any sRNAs that are found. This application is using the Condor DAGMan engine [77] to run application tasks on a cluster of computing nodes to deliver results. It also has a web portal from which end-users can launch and see the annotations of sRNA encoding-genes. Figure 8.6 shows a graphical representation of the SIPHT workflow.

The Montage [57] application was created by the NASA/IPAC Infrared Science Archive. It is an open source toolkit and it can be used to generate custom mosaics of the sky using input images in the Flexible Image Transport System (FITS) format [78]. This workflow of computing tasks is now a standard workflow application and it has been widely used to test workflow enactment systems [43,79,80]. During the production of the final mosaic, the geometry of the output is calculated from the geometry of the input images. The inputs are re-projected to be of the same spatial scale and rotation. The background emissions in the images are then corrected to be of the same level in all images. The re-projected, corrected images are co-added to form the final mosaic. Figure 8.7 shows the Directed Acyclic Graph (DAG) representation of the Montage application for one region of the sky. Through the use of the Pegasus Workflow Management System [26], this application has been successfully enabled in the TeraGrid environment [81] and also in the Amazon EC2/S3 cloud [43].

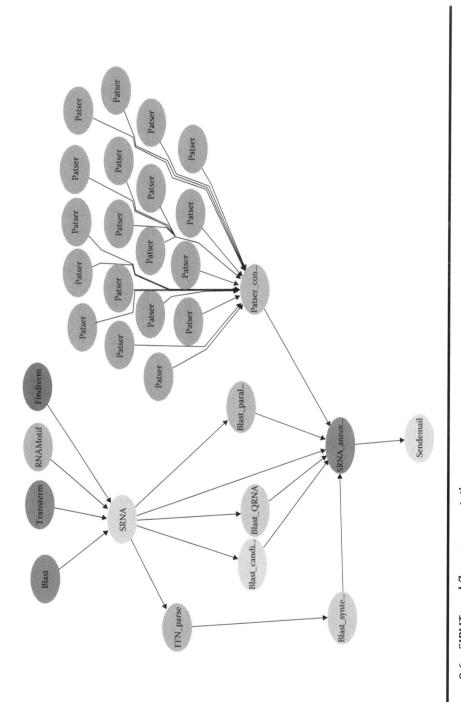

**Figure 8.6    SIPHT workflow representation.**

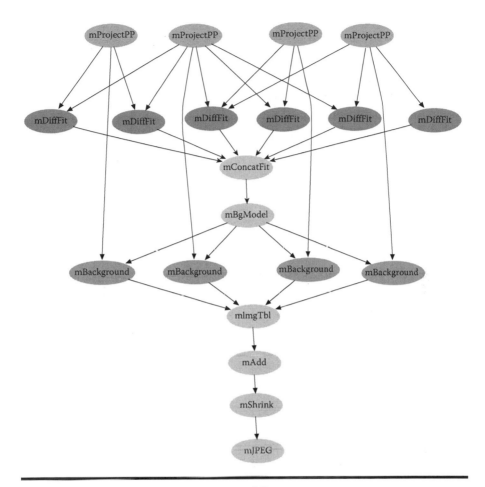

**Figure 8.7    Example of one Montage workflow.**

These two examples from different science fields illustrate the use of scientific workflows. In contrast to the tightly coupled parallel applications, the communication occurs at the end of the execution of one program and usually the communication is done via a file transfer. The characterization of such applications requires identifying all the programs involved in the computation and understanding their computational characteristics such as execution time, amount of storage needed, and software requirements.

Not all workflows are based on standalone computations such as those described above. Some workflows are rather an orchestration of service invocations. These types of workflows are often common in biology, where large amounts of databases and computational tools are made available to the community as research products and models. For example, the Taverna Workbench tool [28,72] provides access to web services through a graphical user interface. Figure 8.8 shows an example of

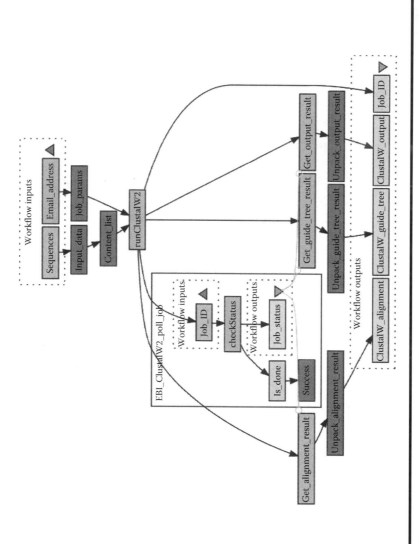

Figure 8.8 EBI ClustalW2 workflow. (From McWilliam, H., EBI ClustalW2, http://www.myexperiment.org/workflows/203. With permission.)

a Taverna workflow shared through the *myExperiment.org portal* [82]. This application performs a ClustalW [83] multiple sequence alignment using the EBI's ClustalW2 web service [84]. The input parameters are the set of sequences to align and the e-mail address of the user. The results are the alignment, the guide tree used to produce the final alignment, the job ID, and the output of the ClustalW program.

## 8.4 Discussion

In this section, we aim to identify appropriate execution environments for different types of applications. The Table 8.1 indicates which resources are appropriate given the characteristics of the application in terms of computational, storage, and communication needs as well as in terms of the desired resource availability, cost, and desired security.

Ease of use is another characteristic that one could explore in the context of the various computing environments. However, ease of use is dependent on the user's knowledge and familiarity with the various infrastructures. In all cases, however, users need to learn new technologies and tools.

## 8.5 Conclusions

In this chapter, we described three main distributed computing environments that are being used to advance science. We also described some of the programming models that scientists use to perform computations in distributed environments. We also illustrated the features of grids, clouds, and volunteer computing that are appropriate for various application characteristics.

As we look at the developments in the area of computing, we can see how over time, computer manufacturers and software providers are providing ever-increasing capabilities. Until not long ago, a computing center would purchase high-performance hardware and a service contract from a computer manufacturer such as IBM, and although this model of compute cycle acquisition is still present, we see more businesses providing more of the services backed by large scale data and compute centers. In this model, the revenues to the companies are not a single large-purchase, but are rather potentially growing over time. This model can also potentially allow businesses to keep their customers for a longer term as they provide ever more increasing functionality. The cost of maintenance of computing resources can also be potentially lowered, because the maintenance is concentrated in the large-scale centers and can be done in a flexible way without exposing the changes to the users. This is in contrast to the current model, where computer technicians need to be dispatched to customer sites and need to restore the compute systems to the specifications of the customer.

**Table 8.1  Criteria to Consider When Selecting a Computational Environment**

| Application Characteristics/ Suitability of a Computing Environment | Grids | Clouds | Volunteer Computing |
|---|---|---|---|
| **Computations** | | | |
| Single processor stand-alone codes | Yes, but compute site policies often prefer multi-processor applications | Yes, but make sure to pick the right virtual resource instance with 1 core | Yes |
| Multi-processor stand-alone codes | Yes, but need to be aware of wallclock time (checkpoint long computations) | Only for a small number of cores—need to pick the right instance and create the right VM with MPI or OpenMP | No |
| Service-based applications | Not the best environment because of wallclock limitations and firewall issues | Yes, may want to consider increasing the number of service instances as the computational load increases | No |
| **Computations** | | | |
| Time-critical computations | Yes, if resource provisioning is employed or priority queues are provided | Yes | No |
| **Data communications (in tightly coupled and workflow-based applications)** | | | |
| Frequent message-based inter-processor communications | Yes, although long duration applications with times greater than wallclock time need to be checkpointed | Only for parallel codes with small numbers of cores (right now ≤8); for larger numbers of cores, need to set up messaging over the virtualized network which can be slow | No |

| | | | |
|---|---|---|---|
| Infrequent message-based communications | Yes | Yes, but for larger numbers of processors need to set up MPI across the VMs | No |
| Infrequent communications (based on files for example) | Yes, although if too many files are being read and written, may want to consider the use of resources with parallel file systems such as Luster [86]. | Yes, but need to decide whether to use the cloud storage system, or set up a file system between VM instances, or perform communications via storage external to the cloud | No |
| **Data storage** | | | |
| Small data footprint | Yes | Yes, can fit within a VM or be hosted on the cloud storage service | Yes, limited to megabytes |
| Large data footprint | Yes, but may have to put data in a specialized storage system, such as SRM [87]. | Yes, but an appropriate compute instance may have to be chosen and cloud storage used | No |
| **Software** | | | |
| Legacy software | Yes, if the environment is right | Yes, if the VM can be created | Probably not a good idea, because the number of potential resources can be small |

*(continued)*

**Table 8.1 (continued)  Criteria to Consider When Selecting a Computational Environment**

| Application Characteristics/ Suitability of a computing environment | Grids | Clouds | Volunteer Computing |
|---|---|---|---|
| Software requiring restrictive licenses | Only if already installed on the site | Probably no, issue of licensing on VMs can be limiting | No |
| Software requiring specialized libraries | Yes, but may require assistance from system administrators to install and configure | Yes, can be put in a VM | Yes, although needs small data footprint. The applications needs to be portable |
| **Resources** | | | |
| Cost | None, but the user needs to apply for cycles (TeraGrid) or work within the policies of a VO (OSG) | In commercial clouds, costs usually include the cost of the compute instance, storage, and data transfer in and out of the cloud | None |

| | | | |
|---|---|---|---|
| Amount of resources available | Depends on the cycle allocation and/or on the VO policy | In theory, unlimited; in practice, special agreements with providers need to be made to acquire significant resources | Depends on the popularity of the project |
| Resource availability—startup time of applications | Depends on resource load and site policies, users compete for resources | Minutes | Can vary greatly, depends on the readiness of volunteers to provide resources to the project |
| Security | X509 certificate-based (users need to acquire a certificate from a trusted authority—campus or grid operations) | X509 certificate-based (users need to acquire a certificate from the cloud provider); other security models can be deployed inside the VMS | Computations are sandboxed and data are encrypted |
| Network performance between processors | High-performance connectivity | Commodity gigabit Ethernet | Consumer-grade Internet |

It will be interesting to see how cloud computing evolves and how it can be made relevant to science applications. Will the campus and national computing centers disappear?

# References

1. D. Thain et al., Distributed computing in practice: The Condor experience [Research articles], *Concurrency and Computation: Practice and Experience*, 17, 323–356, 2005.
2. I. Foster et al., The anatomy of the grid: Enabling scalable virtual organizations, *The International Journal of High Performance Computing Applications*, 15, 200–222, 2001.
3. E. Korpela et al., SETI@home: Massively distributed computing for SETI, *Computing in Science and Engineering*, 3, 5, 2001.
4. G. Lawton, Moving the OS to the Web, *Computer*, 41, 4, 2008.
5. Enabling Grids for E-sciencE (EGEE). Available: http://www.eu-egee.org/
6. The Pacific Rim Application and Grid Middleware Assembly. Available: http://www.pragma-grid.net
7. TeraGrid. Available: http://www.teragrid.org/
8. Open Science Grid. Available: www.opensciencegrid.org
9. DutchGrid: Large-scale distributed computing in the Netherlands. Available: http://www.dutchgrid.nl/
10. Amazon Elastic Compute Cloud. Available: http://aws.amazon.com/ec2/
11. Google App Engine. Available: http://code.google.com/appengine/
12. IBM Cloud Computing. http://www.ibm.com/ibm/cloud/
13. Windows Azure Platform. Available: http://www.microsoft.com/azure/
14. L. Youseff et al., Toward a unified ontology of cloud computing, in *Grid Computing Environments Workshop (GCE '08)*, Austin, TX, 2008.
15. World Community Grid. Available: http://www.worldcommunitygrid.org/
16. OurGrid community. Available: http://www.ourgrid.org/
17. Distributed European Infrastructure for Supercomputing Applications. Available: http://www.deisa.eu/
18. EGEE: CIC Operations Portal. Available: http://cic.gridops.org/index.php?section=home&page=volist
19. EGEE user forum. Available: http://egee-uf3.healthgrid.org/
20. EGEE training event. Available: http://www.egee.nesc.ac.uk/schedreg/index.cfm
21. V. Talwar et al., An environment for enabling interactive grids, in *Symposium on High Performance Distributed Computing (HPDC'03)*, Seattle, WA, 2003.
22. H. Xiao et al., An implementation of interactive jobs submission for grid computing portals, in *Proceedings of the 2005 Australasian Workshop on Grid Computing and E-Research*, vol. 44, Newcastle, Australia: Australian Computer Society, Inc., Darlinghurst, Australia, 2005, pp. 67–70.
23. I. Sfiligoi, Making science in the Grid world: Using glideins to maximize scientific output, in *Nuclear Science Symposium Conference Record*, Honolulu, HI, 2007, pp. 1107–1109.
24. E. Deelman et al., GriPhyN and LIGO, Building a virtual data Grid for gravitational wave scientists, in *High Performance Distributed Computing (HPDC'02)*, Edinburgh, Scotland, 2002.

25. D. Lingrand et al., Modeling the latency on production grids with respect to the execution context, *Parallel Computing (PARCO)*, 35, 493–511, 2009. http://rainbow.polytech.unice.fr/publis/lingrand-glatard-etal:2009.pdf

26. E. Deelman et al., Pegasus: A framework for mapping complex scientific workflows onto distributed systems, *Scientific Programming Journal*, 13, 219–237, 2005.

27. T. Fahringer et al., ASKALON: A tool set for cluster and Grid computing, *Concurrency and Computation: Practice and Experience*, 17, 143–169, 2005.

28. T. Oinn et al., Taverna: A tool for the composition and enactment of bioinformatics workflows, *Bioinformatics*, 20, 3045–3054, 2004.

29. SAGA—ASimpleAPI for GridApplications. Available: http://saga.cct.lsu.edu/

30. S. Jha et al., Grid interoperability at the application level using SAGA, in *International Grid Interoperabilty and Interoperation Workshop (IGIIW 2007)*, Bangalore, India, 2007.

31. List of TeraGrid Science Gateways. Available: http://teragrid.org/gateways/gateway_list.php

32. Online Simulation and more for Nanotechnology. Available: http://nanohub.org/

33. GLite: Lightweight Middleware for Grid Computing. Available: http://glite.web.cern.ch/glite/

34. Apex: Salesforce on-demand programming language andframework. Available: http://developer.force.com/

35. Google Apps. Available: http://www.google.com/apps/intl/en/business/index.html

36. Salesforce: Customer Relationships Management Solutions. Available: http://www.salesforce.com/crm/

37. GoGRID. http://www.gogrid.com/

38. Amazon Simple Storage Service. Available: http://aws.amazon.com/s3/

39. D. Nurmi et al., The eucalyptus open-source cloud-computing system, in *Cluster Computing and the Grid CCGRID'09*, Shanghai, China, 2009, pp. 124–131.

40. OpenNebula: Open source toolkit for cloud computing. Available: http://www.opennebula.org

41. Nimbus. Available: http://workspace.globus.org/

42. Science Clouds. Available: http://workspace.globus.org/clouds/

43. E. Deelman et al., The cost of doing science on the cloud: the Montage example, in *SC '08: Proceedings of the 2008 ACM/IEEE conference on Supercomputing*, Austin, TX, 2008, pp. 1–12.

44. K. Keahey and T. Freeman, Science Ccouds: Early experiences in cloud computing for scientific applications, in *Cloud Computing and Its Applications (CCA-08)*, Chicago, IL, 2008.

45. A. Matsunaga et al., CloudBLAST: Combining mapreduce and virtualization on distributed resources for bioinformatics applications, in *eScience '08*, Indianapolis, IN, 2008.

46. L. Youseff et al., Evaluating the performance impact of xen on MPI and process execution for HPC systems, in *Virtualization Technology in Distributed Computing (VTDC 2006)*, Tampa, FL, 2006.

47. P. Barham et al., Xen and the art of virtualization, in *19th ACM Symposium on Operating Systems Principles (SOSP-03)*, Bolton Landing, NY, 2003, pp. 163–167.

48. ALADDIN-G5K. Available: https://www.grid5000.fr

49. R. Bolze et al., Grid'5000: A large scale and highly reconfigurable experimental grid testbed, *International Journal of High Performance Computing Applications*, 20, 481–494, 2006.

50. D. P. Anderson, BOINC: A system for public-resource computing and storage, in *Fifth IEEE/ACM International Workshop on Grid Computing*, Pittsburgh, PA, 2004.

51. D. P. Anderson and K. Reed, Celebrating diversity in volunteer computing, in *Hawaii International Conference on System Sciences (HICSS'09)*, Waikoloa, HI, 2009.

52. V. Bertis et al., Large scale execution of a bioinformatic application on a volunteer grid, in *Workshop on Parallel and Distributed Scientific and Engineering Computing (PDSEC08)*, Miami, FL, 2008.

53. Grid MP overview. Available: http://www.univaud.com/hpc/products/grid-mp/

54. F. Cappello et al., Computing on large-scale distributed systems: XtremWeb architecture, programming models, security, tests and convergence with grid, *Future Generation Computer Systems*, 21, 417–437, 2005.

55. BOINC projects list. Available: http://boinc.berkeley.edu/projects.php

56. Z. D. Wigder, 2009, Global Online Population Forecast, 2008 to 2013. Available: http://www.forrester.com/Research/Document/Excerpt/0,7211,53355,00.html

57. Montage project. Available: http://montage.ipac.caltech.edu/

58. J. Napper and P. Bientinesi, Can cloud computing reach the top500? in *Proceedings of the Workshop on UnConventional High Performance Computing*, New York, 2009.

59. D. Kondo et al., Cost-benefit analysis of cloud computing versus desktop grids, in *18th International Heterogeneity in Computing Workshop*, Rome, Italy, 2009.

60. E. Walker, The real cost of a CPU hour, *Computer*, 42, 35–41, 2009.

61. V. Breton et al., Grid added value to address malaria, in *Cluster Computing and the Grid Workshops*, Singapore, 2006.

62. H.-C. Lee et al., Grid-enabled high-throughput in silico screening against influenza A neuraminidase, *IEEE Transactions on NanoBioscience*, 5, 288–295, 2006.

63. D. A. Stainforth et al., Uncertainty in predictions of the climate response to rising levels of greenhouse gases, *Nature*, 433, 403–406, 2005.

64. B. Allcock et al., High-performance remote access to climate simulation data: A challenge problem for data grid technologies, in *SuperComputing (SC'01)*, Denver, CO, 2001.

65. MPI: Message Passing Interface. Available: http://www.mpi-forum.org/

66. PVM: Parallel Virtual Machine. http://www.csm.ornl.gov/pvm/

67. TOP500: Supercomputer sites. Available: http://www.top500.org/

68. A. Petitet et al., HPL—A portable implementation of the high-performance linpack benchmark for distributed-memory computers. Available: http://www.netlib.org/benchmark/hpl/

69. S. E. Minkoff, Spatial parallelism of a 3D finite difference velocity-stress elastic wave propagation code, *SIAM Journal on Scientific Computing*, 24, 1–19, 2002.

70. T. Bohlen, Parallel 3D viscoelastic finite difference seismic modelling, *Computers and Geosciences*, 28, 887–899, 2002.

71. E. Deelman et al., Managing large-scale workflow execution from resource provisioning to provenance tracking: The cybershake example, in *e-Science*, Amsterdam, the Netherlands, 2006.

72. T. Oinn et al., Taverna/myGrid: Aligning a workflow system with the life sciences community, in *Workflows for e-Science*, I. J. Taylor et al., Eds., ed: Springer-Verlag London Ltd., Godalming, U.K., 2007, pp. 300–319.

73. I. J. Taylor et al., Eds., *Workflow for e-Science*, Springer, New York, 2007.

74. S. Bharathi et al., Characterization of scientific workflows, in *The Third Workshop on Workflows in Support of Large Scale Science (WORKS08)*, Austin, TX, 2008.

75. J. Montagnat et al., Workflow-based data parallel applications on the EGEE production grid infrastructure, *Journal of Grid Computing*, 6, 369–383, 2008.
76. J. Livny et al., High-throughput, kingdom-wide prediction and annotation of bacterial non-coding RNAs, *PLoS ONE*, 3(9), e3197, 2008.
77. DAGMan: Directed Acyclic Graph Manager. Available: http://www.cs.wisc.edu/condor/dagman
78. FITS: Flexible Image Transport System. Available: http://fits.gsfc.nasa.gov/
79. A. Barker et al., Eliminating the middleman: Peer-to-peer dataflow, *Presented at the Proceedings of the 17th International Symposium on High Performance Distributed Computing*, Boston, MA, 2008.
80. S.-M. Park and M. Humphrey, Data throttling for data-intensive workflows, in *IEEE International Symposium on Parallel and Distributed Processing (IPDPS 2008)*, Miami, FL, 2008.
81. N. Anagnostou et al., Montage: Experiences in astronomical image mosaicking on the teragrid, in *SuperComputing (SC'04)*, Pittsburgh, PA, 2004.
82. D. D. Roure et al., myExperiment: Defining the social virtual research environment, *Presented at the Proceedings of the 2008 Fourth IEEE International Conference on eScience*, Indianapolis, IN, 2008.
83. M. A. Larkin et al., Clustal W and Clustal X version 2.0, *Bioinformatics*, 23, 2947–2948, Nov 01 2007.
84. EBI's ClustalW2 web service. Available: http://www.ebi.ac.uk/Tools/webservices/services/clustalw2
85. H. McWilliam, EBI ClustalW2. Available: http://www.myexperiment.org/workflows/203
86. Lustre file system. Available: www.lustre.org
87. A. Shoshani et al., Storage resource managers: Middleware components for grid storage, in *The Nineteenth IEEE Symposium on Mass Storage Systems (MSS'02)*, College Park, MA, 2002.

# Chapter 9

# Granules: A Lightweight Runtime for Scalable Computing with Support for Map-Reduce

Shrideep Pallickara, Jaliya Ekanayake, and Geoffrey Fox

## Contents

# 9.1 Introduction

Cloud computing has gained significant traction in recent years. By facilitating access to an elastic (meaning the available resource pool that can expand or contract over time) set of resources, cloud computing has demonstrable applicability to a wide range of problems in several domains.

Appealing features within cloud computing include access to a vast number of computational resources and inherent resilience to failures. The latter feature arises, because in cloud computing the focus of execution is not a specific, well-known resource but rather the best available one. Another characteristic of a lot of programs that have been written for cloud computing is that they tend to be stateless. Thus, when failures do take place, the appropriate computations are simply relaunched with the corresponding datasets.

Among the forces that have driven the need for cloud computing are falling hardware costs and burgeoning data volumes. The ability to procure cheaper, more powerful CPUs coupled with improvements in the quality and capacity of networks have made it possible to assemble clusters at increasingly attractive prices. The proliferation of networked devices, Internet services, and simulations has resulted in large volumes of data being produced. This, in turn, has fueled the need to process and store vast amounts of data. These data volumes cannot be processed by a single computer or a small cluster of computers. Furthermore, in most cases, this data can be processed in a pleasingly parallel fashion. The result has been the aggregation of a large number of commodity hardware components in vast data centers.

Map-Reduce [1], introduced by Dean and Ghemawat at Google, is the most dominant programming model for developing applications in cloud settings. Here, large datasets are split into smaller, more manageable sizes, which are then processed by multiple *map* instances. The results produced by individual map functions are then sent to *reducers*, which collate these partial results to produce the final output. A clear benefit of such concurrent processing is a speed-up that is proportional to the number of computational resources. Map-Reduce can be thought of as an instance of the Single Program/Process, Multiple Data (SPMD) [2] programming model for parallel computing introduced by Federica Darema. Applications that can benefit from Map-Reduce include data and/or task-parallel algorithms in domains such as information retrieval, machine learning, graph theory, and visualization, among others.

In this chapter, which is an extended version of our paper [21], we describe Granules [3], a lightweight streaming-based runtime for cloud computing. Granules allows processing tasks to be deployed on a single resource or a set of resources. Besides the basic support for Map-Reduce, we have incorporated support for variants of the Map-Reduce framework that are particularly suitable for scientific applications. Unlike most Map-Reduce implementations, Granules uses streaming for disseminating intermediate results, as opposed to using file-based communications. This leads to demonstrably better performance (see benchmarks in Section 9.7).

This chapter is organized as follows. In Section 9.2, we provide a brief overview of the NaradaBrokering substrate that we use for streaming. We discuss some of the core elements of Granules in Section 9.3. Section 9.4 outlines our support for Map-Reduce and for the creation of complex computational pipelines. Section 9.5 describes the process of developing and deploying applications using Granules. In Section 9.6, we describe related work in this area. In Section 9.7, we profile several aspects of the Granules runtime, and where possible, contrast its performance with comparable systems, such as Hadoop, Dryad, and MPI (Message Passing Interface). In Section 9.8, we present our conclusions.

## 9.2 NaradaBrokering

Granules uses the NaradaBrokering [4–6] streaming substrate (developed by us) for all its streams disseminations. The NaradaBrokering content distribution network (depicted in Figure 9.1) comprises a set of cooperating router nodes known as *brokers*. Producers and consumers do not directly interact with each other. Entities, which are connected to one of the brokers within the broker network, use their

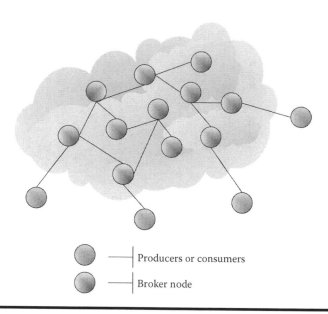

**Figure 9.1  NaradaBrokering broker network.**

hosting broker to funnel streams into the broker network and, from thereon, to other registered consumers of those streams.

NaradaBrokering is application independent and incorporates several services to mitigate network-induced problems as streams traverse domains during disseminations. This system provisions easy-to-use guarantees while delivering consistent and predictable performance that is adequate for use in real-time settings.

Consumers of a given data stream can specify, very precisely, the portions of the data stream that they are interested in consuming. By preferentially deploying links during disseminations, the routing algorithm [4] in NaradaBrokering ensures that the underlying network is optimally utilized. This preferential routing ensures that consumers receive only those portions of streams that are of interest to them. Since a given consumer is typically interested in only a fraction of the streams present in the system, preferential routing ensures that a consumer is not deluged by streams that it will subsequently discard.

The system incorporates support for reliable streaming and secure streaming. In reliable streaming, the substrate copes with disconnects and process/link failures of different components within the system with the ability to fine-tune redundancies [5] for a specific stream. Secure streaming [6] enforces the authorization and confidentiality constraints associated with the generation and consumption of secure streams while coping with denial-of-service attacks.

Some of the domains that NaradaBrokering has been deployed in include earthquake science, particle physics, environmental monitoring, geosciences, geographic information system (GIS) systems, and defense applications.

## 9.3 Granules

Granules orchestrates the concurrent execution of processing tasks on a distributed set of machines. Granules is itself distributed, and its components permeate not only the computational resources on which it interleaves processing, but also the desktop from where the applications are being deployed in the first place. The runtime manages the execution of a set of processing tasks through various stages of their life cycle: deployment, initialization, execution, and termination. Figure 9.2 depicts the various components that comprise Granules.

### 9.3.1 Computational Task

The most fundamental unit in Granules is the notion of a *computational task*. This computational task encapsulates processing functionality, specifies its scheduling strategy, and operates on different types of datasets. These computational tasks can take on additional interchangeable roles (such as map and reduce) and, when cascaded, can form complex execution pipelines.

Computational tasks require the domain specialists to specify processing functionality. This processing typically operates upon a collection of datasets encapsulated within the computational task.

The computational task encapsulates functionality for processing for a given fine-grained unit of data. This data granularity could be a packet, a file, a set of files, or a database record. For example, a computational task can be written to evaluate a regular expression query (grep) on a set of characters, a file, or a set of files. In some

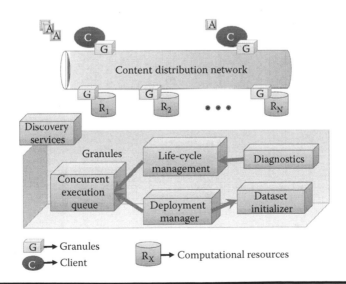

**Figure 9.2** **Overview of the Granules runtime.**

cases, there will not be a specific dataset; rather, each computational task instance initializes itself using a random-seed generator.

Computational tasks include several metadata, such as versioning information, time stamps, domain identifiers, and computation identifiers. Individual instances of the computational tasks include instance identifiers and task identifiers, which in turn allows us to group several related computational tasks together.

### 9.3.2 Datasets and Collections

In Granules, datasets are used to simplify access to the underlying data type. Datasets currently supported within Granules include streams and files; support for databases is being incorporated. For a given data type, besides managing the allocation and reclamation of assorted resources, Granules also mediates access to it. For example, Granules performs actions related to simplifying the production and consumption of streams, reading and writing of files, and transactional access to databases.

A data collection is associated with every computational task. A data collection represents a collection of datasets, and maintains information about the type, number, and identifiers associated with every encapsulated dataset.

All that the domain specialist needs to specify is the number and type of datasets involved. The system imposes no limits on the number of datasets within a dataset collection. During initializations of the dataset collection, depending on the type of the constituent datasets, Granules subscribes to the relevant streams, configures access to files on networked file systems, and sets up connections Java Database Connectivity (JDBC) to the databases.

Dataset collections allow observers to be registered to track data availability, dataset initializations, and closure. This simplifies data processing, since it obviates the need to perform polling.

### 9.3.3 Specifying a Scheduling Strategy

Computational tasks specify a scheduling strategy, which in turn governs their lifetimes. Computational tasks can specify their scheduling strategy along three dimensions (see Figure 9.3). The *counts* axis specifies the number of times a computational task needs to be executed. The *data driven* axis specifies that the computational task needs to be scheduled for execution whenever data is available on any one of its constituent datasets. The *periodicity* axis specifies that computational tasks be periodically scheduled for execution at predefined intervals (specified in ms).

Each of these axes can extend to infinity, in which case, it constitutes a *stay-alive* primitive. A domain

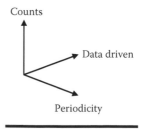

**Figure 9.3 Dimensions for scheduling strategy.**

specialist can also specify a custom scheduling strategy that permutes along these three dimensions. Thus, one can specify a scheduling strategy that limits a computational task to be executed a maximum of 500 times either when data is available or at regular intervals.

A computational task can change its scheduling strategy during execution, and Granules will enforce the newly established scheduling strategy during the next *round* of execution (Section 9.3.5). This scheduling change can be a significant one—from data driven to periodic. The scheduling change could also be a minor one with changes to the number of times the computation needs to be executed, or with an update to the periodicity interval.

In addition to the aforementioned primitives, another primitive—*stay alive until termination condition reached*—can be specified. In this case, the computational task continues to be "stay alive" until the computational task asserts that its termination condition has been reached. The termination condition overrides any other primitives that may have been specified and results in the garbage collection of the computational task.

### 9.3.4 Finite-State Machine for a Computational Task

At a given computational resource, Granules maintains a finite-state machine (FSM) for every computational task. This FSM, depicted in Figure 9.4, has four states: initialize, activated, dormant, and terminate.

The transition triggers for this FSM include external requests, elapsed time intervals, data availability, reset counters, and assertions of the termination condition being reached.

When a computational task is first received in a deployment request, Granules proceeds to initialize the computational task. The FSM created for this computational task starts off in the *initialize* state.

If, for some reason, the computational task cannot proceed in its execution, either because the datasets are not available or the start-up time has not yet elapsed, the computational task transitions into the *dormant* state. If there were problems in initialization, the computational task transitions into the *terminate* state.

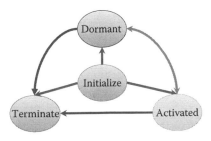

**Figure 9.4    FSM for a computational task.**

If, on the other hand, the computational task was initialized successfully, and is ready for execution with accessible datasets, it transitions into the *activated* state.

## 9.3.5 Interleaving Execution of Computational Tasks

At each computational resource, Granules maintains a pool of worker threads to manage and interleave the concurrent execution of multiple computational tasks.

When a computational task is activated and ready for execution, it is moved into the activated queue. As and when worker threads become available, the computational tasks are pulled from the first in first out (FIFO) queue and executed in a separate thread. Upon completion of the computational task, the worker thread is returned back to the thread-pool, to be used to execute other pending computational tasks within the activated queue. The computational task is placed either in the dormant queue or scheduled for garbage collection depending on the state of its FSM.

After a computational task has finished its latest (or the first) round of execution, checks are made to see if it should be terminated. To do so, the scheduling strategy associated with the computational task is retrieved. If a computational task needs to execute a fixed number of times, a check is made to see if the counter has reset. If the computational task specifies a stay-alive primitive based either on data availability or periodicity, checks are made to see if the datasets continue to be available or if the periodicity interval has elapsed. A check is also made to see if the computational task has asserted that its termination condition has been reached.

If none of these checks indicate that the computational task should be terminated, it is scheduled for another round of execution or it transitions into the dormant state. A computational task can continually toggle between the dormant and the activated state till a termination condition has been reached.

### 9.3.5.1 Sizing Thread-Pools

The number of worker threads within the thread-pool is configurable. In general, the number of threads needs to be balanced so that the accrued concurrency gains are not offset by context-switching overheads among the threads. As a general rule, it is a good idea to set this number to be approximately equal to the number of execution pipelines available on a given machine. Thus, for a quad-core CPU with two execution pipelines per core, the thread-pool will be set up to have approximately eight threads.

## 9.3.6 Diagnostics

In Granules, a user can track the status of a specific computational task or collections (job) of computational tasks. The system maintains diagnostic information about every computational task. This includes information about the number of times a computational task was scheduled for execution, its queuing overheads, its

CPU-bound time, the time it was memory-resident, and the total execution time. A computational task can also assert that diagnostic messages be sent back to the client during any (or some) of its state transitions. On the client side, an observer can be registered for collections of computational tasks to track their progress without the need to actively poll individual computational tasks.

## 9.4 Support for Map-Reduce in Granules

Map-Reduce is the dominant framework used in cloud computing settings. In Map-Reduce, a large dataset is broken up into smaller chunks that are concurrently operated upon by map function instances. The results from these map functions (usually, *<key, value>* pairs) are combined in the reducers, which collate the values for individual keys. Typically, there are multiple reducers, and the outputs from these reducers constitute the final result. This is depicted in Figure 9.5.

The Map-Reduce framework has several advantages. First, the domain scientist only needs to provide the Map-Reduce functionality and the datasets. Second, it is the responsibility of the framework to transparently scale as the number of available resources, and the problem size, increases. Finally, the orchestration of the concurrent data-parallel execution is managed by the framework.

In traditional Map-Reduce, intermediate stages exchange results using a set of *<key, value>* pairs. We have incorporated support for this basic result type. But we have also incorporated support for exchange of primitive data types, such as `int`, `short`, `boolean`, `char`, `long`, `float`, and `double`. We have also incorporated support for exchanging arrays ([]) and 2D arrays ([][]) of these primitive data types. There is also support for exchanging `Objects` that encapsulated compound data types, along with arrays and 2D arrays of these `Objects`.

The intermediate results in most Map-Reduce implementations utilize file IO for managing results produced by the intermediate stages. The framework then notifies appropriate reducers to *pull* or retrieve these results for further processing.

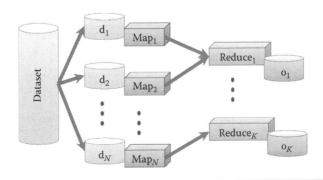

**Figure 9.5    Basic Map-Reduce framework.**

Depending on the application, the overheads introduced by performing such disk-IO can be quite high. In Granules, we use streaming to *push* these results onto appropriate reducers. Streaming, as validated by our benchmarks (described in Section 9.7), is significantly faster, and we think that there are several classes of applications that can benefit from this.

Additionally, since the results are being streamed as and when they have been computed, successive stages have access to partial results from preceding stages instead of waiting for the entire computation to complete. This is particularly useful in situations where one is interested in getting as many results as possible within a fixed amount of time.

### 9.4.1 Two Sides of the Same Coin

In Granules, map and reduce are two roles associated with the computational task. These roles inherit all the computational task functionality, while adding functionality specific to their roles.

The map role adds functionality related to adding, removing, tracking, and enumerating the reducers associated with the map function. Typically, a map function has one reducer associated with it. In Granules, we do not limit the number of reducers associated with a map function. This feature can be used to fine-tune redundancies within a computational pipeline.

The reduce role adds functionality related to adding, removing, tracking, and enumerating maps associated with it. The reducer has facilities to track output generated by the constituent maps. Specifically, a reducer can determine if partial or complete outputs have been received from the maps. The reduce role also incorporates support to detect and discard any duplicate outputs that may be received.

The map and reduce roles have facilities to create and publish results. The payloads for these results can be primitive data types that we discussed earlier, Objects encapsulating compound data types, <*key, value*> pairs, arrays, and 2D arrays of the same. In Granules, generated results include sequencing information and metadata specific to the generator. Additionally, an entity is allowed to assert if these results are partial results and/or if the processing has been completed.

Since map and reduce are two roles of the computational task in Granules, they inherit functionality related to scheduling strategy (and life-cycle management), diagnostic strategy, and dataset management.

Individual map and reduce instances toggle between the activated and dormant states (Section 9.3.5) till such time that they are ready to assert that their termination condition has been reached. For example, a reducer may assert that it has reached its termination condition only after it has received, and processed, the outputs of its constituent maps.

## 9.4.2 Setting Up Graphs

Granules supports a set of operations that allow graphs to be set up. Individual maps can add/remove reducers. Similarly, reducers are allowed to add/remove maps. The functions are functionally equivalent. Granules also allows the map and reduce roles to be *interchangeable*: a map can act as a reducer, and vice versa. Figure 9.6 depicts how support for addition/removal of roles combined with role interchangeability can be used to create a graph with a feedback loop. In our benchmarks, involving the *k-means* machine learning algorithm, we have three stages with a feedback loop from the output of stage 2 to its input. Granules manages overheads related to ensuring that the outputs from the map are routed to the correct reducers.

Additionally, Granules can create execution graphs once the numbers of map and reduce instances in a pipeline have been specified. Granules ensures the appropriate linkage of the Map-Reduce instances.

## 9.4.3 Creating Computational Pipelines

Typically, in Map-Reduce, the instances that comprise an execution pipeline are organized in a directed acyclic graph (DAG), with the execution proceeding in sequence through monotonically increasing stages.

In Granules, we have incorporated support for cycles to be present. This allows Granules to feedback the outputs of some stage, within a pipeline, to any of its preceding stages. The system places no restrictions on the span length, or the number, of the feedback in the pipeline. In a sense it can be argued that Granules supports both data- and control-flow graphs. An example of such a computational graph in Granules is depicted in Figure 9.7.

One feature of the computational task plays a role in allowing these loops: the notion of the stay-alive computation. Furthermore, since this is available at the microlevel (computational task), individual stages, collection of stages, or the

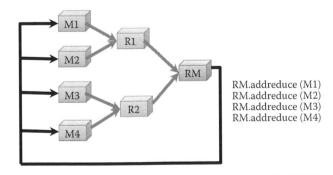

**Figure 9.6   Creating a simple feedback loop.**

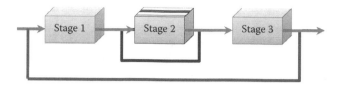

**Figure 9.7    Creating pipelines with cycles.**

computational pipeline itself can be dependent on iterative, periodic, data-driven, or termination conditions.

Granules manages the pipeline complexity. The domain scientist does not need to cope with *fan-in* complexity, which corresponds to the number of units that feed results into a given instance. Once a pipeline has been created, a domain specialist does not have to cope with IO, synchronization, or networking-related issues. The runtime includes facilities to track outputs from preceding stages.

### 9.4.4  Observing the Life Cycle of a Pipeline

At the client side, during the deployment process, Granules allows a life-cycle observer to be registered for an execution pipeline. This observer processes diagnostic messages received from different computational resources running Granules. These diagnostic messages relate to state transitions associated with the different computational task instances (and the map and reduce roles) and the pertinent metrics associated with the computation task. The life-cycle observer reports to the client upon completion of an execution pipeline. The observer also reports errors in the execution of any of the units that comprise the pipeline.

## 9.5  Developing and Deploying Applications Using Granules

In this section, we describe the process of developing and deploying applications using Granules. In both cases, Granules incorporates support for utility classes, whose behavior may be extended to suit specific needs.

### 9.5.1  Developing Applications

Granules simplifies the process of developing applications. Developers simply extend the MapReduceBase class. This class implements functionality that encompasses both the map and reduce roles of a computation. One requirement is that the derived class has exactly one constructor, which does not take any arguments. Developers of the derived class only need to implement the `execute()`

method. Typical steps involved in implementing this method include initialization of the datasets and data structures, processing logic, and specification of a scheduling strategy.

### 9.5.1.1 Initialization

Typically, depending on the type of the dataset, initialization of the datasets involved in the processing is performed automatically. The designer simply specifies the identifiers for the dataset. Initializations of the data structures needed by the computation can be performed either in the *null* constructor or in the execute() method. In the latter case, care must be taken to ensure that the initializations are performed only once across successive invocations of the execute() method.

### 9.5.1.2 Processing Logic

The processing logic within the execute() method is domain specific. This processing would involve either the generation of results, or the management and collation of previously produced results. In the reduce role, it is also possible to check if outputs have been received from all the preceding maps in addition to discarding any duplicate results that were generated.

The generation of results is easy, and the system allows entities to attach different payloads to these results. The system currently allows for the payloads for these results to be *<key, value>* pairs, where the elements of these tuples could be objects that encapsulate compound data types. The system allows instances, arrays([]), and 2D arrays ([][]) of primitive data types such as int, short, long, double, float, and char to be attached as payloads of these results. The system handles the marshaling and un-marshaling of these payloads automatically.

The processing logic also needs to cope with exceptions that will be thrown as results of the processing. These exceptions could result from problems with the datasets, marshaling issues, and networking problems.

### 9.5.1.3 Scheduling Strategy

A computational task can change its scheduling strategy during execution. This change is reflected during the next iteration of the execute() method. The system enforces the newly created scheduling strategy as soon as the current iteration of the execute() method terminates. Computational tasks that have specified a scheduling strategy that constitutes either a stay-alive primitive, or implies a certain number of iterations, can assert that their termination condition has been reached. At this time, the computational task is scheduled for garbage collection as soon as control returns from the execute() method.

## 9.5.2 Deploying Applications Using Granules

Granules provides a helper class, the InstanceDeployer, to enable applications, and the computational tasks that comprise it, to be deployed on a set of resources. This class performs several operations related to initializing communications, resource discovery, and deployment of computations. It is recommended that a deployer be created for each application. This can be done by simply extending the InstanceDeployer.

### 9.5.2.1 Initializing Communications and Resource Discovery

The first step that an application deployer needs to perform is to initialize communications with the content distribution network (NaradaBrokering). This can be performed by invoking the constructor for the base class (InstanceDeployer), which takes a set of properties as its argument. This is typically done by invoking the super(streamingProperties) in the derived class's constructor. Some of the elements that are typically part of this set of properties include the hostname, the port, and the transport type for one of the router nodes within the content dissemination network. Depending on the transport over which communications take place, there would be additional elements that may need to be specified. For example, if the Secure Sockets Layer (SSL) communications are used, additional elements that need to be specified include the locations of the *truststore* and the *keystore* that would be used for secure communications.

Once communications have been established, Granules automatically discovers resources that are currently available. This list could be periodically refreshed should the need arise.

### 9.5.2.2 Initializing and Deploying Computational Tasks

The developer then needs to provide a method that initializes the computational tasks. This involves one or more of the following:

1. *Initializing the Processing Directives associated with an instance*: These directives are used to encode instance-specific information that is accessible only to the instance in question.
2. *Specification of the datasets and collection associated with the computation*: Granules is responsible for configuring access to these datasets.
3. *Linking of the Map-Reduce roles*: Granules ensures that once-linked results produced by the maps are automatically routed to the appropriate reducers.
4. *Specifying the scheduling strategy for the computational tasks*: By default, the exactly-once scheduling strategy is used.
5. *Distribution of datasets across these instances*: Granules incorporates utilities that allow this distribution to be performed efficiently.

To deploy an application, the developer only needs to invoke the `deploy()` method in the InstanceDeployer. This method deploys the computational tasks on the set of resources that were discovered during the initialization phase.

### 9.5.2.3 Tracking/Steering a Deployed Application

The InstanceDeployer implements the JobLifecycleObserver interface, which allows one to track the status of multiple jobs, and the computational tasks that comprise them. Classes that extend the InstanceDeployer have the option to override methods specific to the JobLifecycleObserver interface. Specifically, for a given Job, Granules maintains its registered JobLifecycleObserver and invokes methods on this observer whenever there is an update to the deployment or execution status of the computational tasks that comprise it.

Associated with each Job, Granules maintains a ProgressTracker that maintains information about the execution state of each of the computational tasks that comprise the application. The LifecycleMetrics associated with every computational task includes information about

1. The arrival time for the computational task
2. The queuing overhead for the computational task
3. The total CPU-bound time for the computational task across multiple iterations (if there are any)
4. The processing time for the computational task
5. The current status of the computational task {Awaiting Data, Queued for Execution, Executing, Terminated, Successful, FAILED}

The status of a Job is the cumulative status of the computational tasks that comprise it.

The InstanceDeployer also incorporates methods for tracking/steering a computation. There are methods to refresh the status of a specific computational task or the entire Job. These methods result in updates to the life-cycle metrics of the relevant computational tasks. Additionally, Granules also allows computational tasks to be aborted when they are in execution. The system allows either a specific computational task to be suspended or the entire Job.

## 9.6 Related Work

The original Map-Reduce paper [1] by Ghemawat and Dean described how their programming abstraction was being used in the Google search engine and other data-intensive applications. This work was itself inspired by *map* and *reduce* primitives present in Lisp and other functional programming languages. Google Map-Reduce is written in C++ with extensions for Java and Python. Sawzall [7] is an interpreted, procedural programming language used by Google to develop Map-Reduce applications.

Hadoop [8] was originally developed at Yahoo, and is now an Apache project. It is by far the most widely used implementation of the Map-Reduce framework. In addition to the vast number of applications at Yahoo, it is also part of the Google/IBM initiative to support university courses in distributed computing. Hadoop is also hosted as a framework over Amazon's EC2 [9] cloud. Unlike Granules, Hadoop supports only exactly-once semantics, meaning that there is direct support within the framework for map and reduce functions to maintain state.

Hadoop uses the Hadoop Distributed File System (HDFS) files for communicating intermediate results between the map and reduce functions, while Granules uses streaming for these disseminations, thus allowing access to partial results.

HDFS allows for replicated, robust access to files. During the data-staging phase, Hadoop allows the creation of replicas on the local file system; computations are then spawned to exploit data locality. Hadoop supports automated recovery from failures. Currently, Granules does not incorporate support for automated recovery from failures; this will be the focus of our future work in this area. Here, we plan to harness the reliable streaming capabilities available in NaradaBrokering.

The most dominant model for developing parallel applications in the high performance computing (HPC) community is the SPMD [2] model (first proposed by Federica Darema) in tandem with the MPI [10] library. The SPMD model is a powerful one, and Map-Reduce can in fact be thought of as an instance of the SPMD model. The use of MPI has, however, not been as widespread outside the scientific community.

Microsoft Research's Dryad [11] is a system designed as a programming model for developing scalable parallel and distributed applications. Dryad is based on DAGs. In this model, sequential programs are connected using one-way channels. It is intended to be a super-set of the core Map-Reduce framework. Dryad provides job management and autonomic capabilities, and makes use of the Microsoft Shared Directory Service. However, since Dryad is developed based on DAGs, it is not possible to develop systems that have cycles in them. For example, in our benchmarks, we were not able to implement the *k-means* machine learning algorithm [12] using the basic Dryad framework.

Phoenix [13] is an implementation of Map-Reduce for multi-core and multiprocessor systems. A related effort is Qt Concurrent [14], which provides a simplified implementation of the Map-Reduce framework in C++. Qt Concurrent automatically optimizes thread utilizations on multi-core machines depending on core availability. Disco [15], from Nokia, is an open-source Map-Reduce runtime developed using the Erlang functional programming language. Similar to the Hadoop architecture, Disco stores the intermediate results in local files and accesses them using HTTP connections from the appropriate reduce tasks.

Holumbus [16] includes an implementation of the Map-Reduce framework, developed in the Haskell functional programming language at the FH Wedel University of Applied Sciences, Germany.

Skynet [17] is an open-source Ruby-based implementation of the Map-Reduce framework. Skynet utilizes a peer-recovery system for tracking the constituent tasks. Peers track each other and, once failure is detected, can spawn a replica of the failed peer.

We had originally developed a prototype implementation of Map-Reduce, CGL-MapReduce [18], which implemented Map-Reduce using streaming (once again, using NaradaBrokering) with the ability to "keep alive" map instances. Granules represents an overhaul, and incorporates several new capabilities, such as built-in support for sophisticated life-cycle management (periodicity, data driven, and termination conditions), powerful creation and duplicate detection of results, and diagnostics in addition to the ability to create complex computational pipelines with feedback loops in multiple stages. The code base for the Granules (available for download) runtime has also been developed from scratch.

## 9.7 Benchmarks

In our benchmarks, we profile several aspects of the Granules' performance. We are specifically interested in determining system performance for different life cycles associated with the computational tasks. The different life cycles we benchmark include exactly-once, iterative, periodic, and data-driven primitives. Where possible, we contrast the performance of Granules with comparable systems, such as Hadoop, Dryad, and MPI. It is expected that these benchmarks would be indicative of the performance that can be expected in different deployments.

All machines involved in these benchmarks have four dual-core CPUs, a 2.4 GHz clock, and an 8 GB RAM. These machines were hosted on a 100 Mbps LAN. The Operating System on these machines is Red Hat Enterprise Linux version 4. All Java processes executed within version 1.6 of Sun's Java Virtual Machine (JVM). We used version 3.4.6 of the gcc complier for C++, and for MPI we used version 7.1.4 of the Local Area Multicomputer (LAM) MPI [19].

### 9.7.1 Streaming Substrate

Since we use the NaradaBrokering streaming substrate for all communications between entities, we present a simple benchmark to give the reader an idea of the costs involved in streaming. Our results outline the communication latencies in a simplified setting involving one producer, one consumer, and one broker. The communication latencies are reported for stream fragments with different payload sizes. Additional NaradaBrokering benchmarks in distributed settings can be found in [4,5].

Two cluster machines were involved in this benchmark. The producer and consumer were hosted on the same machine to obviate the need to account for clock

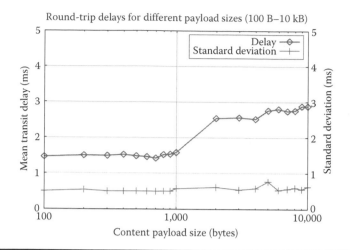

**Figure 9.8 Streaming overheads in cluster settings.**

drifts while measuring latencies for streams issued by the producer, and routed by the broker (hosted on the second machine) to the consumer.

The reported delay, in the results depicted in Figure 9.8, is the average of 50 samples for a given payload size, the standard deviation for these samples also being reported. The $Y$-axis for the standard deviation is the axis on the right side (blue) of the graph. Streaming latencies vary from 750 µs/hop for 100 bytes to 1.5 ms/hop for a stream fragment of 10 kB in cluster settings.

## 9.7.2 Information Retrieval: Exactly-Once

In this section, we present results from a simple information retrieval example. Given a set of text files, the objective is to histogram the counts associated with various words in these files. The performance of Granules is contrasted with that of Hadoop and Dryad. The Dryad version to which we have access uses C#, LINQ, and file-based communications using the Microsoft Shared Directory Service. The OS involved in the Dryad benchmarks is Windows XP.

For this benchmark, we vary the cumulative size of the datasets that need to be processed. The total amount of data that is processed is varied from 20 GB to 100 GB. There were a total of 128 map instances that were deployed on the five machines involved in the benchmark.

The results depicted in Figure 9.9 demonstrate the benefits of using streaming as opposed to file-based communications. As the size of the datasets increases, there is a concomitant increase in the number and size of the intermediate results (file based). This contributes to the slower performance of Hadoop and Dryad. We expect the performance of Dryad's socket-based version to be faster than their file-based version.

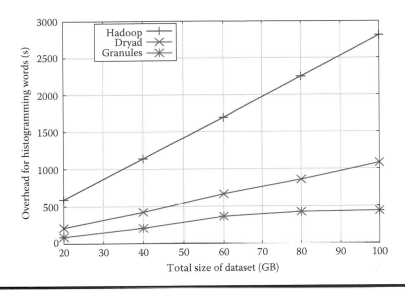

**Figure 9.9** **Processing time for histogramming words.**

## 9.7.3 k-Means: Iterative

Machine learning provides a fertile ground for iterative algorithms. In our benchmarks, we considered a simple algorithm in the area of unsupervised machine learning: *k-means*. Given a set of $n$ data points, the objective is to organize these points into $k$ clusters.

The algorithm starts off by selecting $k$ centroids, and then associates different data points within the dataset to one of the clusters based on their proximity to the centroids. For each of the clusters, new centroids are then computed. The algorithm is said to converge when the cumulative Euclidean distance between the centroids in successive iterations is less than a predefined threshold.

In *k-means*, the number of iterations depends on the initial choice of the centroids, the number of data points, and the specified error rate (signifying that the centroid movements are acceptable). The initial set of data points is loaded at each of the map functions. Each map is responsible for processing a portion of the entire dataset. What changes from iteration to iteration are the centroids. The output of each map function is a set of centroids.

The benchmarks, which were run on five machines, also contrast the performance of Granules with MPI using a C++ implementation of the *k-means* algorithm.

The graphs depicted in Figure 9.10 have been plotted on a log-log graph so that the trends can be visualized a little better. We varied the number of data points in the dataset from $10^5$ to $4 \times 10^7$. The results indicate that Hadoop's performance is orders of magnitude slower than Granules and MPI. In Hadoop,

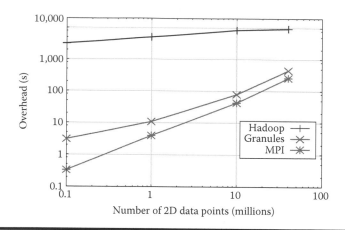

**Figure 9.10**   **Performance of the *k-means* algorithm.**

these centroids are transferred using files, while Granules uses streaming. Furthermore, since Hadoop does not support iterative semantics, map functions need to be initialized and the datasets need to be reloaded using HDFS. Though these file-system reads are being performed locally (thanks to HDFS and data collocation), these costs can still be prohibitive, as evidenced in our benchmarks. Additionally, as the size of the dataset increases, the performances of the MPI/C++ implementation of *k-means* and the Granules/Java implementation of *k-means* start to converge.

## 9.7.4  Periodic Scheduling

In this section, we benchmark the ability of Granules to periodically schedule tasks for execution. For this particular benchmark, we initialized 10,000 map functions that needed to be scheduled for execution every 4 s.

The objective of this benchmark is to show that a single Granules instance can indeed enforce periodicity for a reasonable number of map instances.

Figure 9.11 depicts the results of periodic executions of 10,000 maps for 17 iterations. The graph depicts the spacing in the times at which these maps are scheduled for execution. The $X$-axis represents a specific map instance (assigned IDs from 1 to 10,000), and the $Y$-axis represents the spacing between the times at which a given instance was scheduled. Each map instance reports 17 values.

The first time a computational task is scheduled for execution, a base time, $t_b$, is recorded. Subsequent iterations report the difference between the base time, $t_b$, and the current time, $t_c$. In almost all cases, the spacing between the successive executions for any given instance was between 3.9 and 4.1 s. In some cases, there is a small notch; this reflects cases where the first execution was delayed by a small

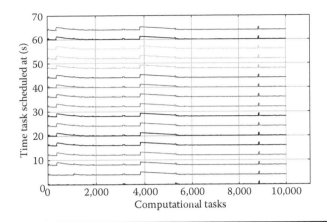

**Figure 9.11  Periodic scheduling of 10,000 computational tasks.**

amount, the (constant) impact of which is reflected in subsequent iterations for that map instance.

## 9.7.5 Data Driven

In this section, we describe the performance of matrix multiplication using Granules. In this case, the object is to measure the product of two dense $16,000 \times 16,000$ matrices, that is, each matrix has 256 million elements with predominantly non-zero values.

The matrix multiplication example demonstrates how computational tasks can be "stay alive," and be scheduled for execution when data is available. The maps are scheduled for execution as and when the data is available for the computations to proceed.

For this benchmark, we vary the number of machines involved in the experiment from 1 to 8. There are a total of 16,000 map instances. At a given time, each of these maps processes portions of the rows and columns that comprise the matrix. Each Granules instance copes with a fragment of more than 2000 concurrent streams. In total, every Granules instance copes with 32,000 distinct streams.

The results for the processing times (plotted on a log-log scale) can be seen in Figure 9.12. In general, as the number of available machines increases, there is a proportional improvement in the processing time. Our plots of the speed-up (Figure 9.13) in processing times with the availability of additional machines reflect this.

In general, these graphs demonstrate that Granules can bring substantial benefits to data-driven applications by amortizing the computational load on a set of machines. Domain scientists do not need to write a single line of networking code; Granules manages this in a transparent fashion for the applications.

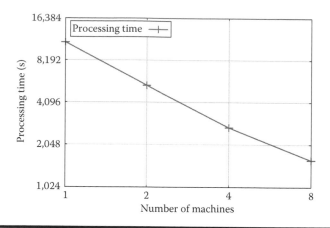

**Figure 9.12    Processing time for matrix multiplication on different machines.**

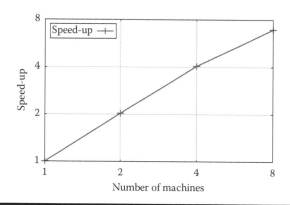

**Figure 9.13    Speed-up for matrix multiplication.**

## 9.7.6 Assembling mRNA Sequences

This section describes the performance of Granules in orchestrating the execution of applications developed in languages other than Java. The application we consider is the CAP3 [20] messenger Ribonucleic acid (mRNA) sequence assembly application (C++) developed at Michigan Tech.

An Expressed Sequence Tag (EST) corresponds to mRNAs transcribed from genes residing on chromosomes, individual EST sequences represent a fragment of mRNA. CAP3 allows us to perform EST assembly to reconstruct full-length mRNA sequences for each expressed gene.

Our objective as part of this benchmark was also to see how Granules can be used to maximize core utilizations on a machine. CAP3 takes as input a set of files. In our benchmark, we need to process 256 files during the assembly.

On a given machine, we fine-tuned the concurrency by setting the number of worker threads within the thread-pool to different values. By restricting the number of threads, we also restricted the amount of concurrency and the underlying core utilizations. We started off by setting the worker-pool size to 1, 2, 4, and 8 on 1 machine, and then used 8 worker threads on 2, 4, and 8 machines. This allowed us to report results for 1, 2, 4, 8, 16, 32, and 64 cores.

The results of our benchmark in terms of processing costs and the speed-ups achieved are depicted in Figures 9.14 and 9.15, respectively. In general, as the number of available cores increases, there is a corresponding improvement in execution times.

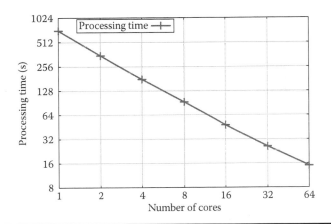

**Figure 9.14   Processing time for EST assembly on different cores using Granules and CAP3.**

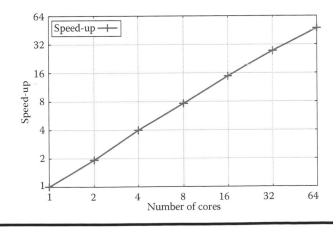

**Figure 9.15   Speed-up for EST assembly using Granules and CAP3.**

The results demonstrate that, when configured correctly, Granules can maximize core utilizations on a given machine. The graphs plotted on a log-log scale indicate that for every doubling of the available cores, the processing time for assembling the mRNA sequences reduces by half (approximately). The Granules runtime reads the thread-pool sizing information from a configuration file; we will be investigating mechanisms that will allow us to dynamically size these thread-pools.

## 9.8 Conclusions

In this chapter, we described the Granules runtime. Rich life-cycle support within Granules allows computations to retain state, which in turn is particularly applicable for several classes for scientific applications.

Granules allows complex computational graphs to be created. As discussed, these graphs can encapsulate both control flow and data flow. Granules enforces the semantics of complex distributed computational graphs that have one or more feedback loops. The domain scientist does not have to cope with IO, threading, synchronization, or networking libraries while developing applications that span multiple stages, with multiple distributed instances comprising each stage. These computational pipelines can be dependent on iterative, periodic, data-driven, or termination conditions.

Demonstrable performance benefits have been accrued by Granules as a result of using streaming for disseminating intermediate results.

Granules' rich life-cycle support, and its performance when contrasted with comparable systems, underscores the feasibility of using Granules in several settings. As part of our future work, we will be investigating support for autonomic error detection and recovery within Granules.

## References

1. J. Dean and S. Ghemawat, Mapreduce: Simplified data processing on large clusters, *Communications of the ACM*, 51, 107–113, January 2008.
2. F. Darema, SPMD model: Past, present and future, *Recent Advances in Parallel Virtual Machine and Message Passing Interface: Eighth European PVM/MPI Users' Group Meeting*, Santorini/Thera, Greece, 2001.
3. S. Pallickara, J. Ekanayake, and G. Fox, An overview of the granules runtime for cloud computing (Short Paper), *Proceedings of the IEEE International Conference on e-Science*, Indianapolis, IN, 2008.
4. S. Pallickara and G. Fox, Naradabrokering: A middleware framework and architecture for enabling durable peer-to-peer grids, *Proceedings of the ACM/IFIP/USENIX International Middleware Conference Middleware-2003*, Rio de Janeiro, Brazil, 2003, pp. 41–61.

5. S. Pallickara et al., A framework for secure end-to-end delivery of messages in publish/subscribe systems, *Proceedings of the Seventh IEEE/ACM International Conference on Grid Computing (GRID 2006)*, Barcelona, Spain, 2006.

6. S. Pallickara, H. Bulut, and G. Fox, Fault-tolerant reliable delivery of messages in distributed publish/subscribe systems, *Fourth IEEE International Conference on Autonomic Computing*, Jacksonville, FL, June 2007, p. 19.

7. R. Pike, S. Dorward, R. Griesemer, and S. Quinlan, Interpreting the data: Parallel analysis with Sawzall, *Scientific Programming Journal*, Special Issue on Grids and Worldwide Computing Programming Models and Infrastructure, 13(4), 227–298, 2005.

8. Apache Hadoop, http://hadoop.apache.org/core/

9. S. Garfinkel, An evaluation of amazon's grid computing services: EC2, S3 and SQS, Technical Report TR-08-07, Harvard University, Cambridge, MA, August 2007.

10. Message Passing Interface Forum, MPI: A message passing interface, *Proceedings of Supercomputing'93*, Portland, OR, IEEE Computer Society Press, Washington, DC, November 1993, pp. 878–883.

11. M. Isard, M. Budiu, Y. Yu, A. Birrell, and D. Fetterly, Dryad: Distributed data-parallel programs from sequential building blocks, *European Conference on Computer Systems*, Lisbon, Portugal, March 2007.

12. J. B. MacQueen, Some methods for classification and analysis of multivariate observations, *Proceedings of Fifth Berkeley Symposium on Mathematical Statistics and Probability*, Vol. 1, Berkeley, CA, University of California Press, Berkeley, CA, 1967, pp. 281–297.

13. C. Ranger, R. Raghuraman, A. Penmetsa, G. R. Bradski, and C. Kozyrakis, Evaluating mapreduce for multi-core and multiprocessor systems, *Proceedings of the International Symposium on High-Performance Computer Architecture (HPCA)*, Phoenix, AZ, 2007, pp. 13–24.

14. Qt Concurrent, Simplified mapreduce in C++ with support for multicores, April 2009, http://labs.trolltech.com/page/Projects/ Threads/ QtConcurrent

15. Disco project, http://discoproject.org/

16. S. Schlatt, T. Hübel, S. Schmidt, and U. Schmidt, The Holumbus distributed computing framework and mapreduce in Haskell, 2009, http://holumbus.fh-wedel.de/trac

17. A. Pisoni, Skynet: A ruby mapreduce framework, April 2009, http://skynet.rubyforge.org/

18. J. Ekanayake, S. Pallickara, and G. Fox, Map-reduce for scientific applications, *Proceedings of the IEEE International Conference on e-Science*, Indianapolis, IN, 2008.

19. J. M. Squyres and A. Lumsdaine, A component architecture for LAM/MPI, *Proceedings of Euro PVM/MPI*, Venice, Itlay, October 2003.

20. X. Huang and A. Madan, CAP3: A DNA sequence assembly program, *Genome Research*, 9, 868–877, 1999.

21. S. Pallickara, J. Ekanayake, and G. Fox, Granules: A lightweight, streaming runtime for cloud computing with support for map-reduce, *Proceedings of the IEEE International Conference on Cluster Computing (CLUSTER 2009)*, New Orleans, LA, 2009.

# Chapter 10

# Dynamic and Adaptive Rule-Based Workflow Engine for Scientific Problems in Distributed Environments

Marc Frincu and Ciprian Craciun

## Contents

## 10.1 Introduction

Currently, there is a great tendency toward creating and implementing new Distributed System paradigms, such as Grid and Cloud Computing, which allow users to both store data and execute applications in a distributed environment without having to be concerned about resource and computational restrictions provided by their personal computers. More and more business and scientific applications rely on the use of Distributed Systems to solve complex tasks in a completely transparent manner so that users would not have to be concerned about where the data is stored or the application is being executed, but instead be focused on the result of the desired job. Together with the occurrence of specific user requirements that need a Distributed System to be solved, there have also appeared applications that need to be solved in a finite number of steps and in certain periods of time. These applications usually consist of several tasks linked together by a workflow that can have at least one entry and exit point.

We should note that workflows have been extensively used in business applications as well as science for solving specific problems. There is a consistent branch of computer science that deals with the subject of business applications by providing businessmen with tools that allow them to focus on modeling and supervising business activities rather than on actual implementation or execution. In what concerns the current chapter, we will deal only with scientific workflows, although the ideas presented here can be applied without major modifications for the business case. On the other hand, scientific workflows arise from various fields, such as applied mathematics, physics, chemistry, biology, geography, or history, which use complex problems that require breaking them into atomic tasks that can be later independently executed. In order to obtain a greater efficiency, these tasks can be executed inside a Distributed System transparent from the user point of view and orchestrated by using either a centralized or a distributed approach. During the workflow's execution, the user would be unaware of the places where tasks are being executed and of the internal logic driving the process. The main interest of the user would be the result itself, which would be sent back after the workflow's execution has ended. This way of solving problems is similar to the one followed by Grid and, more recently, Cloud Computing.

The enactment of scientific workflows requires complex coordination between workflow activities and entities belonging to the Grid or Cloud. Aspects regarding the coordination usually include large amounts of required computation and data storage elements, services, data discovery and selection mechanisms, control and data dependency handling, preparing activities for execution, failure handlers, etc.

As for this Chapter, the difference between Grid and Cloud Computing with regard to the way a workflow is executed is that of concept: Both Grids and Clouds are viewed as resource pools offering services for certain jobs. Among the disadvantages that Grids may have over Clouds, we can enumerate issues related to licensing, legal or political issues, lack of virtualization support, complex architectures, tools and technologies, etc. However, Grids have also managed to offer easy access to their resources in the form of state-full Grid Services, which allow users to submit jobs without having to know any details on the underlying platform. Also Grid Services permit users to later query the result of their computation and offer digital certificates as security mechanisms. In addition, Clouds offer virtualization, and thus they are capable of running multiple virtual machines on the same resource. For the scientific domain, this can be seen as an advantage by running solutions that require different platforms on the same physical machine.

Distributed Systems are dynamic in nature and consequently susceptible both to network and resource failures as well as to changes in their workload. Therefore, a workflow orchestration engine needs to be able to adapt to this unpredictable behavior. Furthermore, workflows must allow dynamic evolution during runtime in case the workflow definitions have been modified. These definitions could concern changes in task dependencies or description, or changes in the method a task should be solved and could occur naturally in any workflow due to task migration, synchronization, occurrences of augmented solution providers, etc. All these issues need to be dealt with automatically because a manual approach or workflow abortion could prove to be inefficient due to various reasons, such as workflow length and complexity. Automation is also a necessity owing to the fact that the execution happens inside a *cloud* where the user has no control over what happens. Moreover, safe nets in the form of logs, warnings, or errors with the aim of notifying the user of possible wrong results need to be offered. Faulty responses could result from a wrong execution path resulted from improper service selection.

The rest of this chapter will address all these issues by starting with a short introduction in workflow modeling, decomposition, and task semantics. Then a brief overview on present workflow issues and solutions will be addressed followed by the description of a simple workflow formalism intended for self-adaptation and auto-generation. In this direction, some examples of scientific workflows will be given. Finally, several general conclusions will be drawn. The workflows will be placed in a Distributed System context, and where necessary, issues and examples will be explained.

## 10.2 Workflow Modeling

Before addressing service-oriented workflow-related issues, we first need to define what re-searchers understand by workflows, how they help us in describing executable solutions to particular problems, and how they resemble to or diverge from classic approaches such as logic schemes or textual algorithms. These will be introduced by using either generic or concrete examples. An important aspect we need to bear in mind before proceeding is that workflows operate at higher levels and do not get into low-level details (unlike arithmetic operations and file IO).

When solving a particular problem, one of the first steps, as far as basic software engineering is concerned, is to decompose the workflow into smaller problems until we reach a point where there are immediate solutions for each existing subproblem. As a consequence, we obtain a *tree* where each node is a problem to be solved, its direct children are subproblems, and the leaves of the tree are problems with immediate or basic solutions. We can assert that in fact each node represents not only a problem to be solved but also the method by which we aggregate the sub-solutions of the subproblems. Thus, by walking the tree downward (from the root) we obtain the decomposition, whereas by walking the tree upward (from the leaves) we obtain the actual computations that have to be done. What we have seen so far is yet only an instantiation of a more generic problem that has roughly the same solving method but differs only in the actual manipulated values. Therefore, we modify our tree by replacing values with symbolic parameters. As previously mentioned, decomposition needs to be stopped when a certain level of granularity has been reached and the identified subproblems have already known solutions (the histogram equalization in case of image processing, sparse matrix multiplication for mathematical problems, etc.).

Single nodes can be treated as *procedures*, namely, as a single unit of work or a program that efficiently solves the well-defined corresponding subproblem. Such a procedure has an output represented by the solution of the problem, and some inputs consisting of the direct parameters of the subproblem, which are received when invoked.

The procedure itself is stripped of any decomposition responsibility, and its unique purpose is to combine the inputs representing both rightful parameters and solutions of subproblems into desired outputs. As an example (see Figure 10.1), we could consider (although it breaks the granularity rule stated above) computing the Least Common Multiple (LCM) of two numbers, (A and B). To solve this, we have chosen to divide the product of these two numbers by their Greatest Common Divisor (GCD). In order to accomplish it, we have two nodes (procedures), one for computing the LCM having as inputs A, B, and GCD, and one for computing the GCD that receives as inputs A and B. From the previous example, we can see that the real parameters for both procedures are A and B, and that the input GCD for the LCM node is in fact the solution of the GCD subproblem.

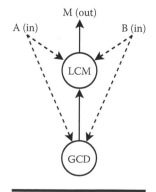

**Figure 10.1   LCM solution tree.**

With more complicated problems, we can clearly notice that by leaving the actual solving method for subproblems outside the procedure itself, we enhance flexibility by allowing the workflow engine to select a method that best matches the particular inputs. In the light of our example, the focus of the solution tree is hence shifting from its nodes to its edges, away from the procedures and toward the data flow between these procedures. Furthermore, we can state that workflows mainly act as glue-code, which binds together applications into complete working meta-applications.

The comparison with the solution tree is incomplete and too particular because we could imagine a situation in which two tasks have a common dependency, as in the case of the Fibonacci recursive function or the Normalized Differential Vegetation Index (NDVI). In this case, modeling the workflow as a tree could lead us to repeat the same calculations twice, which is inefficient in terms of computing resources. In contrast, if nodes were allowed to share subproblem outputs, our problem would be solved and we would be offered a Directed Acyclic Graph (DAG) permitting data reuse. Figures 10.2 and 10.3 give a graphical illustration of the NDVI computation when using both a tree and a graph model. The details of these computations will be described in Section 10.4.

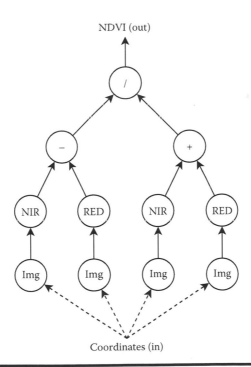

**Figure 10.2   NDVI solution tree.**

Another problem that arises from the previous tree model is that it allows only for one output for each task, Which is not always true for real-life problems. As a simple example, we could, take the integer division of two numbers that has two valid and useful outputs: the quotient and the reminder. In contrast, if we allow only one output for each task we will end up with two tasks, one for the division and one for the reminder, both of them sharing almost the same code and thus leading to execution overhead. Another example could be the split of a color image into its RGB layers. As a consequence, a natural extension to our initial tree model would be to allow a task to return multiple values, and therefore certain parts of the output could be used as inputs in some tasks while others for other tasks. By applying this modification, we also obtain a DAG.

As a remark, we can safely state that the building blocks of workflows are the procedures (the nodes), also called tasks, and the data flow dependencies between them (the edges in our tree). Additionally, we can assume that workflows are deterministic, meaning that for the same inputs we always obtain the same outputs. Also it seems that the natural way of expressing workflows is by modeling them as DAGs, since they not only provide a valuable simplicity in expressing them but also might enhance the overall efficiency of the resulting system.

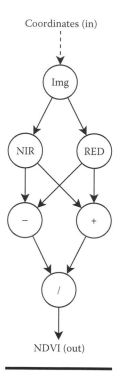

**Figure 10.3 NDVI simplified solution as a DAG.**

## 10.2.1 Workflow Decomposition

In what follows, we will deal with task-dependency-related aspects; explain the most basic workflow *decomposition constructs* as sequence, split, and join; and add to them other special-purpose constructs as decisions and loops. Also we disregard the fact that an edge between two nodes represents the data flow between the output of one and the input of the other, and will treat them as simple execution dependencies. The reason for this assumption is because many workflow engines treat the edges as explicit execution precedence and obtain the data dependency only as a consequence to it. Besides, it is obvious that from such a perspective, variables are indispensable and almost the only means through which tasks can communicate.

A brief overview on the most used constructs is given below.

The *sequence* construct (see Figure 10.4) is similar to the construct from logic schemes meaning that tasks are executed one at a time, starting the next only after the previous one has ended. This construct could come from the fact that the output of the previous task is the input of the next task.

The *split* construct (see Figure 10.5) introduces parallelism into workflows and allows tasks to be executed concurrently. It could be compared with spawning new threads, each of them solving an independent problem.

The *join* construct (see Figure 10.6) represents the end of a split construct and allows parallel paths to join, thus providing a synchronization mechanism. We must note that there is no need for a one-to-one mapping between splits and joins.

The *conditional* construct (see Figure 10.7) must also be added to the list as it is required when decision-making scenarios occur. It can have many flavors ranging from a mere if-condition-else form to a multi-condition construct (similar to the switch case in programming languages), with one sub-workflow for each condition and an additional default one.

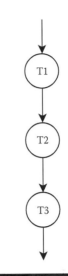

**Figure 10.4  Sequence construct for workflow decomposition.**

Additionally, there are cases when we have to extend the model by including iterative constructs. Such an example is the while-like construct, which takes a condition and a sub-workflow and executes it until the condition is satisfied. Such cases are typical for workflows that contain tasks that are nondeterministic or have side effects. Most implementations try to avoid such situations, and DAG-oriented workflow engines do not support them because they imply a loop.

Although none of the existing workflow engines implicitly support *Map-Reduce* (Dean and Ghemawat, 2004) patterns (see Figure 10.8), they are often used especially in Cloud/Grid Computing due to their capability to express scalability. In what follows, we make an adaptation for workflows as the original design described in the cited paper used a *master* process

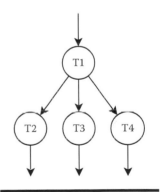

**Figure 10.5  Split construct for workflow decomposition.**

that had to oversee the entire progress, and thus played the role of a simplified orchestration workflow engine. There are normally three basic steps to a Map-Reduce pattern: fan, map, and reduce. First the *fanning* process has the purpose to take one big chunk of data and split it into smaller pieces. It does not appear in the original paper as this resposability was built into the map phase and coordinated by the master process. Then the *mapping* process takes each small piece and applies the needed processing independently and in parallel with the other pieces. Finally, the *reduce* process takes a range of processed data and aggregates them. Considering the NDVI example, we can imagine splitting (fanning) the area into smaller areas in case of large images, computing the NDVI individually (map) for each area, and ultimately putting the puzzle back together into a larger image for the initial bigger area (reduce).

Finally, we can mention trivial constructs, such as task invocation, variable assignment, and basic data manipulation (needed for minor adaptation of mismatching outputs and inputs), which can also be used but are not always part of a workflow language like the basic decomposition constructs.

Workflow languages relying on the previously mentioned constructs need to explicitly express parallelism. This approach has two major shortcomings: first, the user (developer) has to proactively think about the parallelism; second, the engine has almost no liberty to find concurrency (other than explicitly expressed), thus reducing the overall efficiency. As it will be seen later in this chapter, the only workflows that overcome these issues are those based on execution rules following an Event-Condition-Action (ECA) paradigm.

After having explained the basic workflow constructs, we can now further define a *well-formed workflow* from a decomposition perspective. A well-defined workflow is either one identifying with a single task, an instantiation of a single workflow decomposition construct, or any finite combination of the decomposition constructs.

A consequence to the previous definition is that the notions of task and workflow are interchangeable, and in what concerns the rest of the chapter, they can be safely swapped.

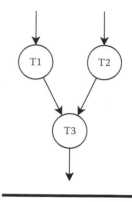

**Figure 10.6 Join construct for workflow decomposition.**

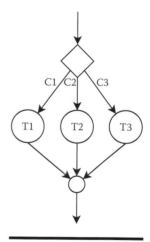

**Figure 10.7 Conditional construct for workflow decomposition.**

## 10.2.2 Task Implementation Model

Workflows can be regarded from two perspectives: the way they are implemented and their semantic aspects In what follows, we have tried to give a small introduction on both topics, starting with implementation and concluding with the semantic part.

When speaking about workflow implementations, we are mainly referring to different frameworks and platforms that provide developers with a common working base in order to implement and use the tasks. The main differences between these platforms are the way in which tasks are implemented and how they obtain

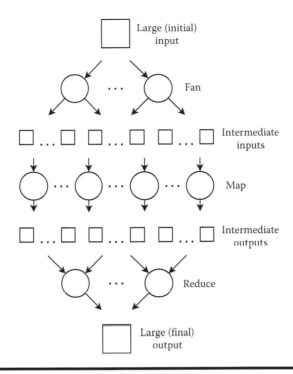

Large (initial) input

Fan

Intermediate inputs

Map

Intermediate outputs

Reduce

Large (final) output

**Figure 10.8    Map-Reduce workflow pattern.**

their inputs and give outputs. More precisely, we can speak either of *process-based* or *service-based* workflows. These two approaches also show how workflows have evolved from chaining offline applications to wrapping applications as services and providing an online interface.

*Process-oriented workflows* have advanced from a mechanism of controlling operating-system processes. Probably the simplest workflow languages may be considered to be shell-scripting languages (like Bash) and make-like tools. The former allows sequential and conditional process chaining, while the latter provides a descriptive rule-like language that even offers automatic parallelism detection. As for the purpose of workflow management, these examples can however be considered rudimentary, since more advanced systems are needed. Nevertheless, all process-based solutions have in common the basic working principles: assuming a list of arbitrary command-line applications with each application provided with the right input/output files, we can construct and execute a workflow solution by chaining these applications in a certain way. A particular aspect is the way these processes (tasks) communicate with one another: they are neither capable of taking (pulling) their own inputs nor submitting (pushing) their outputs, and these facilities must be provided to them by the platform. This aspect is essential in the context Distributed Computing, as outputs from tasks need to be transported to the node requiring them as inputs, thus incurring network load.

With the appearance of Service-Oriented Architectures (SOA), which allow to embed at low-cost processes as Web Services, a shift from process-oriented tasks to *service-oriented* ones was accomplished. The change has brought other advantages as well, namely, in the way inputs and outputs are handled by transforming the command-line arguments and textual configuration files into XML documents, which enclose all the task-required parameters. An interesting and very important aspect concerning Distributed Computing in this service-oriented paradigm is represented by the way in which raw input/output data is handled (for example, large satellite images): instead of relying on the platform to provide file transfer from one node to another, the job is delegated to a distributed storage system, while services explicitly use identifiers of such distributed files as inputs or outputs. Moreover, this abstraction provides the very foundation on which Cloud Computing is built by allowing providers to expose local applications for external use by means of Web Service.

## 10.2.3 Task Semantics

Usually we think of tasks as black boxes that expose a certain interface with strict inputs and outputs and show dependable behaviors. This implies the existence of a contract between the task implementation (what the developer has done) and the task execution (what the user gets). Generally, this contract can have two facets: *syntactic* and *semantic* (in the majority of cases, the former).

From a *syntactic* point of view, a task description reveals to us what type of inputs/outputs it expects to receive/send. For instance, it might tell us that it expects an integer or a list of strings, each matching a certain regular expression. Going even further, it might disclose to us that it awaits a complex compound structure but also provides alternatives. For instance, we can consider an Enterprise Resource Planning (ERP) system where a task could accept a person data type provided either as a structure containing the name, the address, national identifier numbers, or as a unique system-related identifier. These definitions are specific to each workflow engine, and in Business Process Execution Language (BPEL) (WSBPEL, 2007), for example, they are described by using a standard Web Service Web Service Description Language (WSDL). In the case of a make file (which, as stated previously, could be seen as the most elementary workflow engine), it is described in terms of file extensions and file name patterns. In any case, the syntactic contract refers only to data typing (number, string, structure, list, etc.) and some rudimentary conditions (not empty, greater than zero, matching a regular expression, etc.) that make the transition to the semantic perspective.

In the case of the *semantic* contract, some tools and languages may allow us to describe more complex validation rules for both inputs and outputs, and also the relation between them. These rules are named *preconditions* (which logic statements should be true for valid inputs) and *post-conditions* (which logic statements should be true for the outputs and for the relation between inputs and outputs). Although there is no production-ready workflow engine that allows such a perspective, it could be the key to both workflow formal verification and automatic generation. Such a scenario has been proposed in (Lu et al., 2006) and will be overseen in Section 10.6.

## 10.3  Present Workflow Issues and Solutions

Generally, an adaptive workflow engine needs to take into consideration issues related with data integrity; failure handling; open world service assumption; ad hoc workflow design; a multitier abstraction architecture that separates application and user concerns from operational and middleware concerns; support for e-Science lifecycle in which experiments need to be structured, repeatable, and verifiable; data-flow-centric model; etc. Probably the most important problems related to workflow execution are to ensure data integrity and failure handling. The first of them can be solved using either model checking at design time or proper service selection for task execution during runtime. The second one is more problematic as errors could occur in many places and cannot be usually predicted. They include failures of the workflow engine itself, failures of the component services, and failures of the network fabric, which will be briefly discussed in what follows.

Solving workflow engine failures could be achieved by offering a cloning mechanism and creating multiple workflow instances on various resources. Only the initial workflow instance would be active, while the rest of the instances periodically query the active one to check whether it is still running or not. In case of failure to respond to pings, one of the inactive workflows would instead become active and take over the role. To facilitate this operation each time a task changes its status or a rule is added or retracted from the rule base, all the inactive workflows will be notified of the respective event. Consequently, each of them would have an updated view of the overall workflow execution status. As an alternative, a scenario where a workflow is divided into several smaller ones (Lu et al., 2006)—each of them consisting of part of the initial rule base—the part of the workflow that corresponds to these rules can be considered. Yet, these approaches are not completely distributed as they still rely on one or more centralized workflow engines. Instead, an approach in which there does not exist a workflow engine and tasks act as agents with certain requirements, input and output ports, dependencies, and other relevant information, such as task type (initial, intermediate, and final), problem description, etc., could be taken into account. In this case also, two main approaches can be taken. The first one is dependent on a central Task Discovery Mechanism (TDM), but allows tasks to execute independently and without a centralized or distributed orchestrator. Tasks register themselves to the TDM and query it periodically in order to update their status. In addition, tasks still waiting for their dependencies to finish execution also regularly query the TDM to check whether or not their dependencies have finished. A completely distributed approach could be achieved if tasks carried additional information, such as the IDs of their dependencies, and sent at times a broadcast message on a specific port containing besides the dependency ID some query information. Still this scenario is unlikely applicable to large-scale Distributed Systems, which consist of large IP address spaces and where various network security policies would hinder the message from passing through.

Failures of the component services as well can be solved by using rules that allow multiple retries when attempting to access a service, or by using a discovery mechanism that relies on semantic information to retrieve information regarding the possible service alternatives for solving a specific task.

Failures of the network fabric are probably the most difficult issues when dealing with failure handling and recovery. Using a distributed workflow approach, such as the ones formerly described, combined with a mechanism for storing workflow states and resuming them at a later time could provide a certain assurance that the workflow will eventually be executed. However, there remains the issue of time costs with users normally interested in solving their problems under certain deadline constraints where possible.

The failure-related aspects presented in the previous paragraphs also concern users executing scientific workflows, these usually take a lot of time to solve with intervals ranging from a couple of minutes to days or weeks. As a result, workflow engines need to cope with these aspects and try to offer viable solutions so that the workflows would either get executed as a result of some rule-based decisions or would be paused and reactivated once the problems have been solved.

### 10.3.1 Present Workflow Solutions

Presently, there are many solutions that allow the composition and orchestration of tasks, most of them including an SOA-based approach and using either Web or Grid Services as communication end points between services. Composing tasks exposed as services is a preferred approach as it allows service providers to expose software in an easy and uniform way such that anyone complying to the used standards could easily access and use them. In what concerns service composition DAGs or Petri nets can be used to model two different approaches. The first one is based on classic task composition, which is usually accomplished during design time and cannot be easily adapted to support runtime changes as the second one that relies on an ECA. Orchestration engines falling in the first category ordinarily rely on XML-based formalisms to express relations between tasks. In the second case, flow can be seen as made of rules composed of *events* that trigger *actions* implying data updates or task invocations as a result of some *conditions*. This is more suited in case adaptation to system/logical failures or runtime changes in the structure of the workflow are required. Orchestration engines using this approach lean on forward-chaining algorithms, such as RETE (Forgy, 1990), to activate subsequent rules.

While the subject of the topic presented in this chapter is dealt with in a large amount of papers, it is our goal in what follows to present exclusively the most significant and the latest achievements in the field.

### 10.3.1.1 Classic Approaches

Web Service orchestration can be achieved using classic languages, most of them being XML based. One of the most popular standards in service orchestration is the *WS-BPEL 2.0* (WSBPEL, 2007) language. It is an orchestration language aimed, at describing an executable process involving message exchanges with other systems that, in this case, can be exposed as Web Services. Besides this feature, it allows defining and initializing XML- and WSDL-typed variables, support for writing expressions and queries in languages such as XPath 1.0, structured programming by using well-known constructs (including if-then-else, while, sequence, flow, parallel, etc.), encapsulation of logic by using local variables, event and fault handlers, concurrent access to variables, etc. Alternatively, if a non-XML language is preferred, *BPEL script* offers a translation from WS-BPEL 2.0 into a JavaScript and Ruby-syntax-like language. Recently, Charfi and Mezini (2007) proposed an aspect-oriented approach as an alternative to the process-oriented approach of BPEL. In the same paper, the authors also argue that process-oriented composition languages suffer from two main problems. The first one concerns the modularity of the specification as it might not be suited for cases concerning exception handling, access control and authentication, business rules, etc., while the second one concerns the dynamic adaptation during runtime of the service logic. WS-BPEL 2.0 tries to cope with the second issue by introducing dynamic partner binding. Macariu et al. (2008) also try to tackle with the second problem by offering semi-dynamic Web Service composition focused only on a limited class of scientific workflows that concern mathematical problems. Due to its standardization, WS-BPEL 2.0 has been widely adopted as part of many workflow engines, such as ActiveBPEL and Apache-ODE.

*YAWL* (Yet Another Workflow Language) (van der Aalst and ter Hofstede, 2005) can be seen as a viable alternative to BPEL. It is also based on XML including XPath and XQuery to define and manipulate data, and covers most of the existing workflow patterns. It permits dynamic adaptation of workflow models by using worklets and supports design-time model validation, such as detecting deadlocks. Probably the mainly developed feature related with YAWL as far as the work presented in this chapter is concerned with are the worklets (Adams, 2007). They are represented by a set of self-contained workflow processes attached to a specific task and allow dynamic runtime selection depending on the particular work instance context by using a Ripple Down Rules (RDR) approach. RDS allows for rules to be defined in hierarchical order by using binary trees with each node being represented by a rule and having a false and/or true branch. The single node with an exception is the root node that alone has a true branch. The worklet service maintains a set of

RDRs that determine—based on the current data—what worklet should be chosen as a replacement for a specific task during runtime.

*Scufl* is data-flow-centric workflow composition language used by the Taverna (Oinn et al., 2006) workflow engine. Taverna follows a three-tiered architecture approach with Scufl being responsible for linking applications at the user abstraction level. The execution layer interprets the Taverna Data Object Model that handles implicit control flows, while the Freeflue enactment engine manages the invocation of different families of services. Scufl uses a simplified syntax in which collections, control structures, or error-handling mechanisms are implicit with the main components consisting of a set of processors (logical services with one or more input and output ports), a set of data links for connecting data sources to destinations, and coordination links that allow order dependencies where required. The main disadvantage of Scufl is the impossibility of specifying user-defined constraints to either processors or data links. An XML-based version called XScufl (Greenwood, 2004) has also been developed.

Ontology Web Language for Services (*OWL-S*), formerly known as DARPA Agent Markup Language for Services (DAML-S) (Ankolekar et al., 2001), is an ontology-based approach, which can be successfully used in composing Web Services. Composition can be achieved by using the CompositeProcess class part of the process ontology. This class allows users to specify structures such as sequence, split, unordered, join, choice, condition, and iteration. One of the goals of OWL-S is to allow agents to automatically invoke and compose tasks based on their semantic description. In Korhpnen et al. (2003), the DAML-S process model is enhanced with transactional concepts, and the resulting workflow can then be executed using a workflow engine.

Other approaches represent workflows as *DAGs* or rely on the *Job Submission Description Language* (JSDL) (Anjomshoaa et al., 2005). The former is used in projects like Pegasus (Deelman et al., 2005) and Condor (Thain et al., 2003), which rely on Direct Acyclic Graph Manager (DAGMan) to subsequently execute them, while the latter is used in g-Eclipse (Wolniewicz et al., 2007). DAGMan allows for dynamic mapping and some failure-handling features, but is aimed at maximizing processor efficiency, offering a fixed scheduling mechanism and limited control constructs. JSDL is primarily used for describing the submission requirements of individual jobs, and therefore a workflow language is needed to represent job dependencies. g-Eclipse uses an XML format that allows jobs described by using JSDL to be linked together by using one or more input/output ports. In Narayanan and McIlraith (2002), part of DAML-S semantics is transformed to first-order logic and Petri nets. A solution to automatic Web Service composition by using both situation calculus and Petri nets is also proposed.

## 10.3.1.2 ECA-Based Approaches

While workflow languages, such as WS-BPEL, have become standards in Web Service composition, they lack the flexibility and adaptability of rule-based approaches. Moreover, even though enhancements such as worklets allow dynamic runtime task selection, they let the designer (user) think of all the aspects and issues that may appear during the execution of the respective workflow and add them to the rule hierarchy. Hence, in case a scenario for which a correspondent worklet does not exist, it is the conclusion of the last rule satisfied on the path to it that is taken into account. This could infer errors in the overall workflow behavior and result, as wrong decisions could be made on the grounds of insufficient existing knowledge. Worklets are also strongly related with tasks and, as a result, are not meant for dealing with system or network failures. Their best use could therefore be the correct selection of a solution to the problem depicted by the task.

Rule-based languages, such as ECA or CA (Condition Action), allow an alternative declarative approach by allowing (Weigand et al., 2008) *intuitive formal semantics* by exploiting a limited set of primitives, *direct support for business and science policies*, *flexibility* by following alternative execution paths in case of errors or unreachable solutions, *adaptability* by easy insertion and retraction of rules, and *reusability* by their property of being isolated from the process context.

Weigand et al. (2008) describe a CA-based engine called FARAO (FrAmewoRk for Adaptive Orchestration) relying on semantic Web with the goal of offering adaptable service orchestration. FARAO is based on Adaptive Service-Oriented Architecture (ASOA) (Hiel et al., 2008) and uses a shared ontology, which allows rules to refer to data items in terms of it. Thus, changes in the service interface do not influence the orchestration directly as long as it adheres to the ontology. ASOA allows for services to be adapted autonomously or semiautonomously following a monitor-plan-act cycle via a management interface.

Nagl et al. (2006) present a service-oriented rule engine called VIDRE (Vienna Distributed Rules Engine), which uses RuleML (Lee and Sohn, 2003) to represent facts, rules, and queries. It also distributes rules across several rule engines, thus increasing the separation and execution of business rules inside multiple (virtual) organizations.

Other approaches include injecting rules inside the WSDL specifications followed by their deployment on a service executor (Kamada and Mendes, 2007) or using an interceptor (Rosenberg and Dustdar, 2005) for catching BPEL activities. After an activity has been caught, applicable business rules are called via a rule broker service.

The aspect-oriented approach of BPEL, called AO4BPEL (Charfi and Mezini, 2007), also provides a separation of the main activities from the composition logic and follows at the same time the principles of WS-BPEL 2.0. Aspect-oriented programming has been recently acknowledged by many authors as a useful and powerful technique in cases where dynamic application adaptation is required.

AgentWork (Muller et al., 2004) is another workflow engine that allows rule-based adaptation by adding and removing tasks based on ECA rules. Adams (2007) argues that AgentWork does not offer the flexibility of RDR as worklets do and that changes are limited to individual tasks rather than the process-for-task replacement offered by the worklet service.

As it can be noticed from the previous paragraphs, there exist many workflow languages and systems that aim at offering both a standardized solution and a dynamic approach to runtime changes in the workflow execution. Among them the most suited for the job seem to be the ECA approaches, as they offer several advantages like separation of logic represented by rules from data represented by objects, declarative programming useful for applications focused on what to do instead of how to do it, scalability, and centralization of knowledge. These conclusions also arise naturally from what Clouds are and how they work. Clouds are based on virtualized resources that are offered on demand as services. When a user submits a request to a workflow engine exposed as a service, it expects back the result. The workflow engine is responsible for querying the Cloud for any compatible services with its tasks and to call these services once the associated task is ready for execution. The querying can be done based on ECA execution rules and by using some semantic information stored inside the service and task ontologies. This approach allows the user to submit not only pre-created workflows but also only the problem at hand. Based on the latter and on available ontologies, the workflow engine is then able to create the workflow for that particular problem by using a backward-chaining mechanism based on existing execution rules.

## 10.4  Scientific Workflows Examples

The scientific domain relies more and more on Distributed Computing due to large amounts of computations or data requirements. In this frame, the SCIEnce (Macariu et al., 2008) and GiSHEO (Frincu et al., 2009; GiSHEO, 2009) projects aim at providing the user with the possibility to use the advantages of Grids and Clouds for solving problems from two distinct and complementary approaches. The SCIEnce project intends to provide users with access to various Computer Algebra Systems (CASs) and to solve complex problems by using workflows that are executed over a Distributed System transparently to the user. Each task inside a mathematical workflow is represented by an operation that can be solved directly (for example, the GCD or the factorial). The project relies on WS-BPEL 2.0 as the workflow language and on ActiveBPEL as the orchestration engine. To overcome the difficulty of writing in the BPEL language, a simpler and restrictive language called Abstract Workflow Language (AWL) (Macariu et al., 2008) has been created on top of it. Providing scheduling and dynamism to BPEL has proven to be more difficult as initially expected, and there are still some open issues that have not entirely met their answers. Among them, we can enumerate the ones related to choosing resources dynamically at runtime or integrating a scheduler inside the engine. The former is of special interest as CASs differ in the algorithms they implement for solving such tasks. Therefore, we should be able to choose dynamically at runtime the most appropriate one for the job, operation which requires comprehensive knowledge on CAS behavior in various scenarios and an appropriate workflow platform.

The GiSHEO project aspires to provide a platform for earth sciences (history or archeology, for instance) by offering access to satellite image processing through means of web services. Although image processing may be trivial when taken separately, there are cases when we need to bind them together into a workflow in order to achieve the desired result. Useful examples come from the field of archeology; assuming that we want to identify ancient human settlements we could apply the following sequence of transformations: gray-level conversion, histogram equalization, quantization, and thresholding. Another example is represented by the NDVI value used in geography and meteorology for determining the presence of vegetation. The NDVI can be easily computed by using the Map-Reduce construct, as it is usually required for large sets of images. For each image in the set, we need to extract the red (RED) and near-infrared (NIR) bands, which will be used to compute the index as (NIR–RED/NIR+RED). After finishing the computations, the construct will return a set of processed NDVI values, which can be further used in statistics or additional processing. The language expressing the workflow has been chosen to be ECA based and orchestrated by an inference engine. The choice of this approach allowed for the rule chain to be automatically discovered in case users only submitted a request for a particular processing and not the entire workflow. The rule-based approach allows the backward-chaining mechanism to determine the path to be taken starting from the desired output. This mechanism also ensures that the solution will be valid since, besides rule selection, the mechanism also offers a semantic check of each selected service.

Despite that the need for a Distributed System is not immediately obvious, it becomes clear once the data required for processing becomes too large to be stored in one place or the services required by tasks are geographically distributed. In the frame of the SCIEnce project, the problem submitted by the user does not necessarily imply large quantities of data but in contrast requires access to CASs exposed as services in various geographical places. One of the dissimilarities between the SCIEnce project and the GiSHEO project lies in the fact that the latter requires a distributed data system as the used images are usually large (several gigabytes each). In this direction, the services must be placed where the data is, or near it, as transfers would imply an overhead that is too great.

The following sections will deal mostly with the workflow formalism and autogeneration method used in the GiSHEO project.

## 10.5  ECA Workflow Formalism

Recently, several papers have sought defining a formalism for describing adaptive workflows. The work carried out by Lu et al. (2006) defines a model based on

Hoare semantics that allows to automatically check if a workflow can be produced from its actual implementation and to synthesize a workflow implementation based on a specification and a task library. The model focuses on formalizing the semantics of the workflow together with its preconditions and post-conditions and on providing a set of inference rules for each of the following control constructs: empty workflow, composition, loop, universal, conjunction, condition, and disjunction.

In Chun et al. (2002), the authors present a knowledge-based workflow model. Ontologies are used to describe tasks and their relationships as well as the compositional rules. Each user is also associated with a user profile, which is evaluated against compositional rules by the composition algorithm. The authors argue that this approach minimizes the workflow evaluations during runtime and automatizes the interagency workflow design.

A workflow formalism based on the High-Order Chemical Language (HOCL) is presented in Nemeth et al. (2005). HOCL derives from the $\gamma$ calculus and has been successfully used to represent self-organizing systems (Banâtre et al., 2007). The work carried out by Nemeth et al. (2005) tries to provide a coordination framework where a higher level of autonomy is provided, workflow activities are able to react and adapt to environmental changes, a distributed enactment that can make decisions based on partial workflow information is achieved, and advanced control structures are supported. One of the main advantages of this approach is the implicit parallelism of the model, which arises from the fact that tasks are viewed as molecules inside a chemical solution and, as in any real reaction, the process takes place in parallel for each present reactive molecule. Solutions can also contain sub-solutions, which in turn can comprise molecules that react. As a general rule, sub-solutions cannot react with the solution before all the reactions inside them have completed.

In what follows, a simple ECA rule-based workflow formalism will be presented. It has been introduced in the GiSHEO project as the starting point of an inference rule-based service composition engine. The reasons for electing such an approach have been already discussed in the previous sections. This approach also shows how we can achieve service composition by using only rules and a forward-chaining engine.

Similar to the formalism described in Chun et al. (2002), where the ontologies for domain services and tasks are the same, the model we propose also considers tasks and services to be interchangeable. A *task T* or likewise a *service S* can be described as a five tuple $\theta = \theta_1 \ \theta_2 \ \theta_3 \ \theta_4 \ \theta_5$, where $\theta_1$ specifies the number of task instances (the default value being one); $\theta_2$ and $\theta_3$ designate, respectively, the input and output ports of the task; $\theta_4$ encloses the preconditions of the tasks (the tasks that need to be executed before it and optional conditions based on the results of their execution); $\theta_5$ holds the operations needed to be carried out by the task; and $\theta_6$ comprehends other semantic information related to it. The semantic information could contain data about preferred services, required system configuration, and system load.

A workflow $W$ can be specified by $\omega = \omega_1\, \omega_2\, \omega_3\, \omega_4\, \omega_5\, \omega_6$, where the elements are the same as for tasks, the only difference being $\omega_6$, which represents the collection of tasks belonging to it. A natural way of representing workflows is by using DAGs consisting of tasks linked together by preconditions. Similar to tasks, workflows must have at least one input and output port. As mentioned in Section 10.2.1, the notion of workflows and tasks is interchangeable, which is also true in the former definition. As an example, we can note the similarity between the workflow and task ontologies, and the particular case where $\omega_6$ contains a single task in which case the two are identical.

In Nemeth et al. (2005), the notion of abstract and concrete workflow is introduced. An *abstract workflow* is seen as a model that expresses the logic of the problem without containing any means of solving it. In order to accomplish this, a mapping of tasks on services is needed. Such a workflow where tasks are mapped on services is called a *concrete workflow*. The same work also emphasizes that in order to provide full dynamism and autonomy, the conversion between an abstract and a concrete workflow must be accomplished during runtime. We further introduce a mapping function for generating a concrete workflow, $f_i: T \rightarrow S$, where $S$ is a service that satisfies the task description $\theta$ for one or more tasks $T \in \omega_6$.

The *evolution function* or *rule* that allows the activation of tasks based on the fulfillment of their preconditions and additional conditional elements can be expressed by a function $r: T^n \xrightarrow{\text{condition}} T^m$, where $T^n$ represents the tasks needed to be completed before the $T^m$ tasks can proceed with, their own execution. The *condition* represents additional criteria that must be satisfied by the $T^n$ tasks. It is also part of the task precondition set $\theta_4$, but we have chosen to emphasize its importance. It can however be safely omitted without loss of generality. The inverse function $r^{-1}$ gives the $\theta_4$ list of preconditions. As an example of a rule function, we could consider a rule such as $r(T_1, T_2) \xrightarrow{T_2.\text{output1}<10,\, T_1.\text{output1}>0} T_3$, where $T_3$ gets executed only after $T_1$ and $T_2$ are completed and if the output on the output1 ports for the two tasks is greater than 0 for $T_1$ and smaller than 10 for $T_2$.

In the same manner, a user profile can be expressed similar to that in Chun et al. (2002) as $u_1 u_2$ where $u_1$ and $u_2$ represent the user's goal service and the user's service preferences, respectively.

The workflow model described before combines the formerly presented model by mixing features such as multiple task instances, implicit parallelism, and integration of resource selection inside the rules found in the HOCL representation of Nemeth et al. (2005) with semantic information and ontologies from Chun et al. (2002). The resulting workflow language is also backward-chaining enabled, allowing for automatic generation and self-adaptation. This is achieved by using the rule function that allows binding together tasks, and its inverse function that allows workflow generation starting from a desired solution. The aim of the formalism is to offer the basis for a simplified language without loss of generality. The following text will show how the constructs presented in Section 10.2.1 can be expressed without introducing any new elements besides the rules themselves.

Rules are defined simply by mentioning the events and conditions that need to take place in order to trigger the execution-consequent tasks. Events are viewed as completed tasks and are placed on the left-hand side of the rule. Linking the output of left-hand-side tasks with the input of right-hand-side tasks is accomplished by variables. For example, the rule $A[a = o1] \rightarrow B[i1 = a]$ links the output port $o1$ of task $A$ with the input port $i1$ of task $B$ through variable $a$. All tasks on the right-hand side get executed in parallel in the same way as multiple rules are triggered simultaneously if their left-hand-side conditions are met. This aspect of rule-based workflows allows for constructs such as split and join to be naturally expressed without introducing additional elements inside the rule. For instance, a (synchronized) join can be expressed as $A[a = o1], B[b = o1] \rightarrow C[i1 = a, i2 = b]$, and a (parallel) split as $A[a = o1] \rightarrow B[i1 = a], C[i1 = a]$. Synchronization between several tasks can also be achieved by adding them into the left-hand side of the rule: $A[b = o1], B \rightarrow C[i1 = b]$. The previous example shows how task $A$ is synchronized with task $B$ and cannot execute until the latter is completed. Conditional rules can be expressed by placing conditions on the variables: $A[a = o1] \rightarrow B[i1 = a]|d < 1$. Loops can also be easily modeled as in the following example consisting of two rules: $A[a = o1], B[b = o1] \rightarrow A[i1 = a, i2 = b]|d < 1$ and $A[a = o1], B[b = o1] \rightarrow C[i1 = a, i2 = b]|d >= 1$. The former rule expresses the condition to reiterate the loop, while the latter expresses the exit condition.

While tasks are executed by services, the choice of the latter is accomplished by the workflow engine through the $f_t$ mapping function. In addition as their ontologies are defined in the same manner, services could easily be added inside the rules if required. This practice is however not recommended as the service selection should be made at runtime based on the most current data by the engine, a specialized scheduler, or the task itself. In the case of GiSHEO, the selection is made by the centralized workflow enactment engine during runtime.

Rules can also specify whether or not the left-hand-side tasks or the number of right-hand-side-produced instances get consumed. In this direction, the formalism allows for tasks to have multiple instances. This feature allows the introduction of explicit sequencing of multiple rules ready for execution. As an example, we can consider the two rules where task $A$ has only one instance: $A[a = o1, \text{consume} = \text{true}] \rightarrow B[i1 = a], A[i1 = a, \text{instances} = 1]$ and $A[a = o1, \text{consume} = \text{true}] \rightarrow C[i1 = a], A[i1 = a, \text{instances} = 1]$. In this example, the rules cannot fire simultaneously, and one of them needs to wait for the other to produce another instance of task $A$. Multiple task instances allow users to express workflows based on nature, such as chemical reactions (Nemeth et al., 2005). Moreover, we can define multiple-rule visibility domains or solutions (if using a chemical metaphor), which allow both grouping of rules and creating sub-workflows that execute based only on rules belonging to a particular domain. When all the rules have triggered (all tasks that can trigger rules have been consumed), the reaction can extend to wider domains.

## 10.6 Workflow Construction

While most applications and frameworks focus on enhancing the execution and debugging of workflows, only a few try to focus on automatic construction or validation. While in the former case they allow the user to create the workflow in an iconographic mode by dragging and dropping or by providing some commonly used blocks, in the latter case they just verify the workflow from the syntactic perspective.

To see why automatic generation or at least guided design is important, we take a typical case found in scientific problems in which the scientist tries to optimize or solve a concrete problem that is part of a bigger problem. We assume that the used method relies on partial results obtained from other methods that had been studied and hopefully implemented by other scientists. In this case, the performance and usually the consequence of the experiments depend not only on the particular solution but also on the way the methods for the dependencies are selected. Additionally, as the scientist has extensive expertise exclusively in a small portion of the enclosing domain, he does not always know how to best choose these dependencies.

Another usage for such facilities is that as the infrastructure and supporting technologies grow, the problems become more and more complex and overwhelm the capacity to choose the right methods. Also a missed opportunity could be the parallelism built into the workflows, which often leads to suboptimal solutions because of the fact that the designer does not always capture all possible parallel scenarios.

Some possible solutions (Chun et al., 2002; Korhonen et al., 2003) have already been described in one of the previous sections. Another one is described in the paper presented by Lu et al. (2006), where the authors focus mainly on formal checking of workflows. Only as a consequence of the implied model's properties is generation taken into account. In this case, each task is defined as follows: $P(\bar{x})$ $T(\bar{x})[Q_1(\bar{x}), \ldots, Q_n(\bar{x})]$, where $\bar{x}$ represents the input parameters, $P(\bar{x})$ is a first-order logic predicate that represents the precondition of task $T$ (the conditions that must be true in order to execute the task), and the $Q_i(\bar{x})$ vectors stand for possible task post-conditions (what should happen after the task execution). It should be noted that this model provides the opportunity for nondeterminism, since only one of the post-conditions could be true. This possibility is more than what is needed in scientific workflows where a simplified model would look like $P(\bar{x})T(\bar{x})[Q(\bar{x})]$. The cited paper also describes a proof-of-concept algorithm for both verification and generation of a workflow.

The drawback for all these automatic solutions is that they imply an all-or-nothing approach where the user either provides all the necessary data, which leads to a complete workflow construction, or nothing is obtained. In our view, a human-assisted approach where the automatic system tries to create a complete workflow and, in case of failure, asks the user for missing pieces would be more appropriate. This is also the case of the workflow engine developed in the frame of the GiSHEO project. The engine partially offers design-time solutions to users by providing a subset of rules that lead to the desired result. Given the user's requirements (parameters) and the desired problem, the engine searches the task ontologies and selects appropriate services. Then starting from the desired problem and by recursively using the previously defined $r^{-1}$ function, it extracts the appropriate rules. If the resulted set contains no rules with preconditions matching the presented parameters, the engine simply shows the obtained chaining and warns the user of the incomplete nature of the workflow. It is then up to the user to revise and submit new input parameters.

As a conclusion, it can be said that even though automatic generation exists, there is still need for human intervention either when incomplete input data is provided or when the result is dependent on the input values and/or intermediate variations of the parameters, which cannot be done automatically.

## 10.7 Conclusions

This chapter has given a brief overview on scientific workflows seen from a Distributed System perspective. In the first part of the chapter, it has been shown that given the increased need of larger storage and computational resources, workflows have migrated toward a distributed approach by using Web Services as end points for their tasks. In this direction, two main approaches regarding classic and rule-based workflow composition have emerged. The latter seems to be more suited to handle issues related to scalability, failure tolerance, data integrity, and scheduling. It also provides implicitly support for task composition through the use of an inference engine. Although scheduling is an important issue related to task execution, it has been intentionally omitted due to the fact that such a problem requires a large amount of space to be properly addressed. As long as the services return a result in a reasonable amount of time, scheduling can be safely ignored. It only becomes a problem when a cost function, such as a time constraint, based on payed access or a deadline is applied to the workflow. In the second part, we have presented a rule-based workflow formalism and language developed as part of the GiSHEO project. Its aim is to facilitate the creation of workflows by specifying a minimal yet complete workflow language, to allow self adaptation during runtime and auto-workflow generation.

Despite the fact that the need for a service-based distributed workflow system or at least a workflow suited for executing distributed tasks through services has become clear in the last decade, much is still to be done. Although the solutions seem at first numerous and independent from each other, there is a tendency toward the inclusion of semantic information, ontologies, and execution rules inside the execution engines. This work has strived to present both an introduction into what workflows for Distributed Computing are (what they are made of and what solutions and problems currently exist) and how service composition can be easily achieved by using rules and semantics.

## Acknowledgment

This research has been partially supported by the European Space Agency PECS Contract no. 98061 GiSHEO: On Demand Grid Services for High Education and Training in Earth Observation.

## References

Adams, M. J. (2007). Facilitating dynamic flexibility and exception handling for workflows. Ph D thesis, Queensland University of Technology, Brisbane, Australia.

Anjomshoaa, A., F. Brisard, M. Drescher et al. (2005). Job submission description language. http://www.ggf.org/documents/GFD.56.pdf (accessed March 30, 2009).

Ankolekar, A., M. Burstein, J. Hobbs et al. (2001). DAML-S: Semantic markup for web services. http://www-2.cs.cmu.edu/softagents/papers/SWWS.pdf (accessed March 30, 2009).

Banâtre, J., P. Fradet, and Y. Radenac (2007). Programming self-organizing systems with the higher-order chemical language. *International Journal of Unconventional Computing* 3(3), 161–177.

Charfi, A. and M. Mezini (2007). Ao4bpel: An aspect-oriented extension to bpel. *World Wide Web 10*(3), 309–344.

Chun, S., V. Atluri, and N. Adam (2002). Domain knowledge-based automatic workflow generation. In *Proceedings of the 13th International Conference on Database and Expert Systems Application* (*DEXA'02*), Aixen Provence, France, pp. 81–92. Springer-Verlag, London, U.K.

Dean, J. and S. Ghemawat (2004). Mapreduce: Simplified data processing on large clusters. In *Proceedings of the Sixth Conference on Symposium on Operating Systems Design and Implementation* (*OSDI'04*), San Francisco, CA, pp. 10–10. USENIX Association, Berkeley, CA.

Deelman, E., G. Singh, M. Su et al. (2005). Pegasus: A framework for mapping complex scientific workflows onto distributed systems. *Scientific Programming 13*(3), 219–237.

Forgy, C. (1990). Rete: A fast algorithm for the many pattern/many object pattern match problem. In *Expert Systems: A Software Methodology for Modern Applications*, ed. P. G. Reith, pp. 324–341. IEEE Computer Society Press, Los Alamitos, CA.

Frincu, M., S. Panica, M. Neagul, and D. Petcu (2009). Gisheo: On demand grid service based platform for eo data processing. In *Proceedings of the Third International Workshop on High Performance Grid Middleware* (*HiperGrid'09*), Bucharest, Romania, pp. 415–422. Politehnica Press, Romania.

GiSHEO (2009). On demand grid services for high education and training in earth observation. http://gisheo.info.uvt.ro (accessed April 22, 2009).

Greenwood, M. (2004). Xscufl language reference. http://www.mygrid.org.uk/wiki/Mygrid/WorkFlow#XScufl_workflow_definitions (accessed March 30, 2009).

Hiel, M., H. Weigand, and W. van den Heuvel (2008). An adaptive service-oriented architecture. In *Enterprise Interoperability III*, eds. K. Mertens, R. Ruggaber, and K. Popplewell, and X. Xu, pp. 197–208. Springer, London, U.K.

Kamada, A. and M. Mendes (2007). Business rules in a service development and execution environment. In *Proceedings of the International Symposium on Communications and Information Technologies*, Sydney, Australia, pp. 1366–1371. IEEE Computer Society, Washington, DC.

Korhonen, J., L. Pajunen, and J. Puustjarvi (2003). Automatic composition of web service workflows using a semantic agent. In *Proceedings of the 2003 IEEE/WIC International Conference on Web Intelligence (WI'03)*, Beijing, China, pp. 566. IEEE Computer Society, Washington, DC.

Lee, J. and M. Sohn (2003). The extensible rule markup language. *Communications of the ACM 46*(5), 59–64.

Lu, S., A. Bernstein, and P. Lewis (2006). Automatic workflow verification and generation. *Theoretical Computer Science 353*(1), 71–92.

Macariu, G., A. Carstea, and M. Frincu (2008). Service-oriented symbolic computing with symgrid. *Scalable Computing: Practice and Experience 9*(2), 11–25. http://www.scpe.org/vols/vol09/no2/SCPE_9_2_04.pdf (accessed April 16, 2009).

Muller, R., G. Greiner, and E. Rahm (2004). Agent work: A workflow system supporting rule-based workflow adaptation. *Data and Knowledge Engineering 51*(2), 223–256.

Nagl, C., F. Rosenberg, and S. Dustdar (2006). Vidre—A distributed service-oriented business rule engine based on ruleml. In *Proceedings of the 10th IEEE International Enterprise Distributed Object Computing Conference (EDOC '06)*, Hong Kong, China, pp. 35–44. IEEE Computer Society, Washington, DC.

Narayanan, S. and S. McIlraith (2002). Simulation, verification and automated composition of web services. In *Proceedings of the 11th International Conference on World Wide Web (WWW'02)*, Honolulu, HI, pp. 77–88. ACM, New York, NY.

Nemeth, Z., C. Perez, and T. Priol (2005). Workflow enactment based on a chemical metaphor. In *SEFM '05: Proceedings of the Third IEEE International Conference on Software Engineering and Formal Methods*, Koblenz, Germany, pp. 127–136. IEEE Computer Society, Washington, DC.

Oinn, T., M. Greenwood, M. Addis et al. (2006). Taverna: Lessons in creating a work-flow environment for the life sciences: Research articles. *Concurrency and Computation: Practice and Experience 18*(10), 1067–1100.

Rosenberg. F. and S. Dustdar (2005). Business rules integration in bpel—A service-oriented approach. In *Proceedings of the Seventh IEEE International Conference on E-Commerce Technology (CEC'05)*, München, Germany, pp. 476–479. IEEE Computer Society, Washington, DC.

Thain, D., T. Tannenbaum, and M. Livny (2003). Condor and the grid. In *Grid Computing: Making the Global Infrastructure a Reality*, eds. F. Berman, A.J.G. Hey, and G. Fox, pp. 299–335. John Wiley & Sons, Chichester, U.K.

van der Aalst, W. M. P. and A. H. M. ter Hofstede (2005). Yawl: Yet another workflow language. *Information Systems 30*(4), 245–275.

Weigand, H., W. van den Heuvel, and M. Hiel (2008). Rule-based service composition and service-oriented business rule management. *Proceedings of the International Workshop on Regulations Modelling and Deployment (ReMoD'08)*, Montpellier, France.

Wolniewicz. P., N. Meyer, M. Stroinski, M. Stuempert, H. Kornmayer. M. Polak, and H. Gjermundrod (2007). Accessing grid computing resources with g-eclipse platform. *Computational Methods in Science and Technology 13*(2), 131–141.

WSBPEL (2007). Web services business process execution language version 2.0. http://docs. oasis-open.org/wsbpel/2.0/wsbpel-v2.0.pdf (accessed March 30, 2009).

# Chapter 11

# Transparent Cross-Platform Access to Software Services Using GridSolve and GridRPC

Keith Seymour, Asim YarKhan, and Jack Dongarra

## Contents

Distributed computing can be daunting even for experienced programmers. Although many projects have been created to facilitate developing distributed applications, they are often quite complex in themselves. While many scientific applications could benefit from distributed computing, the complexity of the programming models can be a high barrier to entry, especially since many of these applications are developed by domain scientists without extensive training in software development. Thus, we believe that the paramount design consideration of a distributed computing model should be ease of use. With this in mind, we discuss GridRPC, which is a model for remote procedure call (RPC) in the context of a computational grid or other loosely coupled distributed computing environment. Then we discuss GridSolve, an implementation of the GridRPC model.

# 11.1 Introduction to RPC and Network-Based Software Services

RPC refers to a mechanism that allows invoking a procedure on a remote machine as if the procedure was implemented locally. The invocation is typically carried out by means of a communications library and "stub" procedures. The library handles packing up the user's data, sending it across the network to the remote machine, and unpacking it there. The process of packing the data into a standard format (especially important for cross-platform scenarios) is referred to as *data marshaling*. Once the data has been transferred, the RPC system invokes the user's procedure and passes the data to it. From this point, the user's procedure takes control and executes until completion. Then the process is reversed to send the results back to the client machine. The "stub" procedures are used to enable linking the programs (since the actual procedure does not exist locally to be linked) and to initiate the RPC process via calls to the RPC library. This standard RPC process is depicted in Figure 11.1.

One of the earliest implementations of RPC was part of the Cedar project at Xerox Palo Alto Research Center [1], although the concept had been discussed for several years prior to the Xerox implementation [2]. Cedar used RPC to enable distributed computing primarily because of the ease-of-use inherent in the RPC paradigm. Procedure calls were considered a well-understood mechanism and provided clean and simple semantics. Around that time, RPC was also being investigated in the context of distributed operating systems. In a critique of RPC as a general communications model for arbitrary applications [3], it is argued (among other things) that since true transparency is impossible, it may be better to design a partially transparent mechanism. If the system is transparent to the point that the programmers really do not know if their calls will be executed locally or remotely, then there could be serious performance implications (e.g., if a sorting routine called a comparison procedure thousands of times, unaware that it would be executed remotely). Most modern RPC-like systems are not aiming for that level of transparency, but the critique raises issues that are still relevant today. In this

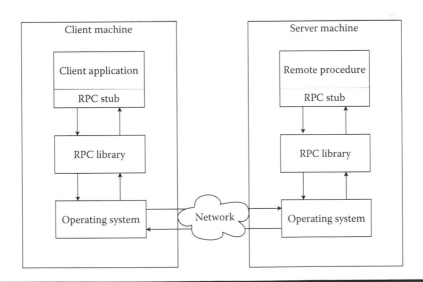

**Figure 11.1   Client–server interaction in standard RPC.**

chapter, we will touch on these and other RPC transparency issues in the context of a grid-based RPC implementation.

The RPC model has several benefits, but the main concern from the perspective of high-performance computing is efficiency. If the user's local machine is slow, but remote resources are fast, RPC can provide an overall reduction in execution time, even including the cost of data marshaling. However, traditional RPC only allows for synchronous calls, that is, once the procedure is invoked, the client program must sit idle until it completes, even if it had other useful computations it could be doing. The synchronous model also prevents submitting multiple parallel RPC requests, which could provide for even better overall performance. Another limitation of the traditional RPC model is that the mapping of RPC request to server is very simplistic, often requiring the use of a specific machine. Intelligent selection of servers could drastically improve the performance. Also the use of client-side stubs requires language-specific generators for all client language bindings. Furthermore, consider the implications of this compilation requirement on interactive computing environments like MATLAB® or Octave, in which cases, the user cannot be expected to compile stubs just to make use of a remote procedure.

RPC remains a useful mechanism due to its elegance and simplicity, but the aforementioned limitations have prompted several extensions to the model, including asynchronous calls, task parallel calls, real-time resource scheduling, fault tolerance, security, and stubless operation. We will be discussing GridRPC, a recent specification of an API (application programming interface) for grid-based RPC, as well as a complete implementation of this API within the GridSolve system.

## 11.2 The GridRPC API

As mentioned in Section 11.1, the difficulty of using most programming models is a hindrance to the widespread adoption of grid computing. One particular programming model that has proven to be viable is an RPC mechanism tailored for the grid, or "GridRPC." Although at a very high-level view the programming model provided by GridRPC is that of standard RPC plus asynchronous coarse-grained parallel tasking, in practice there are a variety of features that will largely hide the dynamicity, insecurity, and instability of the grid from the programmers. As such, GridRPC allows not only enabling individual applications to be distributed, but also can serve as the basis for even higher-level software substrates, such as distributed, scientific components on the grid.

The GridRPC API [4] represents ongoing work to standardize and implement a portable and simple RPC mechanism for grid computing. This standardization effort is being pursued through the Open Grid Forum (previously, Global Grid Forum) Research Group on Advanced Programming Models [5].

In this section, we informally describe the GridRPC model and the functions that comprise the API. A detailed listing of the GridRPC function prototypes can be found in the GridSolve Users' Guide [6].

## 11.2.1 Function Handles and Session IDs

Two fundamental objects in the GridRPC model are *function handles* and *session IDs*. The function handle represents a mapping from a function name to an instance of that function on a particular server. The GridRPC API does not dictate the mechanics of resource discovery, since different underlying GridRPC implementations may use vastly different protocols. Once a particular function-to-server mapping has been established by initializing a function handle, all RPC calls using this function handle will be executed on the server specified in that binding. A session ID is an identifier representing a particular non-blocking RPC call. The session ID is used throughout the API to allow users to obtain the status of a previously submitted non-blocking call, to wait for a call to complete, to cancel a call, or to check the error code of a call.

## 11.2.2 Initializing and Finalizing Functions

The initialize and finalize functions are similar to the MPI initialize and finalize calls. Client GridRPC calls before initialization or after finalization will fail.

- `grpc _ initialize` reads the configuration file and initializes the required modules.
- `grpc _ finalize` releases any resources being used by GridRPC.

## 11.2.3 Remote Function Handle Management Functions

The *function handle management* group of functions allows creating and destroying function handles.

- `grpc _ function _ handle _ default` creates a new function handle using the default server. This could be a predetermined server name or it could be a server that is dynamically chosen by the resource discovery mechanisms of the underlying GridRPC implementation, such as the GridSolve agent.
- `grpc _ function _ handle _ init` creates a new function handle with a server explicitly specified by the user.
- `grpc _ function _ handle _ destruct` releases the memory associated with the specified function handle.
- `grpc _ get _ handle` returns the function handle corresponding to the given session ID (that is, corresponding to that particular non-blocking request).

## 11.2.4 GridRPC Call Functions

A GridRPC call may be either blocking (synchronous) or non-blocking (asynchronous), and it accepts a variable number of arguments (like `printf`) depending on the calling sequence of the particular routine being called.

- `grpc_call` makes a blocking RPC with a variable number of arguments.
- `grpc_call_async` makes a non-blocking RPC with a variable number of arguments.

## 11.2.5 Asynchronous GridRPC Control Functions

The following functions apply only to previously submitted non-blocking requests.

- `grpc_probe` checks whether the asynchronous GridRPC call has completed.
- `grpc_probe_or` checks whether any of the previously issued non-blocking calls in a given set have completed.
- `grpc_cancel` cancels the specified asynchronous GridRPC call.
- `grpc_cancel_all` cancels *all* previously issued calls.

## 11.2.6 Asynchronous GridRPC Wait Functions

The following five functions apply only to previously submitted non-blocking requests. These calls allow an application to express desired nondeterministic completion semantics to the underlying system, rather than repeatedly polling on a set of sessions IDs. (From an implementation standpoint, such information could be conveyed to the OS scheduler to reduce cycles wasted on polling.)

- `grpc_wait` blocks until the specified non-blocking requests have completed.
- `grpc_wait_and` blocks until *all* of the specified non-blocking requests in a given set have completed.
- `grpc_wait_or` blocks until *any* of the specified non-blocking requests in a given set has completed.
- `grpc_wait_all` blocks until *all* previously issued non-blocking requests have completed.
- `grpc_wait_any` blocks until *any* previously issued non-blocking request has completed.

## 11.2.7 Error Reporting Functions

Of course it is possible that some GridRPC calls can fail, so we need to provide the ability to check the error code of previously submitted requests. The following error reporting functions provide error codes and human-readable error descriptions:

- `grpc _ get _ error` returns the error code associated with a given non-blocking request.
- `grpc _ error _ string` returns the error description string, given a numeric error code.
- `grpc _ get _ failed _ sessionid` returns the session ID of the last invoked GridRPC call that caused a failure.

### 11.2.8 Related Work on Network-Enabled Servers

Several Network-Enabled Servers (NES) provide mechanisms for transparent access to remote resources and software. Ninf-G [7] is an implementation of the GridRPC API that can function on top of a variety of grid middleware environments, such as Globus, Condor, and SSH (as of version 5). Ninf-G provides an interface definition language that allows services to be easily added, and client APIs are provided in C and Java. Security, scheduling, and resource management are generally left up to the underlying middleware.

The DIET (Distributed Interactive Engineering Toolbox) project [8] is a client–agent–server RPC architecture, which uses the GridRPC API as its primary interface. A CORBA Naming Service handles the resource registration and lookup, and a hierarchy of agents handle the scheduling of services on the resources. An API is provided for generating service profiles and adding new services, and a C client API exists.

NEOS [9] is a network-enabled problem-solving environment designed as a generic application service provider (ASP). Any application that can be changed to read its inputs from files and write its output to a single file can be integrated into NEOS. The NEOS server acts as an intermediary for all communication. The client data files go to the NEOS server, which sends the data to the solver resources, collects the results, and then returns the results to the client. Clients can use e-mail, Web, socket-based tools, and CORBA interfaces.

Other projects are related to various aspects of GridSolve. For example, task-farming-style computation is provided by the Apples Parameter Sweep Template (APST) project [10], the Condor Master Worker (MW) project [11], and the Nimrod-G project [12]. Request sequencing and workflow management is handled by projects like Condor DAGman [13].

## 11.3 GridSolve: A GridRPC Implementation

GridSolve is a GridRPC-compliant distributed computing system that provides an efficient and easy-to-use programming model for using remote computational resources. Remote resources can provide access to specialized hardware or highly tuned software with the performance and features desired by a computational scientist. The basic goal of GridSolve is to provide an easy-to-use, uniform, portable, and efficient way to access computational resources over a network.

## 11.3.1 Overview and Architecture

The GridSolve system is comprised of a set of loosely connected machines. By loosely connected, we mean that these machines are on the same local, wide, or global area network, and may be administrated by different institutions and organizations. Moreover, the GridSolve system is able to support these interactions in a heterogeneous environment, that is, machines of different architectures, operating systems, and internal data representations can participate in the system at the same time.

Figure 11.2 shows the global conceptual picture of the GridSolve system. In this figure, we can see the three major components of the system: the *client*, the *agent*, and the *servers* (computational or software resources). GridSolve and systems like it are often referred to as grid middleware. GridSolve acts as a glue layer that brings the application or user together with the hardware and/or software needed to complete useful tasks. At the top tier, the GridSolve client library is linked in

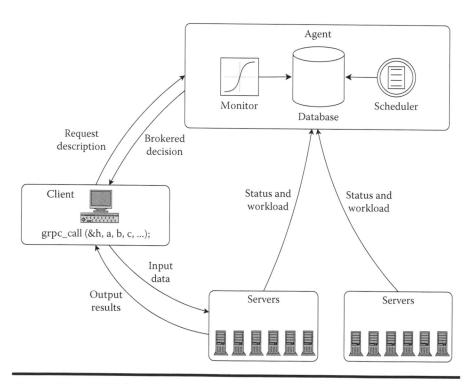

**Figure 11.2   GridSolve architecture showing interactions between client, agent, and servers.**

with the user's application. The application then makes calls to GridSolve's API (GridRPC) for specific services. Through the GridRPC API, GridSolve client-users gain access to aggregate resources without needing to know anything about distributed computing or maintaining software libraries. In fact, the user does not even have to know that remote resources are involved. The GridSolve agent maintains a database of GridSolve servers along with their capabilities (hardware performance and allocated software) and dynamic usage statistics. It uses this information to allocate server resources for client requests. The agent finds servers that will service requests the quickest, balances the load amongst its servers, and keeps track of failed ones. The GridSolve server is a daemon process that awaits client requests. The server can run on single workstations, clusters of workstations, symmetric multiprocessors, or machines with massively parallel processors. A key component of the GridSolve server is a source code generator, which parses a GridSolve Interface Definition Language (gsIDL) file. This gsIDL file contains information that allows the GridSolve system to create new service modules and incorporate new functionalities. In essence, the gsIDL defines an interface and wrapper that GridSolve uses to call functions being incorporated. The (hidden) semantics of a GridSolve request are as follows:

1. Client contacts the agent with a service request description
2. Agent returns a brokered decision containing a list of capable servers
3. Client contacts the server and sends input data
4. Server receives the data and runs appropriate service
5. Client receives the output results or error status from the server

From the user's perspective, the call to GridSolve acts very much like the call to the original function. The GridSolve calls can also be made in an asynchronous fashion, so that the client can either perform other tasks during the RPC call, or the client can submit multiple parallel RPC service requests and then probe for their completion.

## 11.3.2 Transparency and Ease of Use

In addition to the standard GridRPC API, GridSolve provides a number of features that make it easier to use and provide a substantial benefit. These features are intended to make it easier for the service provider to add services, and easier for the user to take advantage of these services.

### 11.3.2.1 Stubless Clients

GridSolve is designed so that the clients do not require client-side stubs to be generated and compiled in order to call remote procedures. This is in contrast with many other RPC systems, where a client stub needs to be generated and bound for each remote function. Several dynamically reconfigurable languages, such as Java and Python, allow clients to incorporate new functionality on the fly, but traditional languages, such as C and Fortran, cannot easily do so. GridSolve accomplishes this by using generalized marshaling routines on the client and the server. Using a stubless client in GridSolve enables it to make new server functionality available to its clients without requiring any changes at the client side. The drawback of this approach is that type-checking cannot be done at the time of calling the GridSolve API. However, this stubless approach fits well with the goal of making GridSolve easy to use. After a client is deployed, no additional changes are required for the client to access new functions deployed at any server.

### 11.3.2.2 Scientific Computing Environments

GridSolve has a strong focus on ease of use, since this is still perceived to be a substantial barrier to the general adoption of distributed and grid computing services. As such, in addition to C and Fortran client interfaces, GridSolve provides client bindings to several high-level SCEs (scientific computing environments), such as MATLAB, Octave, and IDL (Interactive Data Language). In this way, it becomes possible to combine high-performance distributed grid resources with the flexibility, familiarity, and productivity of SCEs. The SCE bindings allow the user to make calls to remote functions in a natural way, and the GridSolve client handles all the details of converting data from the SCEs' internal representations to GridSolve data representations. Then the GridSolve client submits the RPC request to the GridSolve server, and when the remote reply is received, the client converts it back to the natural format for the SCE. This smooth integration with SCEs is one of the most successful features of GridSolve.

### 11.3.2.3 Server Administration

We have implemented a simple technique for adding arbitrary services to a running server. First, the new service should be built as a library or object file. Then the user writes a specification of the service parameters in a gsIDL file. The GridSolve service compiler processes the gsIDL and generates a wrapper, which is automatically compiled and linked with the service library or object files. The services are compiled as external executables with interfaces to the server described in a standard format. The server reexamines its own configuration and installed services periodically to detect new services. In this way, it becomes aware of the additional services without recompilation or restarting of the server itself.

Server administrators may specify arbitrary *server attributes* in a configuration file. These attributes are used to enable filtering or criteria matching in the selection of resources. For example, the server could have attributes describing the machine's architecture or amount of memory. These attributes are sent to the agent and stored in its database so that clients can make complex requests (e.g., only give me x86 servers with more than 2 GB of memory). The agent can very quickly filter service requests using these attributes to find matches with the appropriate servers.

Server administrators can also add *restrictions* in the configuration file. This allows restricting access to the server under certain conditions, such as during peak times or when there are a certain number of jobs already running.

## 11.3.3 Scheduling in GridSolve

Scheduling is essential for achieving an efficient and responsive distributed system. In a distributed, heterogeneous environment like the grid, services can achieve very different performance depending on many factors, including the network conditions, the server speeds, the temporary load on the server, and the efficiency of installed software. These factors need to be accounted for when scheduling service requests onto servers. GridSolve has several alternative scheduling methods available, and the topic of scheduling remains an active research area within GridSolve.

### 11.3.3.1 Agent Scheduling

In agent-based scheduling, the agent uses knowledge of the requested service, information about the parameters of the service request from the client, and the current state of the resources to score the possible servers and return the servers in a sorted order.

When a service is started, the server informs the agent about services that it provides and the computational complexity of those services. This complexity is expressed using two integer constants $a$ and $b$ and is evaluated as $aN^b$, where $N$ is the problem size. At start-up, the server notifies the agent about its computational speed (approximate MFlops from a simple benchmark), and it continually updates the agent with information about its workload. When an agent receives a request for a service with a particular problem size, it uses the service complexity and the server status information to estimate the time to completion on each server providing that service. It orders the servers in terms of time to completion, and then returns the list of servers to the client. The client then sends the service request to the fastest server. If that fails for some reason, the client can resubmit the service request to the next fastest service, thus providing a basic level of fault tolerance. This scheduling heuristic, summarized in Figure 11.3, is known as *Minimum*

for all servers $S_i$ that can provide the desired service
$T_1(S_i)$ = estimated amount of time for computation on $S_i$
$T_2(S_i)$ = estimated time for communicating input and output data
$T(S_i) = T_1(S_i) + T_2(S_i)$ estimated total time using $S_i$
select the server $S_m$ which has the minimum time, where $T(S_m) = \min T(S_i)\ \forall i$

**Figure 11.3    Minimum Completion Time algorithm.**

*Completion Time.* It is simple to implement and works well in many practical cases. Each service request should be assigned to the server that would complete the service in the minimum time, assuming that the currently known loads on the servers will remain constant during the execution and the communication costs between the client and all the servers are the same.

However, the Minimum Completion Time heuristic does not try to maximize the throughput when servers are allowed to run multiple services, and there are many more requested services than available servers. Since an estimate of the execution time for the currently executing service is available, this knowledge could be used to schedule new service requests more intelligently. Some explorations of alternative scheduling heuristics using historical execution trace information are described in [14].

### 11.3.3.2 Server Performance Prediction

The server also plays an important role in helping agent-based scheduling to work effectively. To efficiently schedule an application requires being able to accurately predict the duration of the requests that compose the application. However, predicting the duration of a request is a difficult task. Indeed, the duration might depend on the data (size and values), on the machine where the application is run, and on the implementation of the service. Even when the duration of a service does not depend on the data values (as is the case with many linear algebra kernels), predicting this duration is hard. In GridSolve, the duration of the task is described in the gsIDL file using the highest degree of the complexity polynomial, which gives an approximation of the number of operations the service has to perform when the inputs are known. The server's speed (number of operations per second) is computed by running a simple benchmark when the server is launched. The server periodically updates its current workload, which is used by the agent to scale down the server's speed. Then the estimated duration of the task is computed at runtime by dividing the estimated number of operations by the current speed of the server. However, computing the duration of a service based on the complexity polynomial has several drawbacks.

First, even though the complexity polynomial does not depend on the implementation, different implementations of the same algorithm do not necessarily have the same speed. Assume, for instance, that the service is the matrix multiply routine of the BLAS (Basic Linear Algebra Subroutines). There are a lot of different implementations of the same BLAS API, ranging from reference BLAS (a non-optimized Fortran version) to automatically tuned libraries, such as ATLAS [15], and up to specific implementations optimized for a precise version of a certain CPU, such as the *Goto BLAS* [16]. The complexity of these implementations is always the same ($O(N^3)$, for multiplying matrices of order $N$), but the execution time might be completely different (for instance, the reference BLAS are about six times slower than the vendor-optimized version on some CPUs). This effect is not taken into account by the standard Minimum Completion Time scheduling heuristic in GridSolve.

Moreover, obtaining the speed of the machine with a benchmark assumes that the flop rate of each service is the same as the benchmark. In practice, this is not true because compute-intensive services achieve higher flop rates than data-intensive services. In GridSolve, the server's speed is estimated by running a Linpack benchmark, which performs close to the peak flop rate of the processor. This is appropriate when the requested service is a compute-intensive one, such as for a linear algebra kernel. However, if the service is I/O bound (such as database access) or memory constrained (such as an out-of-core computation), the estimated runtime is likely to be a huge underestimation of the actual runtime.

Finally, for a given service, a slight change of a parameter may lead to a different algorithm and a different time to execute the service. For instance, the matrix–matrix multiply routine of the BLAS (dgemm) performs $C \leftarrow \alpha AB + \beta C$, where $A$, $B$, and $C$ are matrices. It is easy to see that the case $\alpha = 1$ and $\beta = 0$ is completely different from the case $\alpha = 0$ and $\beta = 1$. However, in the current GridSolve model, since the values of $\alpha$ and $\beta$ are not related to the size of the data, they do not appear in the complexity model for the dgemm service.

To solve the problems described above, we propose using a complexity template model for each service that is instantiated on each server for each different use case of the service. This template model consists of a polynomial of the parameters of the problem, and a set of category variables. The polynomial describes the behavior of the service and has coefficients that will be assigned by GridSolve based on the prior execution performance history. The use of categories differentiates the separate performance classes, which cannot be modeled as a continuous complexity function.

GridSolve uses a parametric regression system to compute or update the coefficients for the complexity templates at runtime. Each time the server runs the service, it updates the coefficients of the model using this run and the previous ones. A certain number of previous runs are stored on the server's local disk, which can be reused if the server has to be stopped and restarted. The server periodically sends updates of the coefficients to the agent, which evaluates the expressions at runtime to get an accurate prediction of the execution time of the service. The detailed complexity parameters that the agent receives from the server allow more accurate scheduling decisions to be made.

### 11.3.3.3 Scheduling Using Proxies for Computational Resources

In this server-based approach to scheduling, GridSolve creates server-proxies to delegate the scheduling to specialized scheduling and execution services, such as batch systems, Condor, or LFC (LAPACK for Clusters). The GridSolve agent sees the server-proxy as a single server entity, even though the server-proxy can represent a large number of actual resources, and so the proxy handles the scheduling for these resources rather than the GridSolve agent.

The GridSolve agent can decide to assign the service request to a server-proxy based on several factors (e.g., the proxy can register itself with the agent as a virtual server with a large amount of processing power). The server-proxy will delegate the request to the specialized service (e.g., Condor), which schedules and executes the request. The server-proxy then returns the results back to the client.

### 11.3.3.4 Client Scheduling

Scheduling based purely on computation cost may give poor results because the communication cost can be a very large factor in the overall RPC cost, especially in a WAN environment. While choosing the fastest server may minimize the execution time, if this server is on a distant network, the communication cost can easily overshadow the savings in the execution time.

To eliminate this weakness, we need an estimate of the network performance between the client and the servers that could possibly execute the service. This can be difficult to know ahead of time given the dynamic nature of the system, so we gather the information empirically at the time the call is made. When the client gets a list of servers from the agent, it is sorted based only on the estimate of the computational cost. Normally, the client would simply submit the service request to the first server on the list, but instead we first measure the bandwidth from the client to the top few servers using a simple 32 kB ping-pong benchmark. Given the total data size and the network speed, we compute an estimate of the total communication and computation RPC time for the servers and reorder the list of servers.

There is some cost associated with performing these measurements, but our expectation is that the reduction in the total RPC time will compensate for the overhead. Nevertheless, we try to keep the measurement overhead to a minimum. The time required to perform the measurement will depend on the number of servers that have the requested problem, and the bandwidth and latency from the client to these servers. When the data size is relatively small, the measurements are not performed, because it would take less time to send the data than it would take to perform the measurements. Also, since a given service may be available on many servers, the cost of measuring the network speed to all of them could be prohibitive. Therefore, the number of servers to be measured is limited to those with the highest computational performance. The exact number of measurements is configurable by the client. Once the measurements have been made, they can be cached for a certain amount of time so that subsequent calls on that client do not have to repeat the same measurement. The lifetime of the cached measurements is configurable by the user.

There are many other projects that monitor grid performance (see [17] or [18] for a review). For example, the Network Weather Service (NWS) [19] is a popular general system service that can monitor the performance of network bandwidth and latency (as well as other measures) and provide a statistical forecast for future performance. However, for the GridSolve system, most of the existing systems are inappropriate because clients enter and leave GridSolve dynamically, making it difficult to measure and retain the communication costs between the clients and the full set of servers. Moreover, NWS is required to be configured on each end, which necessitates some expertise that we do not assume. Hence, we have chosen to implement low-overhead probes as a way of building up the communication cost matrix between a client and the servers relevant to that client.

## 11.3.3.5 Task Graph Scheduling

There are two deficiencies associated with the standard RPC-based model when a computational problem essentially forms a workflow consisting of a sequence of tasks, among which there exist data dependencies. First, intermediate results are passed among tasks by first returning to the client, resulting in additional data transport between the client and the servers, which is pure overhead. Second, since the execution of each individual task is a separate RPC session, it is difficult to explore the potential parallelism among tasks where there is no immediate data dependency. Our previous approach to request sequencing partially solves the problem of unnecessary data transport by clustering a sequence of tasks based upon the dependency among them and scheduling them to run collectively. This approach has two limitations. First, the only mode of execution it supports is on a single server. Second, it prevents the potential parallelism among tasks from being explored. Recent work on GridSolve has focused on creating an enhanced request-sequencing technique that eliminates these limitations and solves the above problems. The core features of this work include direct inter-server data transfer and the capability of parallel task execution. The objective of this work is to simplify the parallel execution of data-driven workflow applications in GridSolve.

In GridSolve request sequencing, a request is defined as a single GridRPC call to an available GridSolve service. A data-driven workflow application is constructed as a sequence of requests, among which there may exist data dependencies. For each workflow application, the sequence of requests is scanned, and the data dependency between these requests is analyzed. The output of the analysis is a distributed acyclic graph (DAG) representing the workflow: tasks within the workflow are represented as nodes, and data dependencies among tasks are represented as edges. The workflow scheduler then schedules the DAG to run on the available servers. A set of tasks can potentially be executed concurrently if their dependencies permit it.

In order to eliminate unnecessary data transport when tasks are run on multiple servers, the standard RPC-based computational model of GridSolve has been extended to support direct data transfer among servers. Specifically, in order to avoid the case that intermediate results are passed among tasks via the client, servers must be able to pass intermediate results among each other, without the client being involved.

Recent experiments [20] demonstrated promising benefit from eliminating unnecessary data transfer and exploiting the parallelism found by automatically constructing and analyzing the task graph. The algorithm for workflow scheduling and execution currently used in GridSolve request sequencing is primitive in that it does not take into consideration the differences among tasks and does not consider the overall mutual impact between task clustering and network communication. We are planning to substitute a more advanced algorithm for this primitive one. Additionally, we are currently working on providing support for advanced workflow patterns, such as conditional branches and loops, which are not supported in the current implementation.

## 11.4 RPC Transparency Issues

As we mentioned in the introduction, there are some nontrivial issues to deal with when aiming for a transparent RPC implementation. In this section, we discuss some of these issues within the context of the GridRPC specification and our GridSolve implementation.

### 11.4.1 Parameter Passing

In local procedure calls, arguments are passed by value or by reference. Pass-by-value means that the actual value of the argument is passed to the procedure (e.g., if $x$ has the value 5 and $x$ is passed by value, then the procedure is given the value 5). In contrast, pass-by-reference means that a pointer is passed to the procedure, which must be dereferenced to obtain the actual values (e.g., if the value pointed to by $x$ is stored in memory address $0 \times 100$, then the procedure is given the value $0 \times 100$). Pass-by-reference is useful in a couple of scenarios. First, it allows the procedure to modify the value of an argument, which is not possible in a pass-by-value situation. Also, it is more efficient for passing large data structures, like matrices, because only one address needs to be passed instead of all the values.

In the context of RPC, the problem with pass-by-reference is that the remote machine is in a different address space, so any pointers from the client machine will be meaningless. This could be handled by making requests back to the client when data from the remote pointer is accessed, but that would be very inefficient. The typical approach (and the one implemented in GridSolve) is to pass a copy of the data referenced by the pointer and then restore any modifications to the data upon completion of the RPC. However, in an asynchronous situation, the user needs to be careful because any modifications to the referenced data made after the call but before the results from the RPC are restored would be lost.

Another complication with parameter passing in RPC is that of complex or user-defined data structures. Sun RPC uses XDR (External Data Representation) [21], which is a standard for describing and encoding arbitrary data. In GridSolve, we chose to avoid XDR for performance reasons and because almost all of the procedures we were dealing with used simple data structures like vectors and matrices.

There are trade-offs between transparency, flexibility, simplicity, and efficiency. We gave up some transparency and flexibility to gain simplicity and efficiency.

## 11.4.2 Binding to Servers

RPC binding refers to locating the remote host with the procedure to be invoked and then finding the correct server process on that host. Traditional RPC required specifying the remote host name explicitly. When the user is expected to supply the host names for the remote calls, the veneer of transparency begins to erode. Also, it becomes more than just a transparency issue when asynchronous RPC is considered. In this case, the selection of the remote host to satisfy the request can have a big effect on the performance.

The GridRPC function handle represents a mapping from a service descriptor (in this case, a simple character string) to the remote server that will be used to execute the function. This mapping could be specified by the user or determined by the middleware using simple resource discovery mechanisms or possibly some more sophisticated scheduling algorithms. In the end, the GridRPC specification leaves the issue of binding up to the various implementations.

The normal GridRPC calling sequence is to first initialize the handle and bind to a server using a call to `grpc_function_handle_default()` followed by a call to `grpc_call()` (or one of its brethren) at some point later. In the case of the GridSolve implementation, there is a slight problem with performing the scheduling in this scenario. GridSolve relies on having access to the values of the arguments in `grpc_call()` at the time the scheduling is performed, so it can estimate the execution time and the communication cost of sending the data. However, at the time `grpc_function_handle_default()` is called, we do not know which values will be used in the eventual call, so scheduling is not possible.

To deal with this issue, we allow the user to specify a special host name when initializing the function handle. The special name signifies to the GridSolve internals that the function handle binding should be delayed until the first time the handle is used to make a call. Subsequent calls using that function handle will not change the binding, so the semantics of successive GridRPC calls is not altered.

In terms of transparency, GridSolve does require the user to know the host name of the GridSolve agent, which performs the binding and scheduling, but the user never needs to know any of the server details. This seems like a reasonable trade-off because of multiple benefits provided by the agent.

## 11.4.3 Exception Handling and Fault Tolerance

Whenever communication with remote machines is involved, there is a possibility for new and subtle errors to appear. This can destroy the sense of transparency because now the user must deal with many new failure scenarios, which would never happen with a local procedure call. The GridRPC specification largely avoids attempting to maintain this kind of procedure-level transparency. The GridRPC calls have their own return values and error codes that must be dealt with appropriately. Any errors from the remote procedure itself must be passed back as an output argument of the RPC.

Despite the lack of transparency in exception handling, the GridRPC Specification leaves open the possibility of implementing transparent fault tolerance. In GridSolve, if a call fails, the system will automatically find another server to which to resubmit the job. This is completely transparent, so the user never knows that there were failures in the system. This brings up several issues of how to detect failures. There are many failure scenarios, and the handling of each one is a bit different, but these implementation details do not really affect the user's perception of RPC transparency. The issue of fault tolerance also affects the issue of binding, because when errors occur, the final server handling the request might be different from the one originally selected. GridSolve allows the user to enable or disable the fault-tolerant mode in order to match the desired GridRPC semantics.

### 11.4.4 Data Representation

The internal representation of data is an important issue in RPC because the local and remote machines may have different word lengths, floating-point formats, and byte orderings. If the user has to think about their data representation or data structures, the illusion of transparency is lost. We mentioned XDR earlier as a solution to the issue of passing complex data structures, but XDR also handles conversion of primitive data types between architectures by using a common intermediate representation. The GridRPC specification says nothing about data conversion, so it is left up to the implementors to decide. In GridSolve, we implemented a *receiver makes right* protocol, which allows the client to send data in its native format, which the receiver then converts to its own native format if needed. This avoids having to do two separate conversions (each end converting between native and common representations) as well as avoiding making an extra copy of the data on the sending side. GridSolve is still limited in its support for complex data structures, but we feel the increased efficiency in the common cases is worth making the trade-off.

### 11.4.5 Performance

While we make great effort to ensure good performance in GridSolve, the fact remains that extra communication overhead is inherent in any RPC. It was mentioned in [3] that if you had a truly transparent RPC for arbitrary applications, serious performance degradation could be inadvertently introduced. Of course, GridRPC specifies a different API for remote calls, so users will be aware of which calls are local and which are remote. Nevertheless, to achieve the best performance in an RPC-based application, the developers should carefully consider the ratio of computation time to communication time (since processor power has been increasing faster than communication speed, this issue gets more serious every year). Take matrix multiplication as an example. We compute $C \leftarrow \alpha AB + \beta C$, where $A$, $B$, and $C$ are matrices. For the sake of simplicity, assume that they are all square matrices of size $N \times N$. The communication costs will be on the order of

$$C_{input} = 3 \times \frac{N^2 \times \text{elementsize}}{\text{bandwidth}}$$

$$C_{output} = \frac{N^2 \times \text{elementsize}}{\text{bandwidth}}$$

$$C_{total} = C_{input} + C_{output}$$

where
"elementsize" is the size of each matrix element in bytes
"bandwidth" is the number of bytes per second for the network

Assuming a local network bandwidth of 11 MB/s and an element size of 8 bytes, the communication cost for $N = 3000$ is around 25 s. The computational costs will be on the order of

$$P = \left( \frac{2}{3} N^3 \right) \Big/ M_p$$

where $M_p$ is the performance of the machine in floating-point operations per second. At $N = 3000$ and local machine performance of $M_p = 800\,\text{Mflop/s}$, the local computation cost would be roughly 22.5 s. So, it costs more to send the data (not counting the remote execution time) than it would to just do the computation locally. Since the computation cost is growing faster than the communication cost, there will eventually be a crossover point where it makes sense to do the RPC, but it depends on the performance of the remote machine relative to the local machine as well as the network speed (WANs are often much worse than our 11 MB/s LAN example).

While this example might be discouraging, there are still many favorable scenarios for RPC, especially when taking into account task parallelism. One example is in parameter sweep problems, where the data being distributed is relatively small, and many servers can be used asynchronously and simultaneously to evaluate different input data with the output being collated in some way. Tasks that are suited to RPC computation include Evolutionary Algorithms (genetic algorithms, etc.), Monte Carlo–style algorithms, and optimization algorithms.

### 11.4.6 Security

Unlike with local procedures, when executing a remote procedure, the data is exposed on the network and therefore susceptible to snooping. Security is another area that is not addressed by the GridRPC specification, but the various implementations choose their own strategies. We have not implemented any data encryption methods in GridSolve. It is an important issue, but most of our users are running the entire GridSolve infrastructure on their local networks (e.g., behind firewalls). Because of this, there has not been a huge demand for encryption in GridSolve, but it should be straightforward to add since we have already implemented a transparent data compression module, and encryption could be added to this module at the data transport level.

### 11.4.7 Transparency

Trying to achieve total transparency (even if it is possible) would result in unexpected behavior and unacceptable performance degradation. As it was mentioned earlier, from a design standpoint, total transparency might not be the ideal anyway. We have attempted to design a system that is transparent in the sense of shielding users from unnecessary details and allowing for relatively painless conversion of code to a distributed implementation. The user still retains control over their application in deciding which functions are appropriate for remote processing. But the user does not need to know which server will be used, how the data will be converted, whether the job was resubmitted to another server due to failures, etc. This level of partial transparency allows the GridSolve system to provide better overall performance for the users while leaving the user in control of their application.

## 11.5 Summary

Using distributed grid resources in a simple and effective manner is difficult, though there are multiple programming models that are attempting to meet this challenge. The GridRPC API is a simple and portable programming model providing a standardized mechanism for accessing grid resources. GridSolve provides an implementation of GridRPC and adds a substantial list of features that are designed to make access to grid resources transparent and easier to accomplish. Client bindings for commonly used SCEs (e.g., MATLAB, Octave, and IDL) make it easy for a computational scientist to use grid resources from within their preferred tools. Transparent scheduling via the GridSolve agent relieves the user from having to know the details of the servers and service providers. Service-level fault tolerance provides a simple and usable mode for failure recovery. Task graph scheduling allows the composition of sequences of tasks into an inferred workflow, without requiring additional input from the user. Using all these techniques and more, GridSolve has been working to make the grid easier to use, and further research on this goal continues.

# References

1. A. D. Birrell and B. J. Nelson. Implementing remote procedure calls. *ACM Transactions on Computer Systems*, 2(1): 39–59, 1984.
2. J. E. White. A high-level framework for network-based resource sharing. In *Proceedings of the National Computer Conference*, New York, June 1976.
3. A. S. Tanenbaum and R. van Renesse. A critique of the remote procedure call Paradigm. In *Proceedings of the EUTECO 88 Conference*, Vienna, Austria, pp. 775–783, 1988.
4. K. Seymour, N. Hakada, S. Matsuoka, J. Dongarra, C. Lee, and H. Casanova. Overview of GridRPC: A remote procedure call API for grid computing. In M. Parashar, editor, *GRID 2002*, Baltimore, MD, pp. 274–278, 2002.
5. Global Grid Forum Research Group on Programming Models. http://www.gridforum.org/7_APM/APS.htm
6. J. Dongarra, Y. Li, K. Seymour, and A. YarKhan. Users' guide to GridSolve V0.19. Technical Report, Innovative Computing Laboratory. University of Tennessee, Knoxville, TN, June 2008.
7. Y. Tanaka, H. Nakada, S. Sekiguchi, T. Suzumura, and S. Matsuoka. Ninf-G: A reference implementation of RPC-based programming middleware for grid computing. *Journal of Grid Computing*, 1(1):41–51, 2003.
8. E. Caron, F. Desprez, F. Lombard, J.-M. Nicod, L. Philippe, M. Quinson, and F. Suter. A scalable approach to network enabled servers (research note). *Lecture Notes in Computer Science*, 2400/2002, pp. 239–248, 2002. Springer, Berlin/Heidelberg, Germany.
9. E. Dolan, R. Fourer, J. J. Moré, and T. S. Munson. The NEOS server for optimization: Version 4 and beyond. Technical Report ANL/MCS-P947-0202, Mathematics and Computer Science Division, Argonne National Laboratory, Argonne, IL, February 2002.
10. H. Casanova, G. Obertelli, F. Berman, and R. Wolski. The AppLeS parameter sweep template: User-level middleware for the grid. In *Proceedings of Supercomputing '2000 (CD-ROM )*, Dallas, TX, November 2000, p. 60. IEEE Computer Society, Washington, DC. ISBN 0-7803-9802-5.
11. J. Linderoth, S. Kulkarni, J-P. Goux, and M. Yoder. An enabling framework for master-worker applications on the computational grid. In *Proceedings of the Ninth IEEE Symposium on High Performance Distributed Computing (HPDC9)*, Pittsburgh, PA, pp. 43–50, August 2000.
12. D. Abramson, R. Buyya, and J. Giddy. A computational economy for grid computing and its implementation in the Nimrod-G resource broker. *Future Generation Computer Systems*, 18(8):1061–1074, October 2002.
13. J. Frey, T. Tannenbaum, I. Foster, M. Livny, and S. Tuecke. Condor-G: A computation management agent for multi-institutional grids. *Cluster Computing*, 5:237–246, 2002.
14. Y. Caniou and E. Jeannot. Experimental study of multi-criteria scheduling heuristics for GridRPC systems. In *ACM-IFIP Euro-Par 2004*, Pisa, Italy, September 2004.

15. R. C. Whaley and J. J. Dongarra. Automatically tuned linear algebra software (ATLAS). In ACM, editor, *SC'98: High Performance Networking and Computing: Proceedings of the 1998 ACM/IEEE SC98 Conference: Orange County Convention Center*, November 7–13, 1998, Orlando, FL, 1998. ACM Press and IEEE Computer Society Press, New York and Silver Spring, MD. Best Paper Award for Systems.

16. K. Goto and R. van de Geijn. High-performance implementation of the level-3 BLAS. Technical Report CS-TR-06-23, Department of Computer Sciences, The University of Texas at Austin, Austin, TX, May 5, 2006.

17. D. Lu, Y. Qiao, P. A. Dinda, and F. E. Bustamante. Characterizing and predicting TCP throughput on the wide area network. In *25th International Conference on Distributed Computing Systems (ICDCS 2005)*, June 6–10, 2005, Columbus, OH, pp. 414–424, 2005.

18. S. Zanikolas and R. Sakellariou. A taxonomy of grid monitoring systems. *Future Generation Computer Systems*, 21(1): 163–188, January 2005.

19. R. Wolski, N. T. Spring, and J. Hayes. The network weather service: A distributed resource performance forecasting service for metacomputing. *Future Generation Computer Systems*, 15(5–6): 757–768, 1999.

20. Y. Li, J. Dongarra, K. Seymour, and A. YarKhan. Request sequencing: Enabling Workflow for efficient problem solving in GridSolve. In *International Conference on Grid and Cooperative Computing (GCC 2008)*, Shenzhen, China, October 2008.

21. Sun Microsystems Inc. XDR: External data representation standard. RFC 1014, Sun Microsystems, Inc., June 1987.

*Chapter 12*

# High-Performance Parallel Computing with Cloud and Cloud Technologies

Jaliya Ekanayake, Xiaohong Qiu, Thilina Gunarathne, Scott Beason, and Geoffrey Fox

## Contents

# 12.1 Introduction

Cloud and cloud technologies are two broad categories of technologies related to the general notion of Cloud Computing. By "cloud," we refer to a collection of infrastructure services, such as Infrastructure as a service (IaaS) and Platform as a service (PaaS), provided by various organizations where virtualization plays a key role. By "cloud technologies," we refer to various cloud runtimes, such as Hadoop (ASF, *core*, 2009a), Dryad (Isard et al. 2007), and other MapReduce (Dean and Ghemawat 2008) frameworks, and also the storage and communication frameworks, such as Hadoop Distributed File System (HDFS) and Amazon S3 (Amazon 2009).

The introduction of commercial cloud infrastructure services, such as Amazon EC2, GoGrid (ServePath 2009), and ElasticHosts (ElasticHosts 2009), has allowed users to provision compute clusters fairly easily and quickly, by paying a monetary value for the duration of their usages of the resources. The provisioning of resources happens in minutes, as opposed to hours and days required in the case of traditional queue-based job-scheduling systems. In addition, the use of such virtualized resources allows the user to completely customize the virtual machine (VM) images and use them with ROOT/administrative privileges, another feature that is hard to achieve with traditional infrastructures. The availability of open-source cloud infrastructure softwares, such as Nimbus (Keahey et al. 2005) and Eucalyptus (Nurmi et al. 2009), and open-source virtualization software stacks, such as Xen Hypervisor (Barham et al. 2003), allows organizations to build private clouds to improve the resource utilization of the available computation facilities. The possibility of dynamically provisioning additional resources by leasing from commercial cloud infrastructures makes the use of private clouds more promising.

Among the many applications that benefit from cloud and cloud technologies, the data/compute-intensive applications are the most important. The deluge of data and the highly compute-intensive applications found in many domains, such as particle physics, biology, chemistry, finance, and information retrieval, mandate the use of large computing infrastructures and parallel processing to achieve considerable performance gains in analyzing data. The addition of cloud technologies creates new trends in performing parallel computing. An employee in a publishing company who needs to convert a document collection, terabytes in size, to a different format can do so by implementing a MapReduce computation using Hadoop, and running it on leased resources from Amazon EC2 in just a few hours. A scientist who needs to process a collection of gene sequences using the CAP3 (Huang and Madan 1999) software can use virtualized resources leased from the university's private cloud infrastructure and Hadoop. In these use cases, the amount of coding that the publishing agent and the scientist need to perform is minimal (as each user simply needs to implement a *map* function), and the MapReduce infrastructure handles many aspects of the parallelism.

Although the above examples are successful use cases for applying cloud and cloud technologies for parallel applications, through our research, we have found that there are limitations in using current cloud technologies for parallel applications that require complex communication patterns or require faster communication mechanisms. For example, Hadoop and Dryad implementations of Kmeans clustering applications, which perform an iteratively refining clustering operation, show higher overheads compared to implementations of MPI or CGL-MapReduce (Ekanayake et al. 2008)—a streaming-based MapReduce runtime developed by us. These observations raise questions: What applications are best handled by cloud technologies? What overheads do they introduce? Are there any alternative approaches? Can we use traditional parallel runtimes such as MPI in cloud? If so, what overheads does it have? These are some of the questions we try to answer through our research.

In Section 12.1, we give a brief introduction of the cloud technologies, and in Section 12.2, we discuss with examples the basic functionality supported by these cloud runtimes. Section 12.3 discusses how these technologies map into programming models. We describe the applications used to evaluate and test technologies in Section 12.4. The performance results are discussed in Section 12.5. In Section 12.6, we present details of an analysis we have performed to understand the performance implications of virtualized resources for parallel MPI applications. Note that we use MPI running on non-VMs in Section 12.5 for comparison with cloud technologies. We present our conclusions in Section 12.7.

## 12.2 Cloud Technologies

Cloud technologies such as MapReduce and Dryad have created new trends in parallel programming. The support for handling large data sets, the concept of moving computation to data, and the better quality of services provided by the cloud technologies make them a favorable choice to solve large-scale data/compute-intensive problems.

The granularity of the parallel tasks in these programming models lies in between the fine-grained parallel tasks that are used in message-passing infrastructures such as PVM (Dongarra et al. 1993) and MPI (Forum n.d.), and coarse-grained jobs in workflow frameworks such as Kepler (Ludscher et al. 2006) and Taverna (Hull et al. 2006), in which the individual tasks could themselves be parallel applications written in MPI. Unlike the various communication constructs available in MPI, which can be used to create a wide variety of communication topologies for parallel programs, in MapReduce, the "map→reduce" is the only communication construct available. However, our experience shows that most *composable* applications can easily be implemented using the MapReduce programming model. Dryad supports parallel applications that resemble Directed Acyclic Graphs (DAGs), in which the vertices represent computation units, and the edges represent communication channels between different computation units.

In traditional approaches, once parallel applications are developed, they are executed on compute clusters, supercomputers, or grid infrastructures (Foster 2001), where the focus on allocating resources is heavily biased by the availability of computational power. The application and the data both need to be moved to the available computational resource in order for them to be executed. These infrastructures are highly efficient in performing compute-intensive parallel applications. However, when the volume of data accessed by an application increases, the overall efficiency decreases due to the inevitable data movement. Cloud technologies such as Google MapReduce, Google File System (GFS) (Ghemawat et al. 2003), Hadoop and HDFS, Microsoft Dryad, and CGL-MapReduce adopt a more data-centered approach to parallel runtimes. In these frameworks, the data is staged in data/compute nodes of clusters or large-scale data centers, such as in the case of Google. The computations move to the data in order to perform the data processing. Distributed file systems, such as GFS and HDFS, allow Google MapReduce and Hadoop to access data via distributed storage systems built on heterogeneous compute nodes, while Dryad and CGL-MapReduce support reading data from local disks. The simplicity in the programming model enables better support for quality of services such as fault tolerance and monitoring.

### 12.2.1 Hadoop

Apache Hadoop has a similar architecture to Google's MapReduce runtime, where it accesses data via HDFS, which maps all the local disks of the compute nodes to a single file system hierarchy, allowing the data to be dispersed across all the data/ computing nodes. HDFS also replicates the data on multiple nodes so that failures of any nodes containing a portion of the data will not affect the computations that use that data. Hadoop schedules the MapReduce computation tasks depending on the data locality, improving the overall I/O (input/output) bandwidth. The outputs of the *map* tasks are first stored in local disks until later, when the *reduce* tasks access them (pull) via HTTP connections. Although this approach simplifies the fault-handling mechanism in Hadoop, it adds a significant communication overhead to the intermediate data transfers, especially for applications that produce small intermediate results frequently.

## 12.2.2 Dryad and DryadLINQ

Dryad is a distributed execution engine for coarse-grained data parallel applications. It combines the MapReduce programming style with dataflow graphs to solve the computation tasks. Dryad considers computation tasks as DAGs, where the vertices represent computation tasks and the edges act as communication channels over which the data flows from one vertex to another. The data is stored in (or partitioned to) local disks via the Windows shared directories and metadata files, and Dryad schedules the execution of vertices depending on the data locality. (*Note*: The academic release of Dryad only exposes the DryadLINQ (Yu et al. 2008) API for programmers. Therefore, all our implementations are written using DryadLINQ, although it uses Dryad as the underlying runtime.) Dryad also stores the output of vertices in local disks, and the other vertices that depend on these results access them via the shared directories. This enables Dryad to re-execute failed vertices, a step that improves fault tolerance in the programming model.

## 12.2.3 CGL-MapReduce

CGL-MapReduce is a lightweight MapReduce runtime that incorporates several improvements to the MapReduce programming model, such as (1) faster intermediate data transfer via a pub/sub broker network, (2) support for long-running *map/reduce* tasks, and (3) efficient support for iterative MapReduce computations. The architecture of CGL-MapReduce is shown in Figure 12.1 (left). (*Note*: Please note that the CGL-MapReduce is now known as Twister: Iterative MapReduce Runtime.)

The use of streaming enables CGL-MapReduce to send the intermediate results directly from its producers to its consumers, and eliminates the overhead of the file-based communication mechanisms adopted by both Hadoop and Dryad. The support for long-running *map/reduce* tasks enables configuring and reusing *map/reduce* tasks in the case of iterative MapReduce computations, and eliminates the need for reconfiguring or reloading static data in each iteration. This feature comes with the distinction of "static data" and "dynamic data" that we support in CGL-MapReduce. We refer to any data set that is static throughout the computation

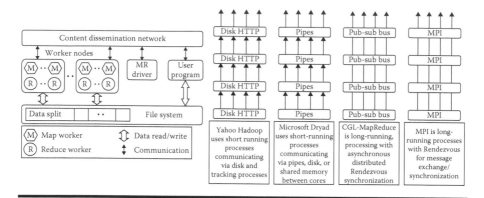

**Figure 12.1** **(Left) Components of CGL-MapReduce. (Right) Different synchronization and intercommunication mechanisms used by parallel runtimes.**

as "static data," and the data that is changing over the computation as "dynamic data." Although this distinction is irrelevant to the MapReduce computations that have only one *map* phase followed by a *reduce* phase, it is extremely important for iterative MapReduce computations, in which the map tasks need to access a static (fixed) data again and again. Figure 12.1 (right) highlights the synchronization and communication characteristics of Hadoop, Dryad, CGL-MapReduce, and MPI.

Additionally, CGL-MapReduce supports the distribution of smaller variable data sets to all the *map* tasks directly, a functionality similar to *MPI_Bcast()* that is often found to be useful in many data analysis applications. Hadoop provides a similar feature via its distributed cache, in which a file or data is copied to all the compute nodes. Dryad provides a similar feature by allowing applications to add resources (files) that will be accessible to all the vertices. With the above features in place, CGL-MapReduce can be used to implement iterative MapReduce computations efficiently. In CGL-MapReduce, data partitioning and distribution is left to the users to handle, and it reads data from shared file systems or local disks. Although the use of streaming makes CGL-MapReduce highly efficient, implementing fault tolerance with this approach is not as straightforward as it is in Hadoop or Dryad. We plan to implement fault tolerance in CGL-MapReduce by re-execution of failed *map* tasks and redundant execution of *reduce* tasks.

## 12.2.4 MPI

MPI, the de facto standard for parallel programming, is a language-independent communications protocol that uses a message-passing paradigm to share the data and state among a set of cooperative processes running on a distributed memory system. MPI specification (Forum, MPI) defines a set of routines to support various parallel programming models, such as point-to-point communication, collective communication, derived data types, and parallel I/O operations.

Most MPI runtimes are deployed in computation clusters where a set of compute nodes are connected via a high-speed network connection yielding very low communication latencies (typically in microseconds). MPI processes typically have a direct mapping to the available processors in a compute cluster or to the processor cores in the case of multi-core systems. We use MPI as the baseline performance measure for the various algorithms that are used to evaluate the different parallel programming runtimes. Table 12.1 summarizes the different characteristics of Hadoop, Dryad, CGL-MapReduce, and MPI.

## 12.3 Programming Models

When analyzing applications written in the MapReduce programming model, we can identify three basic execution units, namely, (1) map-only, (2) map-reduce, and (3) iterative map-reduce. Complex applications can be built by combining these three basic execution units under the MapReduce programming model. Table 12.2 shows the data/computation flow of these three basic execution units, along with examples.

In the MapReduce programming model, the tasks that are being executed at a given phase have similar executables and similar input and output operations. With zero *reduce* tasks, the MapReduce model reduces to a map-only model, which can be applied to many "embarrassingly parallel" applications. Software systems such as batch queues, Condor (Condor 2009), Falkon (Raicu et al. 2007), and SWARM (Pallickara and Pierce 2008) all provide similar functionality by scheduling large numbers of individual maps/jobs. Applications that can utilize a "reduction" or an "aggregation" operation can use both phases of the MapReduce model, and, depending on the "associative" and "commutative" nature of the reduction operation, multiple reduction phases can be applied to enhance the parallelism. For example, in a histogramming operation, the partial histograms can be combined in any order and in any number of steps to produce a final histogram.

The "side effect–free" nature of the MapReduce programming model does not promote iterative MapReduce computations. Each of the *map* and *reduce* tasks are considered as atomic execution units with no state shared in between executions. In parallel runtimes, such as those of the MPI, the parallel execution units live throughout the entire life of the program; hence, the state of a parallel execution unit can be shared across invocations. We propose an intermediate approach to develop MapReduce computations. In our approach, the *map/reduce* tasks are still considered free from side effects, but the runtime allows configuring and reusing the *map/reduce* tasks. Once configured, the runtime caches the *map/reduce* tasks. This way, both *map* and *reduce* tasks can keep the static data in memory, and can be called iteratively without loading the static data repeatedly.

Hadoop supports configuring the number of *reduce* tasks, which enables the user to create "map-only" applications by using zero *reduce* tasks. Hadoop can be

**Table 12.1 Comparison of Features Supported by Different Parallel Programming Runtimes**

| Feature | Hadoop | Dryad | CGL-MapReduce | MPI |
|---|---|---|---|---|
| Programming model | MapReduce | DAG-based execution flows | MapReduce with a *Combine* phase | Variety of topologies constructed using the rich set of parallel constructs |
| Data handling | HDFS | Shared directories/local disks | Shared file system/local disks | Shared file systems |
| Intermediate data communication | HDFS/point to point via HTTP | Files/TCP pipes/shared memory FIFO | Content distribution network (NaradaBrokering (Pallickara and Fox 2003)) | Low-latency communication channels |
| Scheduling | Data locality/rack aware | Data locality/network topology–based runtime graph optimizations | Data locality | Available processing capabilities |
| Failure handling | Persistence via HDFS, re-execution of map and reduce tasks | Re-execution of vertices | Currently not implemented (re-executing map tasks, redundant reduce tasks) | Program-level check-pointing OMPI (Gabriel et al. 2004), FT MPI |
| Monitoring | Monitoring support of HDFS, monitoring MapReduce computations | Monitoring support for execution graphs | Programming interface to monitor the progress of jobs | Minimal support for task-level monitoring |
| Language support | Implemented using Java; other languages are supported via Hadoop streaming | Programmable via C#, DryadLINQ provides LINQ programming API for Dryad | Implemented using Java; other languages are supported via Java wrappers | C, C++, Fortran, Java, C# |

**Table 12.2 Three Basic Execution Units under the MapReduce Programming Model**

| Map-Only | Map-Reduce | Iterative Map-Reduce |
|---|---|---|
| (diagram: Input → map() → Output) | (diagram: Input → map() → reduce() → Output) | (diagram: Input → map() → reduce() → Output, with feedback loop) |
| Cap3 analysis (we will discuss more about this later) | HEP data analysis (we will discuss more about this later) | Expectation maximization algorithms |
| Converting a collection of documents to different formats, processing a collection of medical images, and brute-force searches in cryptography; parametric sweeps | Histogramming operations, distributed search, and distributed sorting; information retrieval | Kmeans clustering, matrix multiplication |

used to implement iterative MapReduce computations, but the framework does not provide additional support to implement them efficiently. The CGL-MapReduce supports all the above three execution units, and the user can develop applications with multiple stages of MapReduce by combining them in any order. Dryad execution graphs resembling the above three basic units can be generated using DryadLINQ operations. DryadLINQ adds the LINQ programming features to Dryad where the user can implement various data analysis applications using LINQ queries, which will be translated to Dryad execution graphs by the compiler. However, unlike in the MapReduce model, Dryad allows the concurrent vertices to have different behaviors and different I/O characteristics, thus enabling a more workflow-style programming model. Dryad also allows multiple communication channels in between different vertices of the dataflow graph. Programming languages such as Swazall (Pike et al. 2005), introduced by Google for its MapReduce runtime, enable high-level language support for expressing MapReduce computations, and the Pig (ASF, *pig*, 2009b) available as a subproject of Hadoop allows query operations on large data sets.

Apart from these programming models, there are other software frameworks that one can use to perform data/compute-intensive analyses. Disco (Nokia 2009) is an open-source MapReduce runtime developed using a functional programming language named Erlang (Ericsson 2009). The Disco architecture shares clear similarities with both Google and Hadoop MapReduce architectures. Sphere (Gu and Grossman 2009) is a framework that can be used to execute user-defined functions in parallel on data stored in a storage framework named Sector. Sphere can also perform MapReduce-style programs, and the authors compare its performance with Hadoop for tera-sort applications. All-Pairs (Moretti et al. 2009) is an abstraction that can be used to solve the common problem of comparing all the elements in a data set with all the elements in another data set by applying a given function. This problem can be implemented using Hadoop and Dryad as well, and we discuss a similar problem in Section 12.4.4. We can also develop an efficient iterative MapReduce implementation using CGL-MapReduce to solve this problem. The algorithm is similar to the matrix multiplication algorithm that we explain in Section 12.4.3.

MPI and threads are two other programming models that can be used to implement parallel applications. MPI can be used to develop parallel applications in distributed memory architectures, whereas threads can be used in shared memory architectures, especially in multi-core nodes. The low-level communication constructs available in MPI allow users to develop parallel applications with various communication topologies involving fine-grained parallel tasks. The use of low-latency network connections between nodes enables applications to perform a large number of inter-task communications. In contrast, the next-generation parallel runtimes, such as MapReduce and Dryad, provide a small number of parallel constructs, such as "map-only," "map-reduce," "Select," "Apply," and "Join," and do not require high-speed communication channels. These constraints require adopting parallel algorithms that perform coarse-grained parallel tasks and less communication. The use of threads is a natural approach in shared memory architectures, where communication between parallel tasks reduces to the simple sharing of pointers via the shared memory. However, the operating system's support for user-level threads plays a major role in achieving better performances using multi-threaded applications. We will discuss the issues in using threads and MPI in more detail in Section 12.5.4.2.

# 12.4 Data Analyses Applications

## 12.4.1 CAP3—Sequence Assembly Program

CAP3 is a DNA sequence assembly program developed by Huang and Madan (1999) that performs several major assembly steps: These steps include computation of overlaps, construction of contigs, construction of multiple sequence alignments, and generation of consensus sequences to a given set of gene sequences. The program reads a collection of gene sequences from an input file (FASTA file format) and writes its output to several output files, as well as the standard output:

Input.fsa → CAP3 → Stdout + Other output files

The program structure of this application fits directly with the "map-only" basic execution unit, as shown in Table 12.2. We implemented a parallel version of CAP3 using Hadoop, CGL-MapReduce, and DryadLINQ. Each *map* task in Hadoop and in CGL-MapReduce calls the CAP3 executable as a separate process for a given input data file (the input "Value" for the *map* task), whereas in DryadLINQ, a "homomorphic Apply" operation calls the CAP3 executable on each data file in its data partition as a separate process. All the implementations move the output files to a predefined shared directory. This application resembles a common parallelization requirement, where an executable script, or a function in a special framework such as MATLAB® or R, needs to be executed on each input data item. The above approach can be used to implement all these types of applications using any of the above three runtimes.

## 12.4.2 High-Energy Physics

Next, we applied the MapReduce technique to parallelize a High-Energy Physics (HEP) data analysis application, and implemented it using Hadoop, CGL-MapReduce, and Dryad. The HEP data analysis application processes large volumes of data, and performs a histogramming operation on a collection of event files produced by HEP experiments. The details regarding the two MapReduce implementations and the challenges we faced in implementing them can be found in Ekanayake et al. (2008). In the DryadLINQ implementation, the input data files are first distributed among the nodes of the cluster manually. We developed a tool to perform the manual partitioning and distribution of the data. The names of the data files available in a given node were used as the data to the DryadLINQ program. Using a homomorphic "Apply" operation, we executed a ROOT-interpreted script on groups of input files in all the nodes. The output histograms of this operation were written to a predefined shared directory. Next, we used another "Apply" phase to combine these partial histograms into a single histogram using DryadLINQ.

## 12.4.3 Iterative MapReduce—Kmeans Clustering and Matrix Multiplication

Parallel applications that are implemented using message-passing runtimes can utilize various communication constructs to build diverse communication topologies. For example, a matrix multiplication application that implements Fox's Algorithm (Fox et al. 1987) and Cannon's Algorithm (Johnsson et al. 1989) assumes parallel processes to be in a rectangular grid. Each parallel process in the grid communicates with its left and top neighbors, as shown in Figure 12.2 (left). The current cloud runtimes, which are based on dataflow models such as MapReduce and

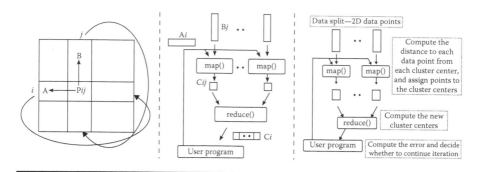

**Figure 12.2 (Left) Communication topology of Cannon's Algorithm implemented using MPI. (Middle) Communication topology of matrix multiplication application based on MapReduce. (Right) Communication topology of Kmeans clustering implemented as a MapReduce application.**

Dryad, do not support this behavior, in which the peer nodes communicate with each other. Therefore, implementing the above type of parallel applications using MapReduce or DryadLINQ requires adopting different algorithms.

We have implemented matrix multiplication applications using Hadoop and CGL-MapReduce by adopting a row/column decomposition approach to split the matrices. To clarify our algorithm, let us consider an example where two input matrices, A and B, produce matrix C, as the result of the multiplication process. We split the matrix B into a set of column blocks and the matrix A into a set of row blocks. In each iteration, all the *map* tasks process two inputs: (1) a column block of matrix B and (2) a row block of matrix A. Collectively, they produce a row block of the resultant matrix C. The column block associated with a particular *map* task is fixed throughout the computation, while the row blocks are changed in each iteration. However, in Hadoop's programming model (a typical MapReduce model), there is no way to specify this behavior. Hence, it loads both the column block and the row block in each iteration of the computation. CGL-MapReduce supports the notion of long-running *map/reduce* tasks, where these tasks are allowed to retain static data in the memory across invocations, yielding better performance for "iterative MapReduce" computations. The communication pattern of this application is shown in Figure 12.2 (middle).

Kmeans clustering (Macqueen 1967) is another application that performs iteratively refining computation. We also implemented Kmeans clustering applications using Hadoop, CGL-MapReduce, and DryadLINQ. In the two MapReduce implementations, each *map* task calculates the distances between all the data elements in its data partition and all the cluster centers produced during the previous run. It then assigns data points to these cluster centers, based on their Euclidian distances. The communication topology of this algorithm is shown in Figure 12.2 (right). Each *map* task produces partial cluster centers as the output; these are then combined at a *reduce* task to produce the current cluster centers. These current cluster centers are used in the next iteration, to find the next set of cluster centers. This process continues until the overall distance between the current cluster centers and the previous cluster centers reduces below a predefined threshold. The Hadoop implementation uses a new MapReduce computation for each iteration of the program, while CGL-MapReduce's long-running *map/reduce* tasks allow it to reuse *map/reduce* tasks. The DryadLINQ implementation uses various DryadLINQ operations, such as "Apply," "GroupBy," "Sum," "Max," and "Join," to perform the computation, and it also utilizes DryadLINQ's "loop unrolling" support to perform multiple iterations as a single-large query.

## 12.4.4 Alu Sequencing Studies

### 12.4.4.1 Alu Clustering

The Alu clustering problem (Batzer and Deininger 2002) is one of the most challenging problems for sequence clustering, because Alus represent the largest repeat families in human genome. There are about 1 million copies of Alu sequences in human genome, in which most insertions can be found in other primates and only a small fraction (~7000) are human specific. This indicates that the classification of Alu repeats can be deduced solely from the 1 million human Alu elements. Notably, Alu clustering can be viewed as a classical case study for the capacity of computational infrastructures, because it is not only of great intrinsic biological interest, but also a problem of a scale that will remain as the upper limit of many other clustering problems in bioinformatics for the next few years, for example, the automated protein family classification for a few millions of proteins predicted from large metagenomics projects.

### 12.4.4.2 Smith–Waterman Dissimilarities

We identified samples of the human and chimpanzee Alu gene sequences using Repeatmasker (Smith et al. 2004) with Repbase Update (Jurka 2000). We have been gradually increasing the size of our projects with the current largest samples having 35,339 and 50,000 sequences, and these require a modest cluster, such as Tempest (768 cores), for processing in a reasonable time (a few hours, as shown in Section 12.5). Note from the discussion in Section 12.4.4.1 that we are aiming at supporting problems with a million sequences—quite practical today on TeraGrid, and equivalent facilities given basic analysis steps scale like $O(N^2)$.

We used an open-source version NAligner (Smith–Waterman software) of the Smith–Waterman–Gotoh (SW-G) algorithm (Smith and Waterman 1981, Gotoh 1982) modified to ensure low start-up effects by each thread processing large numbers (above a few hundreds) at a time. The memory bandwidth needed was reduced by storing data items in as few bytes as possible.

### 12.4.4.3 The O(N²) Factor of 2 and Structure of Processing Algorithm

The Alu sequencing problem shows a well-known factor-of-2 issue present in many $O(N^2)$ parallel algorithms, such as those in direct simulations of astrophysical stems. We initially calculate in parallel the distance, $D(i,j)$, between points (sequences) $i$ and $j$. This is done in parallel over all processor nodes selecting criteria $i < j$ (or $j > i$ for the upper triangular case) to avoid calculating both $D(i,j)$ and the identical $D(j,i)$. This can require substantial file transfer, as it is unlikely that nodes requiring $D(i,j)$ in a later step will find that it was calculated on nodes where it is needed.

For example, the MDS (Multi Dimensional Scaling) and PW (PairWise) clustering algorithms, described in Fox et al. (2008), require a parallel decomposition where each of $N$ processes (MPI processes, threads) has $1/N$ of sequences, and for this subset $\{i\}$ of sequences stores in memory $D(\{i\},j)$ for all sequences j and the subset $\{i\}$ of sequences for which this node is responsible. This implies that we need $D(i,j)$ and $D(j,i)$ (which are equal) stored in different processors/disks. This is a well-known collective operation in MPI called either gather or scatter.

### 12.4.4.4 Dryad Implementation

We developed a DryadLINQ application to perform the calculation of pairwise SW-G distances for a given set of genes by adopting a coarse-grained task decomposition approach that requires minimum inter-process communication to ameliorate the higher communication and synchronization costs of the parallel runtime. To clarify our algorithm, let us consider an example where $N$ gene sequences produce a pairwise distance matrix of size $N \times N$. We decompose the computation task by considering that the resultant matrix groups the overall computation into a block matrix of size $D \times D$, where $D$ is a multiple (>2) of the available computation nodes. Due to the symmetry of the distances $D(i,j)$ and $D(j,i)$, we only calculate the distances in the blocks of the upper triangle of the block matrix, as shown in Figure 12.3 (left). The blocks in the upper triangle are partitioned (assigned) to the available compute nodes, and an "Apply" operation is used to execute a function to calculate $(N/D) \times (N/D)$ distances in each block. After computing the distances in each block, the function calculates the transpose matrix of the resultant matrix, which corresponds to a block in the lower triangle, and writes both these matrices into two output files in the local file system. The names of these files and their block numbers are communicated back to the main program. The main program sorts the files based on their block numbers and performs another "Apply" operation to combine the files corresponding to a row of blocks in a single-large row block, as shown in Figure 12.3 (right).

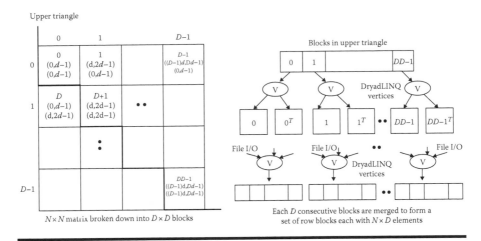

**Figure 12.3** **Task decomposition (left) and DryadLINQ vertex hierarchy (right) of the DryadLINQ implementation of SW-G pairwise distance calculation application.**

## 12.4.4.5 MPI Implementation

The MPI version of SW-G calculates pairwise distances using a set of either single- or multi-threaded processes. For $N$ gene sequences, we need to compute half of the values (in the lower triangular matrix), which is a total of $M = N \times (N - 1)/2$ distances. At a high level, computation tasks are evenly divided among P processes and execute in parallel, namely, the computation workload per process is $M/P$. At a low level, each computation task can be further divided into subgroups and run in $T$ concurrent threads. Our implementation is designed for flexible use of a shared memory multi-core system and distributed memory clusters (tight-coupled to medium-tight-coupled communication technologies, such threading and MPI). We provide options for any combinations of thread versus process versus node, as shown in Figure 12.4. The real computation workload per parallel unit is decided by $M/(T \times P \times \#$ nodes).

As illustrated in Figure 12.4, the data decomposition strategy runs a "space-filling curve through the lower triangular matrix" to produce equal numbers of pairs for each parallel unit such as process or thread. It is necessary to map indexes in each pairs group back to corresponding matrix coordinates $(i,j)$ for constructing a full matrix later on. We implemented a special function, "PairEnumerator," as the convertor. We tried to limit runtime memory usage for performance optimization. This is done by writing a triple of $i,j$ and also writing the distance value of pairwise alignment to a stream writer, and the system flushes accumulated results to a local file periodically. As the final stage, individual files are merged to form a full distance matrix.

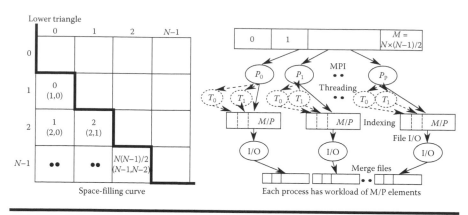

**Figure 12.4** Task decomposition (left) and MPI (right) implementation of SW-G pairwise distance calculation application.

## 12.5 Evaluations

### 12.5.1 Introduction

For our evaluations, we used three compute clusters (details are given in Table 12.3) with two 32-node clusters having almost identical hardware configurations and one latest 32-node cluster of 24-core machines with Infiniband connections. DryadLINQ and the MPI application that performs SW-G computation were run on the Windows cluster (Ref B, Ref C), while Hadoop, CGL-MapReduce, and other MPI applications were run on the Linux cluster (Ref A). We measured the performance of these applications, and present the results in terms of parallel overhead defined for parallelism $P$ by

$$f(P) = \frac{P \times T(P) - T(1)}{T(1)} \tag{12.1}$$

where
  $P$ denotes parallelism (e.g., processes, threads, and *map* tasks) used
  $T$ denotes time as a function of the number of parallel processes used

$T(1)$ is replaced in practice by $T(S)$, where $S$ is the smallest number of processes that can run the job. We used Hadoop release 0.20, the academic release of DryadLINQ, Microsoft MPI, and OpenMPI (OMPI) version 1.3.2 for our evaluations.

### 12.5.2 CAP3 and Particle Physics Case Studies

The results of our performance measurements for CAP3 and particle physics are shown in Figures 12.5 through 12.8.

**Table 12.3    Different Computation Clusters Used for the Analyses**

| Feature | Linux Cluster (Ref A) | Windows Cluster (Ref B) | Windows Cluster (Ref C) |
|---|---|---|---|
| # Node | 32 | 32 | 32 |
| CPU | Intel(R) Xeon(R) CPU L5420 2.50 GHz | Intel(R) Xeon(R) CPU L5420 2.50 GHz | Intel(R) Xeon(R) CPU E7450 2.40 GHz |
| # CPU/# cores | 2/8 | 2/8 | 4/24 |
| Total cores | 256 | 256 | 768 |
| Memory | 32 GB | 16 GB | 48 GB |
| Disk | 1 disk of Western Digital Caviar RE 160 GB SATA 7200 | 2 disks of 1000 GB (1 TB) Ultrastar A7K1000 7200 | 2 HP 146 GB 10K 2.5 SAS HP SP HDD |
| Network | Gigabit Ethernet | Gigabit Ethernet | 20 Gbps Infiniband |
| Operating system | Red Hat Enterprise Linux Server release 5.3 — 64 bit | Windows Server Enterprise — 64 bit | Windows Server 2008 HPC Edition (Service Pack 1) |

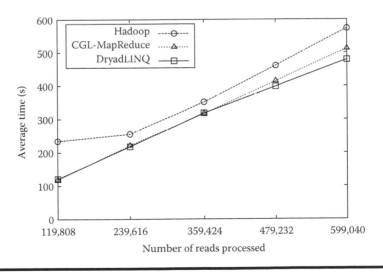

**Figure 12.5    Performance of the CAP3 application—average time (in s) against the number of gene reads processed.**

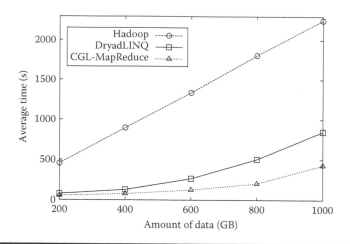

**Figure 12.6 Performance of the HEP data analysis application—average time (in s) against the amount of input data processed (in GB).**

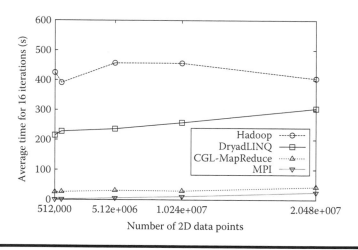

**Figure 12.7 Overhead induced by different parallel programming runtimes for the Kmeans clustering application—overhead against the number of 2D data points clustered. (*Note*: Both axes are in log scale.)**

From these results, it is clearly evident that the cloud runtimes perform competitively well for both "map-only-style" and "map-reduce-style" applications. In the HEP data analysis, both CGL-MapReduce and DryadLINQ access input data from local disks, where the data is partitioned and distributed beforehand. Currently, HDFS can be accessed using Java or C++ clients only, and the ROOT-interpretable scripts (ROOT—data analysis framework developed at CERN) are

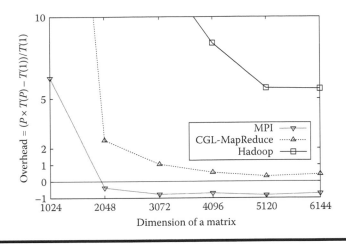

**Figure 12.8 Overhead induced by different parallel programming runtimes for the matrix multiplication application—overhead against the dimension of an input matrix.**

not capable of accessing data from HDFS. Therefore, we placed the input data in the IU (Indiana University) Data Capacitor—a high-performance parallel file system based on the Lustre file system, and programmed the *map* task in Hadoop to directly access data from it. The performance results show that this dynamic data movement in the Hadoop implementation incurred considerable overhead to the computation, while the ability of reading input data from local disks gave significant performance improvement to both DryadLINQ and CGL-MapReduce, as compared to the Hadoop implementation.

## 12.5.3 Kmeans and Matrix Multiplication Case Studies

For an iterative class of applications, cloud runtimes show considerably high overheads, compared to the MPI and CGL-MapReduce versions of the same applications; the results shown in Figures 12.7 and 12.8 imply that, for these types of applications, we still need to use high-performance parallel runtimes or alternative approaches. (*Note*: The negative overheads observed in the matrix multiplication application are due to the better utilization of a cache by the parallel application than the single-process version.) CGL-MapReduce shows a close performance closer to the MPI for large data sets in the case of Kmeans clustering and matrix multiplication applications, an outcome that highlights the benefits of supporting iterative computations and the faster data communication mechanism present in CGL-MapReduce.

## 12.5.4 Alu Sequence Analysis Case Study

### 12.5.4.1 Performance of Smith–Waterman–Gotoh Algorithm

We performed the Dryad and MPI implementations of Alu SW-G distance calculations on two large data sets and obtained the following results.

There is a short partitioning phase for DryadLINQ, and then both approaches calculate the distances and write these out to intermediate files, as discussed in Section 12.4. We note that the merge time is currently much longer for MPI than DryadLINQ, while the initial steps are significantly faster for MPI. However, the total times in Table 12.4 indicate that both MPI and DryadLINQ implementations perform well for this application, with MPI a few percent faster with current implementations. As expected, the times scale proportionally to the square of the number of distances. On 744 cores, the average time of 0.0067 ms/pair that corresponds to roughly 5 ms/pair calculated per core is used. The coarse-grained Dryad application performs competitively with the tightly synchronized MPI application. It proves once more the applicability of the cloud technologies for the composable applications.

### 12.5.4.2 Threaded Implementation

In Section 12.5.4.1, we looked at using MPI with one process per core and compared this with a threaded implementation, with each process having several threads. Labeling the configuration as $t \times m \times n$ for $t$ threads per process, $m$ MPI processes per node, and $n$ nodes, we compare choices of $t$, $m$, and $n$ in Figure 12.9.

**Table 12.4  Comparison of DryadLINQ and MPI Technologies on Alu Sequencing Application with SW-G Algorithm**

| Technology | | Total Time (s) | Time per Pair (ms) | Partition Data (s) | Calculated and Output Distance (s) | Merge Files (s) |
|---|---|---|---|---|---|---|
| Dryad | 50,000 sequences | 17200.413 | 0.0069 | 2.118 | 17104.979 | 93.316 |
| | 35,339 sequences | 8510.475 | 0.0068 | 2.716 | 8429.429 | 78.33 |
| MPI | 50,000 sequences | 16588.741 | 0.0066 | N/A | 13997.681 | 2591.06 |
| | 35,339 sequences | 8138.314 | 0.0065 | N/A | 6909.214 | 1229.10 |

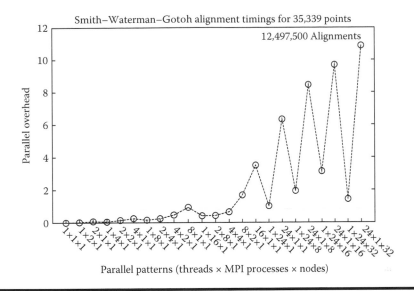

**Figure 12.9  Performance of Alu gene alignments for different parallel patterns.**

The striking result for this step is that MPI easily outperforms the equivalent threaded version of this embarrassingly parallel step. In Figure 12.9, all the peaks in the overhead correspond to patterns with large values of t. Note that the MPI intranode $1 \times 24 \times 32$ pattern completes the full 624 billion alignments in 2.33 h—4.9 times faster than the threaded implementation $24 \times 1 \times 32$. This 768-core MPI run has a parallel overhead of 1.43 corresponding to a speedup of 316.

The SW-G alignment performance is probably dominated by memory bandwidth issues, and we are pursuing several points that could affect this, though it is not at our highest priority as SW-G is not the dominant step. We have tried to identify the reason behind the comparative slowness of threading. Using Windows monitoring tools, we found that the threaded version has about a factor of 100 more context switches than in the one-thread-per-process MPI version. This could lead to a slowdown of the threaded approach and correspond to Windows handling of paging of threads with large memory footprints.

## 12.6  Performance of MPI on Clouds

After the previous observations, we analyzed the performance implications of cloud for parallel applications implemented using MPI. Specifically, we were trying to find the overhead of virtualized resources, and understand how applications with different communication-to-computation (C/C) ratios perform on cloud resources. We also evaluated different CPU-core assignment strategies for VMs, in order to understand the performance of VMs on multi-core nodes.

Commercial cloud infrastructures do not allow users to access the bare-hardware nodes, in which the VMs are deployed, a must-have requirement for our analysis. Therefore, we used a Eucalyptus-based cloud infrastructure deployed at our university for this analysis. With this cloud infrastructure, we have complete access to both VM instances and to the underlying bare-metal nodes, as well as the help of the administrators; as a result, we could deploy different VM configurations, allocating different CPU cores to each VM. Therefore, we selected the above cloud infrastructure as our main test bed.

For our evaluations, we selected three MPI applications with different communication and computation requirements, namely, (1) the matrix multiplication, (2) Kmeans clustering, and (3) the Concurrent Wave Equation Solver. Table 12.5 highlights the key characteristics of the programs that we used as benchmarks.

## 12.6.1 Benchmarks and Results

The Eucalyptus (version 1.4) infrastructure we used is deployed on 16 nodes of an iDataplex cluster, each of which has 2 Quad Core Intel Xeon processors (for a total of 8 CPU cores) and 32 GB of memory. In the bare-metal version, each node runs a Red Hat Enterprise Linux Server release 5.2 (Tikanga) operating system. We used the OMPI version 1.3.2 with the gcc version 4.1.2. We then created a VM image from this hardware configuration, so that we would have a similar software environment on the VMs once they were deployed. The virtualization is based on the Xen hypervisor (version 3.0.3). Both bare-metal and virtualized resources utilized gigabit Ethernet connections.

When VMs are deployed using Eucalyptus, it allows us to configure the number of CPU cores assigned to each VM image. For example, with 8 core systems, the CPU-core allocation per VM can range from 8 cores to 1 core per VM, resulting in several different CPU-core assignment strategies. In an Amazon EC2 infrastructure, the standard instance type has half a CPU per VM instance (Evangelinos and Hill 2008). In the current version of Eucalyptus, the minimum number of cores that we can assign for a particular VM instance is 1; hence, we selected five CPU-core assignment strategies (including the bare-metal test) listed in Table 12.6.

We ran all the MPI tests, on all five hardware/VM configurations, and measured the performance and calculated speedups and overheads. We calculated two types of overheads for each application using formula (1). The total overhead induced by virtualization and parallel processing is calculated using the bare-metal single-process time as $T(1)$ in formula (1). The parallel overhead is calculated using the single-process time from a corresponding VM as $T(1)$ in formula (1).

In all the MPI tests we performed, we used the following invariant to select the number of parallel processes (MPI processes) for a given application:

Number of MPI processes = Number of CPU cores used

**Table 12.5 Computation and Communication Complexities of Different MPI Applications Used**

| *Application* | *Matrix Multiplication* | *Kmeans Clustering* | *Concurrent Wave Equation* |
|---|---|---|---|
| Description | Implements Cannon's Algorithm<br><br>Assume a rectangular process grid (Figure 12.1, left) | Implements Kmeans Clustering algorithm<br><br>A fixed number of iterations are performed in each test | A vibrating string is decomposed (split) into points, and each MPI process is responsible for updating the amplitude of a number of points over time |
| Grain size (*n*) | The number of points in a matrix block handled by each MPI process | The number of data points handled by a single MPI process | Number of points handled by each MPI process |
| Communication pattern | Each MPI process communicates with its neighbors both row-wise and column-wise | All MPI processes send partial clusters to one MPI process (rank 0); rank 0 distributes the new cluster centers to all the nodes | In each iteration, each MPI process exchanges boundary points with its nearest neighbors |
| Computation per MPI process | $[O((\sqrt{n})]^3)$ | $O(n)$ | $O(n)$ |
| Communication per MPI process | $[O((\sqrt{n})]^2) = O(n)$ | $O(1)$ | $O(1)$ |
| C/C | $O\left(\dfrac{1}{\sqrt{n}}\right)$ | $O\left(\dfrac{1}{n}\right)$ | $O\left(\dfrac{1}{n}\right)$ |
| Message size | $(\sqrt{n})^2 = n$ | $D$—where $D$ is the number of cluster centers<br><br>$D \ll n$ | Each message contains a double value |
| Communication routines used | *MPI_Sendrecv_replace()* | *MPI_Reduce()*<br>*MPI_Bcast()* | *MPI_Sendrecv()* |

**Table 12.6 Different Hardware/VM Configurations Used for Our Performance Evaluations**

| Ref | Description | Number of CPU Cores Accessible to the Virtual or Bare-Metal Node | Amount of Memory (GB) Accessible to the Virtual or Bare-Metal Node | Number of Virtual or Bare-Metal Nodes Deployed |
|---|---|---|---|---|
| BM | Bare-metal node | 8 | 32 | 16 |
| 1-VM-8-core | 1 VM instance per bare-metal node | 8 | 30 (2 GB is reserved for dom0) | 16 |
| 2-VM-4-core | 2 VM instances per bare-metal node | 4 | 15 | 32 |
| 4-VM-2-core | 4 VM instances per bare-metal node | 2 | 7.5 | 64 |
| 8-VM-1-core | 8 VM instances per bare-metal node | 1 | 3.75 | 128 |

For example, for the matrix multiplication application, we used only half the number of nodes (bare-metal or VMs) available to us, so that we had 64 MPI processes = 64 CPU cores. (This is mainly because the matrix multiplication application expects the MPI processes to be in a square grid, in contrast to a rectangular grid). For Kmeans clustering, we used all the nodes, resulting in a total of 128 MPI processes utilizing all 128 CPU cores. Some of the results of our analysis highlighting the different characteristics we observed are shown in Figures 12.10 through 12.17.

For the matrix multiplication, the graphs show very close performance characteristics in all the different hardware/VM configurations. As we expected, the bare-metal has the best performance and speedup values, compared to the VM configurations (apart from the region close to the matrix size of 4096 × 4096, where the VM performed better than the bare-metal; we have performed multiple tests at this point, and found that it is due to the cache performances of the bare-metal node). After the bare-metal, the next-best performance and speedups were recorded in the case of 1 VM per bare-metal node configuration, in which the performance difference was mainly due to the overhead induced by the virtualization. However, as we increased the number of VMs per bare-metal node, the overhead increased

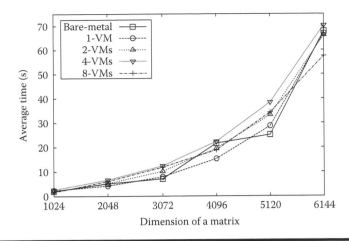

**Figure 12.10 Performance of the matrix multiplication application—average time (in s) against the size of a matrix (number of MPI processes = 64).**

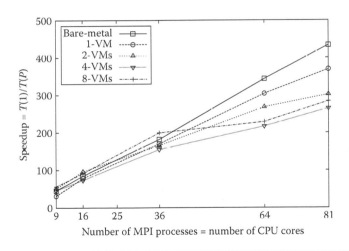

**Figure 12.11 Speedup of the matrix multiplication application—speedup against the number of MPI processes = number of CPU cores used (fixed matrix size = 5184 × 5184).**

as well. At 81 processes, the 8 VMs per node configuration shows about a 34% decrease in speedup compared to the bare-metal results.

In Kmeans clustering, the effect of virtualized resources is much clearer than in the case of matrix multiplication. All VM configurations show a lower performance compared to the bare-metal configuration. In this application, the amount of data transferred between MPI processes is extremely low compared to the

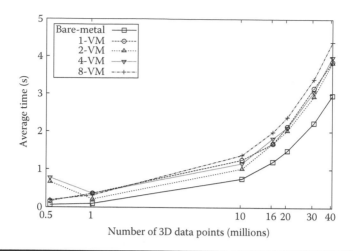

**Figure 12.12    Performance of Kmeans clustering—average time (in s) against the number of 3D data points clustered (number of MPI processes = 128).**

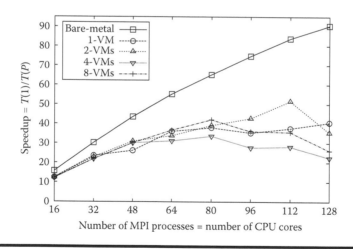

**Figure 12.13    Speedup of Kmeans clustering—speedup against the number of MPI processes = number of CPU cores used (number of data points = 860,160).**

amount of data processed by each MPI process, and also in relation to the amount of computations performed. Figures 12.14 and 12.15 show the total overhead and the parallel overhead for Kmeans clustering under different VM configurations. From these two calculations, we found that, for VM configurations, the overheads are extremely large for data-set sizes of less than 10 million points, for which the bare-metal overhead remains less than 1 (for all cases). For larger data sets, such as those of 40 million points, all overheads reached less than 0.5. The slower speedup

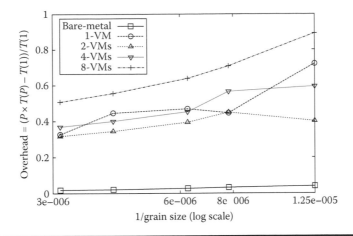

**Figure 12.14 Total overhead of Kmeans clustering—overhead against 1/grain size, grain size = number of 2D data points per parallel task (number of MPI processes = 128).**

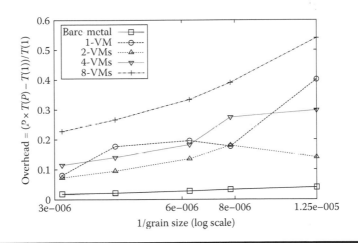

**Figure 12.15 Parallel overhead of Kmeans clustering—parallel overhead against 1/grain size (number of MPI processes = 128).**

of the VM configurations (shown in Figure 12.13) is due to the use of a smaller data set (~800K points) to calculate the speedups. The overheads are extremely large for this region of the data sizes, and hence, this resulted in lower speedups for the VMs.

The concurrent wave equation splits a number of points into a set of parallel processes, and each parallel process updates its portion of the points in some

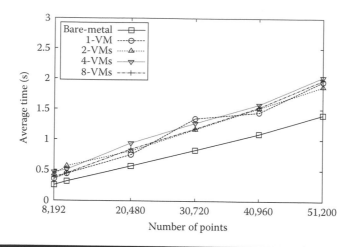

**Figure 12.16** **Performance of the Concurrent Wave Equation Solver—average time (in s) against the number of points computed (number of MPI processes = 128).**

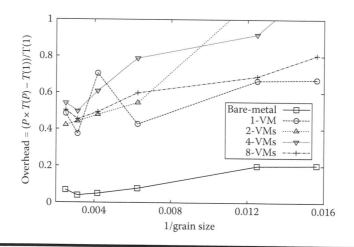

**Figure 12.17** **Total overhead of the Concurrent Wave Equation Solver—overhead against 1/grain size, grain size = number of points assigned per parallel task (number of MPI processes = 128).**

number of steps. An increase in the number of points increases the amount of computations performed. Since we fixed the number of steps in which the points were updated, we obtained a constant amount of communication in all the test cases, resulting in a C/C ratio of $O(1/n)$. In this application also, the difference in performance between the VMs and the bare-metal version was clearer, and at the highest grain size, the total overhead of 8 VMs per node is about seven times higher than the overhead of the bare-metal configuration. The performance differences between the different VM configurations became smaller with the increase in grain size.

From the above experimental results, we can see that the applications with lower C/C ratios experienced a slower performance in virtualized resources. When the amount of data transferred between MPI processes is large, as in the case of the matrix multiplication, the application is more susceptible to the bandwidth than the latency. From the performance results of the matrix multiplication, we can see that the virtualization has not affected the bandwidth considerably. However, all the other results show that the virtualization has caused considerable latencies for parallel applications, especially with smaller data transfer requirements. The effect on latency increases as we use more VMs in a bare-metal node.

According to the Xen para-virtualization architecture (Barham et al. 2003), domUs (VMs that run on top of a Xen para-virtualization) are not capable of performing I/O operations by themselves. Instead, they communicate with dom0 (privileged OS) via an event channel (interrupts) and the shared memory, and then the dom0 performs the I/O operations on behalf of the domUs. Although the data is not copied between domUs and dom0, dom0 needs to schedule the I/O operations on behalf of domUs. Figure 12.18 (left) and (right) shows this behavior in the 1 VM per node and 8 VMs per node configurations, respectively, that we used.

In all the above parallel applications we tested, the timing figures measured correspond to the time for computation and communication inside the applications. Therefore, all the I/O operations performed by the applications are network dependent. From Figure 12.19 (right), it is clear that dom0 needs to handle eight event channels when there are eight VM instances deployed on a single bare-metal node. Although the eight MPI processes run on a single bare-metal node, since they are in different virtualized resources, each of them can only communicate via dom0. This explains the higher overhead in our results for 8 VMs per node configuration. The architecture reveals another important feature as well, that is, in the case of the 1 VM per node configuration, when multiple processes

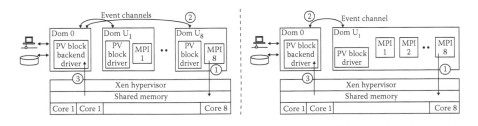

**Figure 12.18** **(Left) Communication between dom0 and domU when 1 VM per node is deployed. (Right) Communication between dom0 and domUs when 8 VMs per node are deployed.**

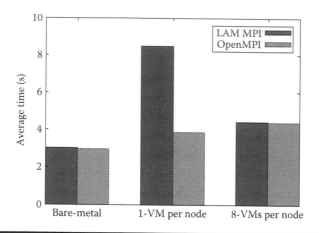

**Figure 12.19 LAM versus OMPI under different VM configurations.**

(MPI or others) that run in the same VM communicate with each other via the network, all the communications must be scheduled by dom0. This results in higher latencies. We could verify this by running the above tests with LAM MPI (a predecessor of OMPI, which does not have improved support for in-node communications for multi-core nodes). Our results indicate that, with LAM MPI, the worst performance for all the tests occurred when 1 VM per node was used. For example, Figure 12.19 shows the performance of Kmeans clustering under bare-metal, 1 VM per node, and 8 VMs per node configurations. This observation suggests that, when using VMs with multiple CPUs allocated to each of them for parallel processing, it is better to utilize parallel runtimes, which have better support for in-node communication.

Several others have also performed relevant research on the performance implications of virtualized resources. Youseff et al. (2006) present an evaluation of the performance impact of Xen on MPI. According to their evaluations, the Xen does not impose considerable overheads for HPC (high-performance computing) applications. However, our results indicate that the applications that are more sensitive to latencies (smaller messages, lower C/C ratios) also experience higher overheads under virtualized resources, and this overhead increases as more and more VMs are deployed per hardware node. From their evaluations, it is not clear how many VMs they deployed on the hardware nodes, or how many MPI processes were used in each VM. According to our results, these factors cause significant changes in possible results. Running 1 VM per hardware node produces a VM instance with a similar number of CPU cores, such as in a bare-metal node. However, our results indicate that, even in this approach, if the parallel processes inside the node communicate via the network, the virtualization may produce higher overheads under the current VM architectures.

Evangelinos and Hill (2008) discuss the details of their analysis of the performance of HPC benchmarks on the EC2 cloud infrastructure. One of the key observations noted in their paper is that both the OMPI and the MPICH2-nemsis show extremely large latencies, while the LAM MPI, the GridMPI, and the MPICH2-scok show smaller, smoother latencies. This observation is similar to what we observed with the LAM MPI in our tests, and the same explanation holds valid for their observation as well.

Walker (2008) presents benchmark results of the performance of HPC applications using "high-CPU extra-large" instances provided by EC2, and on a similar set of local hardware nodes. The local nodes are connected using Infiniband switches, whereas the Amazon EC2 network technology is unknown. The results indicate about a 40%–1000% performance degradation on the EC2 resources, compared to the local cluster. Since the differences in operating systems and the compiler versions between the VMs and bare-metal nodes may cause variations in results, for our analysis, we used a cloud infrastructure over which we have complete control. In addition, we used similar software environments in both VMs and bare-metal nodes. In our results, we noticed that applications that are more susceptible to latencies experience a higher performance degradation (around 40%) under virtualized resources. Bandwidth does not seem to be a consideration in private cloud infrastructures.

Gavrilovska et al. (2007) discuss several improvements over the current virtualization architectures to support HPC applications, such as HPC hypervisors and self-virtualized I/O devices. We notice the importance of such improvements and research. In our experimental results, we used hardware nodes with 8 cores, and deployed and tested up to 8 VMs per node in these systems. Our results show that the virtualization overhead increases with the number of VMs deployed on a hardware node. These characteristics will have a larger impact on systems having more CPU cores per node. A node with 32 cores running 32 VM instances may produce very large overheads under the current VM architectures.

## 12.7 Conclusions and Future Work

We have described several different studies of clouds and cloud technologies on both real applications and standard benchmark. These address different aspects of parallel computing using either traditional (MPI) or the new cloud-inspired approaches. We find that cloud technologies work well for most pleasingly parallel problems ("map-only" and "map-reduce" classes of applications). In addition, their support for handling large data sets, the concept of moving computation to data, and the better quality of services provided such as fault tolerance and monitoring, all serve to simplify the implementation details of such problems. Applications with complex communication patterns observe higher overheads when implemented using cloud technologies, and even with large data sets, these overheads limit the usage of cloud technologies for such applications. Enhanced MapReduce runtimes, such as CGL-MapReduce, allow iterative-style applications to utilize the MapReduce programming model, while incurring minimal overheads, as compared to other runtimes, such as Hadoop and Dryad.

Handling large data sets using cloud technologies on cloud resources is an area that needs more research. Most cloud technologies support the concept of moving computation to data where the parallel tasks access data stored in local disks. Currently, it is not clear to us whether this approach would work well with the VM instances that are leased only for the duration of use. A possible approach is to stage the original data in high-performance parallel file systems or Amazon S3–type storage services, and then move the data to the VMs each time they are leased to perform computations.

MPI applications that are sensitive to latencies experience moderate-to-higher overheads when performed on cloud resources, and these overheads increase as the number of VMs per bare-hardware node increases. For example, in Kmeans clustering, 1 VM per node shows a minimum of an 8% total overhead, while 8 VMs per node show at least a 22% overhead. In the case of the Concurrent Wave Equation Solver, both these overheads are around 50%. Therefore, we expect the CPU-core assignment strategies, such as half a core per VM, to produce very high overheads for applications that are sensitive to latencies. Applications that are not susceptible to latencies, such as those that perform large data transfers and/or higher C/C ratios, show minimal total overheads in both bare-metal and VM configurations. Therefore, we expect that the applications developed using cloud technologies will work fine with cloud resources, because the milliseconds-to-seconds latencies that they already have under the MapReduce model will not be affected by the additional overheads introduced by the virtualization. This is also an area we are currently investigating. We are also building applications (biological DNA sequencing) whose end-to-end implementation from data processing to filtering (data-mining) involves an integration of MapReduce and MPI (Fox et al. 2008).

# Acknowledgments

We would like to thank Joe Rinkovsky and Jenett Tillotson from University Information Technology Services, Indiana University (IU UITS), for their dedicated support in setting up a private cloud infrastructure and helping us with various configurations associated with our evaluations. We would also like to thank the Advanced Research Services and Tools (ARTS) team at Microsoft Research for their support on hardware and software infrastructures. We are grateful to Mina Rho and Haixu Tang from the Indiana University School of Informatics and Computing for their help in understanding Alu sequence clustering and providing human and chimpanzee gene sequence data.

# References

Amazon.com, Inc. 2009. Simple Storage Service (S3). http://aws.amazon.com/s3

ASF. 2009a. Apache Hadoop Core. http://hadoop.apache.org/core

ASF. 2009b. Apache Hadoop Pig. http://hadoop.apache.org/pig/

Barham, P., B. Dragovic et al. 2003. Xen and the art of virtualization. *Proceedings of the 19th ACM Symposium on Operating Systems Principles*, Bolton Landing, NY.

Batzer, M.A. and P.L. Deininger. 2002. Alu repeats and human genomic diversity. *Nat. Rev. Genet.* **3**(5): 370–379.

Condor Team. 2009. Condor DAGMan. http://www.cs.wisc.edu/condor/dagman/

Dean, J. and S. Ghemawat. 2008. MapReduce: Simplified data processing on large clusters. *Commun. ACM* **51**(1): 107–113.

Dongarra, J., C.A. Geist et al. 1993. Integrated PVM framework supports heterogeneous network computing. *Comput. Phys.* 7(2): 166–175.

Ekanayake, J., S. Pallickara et al. 2008. MapReduce for data intensive scientific analyses. *IEEE Fourth International Conference on eScience '08*, Indianapolis, IN.

ElasticHosts Ltd. 2009. Cloud Hosting. http://www.elastichosts.com/

Ericsson 2009. Erlang programming language. http://www.erlang.org/

Evangelinos, C. and C. Hill. 2008. Cloud computing for parallel scientific HPC applications: Feasibility of running coupled atmosphere-ocean climate models on Amazon's EC2. *The First Workshop on Cloud Computing and its Applications (CCA'08)*, Chicago, IL.

Forum, MPI. n.d. MPI (Message Passing Interface). http://www.mcs.anl.gov/research/projects/mpi/

Foster, I. 2001. The anatomy of the grid: Enabling scalable virtual organizations. *Int. J. Supercomput. Appl.* **15**: 200–222.

Fox, G.C., A. Hey, and S. Otto. 1987. Matrix algorithms on the hypercube I: Matrix multiplication. *Parallel Comput.* **4**: 17.

Fox, G., S. Bae et al. 2008. Parallel data mining from multicore to cloudy grids. *Proceedings of the International Advanced Research Workshop on High Performance Computing and Grids (HPC2008)*, Cetraro, Italy.

Gabriel, E., G.E. Fagg et al. 2004. Open MPI: Goals, concept, and design of a next generation MPI implementation. *Proceedings of the 11th European PVM/MPI Users' Group Meeting.* Budapest, Hungary.

Gavrilovska, A., S. Kumar et al. March 2007. Abstract high-performance hypervisor architectures: Virtualization in HPC systems. *Proceedings of the HPCVirt 2007*, Lisbon, Portugal.

Ghemawat, S., H. Gobioff et al. 2003. The Google file system. *SIGOPS Oper. Syst. Rev.* **37**(5): 29–43.

Gotoh, O. 1982. An improved algorithm for matching biological sequences. *J. Mol. Biol.* **162**: 705–708.

Gu, Y. and R.L. Grossman. 2009. Sector and sphere: The design and implementation of a high-performance data cloud. *Philos. Trans. A: Math Phys. Eng. Sci.* **367**(1897): 2429–2445.

Huang, X. and A. Madan. 1999. CAP3: A DNA sequence assembly program. *Genome Res.* **9**(9): 868–877.

Hull, D., K. Wolstencroft et al. 2006. Taverna: A tool for building and running workflows of services. *Nucleic Acids Res.* 34(Web Server issue): W729–32.

Isard, M., M. Budiu et al. 2007. Dryad: Distributed data-parallel programs from sequential building blocks. *SIGOPS Oper. Syst. Rev.* **41**(3): 59–72.

Johnsson, S.L., T. Harris et al. 1989. Matrix multiplication on the connection machine. *Proceedings of the 1989 ACM/IEEE Conference on Supercomputing*, Reno, NV. ACM, New York.

Jurka, J. 2000. Repbase update: A database and an electronic journal of repetitive elements. *Trends Genet.* **9**:418–420.

Keahey, K., I. Foster et al. 2005. Virtual workspaces: Achieving quality of service and quality of life in the Grid. *Sci. Program.* **13**(4): 265–275.

Ludscher, B., I. Altintas et al. 2006. Scientific workflow management and the Kepler system [research articles]. *Concurr. Comput. Pract. Exp.* **18**(10): 1039–1065.

Macqueen, J. 1967. Some methods for classification and analysis of multivariate observations. *Proceedings of the Fifth Berkeley Symposium on Mathematical Statistics and Probability*, Vol. 1: *Statistics*, Berkeley, CA, pp. 281–297.

Moretti, C., H. Bui et al. 2009. All-pairs: An abstraction for data intensive computing on campus grids. *IEEE Trans. Parallel Distrib. Syst.* **21**(1): 33–46.

Nokia. 2009. Disco project. http://discoproject.org/

Nurmi, D., R. Wolski et al. 2009. The eucalyptus open-source cloud-computing system. *Proceedings of the Ninth IEEE/ACM International Symposium on Cluster Computing and the Grid*, Shanghai, China.

Pallickara, S. and G. Fox. 2003. NaradaBrokering: A distributed middleware framework and architecture for enabling durable peer-to-peer grids. *Proceedings of the ACM/IFIP/USENIX 2003 International Conference on Middleware*, Rio de Janeiro, Brazil. Springer-Verlag, New York.

Pallickara, S. L. and M. Pierce. 2008. SWARM: Scheduling large-scale jobs over the loosely-coupled HPC clusters. *Proceedings of the IEEE Fourth International Conference on eScience '08 (eScience, 2008)*, Indianapolis, IN.

Pike, R., S. Dorward et al. 2005. Interpreting the data: Parallel analysis with Sawzall. *Sci. Program.* **13**(4): 277–298.

Raicu, I., Y. Zhao et al. 2007. Falkon: A fast and light-weight tasK executiON framework. *Proceedings of the 2007 ACM/IEEE Conference on Supercomputing*, Reno, NV. ACM, New York.

ServePath. 2009. GoGrid Cloud Hosting. http://www.gogrid.com/

Smith, T.F. and M.S. Waterman. 1981. Identification of common molecular subsequences. *J. Mol. Biol.* **147**:195–197.

Smith, A.F.A., R. Hubley, and P. Green. 2004. Repeatmasker. http://www.repeatmasker.org

Smith Waterman Software. http://jaligner.sourceforge.net/naligner/

Vermorel, J. 2005. NAligner (Smith Waterman software with Gotoh enhancement). http://jaligner.sourceforge.net/naligner/

Walker, E. 2008. Benchmarking Amazon EC2 for high-performance scientific computing. http://www.usenix.org/publications/login/2008–10/openpdfs/walker.pdf.

Youseff, L., R. Wolski et al. 2006. Evaluating the performance impact of Xen on MPI and process execution for HPC systems. *Proceedings of the First International Workshop on Virtualization Technology in Distributed Computing*, Tampa, FL.

Yu, Y., M. Isard et al. 2008. DryadLINQ: A system for general-purpose distributed data-parallel computing using a high-level language. *Proceedings of the Symposium on Operating System Design and Implementation (OSDI )*, San Diego, CA.

*Chapter 13*

# BioVLAB: Bioinformatics Data Analysis Using Cloud Computing and Graphical Workflow Composers

Youngik Yang, Jong Youl Choi, Chathura Herath, Suresh Marru, and Sun Kim

## Contents

# 13.1 Introduction

Recent advances in high-throughput instrument technologies allow small research labs to obtain data for scientific projects of their interest in a cost-effective way. In biology and medicine, this opened a door to a genome-wide study. Unfortunately, many small research labs are unable to afford the analysis of such data since the data analysis task requires bioinformatics experts and a good computing infrastructure to process and analyze a large amount of data. We have been developing a novel bioinformatics computing architecture, called BioVLAB, using Amazon cloud computing and the Linked Enviroments for Atmospheric Discovery (LEAD)/OGCE (Open Grid Computing Environments) scientific workflow system. The emergence of cloud computing enables biologists to perform data analysis tasks without worrying about computing resources and related issues such as system administration and resource allocation. The BioVLAB architecture is based on the LEAD/OGCE workflow system that includes a front-end graphical workflow system named XBaya, which allows biologists to run tasks in an intuitive way. XBaya empowers users to visually monitor workflow execution in real time and provides controls to modify the workflow and steer it according to their scientific needs. The workflow system presents an elegant abstraction so that biologists can focus on science while the system deals with all cloud computing and local resource interactions.

Using the BioVLAB architecture, we have developed three experimental systems: BioVLAB-protein, for a simple protein sequence analysis; BioVLAB-microarray, for analyzing microarray data from NCBI's (*National Center for Biotechnology Information*) GEO (Gene Expression Omnibus); and BioVLAB-MMIA (microRNA and mRNA integrated analysis), for the combined analysis of gene and microRNA expression data. This chapter discusses the BioVLAB system architecture and the three prototype systems.

# 13.2 Motivation to Use Cloud Computing

Cloud computing is becoming important in both academia and industry, since the recent advancement in new technologies—such as high throughput computing based on multi-core/multi-process architecture, cost-efficient memory and data capacity, and virtualization techniques—is changing the traditional concept of data analysis into a data-intensive way. For many years in research communities, data analysis using computers mainly depends on the capacity of local, small set of computers. However, in the current situation, we are now witnessing a burst of data, and such small sets of computing nodes are not enough to keep up with the fast generation of huge volume of data. Many researchers are now trying to use the full capacity of computing powers by utilizing parallelism or a form of multiple computers, called computer clusters or grids, for data-intensive computing. Another important characteristic of cloud computing is elasticity that allows users to purchase computing power only for the capacity and duration that the users need. Especially, this is an important, new opportunity for small research labs that do not have high-performance computing infrastructure in place.

Currently, a handful of cloud-computing services are available to the public or are ready for release in the near future. Among them, the Amazon Elastic Compute Cloud (also known as EC2) is the first cloud-computing service in which users can "rent" multiple or hundreds of computing units in an on-demand manner. As seen in our previous work [1] and Amazon's report [2], many services and applications have been developed for running in Amazon EC2. Microsoft is also testing a cloud-computing service, called Azure, to provide an Internet-scale cloud service platform. By collaborating with academia, HP, Intel, and Yahoo, Microsoft has recently launched a cloud computing test bed, called M45, to provide a globally distributed Internet-scale testing environment to support various academic researches.

## 13.3  System Architecture and Components

The BioVLAB system is based on the LEAD/OGCE workflow infrastructure. The implementation of this infrastructure heavily uses Service-Oriented Architecture (SOA) concepts. This architecture can be classified into three major layers. As shown in Figure 13.1, the topmost layer is the user interaction layer. The XBaya Graphical User Interface (GUI) serves as the user-facing interface, enabling biologists to construct, execute, and monitor workflow executions. The entire workflow system can be operated as a custom desktop application or can be coupled with the OGCE- based web portal interface.

The second layer represents various middleware components comprising of a workflow composition API (application programming interface), an execution engine, and monitoring capabilities. These components are further detailed in Section 13.3.1. The middleware layer also includes a web service wrapper called GFac (generic factory), which wraps command-line scientific applications into web services. These wrapped application services can be invoked stand-alone or can be orchestrated into workflows.

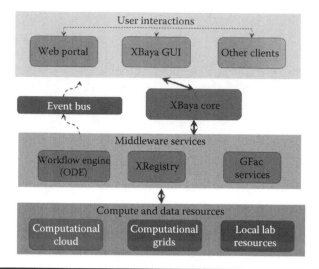

**Figure 13.1  BioVLAB architecture.**

The third layer represents various computing and data resources from local workstations to computational clouds like Amazon EC2. The GFac toolkit has a built-in functionality to manage all data transfers and jobs. The toolkit accepts a request from the workflow execution system and translates this request into data movement, and computes job submission to local, grid, or cloud computing resources. The wrapped application service is registered with a web service registry called XRegistry, which is used by the workflow GUI to browse and construct the registered services into workflows.

## 13.3.1 User Interaction Layer

The main components of the user interaction layer are the workflow system and the web portal.

### 13.3.1.1 Workflow Composer and Execution Engine

The concept of workflow has been introduced in scientific research communities to enable a batch execution of multiple tasks on behalf of users. By using such workflows, we can reduce a user's involvement and release the burden of repeating tedious tasks. Among various workflow composer and execution engines available in the public domain, BioVLAB uses XBaya, a graphical workflow composer and execution engine.

Using XBaya, a user can compose a workflow with ease by performing simple drag and drop from the workbench, which displays the available applications users can include, and execute the workflow graph instantly. After executing a workflow,

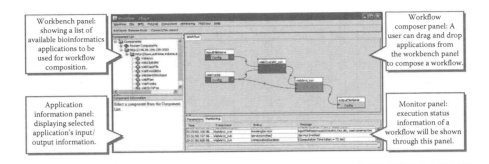

**Figure 13.2  Components of XBaya.**

XBaya can report to users the execution status of the workflow. Detailed status messages will be displayed on the monitor panel, as shown in Figure 13.2.

In Section 13.3.1.2, we will explain XBaya in detail.

## 13.3.1.2 XBaya—Workflow System

XBaya, a scientific workflow tool, is the main point of interaction for the scientist dealing with the workflow system, and it provides a high-level SOA-based programming model to interact with the service layer of the workflow system. This scientific workflow-programming model has been recognized as the accepted standard across different scientific disciplines and the preferred programming model for scientific computing. This section focuses on describing the modes of operation of the XBaya workflow tool.

The XBaya workflow system facilitates three modes of operation with respect to the different stages of workflow execution:

1. Workflow composition
2. Workflow orchestration
3. Workflow monitoring

Besides interacting with these different phases of workflow life cycle, XBaya also manages authentication and authorization of workflow users and provides a comprehensive security infrastructure based on the GSI (Grid Security Infrastructure) [35], while facilitating user authorizations as well as user groups.

### 13.3.1.2.1 Workflow Composition

XBaya is a pure SOA-based workflow system, and the workflow activities are either pure web services or workflow control structures. The web services can be abstract services that can be instantiated to actual service just in time when they are needed for the workflow, or they can be concrete services deployed by a third party. The control structures provided by XBaya on the other hand consist of conditional branching structures, commonly known as if-else conditions and parallel processing structures like for-each blocks that facilitate doing parallel transforms to array data structures. Besides services and control structures, sometimes, certain data structures require minor transformations, and many workflow systems provide widget components to facilitate such requirements (e.g., regEx widget for string comparison). XBaya provides the flexibility for the workflow user to implement a widget as the workflow is composed, by implementing a Java skeleton that captures the widget functionality in a Java operation.

The workflow system consists of a registry service, named XRegistry [36], which allows resource sharing in a secure manner. This is a registry that is also used by other components, like GFac, for resource storage and lookups. The registry interface not only allows resource sharing and service discovery, but also provides a mechanism to protect the application service from unauthorized access, thus preventing unauthorized users from having access to scientific applications. The service authors could create their services using a GFac toolkit and register them in the XRegistry as abstract services, and XBaya allows users to query these services and import them to be used in composition. Besides looking up XRegistry, XBaya allows third-party web services to be included in the workflow either by importing the WSDL (*Web Services Description Language*) file of the service or by providing the End Point Reference (EPR) of the web service. Further, as shown in Figure 13.3, the XBaya workbench provides an interactive and easy drag-and-drop interface for workflow composition.

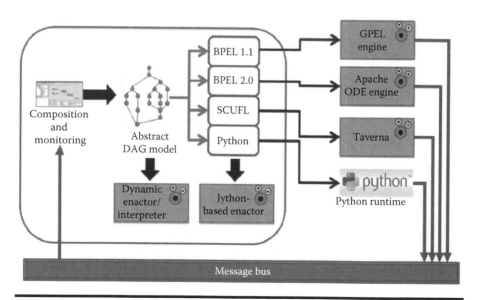

**Figure 13.3　Architecture of the XBaya workflow system.**

## 13.3.1.2.2 Workflow Orchestration

XBaya provides a high-level workflow description language, referred to as the Abstract DAG model in Figure 13.3, that is independent of conventional workflow execution languages. This allows the composition of the workflow to be completely decoupled from the execution, as well as the workflow to be transformed into different workflow-execution languages easily. The different workflow-enactment environments do have their merits and demerits, and depending on the domain science, the optimal workflow-enactment environment should be chosen to capitalize on the merits. For example, the Apache Orchestration Director Engine (ODE) [37] workflow engine is well equipped to handle long-running workflows in a scalable manner, whereas the XBaya dynamic enactor would provide dynamic user interaction during workflow execution, thus providing better steering of the workflow. Figure 13.3 provides the architecture of the XBaya workflow tool, and how the interaction with different workflow engines would take place, as well as how the Abstract DAG model may get compiled into each execution environment as necessary. In this chapter, the focus would be on the XBaya dynamic workflow enactor/interpreter, because the flexibilities provided by the dynamic workflow enactor seem to fit the bioinformatics domain while fulfilling the other necessary requirements expected of the workflow system.

The following sets of features capture the interactive and dynamic aspects of the workflows that are provided by the XBaya workflow system. We define an activity to be an encapsulation of logic that can be represented as an XBaya workflow node.

1. Deviations during workflow execution when workflow definition is static:
   a. Fault handling
   b. Dynamic change workflow inputs, workflow rerun
   c. Dynamic change in point of execution, workflow smart rerun
   d. Pause execution, step through execution, and debug points
2. On-the-fly workflow composition when workflow definition changes:
   a. Dynamic addition of activities to the workflow
   b. Dynamic removal or replacement of activity from the workflow

These two sets are organized in a way that the first set captures the dynamic interactions that do not require changes to the workflow definition while it is executing. In other words, the workflow definition remains static during the dynamic interactions. The second set in the taxonomy are the dynamic interactions that would change the definition of the workflow.

Since some of the features require the workflow definition to be changed while it is being executed, compilation of the workflow to a script would be a wrong approach. If the workflow is interpreted one activity at a time, as the user makes changes to the workflow, these changes would automatically be picked up when the interpreter visits those nodes of the workflow. In XBaya, the workflows are interpreted rather than compiled, and the result of execution of each activity is check-pointed. The interpretation allows the workflow definition to be changed dynamically, while the check-pointing allows the parts of the workflows to be run again as necessary. These dynamic features allow scientists to monitor the workflows as they execute and make real-time changes to the workflows and steer their scientific application to achieve better results.

### 13.3.1.2.3 Workflow Monitoring

The XBaya workflow system provides a real-time monitoring interface for the workflows to evaluate the progress of an experiment. Figure 13.4 shows a workflow in the middle of the execution where the different colors of the components show the execution status of that particular component (gray: complete, green: running, and yellow: waiting). The monitoring infrastructure of the workflow is completely decoupled with the workflow execution so that the workflow can be run with or without monitoring. The workflow system employs a WS-Eventing-based [38] publish/subscribe messaging system as a message bus to gather the progress of the workflow that is happening in distributed locations and services, and the XBaya monitoring interface would listen to those notifications sent by the workflow activities and reflect the progress of the workflow in the workbench.

### 13.3.1.3 Web Portal

The management of our system as an administrator or the access of stored data as an individual user can be performed through the portal interface called web

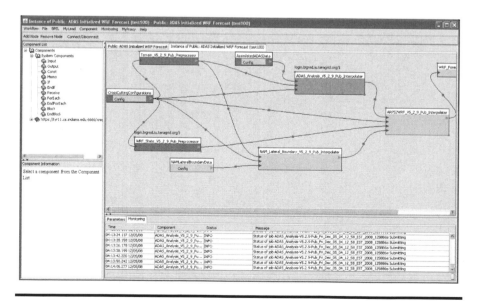

**Figure 13.4    Illustration of workflow monitoring.**

portal. We built a web portal by using the OGCE portal [3]. As an administrator, the management of registered applications that users are allowed to execute can be performed easily through GFac's registry portlet that we have deployed in our system. User management and access control can also be done through the portlet interface provided by OGCE.

The user can upload and download inputs and outputs of bioinformatics applications, which are stored in the remote storage services, such as Amazon EC2 and Microsoft's Application-Based Storage, through our web portal simply by using a web browser.

## 13.3.2 Middleware Services

Most bioinformatics applications lack interoperability, and they are mostly standalone and platform-dependent; thus, it requires significant efforts to execute multiple applications in a single environment. In our system, we deploy the Generic Service Toolkit, known as GFac, to convert any command-line bioinformatics application into a web service, which is accessible by XBaya.

### 13.3.2.1 Generic Factory

GFac wraps a command-line application into a web service. The toolkit also handles file staging, job submission, and monitoring. Furthermore, the wrapped service acts as the extensible runtime around which extensions like sharing, auditing, resource brokering, and urgent computing may be implemented.

The service toolkit includes a GFac service for on-demand creation of application services, and a service runtime that provides logic for application services. A user defines his applications, deployment information, and mapping to the service, as three deployment descriptors: application, host, and service description documents. The host description documents include Java and toolkit installation locations and temporary working directories, and if it is a compute host description, it includes the remote access mechanisms for file transfers and job submissions. On the other hand, the application deployment descriptions define application installation location and execution information about the application itself. Finally, the service description documents define input, output, and other application configuration information.

When a user requests a new application service, the factory service chooses a host from registered service hosts, and starts a new application service on this host. If multiple service hosts are registered, the factory service will provide load-balancing by choosing a host in a round-robin fashion. The newly created service fetches deployment descriptors from the registry and configures itself according to the contract defined by the service and according to application descriptions. After a successful initialization, the service registers its WSDL in the registry service so that it can be used by other workflow executions, and the service self-shutdown, after a given period of inactivity.

When an application service is invoked, the service parses the request and identifies the parameters that should be passed into the underlying application. As mentioned earlier, a typical application service invocation involves two hosts: the service host, where the service instance is running, and the application host, where the application is executed. Services and applications have a one-to-many mapping, where multiple application descriptions correspond to different installations of the same application. After deciding the best application host to execute the application, the input data files specified by input parameters are staged to this application host and the underlying application is executed using a job submission mechanism. The service monitors the status of the remote application and publishes frequent activity information to the event bus. Once the invocation is complete, the application service tries to determine the results of the application invocation by searching the standard output for user-defined patterns or by listing prespecified locations for the generated data products.

Apart from wrapping a command-line application as a service, the application service provides a number of add-on facilities that are essential for a scientific workflow environment. The application service runtime is implemented using a processing pipeline based on the Chain-of-Responsibility pattern, where inserting interceptors can alter the pipeline. The resulting architecture is highly flexible and extensible, and provides the ideal architectural basis for a system that supports a wide range of requirements. Furthermore, the design has abstracted out common services like file transfer, registry support, notification support, and job submission, allowing different implementations to be switched dynamically or via configurations.

## 13.3.3 Compute and Data Resources

Some bioinformatics applications are computationally intensive and require a powerful high-performance or parallelizable computation environment. To respond to this problem, our system is designed to utilize remote high-performance resources, such as the computing cloud of Amazon EC2 in which a user can create any number of virtual computing instances at any time. Our system can also use public remote storage services, such as Amazon S3 (Simple Storage Service) and Microsoft Application-Based Storage, to store the intermediate or the final output of the workflow execution. For easy-to-use access and management of data stored in the remote services, we provide the web portal in our system.

### 13.3.3.1 Amazon Computing Clouds Services

The BioVLAB system uses Amazon's EC2 and S3 as a computing cloud and a persistent storage, respectively. EC2 provides a computing cloud service where a user can have any number of virtual computing instances in an on-demand manner, and S3 supplies a persistent place to store user data. While the storage in EC2 is volatile, S3 is persistent, reliable, and convenient to access with simple web interfaces.

In EC2, a user can create a customized virtual machine by using his own machine image, called Amazon Machine Image (AMI). For our BioVLAB system, we have created our own customized AMI that contains a Unix-based operating system, all bioinformatics applications we used, and a set of services for workflow execution. By sharing our customized AMI with others, any user can also create a virtual machine with a fully pre-configured BioVLAB system.

## 13.4 Bioinformatics Applications

In this section, we describe three BioVLAB prototype systems.

### 13.4.1 BioVLAB-Protein

As the new sequencing technology enables rapid sequencing of many genomes, new protein sequences are increasingly available; thus, there is an urgent need to decode information of the raw sequences. Protein sequences can be analyzed, executing various sources of applications in bioinformatics, such as Gibbs [4], ClustalW [5], and ARCS [6]. Then, aligned residues can be graphically analyzed using WebLogo [7]. In addition, functions of a protein can be determined by querying against domain databases such as Prosite [8], Pfam [9], and Gene Ontology [10].

Figure 13.5 is a sample workflow for protein sequence analysis with cloud computing. With an input file with multiple protein sequences, the sequences are aligned with a multiple sequence alignment tool, ClustalW. Then, ARCS highlights conserved regions among aligned biological sequences by measuring sequence characteristics based on column correlations.

### 13.4.2 BioVLAB-Microarray

Microarray technology has been widely used in cell dynamics research. This high-throughput technology can measure expression levels of hundreds of thousands of genes in a single batch; thus, it gives a massive amount of valuable information of how a certain cell reacts to cell conditions [11].

This technology is useful in various ways. It can help identify a function of gene that was previously unknown, by inspecting genes with similar expression patterns. Also, examining the co-expression pattern can help identify interaction partners and correlation of genes. In addition, it can be used to detect genes related to a certain disease, and thus possibly discover a target of new medicine.

A typical use case of microarray gene expression includes search for genes with similar expression patterns, extraction of differentially expressed genes, clustering

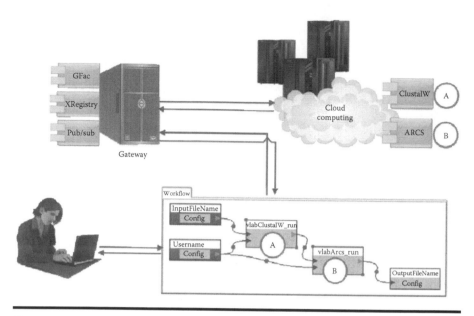

**Figure 13.5  BioVLAB-protein architecture.**

of genes based on expression patterns, component analysis, and protein–protein interaction network by projecting the expression pattern onto an interaction database, such as Database of Interacting Proteins (DIP) [12].

Figure 13.6 is an example workflow of a microarray gene expression analysis in a cloud computing architecture. When the workflow in the figure is executed, a microarray gene expression data is obtained remotely from the NCBI GEO database using the R GEOquery package [13]. Biologists are often interested in statistically differentially expressed genes in an experiment, and can extract such genes based on a statistical test such as False Discovery Rate (FDR) [14], which is the second step in the workflow. We used the limma package [15] to detect the differentially expressed genes. In the next step, the display of the differentially expressed genes as a heat map and various clustering methods can run in parallel. Grouping genes may reveal functions of previously unknown genes, or a meaningful expression pattern. Thus, various clustering methods have been widely used to search hidden information in different views, in microarray experiments. We used several clustering methods, that is, $k$-means clustering [16], quality threshold clustering (QT clustering) [17], and biclustering [18], appeared as nodes in the workflow. Built-in R functions *kmeans* was used for $k$-means clustering. Additional clustering packages such as flexclust [19] and biclust [20] were used for QT clustering and biclustering, respectively.

A graphical summary of microarray gene experiments is shown in Figure 13.7, where we used the GDS38 gene expression data set [21], a time-series gene expression data set for measuring gene expressions in various cell cycle stages in *Saccharomyces*

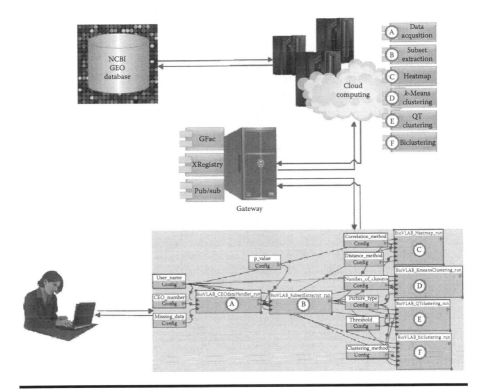

**Figure 13.6  BioVLAB-microarray architecture.**

*cerevisiae* yeast genome. The experimental setup was identical to our previous work [1], and figures were taken from this work. Figure 13.7a is a heat map summary of differentially expressed genes with a *p* value ≤0.05. Figure 13.7b shows the *k*-means clustering result with a scatter plot and a heat map with a cluster size of 3. Figure 13.7c summarizes the result of QT clustering with a radius threshold of 1. The biclustering summary is shown in Figure 13.7d, where the Cheng and Church method [22] was used with a cluster size of 3.

### 13.4.3  BioVLAB-MMIA

MMIA [23] uses an inversely correlated expression pattern between miRNA and mRNA for a combined analysis, since perfect seed-pairing between them is associated with mRNA destabilization [24]. MMIA provides two main results. The first result gives disease information associated with dys-regulated miRNA expression and common transcription factors in upstream regions of the miRNAs. The second provides functional, pathological, and pathway information associated with inversely correlated expressed target mRNAs of the miRNAs. Currently, MMIA considers only humans.

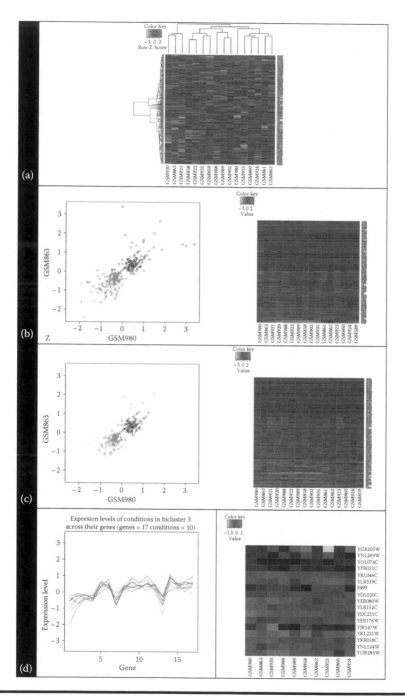

**Figure 13.7** Experimental results: (a) heat map, (b) *k*-means clustering (*k* = 3), (c) QT clustering (radius = 1), and (d) biclustering (cluster size = 3).

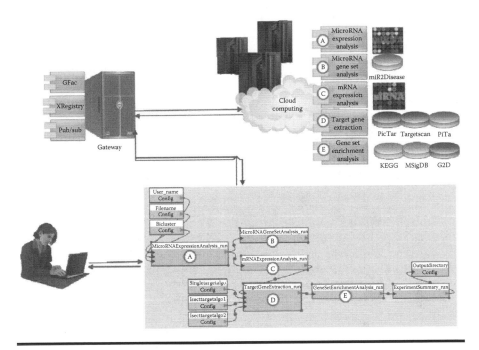

**Figure 13.8   BioVLAB-MMIA architecture.**

We re-implemented the web-based MMIA in a cloud computing environment and named it BioVLAB-MMIA, as shown in Figure 13.8. It consists of five modules. The first module (A in the figure) takes miRNA expression data or mis-regulated miRNA gene list as an input. This module performs a statistical test for identifying down- or up-regulated miRNAs. The second module (B in the figure) finds enriched miRNA gene sets based on the mis-regulated miRNAs. The miRNA gene set database contains two categories. One is the disease-related miRNA gene set [25], and the other is for transcription binding factor sites in promoter regions of miRNA genes [26]. For example, each disease entry has an annotated miRNA gene list in the miRNA gene set database. The third module performs a significance test for the mRNA microarray and reports dys-regulated mRNA genes. The fourth module obtains computational mRNA targets by the mis-regulated miRNAs, and it provides three algorithms: TargetScan version 4.2 [27], PITA [28], and PicTar [29]. This module supports not only a single algorithm but also an intersection between two different algorithms. The fifth module inspects the inversely correlated expression between the selected miRNAs and their previously identified mRNA targets. It also performs a gene set analysis for the inversely expressed target mRNAs of the miRNAs. The precompiled gene sets contain MIT MSigDB [30], KEGG [31], and G2D [32], for functional, pathological, and pathway information, respectively.

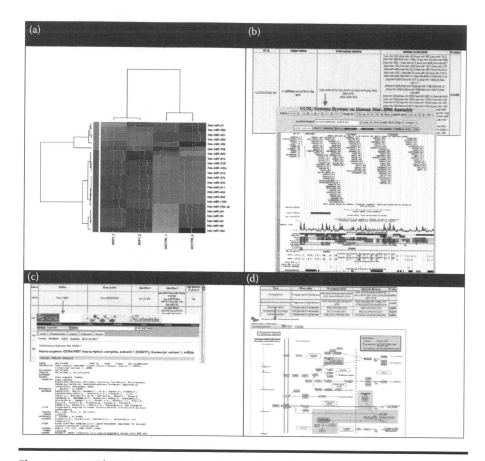

**Figure 13.9** BioVLAB-MMIA experimental results: (a) significantly down-regulated microRNA, (b) microRNA gene set analysis, (c) mRNA targets prediction, and (d) combined analysis of microRNA and mRNA.

Figure 13.9 is a graphical summary of the BioVLAB-MMIA experiment. Figure 13.9a shows a heat map that displays significantly down-regulated genes in an miRNA experiment on human genes. It was obtained after the execution of the first module (node A in the workflow) in the example workflow. Figure 13.9b is a part of the summary table after node B is executed. The USCS genome browser [26] result appearing in Figure 13.9b was obtained by clicking an entry in the summary table. Figure 13.9c corresponds to node D, and shows an example of mRNA target prediction and the details of gene from NCBI that were obtained by clicking an entry. Figure 13.9d is a result of the combined analysis of microRNA and mRNA, which is node E in the workflow. A KEGG map appearing in the figure was obtained by clicking a pathway entry in the summary table. See more details in [33].

## 13.5 Conclusion

We have shown that the approach of combining cloud computing and a graphical workflow composer could be a solution to computational analysis problems in scientific domains such as bioinformatics. The most important outcome of this approach is a possibility of soliciting a much broader participation of small research labs for important data-driven scientific projects by reducing the burden of computer system setup and administration and allowing flexible workflow management. This approach has a potential to significantly speed up advances in scientific domains, biology and medicine in this case. We are currently designing and building a larger system for biological pathway analysis based on our experience in building a web-based pathway system called ComPath [34].

## References

1. Y. Yang, J. Y. Choi, K. Choi, M. Pierce, D. Gannon, and S. Kim, BioVLAB microarray: Microarray data analysis in virtual environment, in *Fourth IEEE International Conference on eScience,* Inidianapolis, IN, 2008, pp. 159–165.
2. Case Studies, http://aws.amazon.com/solutions/case-studies/
3. J. Alameda, M. Christie, G. Fox, J. Futrelle, D. Gannon, M. Hategan, G. Kandaswamy, G. V. Laszewski, M. A. Nacar, M. Pierce, E. Roberts, C. Severance, and M. Thomas, The open grid computing environments collaboration: Portlets and services for science gateways: Research Articles, *Concurr. Comput. Pract. Exp.,* 19, 921–942, 2007.
4. W. Thompson, E. C. Rouchka, and C. E. Lawrence, Gibbs recursive sampler: Finding transcription factor binding sites, *Nucleic Acids Res.,* 31, 3580–3585, July 1, 2003.
5. J. D. Thompson, D. G. Higgins, and T. J. Gibson, CLUSTAL W: Improving the sensitivity of progressive multiple sequence alignment through sequence weighting, position-specific gap penalties and weight matrix choice, *Nucleic Acids Res.,* 22, 4673–4680, November 11, 1994.
6. B. Song, J.-H. Choi, G. Chen, J. Szymanski, G.-Q. Zhang, A. K. H. Tung, J. Kang, S. Kim, and J. Yang, ARCS: An aggregated related column scoring scheme for aligned sequences, *Bioinformatics,* 22, 2326–2332, October 1, 2006.
7. G. E. Crooks, G. Hon, J.-M. Chandonia, and S. E. Brenner, WebLogo: A sequence logo generator, *Genome Res.,* 14, 1188–1190, June 2004.
8. N. Hulo, A. Bairoch, V. Bulliard, L. Cerutti, E. De Castro, P. S. Langendijk-Genevaux, M. Pagni, and C. J. A. Sigrist, The PROSITE database, *Nucleic Acids Res.,* 34, D227–230, January 1, 2006.
9. R. D. Finn, J. Mistry, B. Schuster-Bockler, S. Griffiths-Jones, V. Hollich, T. Lassmann, S. Moxon et al., Pfam: Clans, web tools and services, *Nucleic Acids Res.,* 34, D247–251, January 1, 2006.
10. M. Ashburner, C. A. Ball, J. A. Blake, D. Botstein, H. Butler, J. M. Cherry, A. P. Davis et al., Gene ontology: Tool for the unification of biology, *Nat. Genet.,* 25, 25–29, 2000.

11. Microarrays: Chipping away at the mysteries of science and medicine, in *A Science Primer*. 2008: NCBI, http://www.ncib.nlm.nih.gov/About/primer/microarrays.html

12. L. Salwinski, C. S. Miller, A. J. Smith, F. K. Pettit, J. U. Bowie, and D. Eisenberg, The database of interacting proteins: 2004 update, *Nucleic Acids Res.*, 32, D449–451, January 1, 2004.

13. S. Davis and P. S. Meltzer, GEOquery: A bridge between the gene expression omnibus (GEO) and bioconductor, *Bioinformatics*, 23, 1846–1847, July 15, 2007.

14. W. J. Ewens and G. R. Grant, *Statistical Methods in Bioinformatics*, 2nd Edition, Springer, Heidelberg, Germany, 2005.

15. G. K. Smyth, Linear models and empirical Bayes methods for assessing differential expression in microarray experiments, *Stat. Appl. Genet. Mol. Biol.*, 3, Article 3, Epub, 2004.

16. J. A. Hartigan and M. A. Wong, A k-means clustering algorithm, *Appl. Stat.*, 28, 100–108, 1979.

17. L. J. Heyer, S. Kruglyak, and S. Yooseph, Exploring expression data: Identification and analysis of coexpressed genes, *Genome Res.*, 9, 1106–1115, 1999.

18. S. C. Madeira and A. L. Oliveira, Biclustering algorithms for biological data analysis: A survey, *IEEE/ACM Trans. Comput. Biol. Bioinform.*, 1, 24–25, 2004.

19. F. Leisch, Flexclust: Flexible cluster algorithms, R package, 2005.

20. S. Kaiser and F. Leisch, A toolbox for bicluster analysis in R, University of Munich Department of Statistics: Technical Report, No. 28, 2008.

21. GDS38: Cell cycle, alpha-factor block-release time course. vol. 2008: NCBI GEO, p. http://www.ncbi.nlm.nih.gov/geo/gds/gds_browse.cgi?gds=38.

22. Y. Cheng and G. M. Church, Biclustering of expression data, in *Proceedings of the Eighth International Conference on Intelligent Systems for Molecular Biology*, La Jolla, CA, 2000, pp. 93–103.

23. S. Nam, M. Li, K. Choi, C. Balch, S. Kim, and K. P. Nephew, MicroRNA and mRNA integrated analysis (MMIA): A web tool for examining biological functions of microRNA expression, *Nucleic Acids Res.*, 37, W356–362, May 6, 2009.

24. W. Filipowicz, S. N. Bhattacharyya, and N. Sonenberg, Mechanisms of post-transcriptional regulation by microRNAs: Are the answers in sight?, *Nat. Rev. Genet.*, 9, 102–114, 2008.

25. Q. Jiang, Y. Wang, Y. Hao, L. Juan, M. Teng, X. Zhang, M. Li, G. Wang, and Y. Liu, miR2Disease: A manually curated database for microRNA deregulation in human disease, *Nucleic Acids Res.*, 37, D98–104, January 1, 2009.

26. D. Karolchik, R. M. Kuhn, R. Baertsch, G. P. Barber, H. Clawson, M. Diekhans, B. Giardine et al., The UCSC genome browser database: 2008 update, *Nucleic Acids Res.*, 36, pp. D773–779, January 11, 2008.

27. B. P. Lewis, C. B. Burge, and D. P. Bartel, Conserved seed pairing, often flanked by adenosines, indicates that thousands of human genes are microRNA targets, 120, 15–20, 2005.

28. M. Kertesz, N. Iovino, U. Unnerstall, U. Gaul, and E. Segal, The role of site accessibility in microRNA target recognition, *Nat. Genet.*, 39, 1278–1284, 2007.

29. A. Krek, D. Grun, M. N. Poy, R. Wolf, L. Rosenberg, E. J. Epstein, P. MacMenamin et al., Combinatorial microRNA target predictions, *Nat. Genet.*, 37, 495–500, 2005.

30. A. Subramanian, P. Tamayo, V. K. Mootha, S. Mukherjee, B. L. Ebert, M. A. Gillette, A. Paulovich et al., Gene set enrichment analysis: A knowledge-based approach for interpreting genome-wide expression profiles, *Proc. Natl. Acad. Sci. USA*, 102,15545–15550, October 25, 2005.

31. M. Kanehisa, S. Goto, S. Kawashima, Y. Okuno, and M. Hattori, The KEGG resource for deciphering the genome, *Nucleic Acids Res.*, 32, D277–280, January 1, 2004.

32. C. Perez-Iratxeta, P. Bork, and M. A. Andrade-Navarro, Update of the G2D tool for prioritization of gene candidates to inherited diseases, *Nucleic Acids Res.*, W212–W216, 2007.

33. MMIA, http://cancer.informatics.indiana.edu/mmia

34. K. Choi and S. Kim, ComPath: Comparative enzyme analysis and annotation in pathway/subsystem contexts, *BMC Bioinformatics*, 9, 145, 2008.

35. V. Welch, F. Siebenlist, I. Foster, J. Bresnahan, K. Czajkowski, J. Gawor, C. Kesselman, S. Meder, L. Pearlman, and S. Tuecke, Security for grid services, *Twelfth International Symposium on High Performance Distributed Computing (HPDC-12)*, Seattle, WA, pp. 48–57, 2003.

36. S. Perera, S. Marru, and C. Herath, Workflow infrastructure for multi-scale science gateways, *Proceedings of TeraGrid Annual Conference*, Las Vegas, NV, 2008.

37. Apache ODE, http://ode.apache.org

38. WS-Eventing Specification, http://www.w3.org/Submission/WS-Eventing/

# Chapter 14

# Scale-Out RDF Molecule Store for Efficient, Scalable Data Integration and Querying

Yuan-Fang Li, Andrew Newman, and Jane Hunter

## Contents

# 14.1 Introduction

Resource Description Framework (RDF) and Web Ontology Language (OWL) offer significant potential as technologies designed to support the integration of and reasoning across heterogeneous disparate data sources. Comprehensive datasets from many disciplines, including environmental sciences, biological sciences, social sciences, and health sciences, have been semantically annotated using these languages to facilitate data correlation, integration, and reasoning. The widespread adoption of Semantic Web technologies is being driven by the need to answer complex queries that demand the integration and processing of multiple related but disparate multidisciplinary datasets.

The research work presented in this chapter is part of a bioinformatics project that is aimed at applying Semantic Web technologies to molecular biology data, to enable *in silico* drug discovery and development by identifying candidate therapeutic targets through the analysis of integrated datasets that relate molecular interactions and biochemical pathways with physiological effects, such as compound toxicology and gene–disease associations. Current protein–protein interaction (PPI) data is distributed across a wide range of disparate, large-scale, publicly available databases and repositories. The integration of data in these datasets is required before researchers can perform complex querying and analyses over the data to reveal previously undetected pathways and new drug candidates.

Given the massive scale of the datasets, the wide variety of different naming conventions (Good and Wilkinson 2006), and the different syntactic and semantic representations and descriptions, precise and efficient integration is a very challenging problem. Current tools available for bioinformatics data integration and discovery vary widely in terms of quality, maintenance, and applicability. Although there exist many different tools for performing operations on many different kinds of data (Merelli et al. 2007), there is also a general lack of standards for representing data, and a slow uptake of existing data standards (Good and Wilkinson 2006). In Newman et al. (2008a), we proposed a more standardized approach to the integration of PPI data in RDF through the use of RDF blank nodes, which are used to represent real-world entities such as proteins, interactions, and pathways.

## 14.1.1 Proposed Architecture

Existing RDF databases have typically suffered from limited scalability, and poor or inefficient inferencing and querying.* While some stores offer a high level of scalability for a single node, there is little support for aggregation across multiple nodes. Inferencing is typically limited to either basic operations across large amounts of data or richer inferencing over small amounts of data—for our project, as well as for many other scientific challenges, rich, complex inferencing over large amounts of data[†] is required.

In addition, there are many other problems associated with scientific data analysis that require consideration. These include algorithm intensity, nonlinearity, and limitations on computer component bandwidth (Gray et al. 2005). These issues prevent interactive analysis over derived datasets. In order to overcome these difficulties, Gray recommended a number of mechanisms to expedite and improve scientific data analysis (Gray et al. 2005):

- The use of standardized and precise metadata to describe units, names, accuracy, provenance, capture details, etc., in order to help tools compare and process the data correctly
- The creation and adoption of common terminologies using Semantic Web technologies (RDF and OWL)
- The use of set-oriented processing methods, such as Google's MapReduce (Dean and Ghemawat 2004)

So, while the use of ontologies and other Semantic Web technologies such as RDF can provide the ability to integrate, reason, and process over datasets, the magnitude of the processing required and the size of the datasets prevent a speedy, efficient end-to-end solution. A distributed processing architecture developed by Google, known as MapReduce (Dean and Ghemawat 2004), is becoming increasingly popular. This data-processing technique provides a common way to solve general processing problems and is closely aligned with the way data is acquired from experiments or simulations (Gray et al. 2005). In a MapReduce system, a *map* function takes input key, value pairs and transforms them to output key, value pairs. The *reduce* function takes the values in each unique key and produces output values. The advantages of this architecture are numerous (Dean and Ghemawat 2004, Yang et al. 2007), and include

- A programming model that is abstract, simple, highly parallel, powerful, easy to maintain, and easy to learn
- An ability to efficiently leverage low-end commodity hardware

---

* http://esw.w3.org/topic/TripleStoreScalability
† http://esw.w3.org/topic/LargeTripleStores

- Easy deployment across hundreds to thousands of nodes on internal or external hosting services
- Robustness and ability to recover from data corruption or the loss of individual nodes

Our hypothesis is that Semantic Web applications can benefit from the adoption of a scale-out architecture together with MapReduce data processing, in order to speed up querying, inferencing, and processing over large RDF triple stores of scientific datasets. One such example is our project that focuses on the integration and processing of large-scale PPI data.

## 14.1.2 Case Study

The primary aim of our project is to integrate data from protein datasets, such as MPact (Güldener et al. 2006), the Database of Interacting Proteins (DIP) (Salwinski et al. 2004), IntAct (Kerrien et al. 2007), and the Molecular INTeractions database (MINT) (Chatr-aryamontri et al. 2007), using a common model for proteins and PPI data to enable data harmonization. The common model is represented as an OWL Description Logics (OWL-DL) ontology. This ontology was developed by reusing vocabularies from well-established ontologies, such as Gene Ontology (Ashburner et al. 2000), Cell-Type ontology (Bard et al. 2005), BioPAX (Bader and Cary 2005), PSI-MI (Hermjakob et al. 2004), and others such as National Center for Biotechnology Information (NCBI) taxonomy. Based on this ontology, protein datasets are converted into RDF instances and stored in a distributed RDF triple store, where they are available for subsequent analysis and querying.

Figure 14.1 shows a small RDF graph about a yeast protein with UniProt ID "Q12522," together with other information, such as host species, genomic sequence, and external references, that represents a protein instance in our ontology.

It is one of the objectives of our project to achieve real-time, interactive SPARQL Protocol and RDF Query Language (SPARQL) query response to queries such as "Show me all the human kinases expressed in the liver that are strongly inhibited by at least two compounds and are localized to the nucleus." Such queries are very slow to execute, as they involve many joins and may generate an RDF graph that exceeds available memory. Hence, the bioinformatics application provides us with an ideal test bed and an end-user group for evaluating our *Scale-Out RDF Molecule Store*.

Within the life sciences, the heterogeneity of naming conventions across datasets is a major problem. Each dataset has its own method for protein identification. There have been previous attempts at naming standardization, but they have had limited effect (Good and Wilkinson 2006). In Newman et al. (2007), the authors proposed an "identity reconciliation process" based on the use of RDF "blank" nodes, which provide the hub that links to the relevant entries in different (translated) datasets and creates a single representation encompassing all information about a particular protein, and also enables all three levels of "attitudes" of knowledge representation (record, statement, and domain) (Ruttenberg et al. 2006) pertaining to a particular protein.

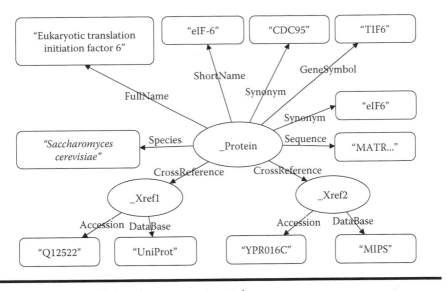

**Figure 14.1    RDF triples about a yeast protein.**

Distributed processing necessitates the need to decompose RDF graphs into smaller units. RDF blank nodes also introduce a number of associated problems that arise during RDF graph decomposition and merging. The most significant problem is that RDF blank nodes are only uniquely identifiable within their enclosing graph—they are not globally addressable. The implication is that arbitrarily breaking down an RDF graph that contains blank nodes will incur loss of information. The concept of RDF molecules (Ding et al. 2005) was proposed to tackle the problem of addressing blank nodes by decomposing an RDF graph losslessly into a set of molecules that distribute updates to graphs. Overcoming this problem will require a number of extensions to RDF molecules that are described in detail in Section 14.3.

## 14.1.3 *Objectives*

The objectives of the work described in this chapter are to investigate solutions to the problems of inefficient semantic querying and reasoning across large-scale triple stores, and co-identification. These two issues hinder the adoption of Semantic Web technologies across many disciplines and applications. The more specific objectives of this work are to investigate and evaluate the following:

- Methods by which the MapReduce scale-out architecture can be used to improve the performance of semantic querying and inferencing over large-scale RDF triples
- The adoption of RDF molecules for decomposing and distributing RDF graphs across computational nodes in the MapReduce architecture

- The use of blank nodes to resolve the co-identification problem
- Extensions to RDF molecules to overcome problems of ambiguity, data loss, and inefficiency introduced by blank nodes

In addition, the aim is to evaluate our proposed Scale-Out RDF Molecule Store in the context of the querying and analysis of large-scale PPIs.

In Section 14.2, we describe related work. Section 14.3 describes the proposed extensions to RDF molecules with hierarchy and ordering. In Section 14.4, we describe the bioinformatics dataset, which will be used for evaluation in Section 14.5, and introduce important components of the system: (a) graph decomposition into molecules and molecule merging, (b) MapReduce-based data integration, and (c) SPARQL querying across cluster. In Section 14.5, we present the initial results of the system's performance of graph decomposition and merging, distributed data integration, and SPARQL querying. Finally, we present our conclusions in Section 14.6.

## 14.2 Related Works

### 14.2.1 Scale-Out Architecture

For a relatively new architecture, scale-out MapReduce systems have already received very promising and positive feedback and evaluation results. Benefits include better price/performance, successful application to many different domains, and open-source implementations.

The MapReduce programming framework (Dean and Ghemawat 2004) was proposed and developed by Google to support distributed computation over a large cluster of commodity-grade hardware. The MapReduce framework consists of higher-order functions, *map* and *reduce*, found in the functional programming language. The *map* function takes as input a (key, value) pair and produces intermediate results, a set of (key, value) pairs. The *reduce* function takes as input the intermediate results with the same (key, value) and produces the final result.

In the MapReduce framework, a large computation task is divided into a map phase and a reduce phase, in which the map and reduce functions are executed in parallel over a cluster of machines. The distribution of input/output files and the *map* and *reduce* tasks, load balancing, and fault tolerance are managed by the MapReduce framework and the underlying distributed file system, thus enabling rapid development of parallelized user programs.

Google's initial work using these MapReduce scale-out techniques has included indexing the Web, statistical analysis of Web site usage, general data storage and querying, map and satellite imagery processing, and social networking (Chang et al. 2006). Similarly, Yahoo has been applying MapReduce to "search and information retrieval, machine learning and data mining, microeconomics, community systems and media experience and design" (The Yahoo! Research Team 2006). Other successful applications include indexing and searching Web documents (Khare et al. 2004), natural language processing (Pantel 2007), learning algorithms for multicore systems (Chu et al. 2007), and simulation (McNabb et al. 2007).

The Hadoop* project provides an open-source implementation of Google's scale-out MapReduce, a system including the Hadoop Distributed File System (HDFS), MapReduce, and HBase (a BigTable clone).

The MapReduce scale-out architecture has been used in Oren et al. (2008) to index documents for open linked data.[†] There have also been initial implementations and research into similar, overlapping areas, including RDF stores using "shared-nothing" clustering, extending MapReduce higher-level operations, and column databases for storing and querying RDF.

The YARS2 federated RDF repository and the SWSE (Semantic Web Search Engine) architecture use a "shared-nothing" approach to achieve scalability (Harth et al. 2007). This has some conceptual similarities to our data acquisition architecture. However, it is still bound to indexing and querying, and does not share the attributes of a MapReduce scale-out solution with its ability to perform arbitrary processing and indexing schemes.

The designs of BigTable and HBase are similar to column databases such as Sybase IQ, LucidDB, Metakit, KDB, C-Store (Stonebraker et al. 2005), and Monet (Boncz 2002). These databases were specifically designed to obtain the best performance from modern hardware architecture. There is also some initial research currently underway investigating the use of C-Store and MonetDB (Muster 2007) for storing and querying RDF data as well as using these databases to handle scientific data (Ivanova et al. 2007). Our approach differs from these approaches in a number of ways:

- We create a generic store for triples of any predicate, rather than creating one table per predicate.
- Our clustered approach differs substantially from their database architecture.
- We do not support ACID (Atomicity, Consistency, Isolation and Durability) database transactions.
- Column databases do not have a MapReduce-like processing framework, and do not combine processing and data management in the same way.

To the best of our knowledge, the work described in this chapter represents the first attempt to apply a scale-out distributed computing approach to expedite the querying and processing of data in a large scale-out RDF triple store. Although in this chapter we use specifically PPI data for performance evaluation, there are undoubtedly many other suitable applications that require the integration and processing of large-scale distributed datasets (e.g., climatology, geosciences, and astronomy).

---

### 14.2.2 RDF Modules

The concept of RDF molecules was first proposed in Ding et al. (2005) as a method that provides the optimum level of granularity between RDF graphs and triples. Given an RDF graph *G*, the set of molecules are the smallest sets of triples into which *G* can be decomposed without loss of information.

Figure 14.2 shows the different granularity levels of various RDF constructs.

There has been previous relevant work in the area of RDF graph decomposition. Below we provide an analysis of three possible approaches to RDF graph decomposition:

- *Named Graphs* (Carroll et al. 2005) enable the specification of an RDF graph through a set of RDF statements. The division of statements into subgraphs is arbitrary in the sense that the ontology author is responsible for manually constructing the subgraphs and naming them. Hence, no automated process is available.
- *Concise Bounded Description* (CBD) (Stickler 2005) is a subgraph of triples about a particular resource *R* and a chain of triples with blank nodes consisting of matching object to subject nodes (ignoring the special case for reification). All triples in a graph where the resource *R* is the subject are added to the subgraph. Next, it recursively adds any triples with blank node subjects already in the subgraph. A drawback of CBD is that it only looks at subject nodes in RDF triples and a CBD created for a resource node may not include all of the information.
- *Minimum Self-Contained Graphs* (MSGs) (Tummarello et al. 2005) is a proposal for the decomposition of an RDF graph into self-contained subgraphs. Given an RDF triple, its corresponding MSG includes (a) the triple itself and, recursively, (b) for all the blank nodes involved in the MSG so far, all the triples of MSGs containing these blank nodes. Compared to CBD, MSG looks for statements to be included in the MSG in both directions. Hence, it results in a lossless decomposition.

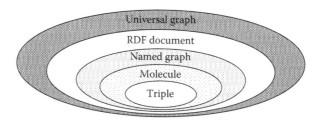

**Figure 14.2** **Relative granularity levels of RDF constructs. (Adapted from Ding, L. et al., *Tracking RDF Graph Provenance Using RDF Molecules*, UMBC, Baltimore, MD, 2005.)**

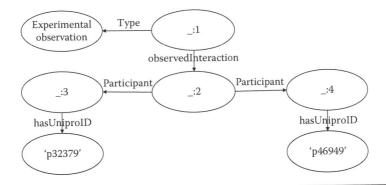

**Figure 14.3    A simple RDF graph modeling a PPI.**

Based on the above analysis, we believe that RDF molecules provide the best approach for our MapReduce RDF store, as they ensure automated, unambiguous, and lossless decomposition and an optimal level of granularity.

Formally, given an RDF graph $G$ and a background ontology $W$, a pair of operators $(d, m)$ are defined for decomposition and merging:

$$M = d(G, W)$$

$$G = m(M, W)$$

where $M$ is the set of molecules as the result of the decomposition of $G$ with regard to $W$ using the decomposition operator $d$. The merging operator $m$ merges $M$ back to the same graph $G$, also with respect to the background ontology $W$. The set of molecules $M$ are mutually independent in the sense that no blank node is shared among them. Hence, they can be individually processed and later merged to construct the RDF graph $G$ losslessly.

Two types of decomposition were defined: *naïve decomposition*, in which no background ontology is consulted, and *functional decomposition*, in which an OWL ontology is queried for functional dependency between nodes.

The diagram shown in Figure 14.3 consists of six triples (in N3 format) that model a physical interaction between two proteins ( _ :3 and _ :4), represented as blank nodes.

The naïve decomposition results in a single molecule consisting of all the above triples, since they are connected by blank nodes.

## 14.3  Extended RDF Molecules

In order to maintain maximal compatibility with other datasets, we decided not to put any restriction on the format of data, hence allowing blank nodes in RDF

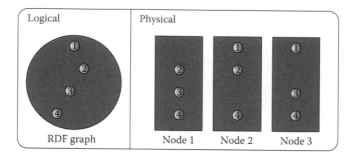

**Figure 14.4    An RDF graph decomposed into molecules that are distributed in a cluster.**

documents. This decision presents a challenge for the distributed processing of RDF documents, as blank nodes are only addressable locally within a document. As stated in Section 14.2.2, RDF molecules provide a mechanism for decomposing an RDF graph into a set of self-contained molecules, each of which contains all (transitively) connected blank nodes. This enables an RDF graph to be losslessly decomposed, distributed for processing, and subsequently merged, as depicted in Figure 14.4.

The original definition of RDF molecules (Ding et al. 2005) has a number of inherent limitations that need to be overcome in order to be used for the RDF graph decomposition and merging, without loss of data or integrity. As can be seen in Figure 14.3, on the top, the absence of hierarchy in the original RDF molecule definition makes it difficult or even impossible to distinguish triples [ _ :2 participant _ :3] and [ _ :2 participant _ :4]. Moreover, the absence of ordering prevents certain important performance benefits, such as rapid retrieval of triples, to be leveraged.

In Sections 14.3.1 through 14.3.3, we present our extensions of RDF molecules that mitigate these problems.

## 14.3.1  Hierarchies

In the original definition, molecules are flat and each molecule contains a set of RDF triples. We believe that having hierarchical molecules helps to better reflect the structure of the underlying RDF document. These extensions to molecules accurately reflect a structure found in biological and other data, and represent relationships found in databases similar to where one relation refers to another via a foreign key.

Another important reason for adding hierarchies is to be able to identify equivalent blank nodes based on context instead of on internal identifiers. Given the same context, we can determine blank node equivalence and remove redundant information.

| Molecule | ::= | *('[' Submolecule ']')\** |
|----------|-----|------------------------------|
| Submolecule | ::= | *RootTriple ( Molecule )?\|NIL* |
| RootTriple | ::= | *Subject Predicate Object* |

**Figure 14.5  Abstract syntax of RDF molecules extended with hierarchies.**

Extended with hierarchies, a molecule is defined recursively as shown in Figure 14.5. An RDF molecule is defined as a (possibly empty) set of submolecules, each of which consists of a root triple and an optional molecule pointed to by this triple. The root triple is an RDF triple. For a given molecule, we define the head triple to be lexicographically the largest, as defined in Section 14.3.2, from the set of root triples.

As described in Section 14.2.2, a molecule in the original definition contains triples, all of which are on a single level. We believe that the incorporation of hierarchies as shown above helps to capture the structure of the underlying RDF triples. Moreover, as RDF graphs capture knowledge, usually there is an inherent structure about the data being represented. Hierarchical RDF molecules allow the representation of this structure explicitly as well.

## 14.3.2 Ordering

The other major extension to molecules that we implemented is ordering. Maintaining ordering is important for the efficient comparison of molecules and triples for graph and molecule merging.

Molecule ordering is defined over triple ordering. The "less-than" relationship between two triples is based on the comparison between their subjects, predicates, and objects, in turn.

For two nodes, the ordering is determined by the following rules:

1. Node type
   a. Blank node type, which is less than
   b. URI reference node type, which is less than
   c. Literal node type
2. Node value
   a. Comparison of string value of the nodes

The ordering of two triples is based on the comparison of their nodes in turn. If subject nodes are equal, predicate nodes are compared. If predicate nodes are equal, then the object nodes must be compared.

The ordering of two molecules is defined over all root triples, and submolecules, recursively.

*Example.* Based on the extended molecule definition, the graph in Figure 14.3 is decomposed into the molecule shown in Figure 14.6. Note that this molecule has

```
{ _ :1 type ExperimentalObservation}
{ _ :1 observedInteraction _ :2}
   { _ :2 participant _ :3 }
      { _ :3 hasUniprotID 'p32379'}
   { _ :2 participant _ :4 }
      { _ :4 hasUniprotID 'p46949''}
```

**Figure 14.6    RDF molecule decomposition of the graph shown in Figure 14.3.**

three hierarchies and the second root triple contains two submolecules. The blank nodes ( _ :3 and _ :4) in these two submolecules are distinguishable because of the hierarchies.

## 14.3.3 Important Algorithms

In this section, we present algorithms for molecule-related operations, such as naïve graph decomposition (no background ontology) and molecule merging. There are a number of advantages associated with this approach compared to the functional approach:

- Less duplication across molecules—functional decomposition will generally result in blank nodes shared across multiple molecules, whereas naïve decomposition will generate one molecule containing all such blank nodes.
- As the decomposition and processing do not need to consult an ontology, it is generally faster and is easier to implement.

As described in Ding et al. (2005), the naïve graph decomposition algorithm decomposes a graph into a set of molecules. The decomposition of a local RDF graph into a set of molecules is described in the pseudocode shown in Figure 14.7. We rely on the equality of the blank node identifiers (a combination of a Universally Unique Identifier (UUID) and a surrogate numeric identifier) when decomposing triples from a local graph.

There are three cases to consider when identifying submolecules:

- If the head triple is a link triple and the triple to add has a subject that is equal to its object, then the triple is added to the head triple.
- If the identified submolecule contains a triple that links to the head of the current molecule, then the current molecule is added to the submolecule and the molecule used from then on is the submolecule. In other words, the contents of the molecule are added to the submolecule, which becomes the molecule used in future operations.
- If the identified submolecule does not contain a triple that links to the current molecule, then it is added to the current molecule.

```
AT is the set of added triples (initially empty).
LGT is a sorted set (order as defined above) of triples from a local
graph.
FOR EACH Triple T from LGT not in AT
    Create a new molecule M adding T.
    IF  T is Grounded THEN
        Add T to AT.
    ELSE
        findEnclosedTriples(M).
    END IF
END FOR
findEnclosedTriples(M)
    T is the HeadTriple of M.
    BTS is a set of all triples which contain T's blank nodes.
    FOR EACH Triple BT from BTS not in AT
        Create a new molecule SM adding BT.
        Add BT to AT.
        findEnclosedTriples(SM)
        IF BT is a Link Triple THEN
            IF BT's object node equals M's subject node THEN
                Add M to SM.
                SM becomes M.
            ELSE
                Add SM to M.
            END IF
        ELSE
            Add BT to M.
        END IF
    END FOR
    Add all triples found to the set AT.
END findEnclosedTriples
```

**Figure 14.7    Graph decomposition algorithm.**

The complexity of the above graph decomposition algorithm can be analyzed as follows. Assume that all basic operations, such as adding one triple to a molecule, comparison between two nodes, getting the subject/object node from a triple, testing whether a triple is a blank node, and creating a molecule, take constant time $O(1)$. The complexity of the algorithm depends on the number of blank nodes of the graph being decomposed. For example, suppose we have a graph $G$ with $n$ triples:

- The best case is when no triple contains blank nodes. In this case, both the subject and object nodes of each triple are tested for blank node. The triples are subsequently added to a new molecule. Four constant-time operations are performed for $n$ triples. Hence, the complexity is linear to the size of the graph $O(n)$.
- The worst case is when all triples share, recursively, some blank nodes and they end up in one molecule with $n$ levels (one triple at a level). In this case,

the molecule is a chain of triples. As a triple is only added to a (sub)molecule once, it is only compared to the head triple of the enclosing molecule once. Hence, only a constant number of basic operations are performed for adding each triple. Hence, the time complexity is still $O(n)$.

Therefore, the complexity of the decomposition algorithm is $O(n)$, linear to the size of the graph. Also note that three indices are maintained for subject (s), predicate (p), and object (o): (s p o), (p o s), and (o s p), where all the triples in the graph are stored in all three indices. By storing these indices in hash maps, the retrieval of triples takes constant time.

The merging of molecules depends on the presence of a one-to-one correspondence between blank nodes. Next, we present the algorithm for finding the mapping between molecules $m_1$ and $m_2$, shown in Figure 14.8.

For each root triple, get the submolecules of $m_1$ and compare them to the triples of $m_2$. If the two triples are equal (using the blank node ID), then the corresponding blank nodes of the two triples are added to the map. This process stops when all levels of one molecule have been considered.

The complexity of the findBlankNodeMap algorithm depends on the number of comparisons between triples of the two molecules. Note that having hierarchies helps to greatly reduce the number of comparisons, as comparisons are only made for submolecules on the same level.

Without loss of generality, let us assume that $m_1$ has fewer levels of submolecules. Let the number of levels of $m_1$ be $m$ and the number of triples on level $i$ be $n_1^i$. For the

```
findBlankNodeMap(m1, m2)
    BM is a map of blank nodes from m1 to m2 (initially empty).
    FOR EACH root triple t1 in m1
        Find the root triple t2 from m2 that corresponds to t1.
        LET sm1 = m1.submolecule for t1.
        LET sm2 = m2.submolecule for t2.
        IF sm1 != null AND sm2 != null THEN
            nm = findBlankNodeMap(sm1, sm2).
            IF nm = empty THEN
                return empty map.
            ELSE
                add nm to BM.
            END IF
        ELSE IF t1.submolecule = null AND t2.submolecule = null THEN
            add map between blank nodes in t1 and t2.
        ELSE
            return empty map.
        END IF
    END FOR
    return BM.
END findBlankNodeMap
```

**Figure 14.8  Algorithm for finding blank node mappings between two molecules.**

first $m$ levels, let the number of triples of molecule $m_2$ be $n_2^i$. Thus, the complexity of the findBlankNodeMap algorithm is

$$C_2^1 = n_1^1 \times n_2^1 + \cdots + n_1^m \times n_2^m = \sum_1^m (n_1^i \times n_2^i)$$

The merging algorithm for the original molecule definition would require the comparison of all proteins, resulting in the complexity $\sum_{i=1}^m n_1^i \times \sum_{i=1}^m n_2^i$, which is strictly larger than the above complexity result and the difference is greater with the increase in the number of levels.

The extended molecules are an important component of the Scale-Out RDF Molecule Store. Together with the scale-out architecture, the molecule store will enable efficient storage, retrieval, querying, and analysis of integrated biomolecular data. In Section 14.4, we give a brief account on the performance evaluation of molecule-related algorithms and the integration process.

## 14.4 Distributed RDF Molecule Store

In this section, we describe the actual test-bed system and the distributed RDF molecule store that we have implemented based on the open-source software project Java RDF Binding (JRDF).* We also describe key system components, including graph decomposition, RDF molecule merging, distributed graph creation, and SPARQL querying across the cluster.

### 14.4.1 Protein–Protein Interaction Test Bed

For the purpose of performance evaluation in the context of our project, we initially selected datasets from DIP, IntAct, MINT, and MPact. In Newman et al. (2008b), an integration process was proposed to (a) represent the datasets as RDF instances compliant with the common ontology and (b) integrate the PPI RDF instances to form new RDF graphs based on UniProt IDs and genomic sequences of proteins, which are represented as RDF blank nodes. In Section 14.4.2, we demonstrate our implementation of the above integration framework using the MapReduce framework as a means of distributing RDF molecules across a cluster. We evaluate its performance.

In PPI networks, a protein has a number of identifiers, external references, a genomic sequence string, and a host organism. The protein may also participate in interactions with other proteins. As discussed in Section 14.1.2, blank nodes

---

* http://jrdf.sourceforge.net/

are used to represent proteins, interactions, external references, etc. Hence, each protein and all of its associated information will belong to a single molecule.

A number of queries have been identified that may reveal previously unrecognized PPIs. For instance, the query "Find all yeast protein–protein interactions that are known to be localized to the endosomal system" helps biologists to filter PPIs integrated across the Gene Ontology, the NCBI taxonomy, and PPI datasets. Given the size of the PPI data and associated datasets (well over 1 billion triples), only a distributed processing environment is capable of performing integration and querying tasks on this scale.

### 14.4.2  RDF Molecule Store

Each node in the cluster contains a local, persistent RDF molecule store that responds to SPARQL queries. Our indexing scheme takes each permutation of an RDF triple (subject, predicate, and object) with an additional molecule ID (m) and its parent molecule ID (i): (spomi, posmi, ospmi, and imspo) to create four ordered indices. This indexing scheme supports efficient addition, retrieval, and removal of molecules and triples in the molecule store. An RDF molecule API defines an indexing adaptor to provide SPARQL query functionality.

### 14.4.3  Graph Decomposition and Molecule Merging

In our approach, we adopted the naïve decomposition algorithm for its simplicity, efficiency, and robustness. This algorithm computes connected components only through edges that connect two blank nodes. Given an RDF graph, the naïve decomposition algorithm decomposes it into a set of RDF molecules, which do not share blank nodes and are therefore mutually independent.

The molecule store merges two molecules if one molecule contains all the properties (or more) of another molecule. In this way, as more molecules are added, redundant molecules are removed (or never added), allowing results from multiple nodes from a query to be merged.

### 14.4.4  Scale-Out Distributed Processing

A MapReduce-style task was developed to transform input datasets into RDF molecules and persist them in the RDF molecule store, in a distributed fashion. A map task takes each data file as input and converts it into a local RDF molecule graph. The reduce task collects RDF molecules from the cluster and puts them in the persistent, distributed molecule store. Developed based on the Hadoop project, this Scale-Out RDF Molecule Store is able to efficiently integrate large amount of source data. This scale-out processing environment has been designed in a way to achieve better load balancing for distributed query answering.

We have implemented a Representational State Transfer (REST)-style distributed SPARQL query engine for RDF molecules based on the JRDF project. One node in the cluster is designated as the *distributed* query server, which issues queries to each individual *local* query-answering server. A SPARQL query is executed in parallel on each local server in the cluster. Local servers compute query results against local indices and return results to the distributed server, which combines the results to provide the final query answer. The overall query-answering time depends on the longest local query-answering time, plus a small round-trip network latency and its own processing overhead.

In Section 14.5, we provide the results of the detailed performance evaluation of the system.

## 14.5 Evaluation Results

In this section, we provide initial performance evaluation results for the critical steps in our methodology: (a) RDF graph decomposition and RDF molecule merging, (b) MapReduce-based integration of PPI data and the distribution of RDF molecules into the cluster, and (c) distributed SPARQL query answering.*

### 14.5.1 Graph Decomposition and RDF Molecule Merging

The graph decomposition and merging algorithms described in Section 14.4 are critical components of the distributed RDF molecule store. Applied sequentially, the two algorithms can decompose an RDF graph into a set of RDF molecules, and then merge them back to form an equivalent graph. In this section, we evaluate the performance of these algorithms by comparing them with Jena (McBride 2002). Jena is, to the best of our knowledge, the only RDF triple store that provides similar functionality, and hence an ideal candidate for performance comparison purposes.

A set of RDF graphs was created for comparison, and the time taken to determine equivalence was measured. The graphs contain triples that have chaining blank nodes, for example, _ :1 p1 _ :2, _ :2 p2 _ :3, _ :3 p3 _ :4. For example, Table 14.1 shows that Jena takes 0.05 s to perform the graph equivalence test when the chain depth is 3 and the chain size is 10 (total graph size is 30). Note that DNF stands for "Did Not Finish" (>900 s).

The RDF molecule approach is faster as the number of chains reaches 100. Moreover, the RDF molecule implementation gives consistently superior performance, as both the number of chains and the chain depth increase. When the chain depth is at least 10 and the number of chains is at least 100 (i.e., graph size is at least 1000), the molecule implementation performs orders of magnitude better than Jena, with Jena not being able to determine equivalence for graph sizes over

---

* All computers used in the experiments in this section have identical setup: Intel Xeon 1.86 GHz with 2 GB main memory running JDK 1.5 on top of Linux (CentOS 5).

**Table 14.1 Time Measurement of Jena and Molecule on Graph Equivalence (in s)**

| Chain Size | Depth | | | |
|---|---|---|---|---|
| | 3 | 5 | 10 | 20 |
| **Jena** | | | | |
| 10 | 0.05 | 0.07 | 0.1 | 0.3 |
| 100 | 0.2 | 0.4 | 1.8 | 9.2 |
| 1,000 | 13.1 | 37.7 | 197.7 | DNF |
| 10,000 | DNF | DNF | DNF | DNF |
| **Molecules** | | | | |
| 10 | 0.06 | 0.0 | 0.1 | 0.2 |
| 100 | 0.2 | 0.3 | 0.4 | 0.7 |
| 1,000 | 0.9 | 1.3 | 2.5 | 5.0 |
| 10,000 | 7.7 | 13 | 26.4 | 57.4 |

20,000. Also note that with the increase of chain size and depth, the performance of molecule implementation exhibits linear degradation, which is in line with our complexity analysis of the algorithms.

## 14.5.2 MapReduce Performance

As mentioned earlier, we employ the MapReduce framework for the integration of PPI (and associated) data and the distribution of RDF molecules across a cluster of computers. A series of tests were performed to evaluate the integration and loading time of the distributed molecule store on both a 2-node and a 3-node cluster.

The MapReduce tasks were run multiple times using 11 input files (a total of 4,164,271 triples and 224,299 molecules). Table 14.2 summarizes the dataset sizes and performance of the various tasks on the two clusters. Note that the last two columns represent the time taken (in s) on the 2-node and the 3-node cluster, respectively.

A number of observations are worth discussing:

■ Tasks 2 and 3 take roughly the same time, despite the fact that task 3 handles 48% more triples and 14% more molecules than task 2.
■ There is a 100% increase in the time taken from task 3 to task 4, although task 4 only handles 44% more triples.

**Table 14.2 Time Measurements of Various MapReduce Tasks on Two Clusters (in s)**

| Task No. | # Triples | # Molecules | 2-Node Cluster | 3-Node Cluster |
|----------|-----------|-------------|----------------|----------------|
| 1 | 363,308 | 10,387 | 201 | 165 |
| 2 | 1,164,446 | 73,357 | 899 | 829 |
| 3 | 1,727,754 | 83,744 | 995 | 895 |
| 4 | 2,488,024 | 138,675 | 1,872 | 1,784 |
| 5 | 2,851,332 | 149,062 | 2,041 | 1,789 |
| 6 | 3,652,470 | 212,032 | 2,098 | 1,883 |
| 7 | 4,164,271 | 224,299 | 3,819 | 2,589 |

■ On the 3-node cluster, tasks 4, 5, 6, and 7 take comparable amount of time to complete, although there is a significant increase in the sizes of the tasks.

The above performance characteristics are due to the nature of the MapReduce framework, in which the map and reduce phases execute in sequence: no reduce task can start unless all map tasks have been finished. Therefore, a very large single-input file in the map phase in tasks 4, 5, 6, and 7 dominated their running time. Preprocessing of large input files to break them into smaller chunks is a viable solution to help reduce the time taken by the map phase. Figure 14.9 gives a more intuitive view of the running time of the different tasks. The horizontal axis represents the number of triples (in millions), and the vertical axis represents time (in s). It can be seen that the slope of the 3-node cluster is much more moderate compared to that of the 2-node cluster.

As shown in Figure 14.9, with the increase of data size, the 3-node cluster shows greater scalability. When the triple number exceeds 2 million, the 3-node cluster exhibits a constant rate of slowdown, whereas the 2-node cluster slows down considerably when processing 4 million triples. It shows that small clusters do not take full advantage of the MapReduce framework as performance suffers from communication overhead and node balancing. We expect that a larger cluster will amortize these overheads and be much more scalable.

The distributed RDF molecule store takes up around 0.5 GB disk space per million triples. This is due to the fact that more indexing information is maintained for RDF molecules (Section 14.4.2) and no compression or other space-saving optimizations have been applied at this time. Previous modeling (Moreira et al. 2007) has shown that the response time of Nutch is essentially constant as the number of servers reaches 2000 nodes with up to 40 GB of data per node. We expect that our implementation of the on-disk, distributed RDF molecule store will conservatively

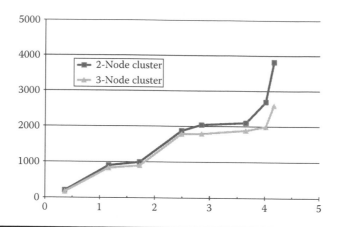

**Figure 14.9    Time measurement of MapReduce conversion tasks.**

reach 160 billion triples with a similar setup. Improving indexing efficiency will easily boost cluster capacity.

## 14.5.3 Distributed SPARQL Query Responses

As mentioned in Section 14.4.4, our SPARQL query engine has been developed by adapting the indexing structure of our RDF molecule store, so that it is compatible with the indexing structure of the JRDF triple store. Hence, comparable query performance and memory usage is expected.

To test the distributed query performance, we ran a mix of five queries about the PPI data on the 2-node and 3-node clusters. These queries have a large range of selectivity (from 0 results to around 2000 results per query), and hence are able to represent the general performance characteristics of the distributed RDF molecule store using real-world data. For example, the SPARQL query in Figure 14.10 returns the full names and UniProt IDs of human (`ncbi:ncbi_taxo_9606_ind`) proteins (`biopax:physicalEntity`) that are known to be localized at the nucleus (`cc:GO_0005634_ind`). Such a query requires the integration of the NCBI organisms' taxonomy, the Cellular Component Gene Ontology, the UniProt protein database, and other PPI databases that contain human data.

Table 14.3 summarizes the average query-answering performance of the 2-node and 3-node clusters (the same clusters used in Section 14.5.2) on the same dataset (task 7 in Table 14.2). As a baseline comparison, the same set of queries is executed against a native Sesame2 RDF triple store.* To make the comparison fair, the Sesame triple store only contains about 33% of the triples of the 3-node cluster (basically, the triples stored on a single compute node in the 3-node cluster,

---

* http://www.openrdf.org/

```
PREFIX rdf:          <http://www.w3.org/1999/02/22-rdf-syntax-ns#>
PREFIX biopax:       <http://www.biopax.org/release/biopax-level2.owl#>
PREFIX biomanta:     <http://biomanta.sourceforge.net/2007/07/biomanta _
                     extension _ 02.owl#>
PREFIX ncbi:         <http://biomanta.sourceforge.net/2007/10/ncbi _ taxo.
                     owl#>
PREFIX  xsd:         <http://www.w3.org/2001/XMLSchema#>
PREFIX  cc:          <http://www.imb.uq.edu.au/biomanta/dev _ ontology#>
SELECT ?name ?id
WHERE {
    ?x rdf:type biopax:physicalEntity.
    ?x biomanta:fromNCBISpecies ncbi:ncbi _ taxo _ 9606 _ ind.
    ?x biomanta:subcellularLocation  cc:GO _ 0005634 _ ind.
    ?x biomanta:hasFullName ?name.
    { ?x biomanta:hasPrimaryRef ?y.
      ?y biopax:DB ?db.
      FILTER ( str(?db) = "uniprotkb"^^xsd:string )
    }.
    ?y biopax:ID ?id.
}
```

**Figure 14.10   An example SPARQL query about PPI.**

**Table 14.3   Performance Statistics for RDF Stores Over Different Queries (in s)**

| Query Performance | Query 1 | Query 2 | Query 3 | Query 4 | Query 5 |
|---|---|---|---|---|---|
| Answer # | 2 | 203 | 203 | 0 | 1762 |
| Single-node Sesame | 4.0 | 0.2 | 284.9 | 1800 | 1800 |
| 2-Node cluster | 19.5 | 2.8 | 5.6 | 6.1 | 19.6 |
| 3-Node cluster | 13.4 | 2.3 | 4.3 | 4.7 | 13.0 |

totaling 1,384,496 triples), as the Sesame triple store runs on a single machine only. Also note that the Sesame query engine was terminated after running for 1800 s for queries 4 and 5* without completion.

Figure 14.11 illustrates that Sesame outperforms both clusters for query 1 and query 2. However, the performance is not significantly different from that of the 3-node cluster. For query 3, both clusters are faster than Sesame. For queries 4 and 5, both clusters are able to complete the computation while the Sesame engine runs for 1800 s before being terminated. Also note that both clusters perform relatively

---

* Each of the local query servers and the Sesame query engine is allocated 1.6 GB of memory.

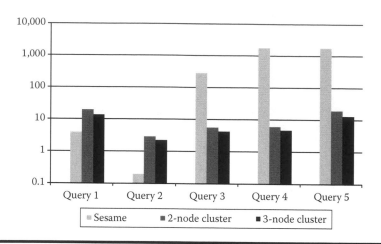

**Figure 14.11 Performance comparison on five SPARQL queries (logarithmic scale).**

*consistently*, whereas there is a great variability in Sesame's performance. Hence, as the cluster size increases, we anticipate that the distributed RDF molecule store will exhibit much greater performance advantage over conventional RDF triple stores.

### 14.5.4 Discussion on Scalability

The scale-out-style MapReduce and Hadoop frameworks were designed for very large-scale data processing that usually involves petabytes of data and thousands of compute nodes. Hence, only larger clusters of at least 10 or 20 nodes are able to enjoy the full benefits of MapReduce. The 2-node and 3-node clusters we used to perform the above experiments are for development and testing purposes only. However, even at this small scale, they show very promising results and exhibit good scalability that would improve further as the cluster size grows. As discussed in Section 14.5.2, a large cluster is able to hold a tremendous amount of RDF triples. Therefore, the benefits of the distributed SPARQL query answering would become more prominent.

## 14.6 Conclusions

Efficient querying and inferencing across large-scale integrated datasets drawn from many distributed, disparate sources is a challenge facing many communities.

Semantic Web technologies, such as RDF, OWL, and SPARQL, are ideal candidates for the task of data integration, as they offer open, unambiguous, and extensible solutions. At the same time, distributed processing paradigms, such as MapReduce, have demonstrated economic and practical ways to index and process massive amounts (petabytes) of data. Hence, the synergistic combination of MapReduce and Semantic Web technologies appears to offer a perfect solution to the problem of large-scale heterogeneous data integration, querying, and reasoning.

However, the co-identification problem (Guha 2004), particularly within disciplines such as life sciences, introduces additional complications. Attempts to standardize naming conventions have had limited impacts. RDF blank nodes, on the other hand, provide a novel way of referring to entities of common interest without creating new names or coming up with new naming conventions. But RDF blank nodes introduce complications when attempting to distribute RDF graphs across a distributed architecture, as they are only locally addressable within the enclosing RDF graph. It has been proposed that the use of RDF blank nodes be banned. We believe that banning the use of a very common language feature in RDF, OWL, and Semantic Web Rule Language (SWRL) (Horrocks et al. 2004) has a detrimental effect on data integration abilities and interoperability.

In a MapReduce framework, it is a necessary first step to decompose large datasets into smaller units for processing. With the ubiquitous presence of blank nodes, RDF graphs provide too coarse a granularity for effective processing, as the context of an entire graph is needed to disambiguate RDF blank nodes. A finer granularity is required to support the distributed integration and processing of RDF data. We believe that RDF molecules provide a finer-grained solution to the semantic integration and distribution/decomposition problem. As such, we have developed optimized algorithms to losslessly decompose an RDF graph into a set of smaller "molecules" and subsequently merge them, enabling MapReduce-style processing of RDF graphs. However, this process revealed that the presence of RDF blank nodes can cause problems of data loss, integrity loss, ambiguity, and slow performance. Consequently, we have had to extend the definition of RDF molecules to include hierarchy and ordering. By incorporating hierarchy, originally flat RDF molecules now contain explicit structural information that is beneficial in enabling more intelligent processing. More importantly, a hierarchy makes it possible to disambiguate blank nodes within a single molecule. The ordering of molecules also provides an efficient way of cross-checking data integrity during the processing of molecules.

In this chapter, we present a MapReduce-based RDF molecule store based on the MapReduce framework. This system supports efficient processing of RDF data by generating and indexing RDF molecules in a clustered, scale-out environment. Critical algorithms for decomposing an RDF graph, and merging RDF molecules and their respective computational complexity are described, implemented, and evaluated for performance. We have compared RDF graph decomposition and merging steps with the graph equivalence algorithm in Jena and obtained promising results. Performance evaluation of distributed data integration has been conducted on a 2-node and a 3-node cluster. Even on this small scale, improvements in the performance and efficiency of SPARQL queries have been shown. We have run a number of SPARQL queries over the distributed RDF molecule store containing more than 4 million triples and compared performance against the Sesame triple store. Comparable performance has been obtained in most cases. And in some cases, the distributed RDF molecule store demonstrates performance orders of magnitude better than Sesame. As greater numbers of triples are loaded into the RDF molecule store and as the size of the cluster grows, we can expect the performance advantage to further increase over traditional RDF triple stores.

Future plans include testing the approach over larger compute clusters using Amazon's Elastic Compute Cloud (EC2).* SPARQL query engine optimization (Stocker et al. 2008) is an important task to boost overall system performance. Future development of additional indexing adaptors would also allow query engines from other RDF triple stores, such as Jena, Sesame, and OpenLink Virtuoso, to be used.

Recently, a number of SPARQL performance benchmarks (Bizer and Schultz 2008, Schmidt et al. 2009) have been proposed. These benchmarks use synthetically, statistically generated datasets to evaluate the performance (query response time) of various SPARQL query engines. Although the data used in these benchmarks are not real-world data, they still provide valuable information about the efficiency of query engines and suggest potential performance improvement avenues. We will conduct proper evaluation of our distributed query engine against these benchmark systems.

An efficient underlying indexing scheme for RDF molecules is vital to the SPARQL query-answering performance. The current indexing scheme extends that of the traditional RDF triple store by appending two molecule indices (parent molecule ID and current molecule ID) to the triple IDs. More efficient indexing schemes, such as the works proposed by Weiss et al. (Weiss et al. 2008), are an important area to work on.

Another important future research direction is the development of a distributed processing environment for the extended RDF molecule store with inference capabilities. We believe that such an environment will greatly enhance our ability to query and reason across large amounts of data efficiently.

# References

Ashburner, M., Ball, C., Blake, J. et al. (2000) Gene ontology: Tool for the unification of biology. *Nature Genetics*, 25, 25–29.

Bader, G. D. and Cary, M. P. (2005) BioPAX—Biological pathways exchange language Level 2, Version 1.0 Documentation. BioPAX.

Bard, J., Rhee, S. Y., and Ashburner, M. (2005) An ontology for cell types. *Genome Biology*, 6: R21.

Bizer, C. and Schultz, A. (2008) Benchmarking the performance of storage systems that expose SPARQL endpoints. *Fourth International Workshop on Scalable Semantic Web Knowledge Base Systems* (*SSWS2008*), Karlsruhe, Germany.

---

* http://aws.amazon.com/ec2/

Boncz, P. A. (2002) Monet: A next-generation DBMS kernel for query-intensive applications. PhD thesis, Universiteit van Amsterdam, Amsterdam, the Netherlands.

Carroll, J. J., Bizer, C., Hayes, P., and Stickler, P. (2005) Named graphs, provenance and trust. *Proceedings of the 14th International Conference on World Wide Web*, Chiba, Japan. ACM, NewYork.

Chang, F., Dean, J., Ghemawat, S. et al. (2006) Bigtable: A distributed storage system for structured data. *USENIX'06: Proceedings of the Seventh Conference on USENIX Symposium on Operating Systems Design and Implementation*, Seattle, WA.

Chatr-aryamontri, A., Ceol, A., Palazzi, L. M. et al. (2007) MINT: The molecular INTeraction database. *Nucleic Acids Research*, 35, 572–574.

Chu, C. T., Kim, S. K., Lin, Y. A. et al. (2007) *Map-Reduce for Machine Learning on Multicore.* MIT Press, Vancouver, Canada.

Dean, J. and Ghemawat, S. (2004) MapReduce: Simplified data processing on large clusters. *Proceedings of the Sixth Conference on Symposium on Operating Systems Design and Implementation*, San Francisco, CA. USENIX Association, Berkeley, CA.

Ding, L., Finin, T., Peng, Y., da Silva, P. P., and McGuinness, D. L. (2005) *Tracking RDF Graph Provenance Using RDF Molecules.* UMBC, Baltimore, MD.

Good, B. M. and Wilkinson, M. D. (2006) The life sciences semantic web is full of creeps! *Briefings in Bioinformatics*, 7, 275–286.

Gray, J., Liu, D. T., Nieto-Santisteban, M. et al. (2005) Scientific data management in the coming decade. *ACM SIGMOD Record*, 34, 34–41.

Guha, R. (2004) Object co-identification on the semantic web. *13th World Wide Web Conference*, New York.

Güldener, U., Münsterkötter, M., Oesterheld, M. et al. (2006) MPact: The MIPS protein interaction resource on yeast. *Nucleic Acids Research*, 34, 436–441.

Harth, A., Umbrich, J., Hogan, A., and Decker, S. (2007) YARS2: A federated repository for searching and querying graph structured data. DERI, Galway, Ireland.

Hermjakob, H., Montecchi-Palazzi, L., Bader, G. et al. (2004) The HUPO PSI's molecular interaction format—A community standard for the representation of protein interaction data. *Nature Biotechnology*, 22, 177–183.

Horrocks, I., Patel-Schneider, P. F., Boley, H. et al. (2004) SWRL: A semantic web rule language combining OWL and ruleML. *W3C Member Submission*. W3C.

Ivanova, M., Nes, N., Goncalves, R., and Kersten, M. (2007) MonetDB/SQL meets skyserver: The challenges of a scientific database. *Proceedings of the 19th International Conference on Scientific and Statistical Database Management*, Banff, Canada.

Kerrien, S., Alam-Faruque, Y., Aranda, B. et al. (2007) IntAct—Open source resource for molecular interaction data. *Nucleic Acids Research*, 35, D561–565.

Khare, R., Cutting, D., Sitaker, K., and Rifkin, A. (2004) Nutch: A flexible and scalable open-source web search engine, CommerceNet Labs Technical Report 04.

McBride, B. (2002) Jena: A semantic web toolkit. *IEEE Internet Computing*, 6, 55–59.

McNabb, A. W., Monson, C. K., and Seppi, K. D. (2007) MRPSO: MapReduce particle swarm optimization. *Proceedings of the Ninth Annual Conference on Genetic and Evolutionary Computation*, London, U.K., p. 177.

Merelli, E., Armano, G., Cannata, N. et al. (2007) Agents in bioinformatics, computational and systems biology. *Briefings in Bioinformatics*, 8, 45.

Moreira, J. E., Michael, M. M., Da Silva, D. et al. (2007) Scalability of the Nutch search engine. *Proceedings of the 21st Annual International Conference on Supercomputing*. Seattle, WA. ACM Press, NewYork.

Muster, P. (2007) Quantitative and qualitative evaluation of a SPARQL front-end for MonetDB. Department of Informatics, University of Zurich, Zurich, Switzerland.

Newman, A., Hunter, J., Li, Y.-F., Bouton, C., and Davis, M. (2007) BioMANTA ontology: The integration of protein–protein interaction data. *Interdisciplinary Ontology Conference (InterOntology08)*, Tokyo, Japan.

Newman, A., Hunter, J., Li, Y.-F., Bouton, C., and Davis, M. (2008a) BioMANTA ontology: The integration of protein–protein interaction data. *Proceedings of Interdisciplinary Ontology Conference 2008 (InterOntology08)*, Tokyo, Japan.

Newman, A., Hunter, J., Li, Y.-F., Bouton, C., and Davis, M. (2008b) A scale-out RDF molecule store for distributed processing of biomedical data. *Semantic Web for Health Care and Life Sciences Workshop (HCLS'08) at the 17th International Conference on World Wide Web (WWW'08)*, Beijing, China.

Oren, E., Delbru, R., Catasta, M. et al. (2008) Sindice.com: A document-oriented lookup index for open linked data. *International Journal of Metadata, Semantics and Ontologies*, 3, 37–52.

Pantel, P. (2007) Data catalysis: Facilitating large-scale natural language data processing. *Proceedings of the International Symposium on Universal Communication (ISUC-07)*, Kyoto, Japan.

Ruttenberg, A., Rees, J., and Zucker, J. (2006) What BioPAX communicates and how to extend OWL to help it. *OWL: Experiences and Directions Workshop*, Athens, GA.

Salwinski, L., Miller, C. S., Smith, A. J. et al. (2004) The database of interacting proteins: 2004 update. *Nucleic Acids Research*, 32, D449–451.

Schmidt, M., Hornung, T., Lausen, G. and Pinkel, C. (2009) SP2Bench: A SPARQL performance benchmark. *IEEE 25th International Conference on Data Engineering (ICDE'09)*, Shanghai, China.

Stickler, P. (2005) CBD—Concise Bounded Description. http://www.w3.org/Submission/CBD/, W3C Member Submission.

Stocker, M., Seaborne, A., Bernstein, A., Kiefer, C., and Reynolds, D. (2008) SPARQL basic graph pattern optimization using selectivity estimation. *Proceeding of the 17th International Conference on World Wide Web*. Beijing, China. ACM, NewYork.

Stonebraker, M., O'Neil, E., O'Neil, P. et al. (2005) C-store: A column-oriented DBMS. *Proceedings of the 31st International Conference on Very Large Data Bases*, Trondheim, Norway, pp. 553–564.

The Yahoo! Research Team (2006) Content, metadata, and behavioral information: Directions for yahoo! research. *IEEE Data Engineering Bulletin*, 29, 10–18.

Tummarello, G., Morbidoni, C., Puliti, P., and Piazza, F. (2005) Signing individual fragments of an RDF graph. *Special Interest Tracks and Posters of the 14th International Conference on World Wide Web*, Chiba, Japan. ACM, NewYork.

Weiss, C., Karras, P. and Bernstein, A. (2008) Hexastore: Sextuple indexing for semantic web data management. *Proceedings of the VLDB Endowment*, 1, 1008–1019.

Yang, H.-C., Dasdan, A., Hsiao, R.-L., and Parker, D. S. (2007) Map-reduce-merge: Simplified relational data processing on large clusters. *Proceedings of the 2007 ACM SIGMOD International Conference on Management of Data*, Beijing, China.

# Chapter 15

# Enabling XML Capability for Hadoop and Its Applications in Healthcare

Jianfeng Yan, Jin Zhang, Ying Yan, and Wen-Syan Li

## Contents

# 15.1 Introduction

Current analytics is limited to structured data (i.e., relational); however, many advanced applications rely on semi-structured data, such as XBRL (eXtensible Business Report Language) for finance and accounting, reporting applications and NewsML (News Markup Language) for publishing and news/media content management. Among these applications that require management of semi-structured data, healthcare is one of the areas that truly relies on XML (Extensible Markup Language) to store and exchange medical and healthcare information. For example, HL7 CDA (Health Level Seven Clinic Document Architecture) has been a standard for electronic interchange of clinical information among healthcare providers, and it has been adapting XML technology in its newer release to extend its capability. Moreover, XML technology is being adapted in modeling and storing medical records in the past decade, as computers are widely used in all systems and laboratories in modern hospitals and clinical centers.

An electronic medical record (EMR) is a computerized legal medical record (i.e., patient record) created in an organization that delivers care, such as hospitals and clinical centers. An EMR has three parts, as illustrated in Figure 15.1 and as follows:

1. *Patient data:* It stores *basic information of a patient,* such as name, address, date of birth, and insurance information. The patient data is usually structured and can be stored in relational tables.
2. *Patient profile:* It usually includes a *summary of the medical history of a patient's family,* such as if the family members have cancers or high blood pressures, as well as the *lifestyle* of a patient, such as if he or she smokes, drinks, and exercises, and if a patient is under heavy pressure at work. The patient profile data is usually structured; however, depending on how many details need to be collected and recorded for the patient profiles, it could also be semi-structured.

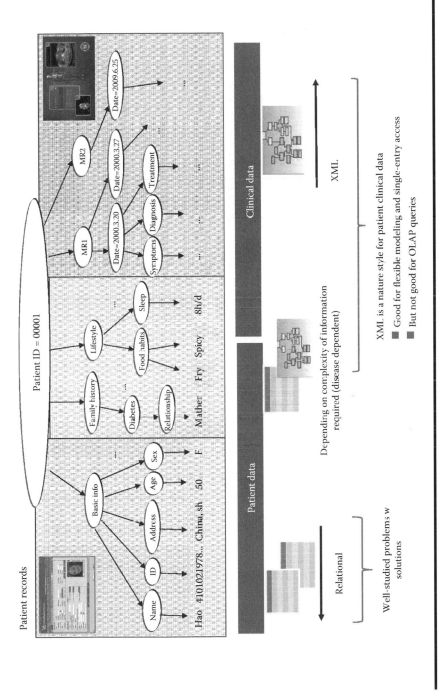

**Figure 15.1   Example of EMR.**

3. *Clinical data:* It stores clinical informatics, including symptoms, diagnosis, and treatments of each hospital visit by a patient. The clinical data is usually semi-structured because of the nature of its diverse data types, possible evolving schema, and tree-like diagnosis and treatment classifications.

A patient record has a unique identifier (Pid, patient ID), usually a social security number or a citizen identification card number. Patient data is documented once when a patient registers at a hospital the first time and it is modified only when his/her personal information or insurance information changes. A patient profile is created when the patient first registers at the hospital and the patient profile is augmented as the patient visits the hospital. A single clinical record, uniquely identified by a unique identifier (CRid, clinical record ID), is used to store symptoms, diagnosis, and treatment of a hospital visit. CRid is usually a number automatically generated by computer systems. Clinical data of a patient is stored in multiple clinical records.

XML is a more desirable format for modeling and storing semi-structured clinical data in EMR applications for its extendibility to model complexity and diverse formats of clinical data; however, EMR systems are usually built on top of the RDBMS (relational database management system) or file systems. Few advanced database systems support native XML storage and retrieval capability, such as IBM DB2 [3]; however, their capability supporting complex healthcare applications on a large set of EMRs is very limited. These complex healthcare applications could include interactive queries that provide diagnosis and treatment assistance to doctors and batched jobs that analyze EMRs to measure treatment effectiveness and to define treatment standard procedure. The complexity arises when the system needs to deal with query conditions on semi-structured parts of EMRs and a potentially large number of query conditions. The response time of query processing on a large EMR database could be tens of minutes to hours for RDBMS-based implementations, or native XML-based implementations if indexing is not designed properly or query processing is parallelized across a cluster of servers.

These applications demand a healthcare informatics system with high *usability* (i.e., supporting healthcare-specific style of query, search, and analytics), *flexibility* (i.e., supporting semi-structured/XML data modeling dealing with evolving data types, schemas, and terminologies), *reliability* (i.e., fault tolerance), *performance* (i.e., fast response time, automated load balance, and the ability to scale up the system when needed), and extendibility (i.e., system's capability to be scaled up as needed). To meet these requirements, it requires a novel data management system since XML presents a different set of challenges to query processing, indexing, parallelism, and distributed computing.

SAP Technology Lab, China, is developing a clouds-enabled information appliance, Xbase, supporting search and analytics on XML-based EMR databases. In light of many recent comparisons of approaches to large-scale data analysis, such as in [22] and existing XML indexing and query processing techniques, we take a hybrid approach to building Xbase. Xbase is the first healthcare-specific analytic engine to be built on top of existing cluster/cloud infrastructure Hadoop [24] (for semi-structured data and search/indexing requiring massive parallelism) and RDBMS (for metadata and structured data). Our implementation of Xbase runs on a large cluster of commodity machines to achieve high scalability in a cost-effective manner.

XML and distributed computing present a different set of challenges to query processing, indexing, and parallelism using existing Hadoop APIs as well as its storage, Hadoop Distributed File System (HDFS) [25], and MapReduce distributed computing framework [8].

In this chapter, we present the architectural design and features of Xbase to meet the requirements of advanced healthcare applications. The key features of Xbase include

■ Native XML storage with support of distributed file systems
■ Query processing and indexing applied directly to native XML structure and content
■ Parallel query processing and index building on top of emerging Hadoop cloud computing infrastructure
■ Being built natively on emerging cloud computing infrastructure Hadoop to achieve almost unlimited distributed storage capability and computation capability

We also describe how our indexing and query processing designs are mapped into the Hadoop infrastructure and MapReduce distributed computing framework as well as why we select Hadoop over other candidates, including Hbase [26], Google's Bigtable [5], Hive [27], and existing column-oriented DBMS, such as Trex [23] and Vertica [29], as the framework for implementation, storage, and computation. The main contribution of this work is sharing the design and engineering experience of our efforts building the first XML database, Xbase, on the emerging and popular cloud computing infrastructure, Hadoop. Xbase is experimentally evaluated, and preliminary results are presented to validate the applicability of our approach.

The rest of this chapter is organized as follows. In Section 15.2, we describe query patterns in healthcare informatics. In Section 15.3, we describe the system architecture of Xbase. In Section 15.4, we describe the index design and indexing phase in Xbase based on available Hadoop computing infrastructure. In Section 15.5, we describe query processing in Xbase. In Section 15.6, we present evaluation results that experimentally validate effectiveness of our system. In Section 15.7, we discuss related work, and conclude the chapter in Section 15.8.

## 15.2 Query Patterns for Healthcare Informatics

Queries in healthcare applications have certain patterns. A healthcare informatics system needs to support both interactive and report-generating/analytic queries. It also needs to incorporate domain knowledge bases, such as classifications of diagnosis, medical terms, treatment procedures, medicine ingredients, and doctors' expertise and their access control lists, in query processing. Another pattern is that there could be a large number of attributes involved in queries, especially for complicated diseases. In real-world cases studied, we observed that there are potentially more than 100 attributes in queries related to heart-related diseases and more than 200 attributes for cancer-related diseases; however, usually a relatively small subset of attributes (i.e., 10%–20%) are specified in a single query. Thus, column-based storage is preferred to save I/O bandwidth. The complexity of queries and analytics is disease/function dependent.

We categorize queries over healthcare informatics into the following four types:

1. Interactive, similarity-based ad hoc queries, such as searching possible diagnosis and treatment of other patients with similar symptoms and profiles
2. BI style analytics, such as batched jobs that analyze cost efficiency for all hospitals in a city grouping by types of diseases, analyze EMR databases to measure treatment effectiveness, and define treatment standard procedure
3. Queries for topic-focused browsing and navigation with aggregation/summarization of information, similar to roll-up and drag-down interactions in typical data warehousing applications
4. Data mining style analytics, such as medical insurance fraud detection and biomedicine-related pattern exploration

In this chapter, we focus on describing our system design aspects related to supporting the first two categories of queries: (1) interactive, similarity-based ad hoc queries and (2) batched report-generating BI style analytics. Xbase is currently built specifically for healthcare applications; thus, we support query syntax commonly used for the two types of queries. For example, a query finding possible diagnosis by searching patients with similar symptoms and profiles ranked by clinical diagnosis code standard may include the following types of conditions:

■ Range, such as $30 < age < 40$
■ Category, such as manifestations = {nephrosis, blindness, polyneuropathy}
■ Boolean, such as sex = female
■ In set, such as if a patient has one or more chronic kidney disease symptoms or if a set of keywords are in a free style doctor notes
■ Path expression, such as `/Pid/emr/treatment [medicine = aspirin]/medicine` (i.e., a query selecting medicine nodes with the medicine

name "aspirin") and `/Pid/emr/diagnose [enteritis] [diabe-tes]` (i.e., a query selecting diagnosed children of the context nodes that have both an enteritis child element and a diabetes child element)

Furthermore, healthcare-related queries are record oriented around Pid and EMRid (i.e., EMR ID). Here, we describe query patterns of healthcare applications. In Section 15.4, we formally define the scope of query syntax and conditions supported in Xbase.

## 15.3 System Architecture of Xbase

As Xbase is designed as an information appliance for healthcare applications, it needs to support EMR-oriented queries and analytics on both content and structure data of EMRs. We utilize RDBMS for patient data and patient-profile-related query conditions, and Hadoop for patient-clinical-data-related query conditions. In this section, we describe the architectural design of Xbase starting with an overview of Hadoop [24].

The Apache Hadoop project develops open-source software for reliable, scalable, and distributed computing. Hadoop includes the following subprojects:

- HBase [26]: A scalable, distributed database that supports structured data storage for large tables.
- HDFS [25]: HDFS is the primary storage system used by Hadoop applications. HDFS creates multiple replicas of data blocks and distributes them on compute nodes throughout a cluster to enable reliable, extremely rapid computations.
- Hive [27,28]: A data warehouse infrastructure that provides data summarization and ad hoc querying.
- MapReduce [8]: A software framework for distributed processing of large data sets on compute clusters.
- Pig [9,20]: A high-level dataflow language and execution framework for parallel computation.

MapReduce is a programming model and an associated implementation for processing and generating large data sets. Users specify a map function that processes a key–value pair to generate a set of intermediate key–value pairs, and a reduce function that merges all intermediate values associated with the same intermediate key. Programs written in this functional style are automatically parallelized and executed on a large cluster of commodity machines. The run-time system of Hadoop takes care of the details of partitioning the input data, scheduling the program's execution across a set of machines, handling machine failures, and managing the required inter-machine communication.

Xbase utilizes Hadoop's HDFS as storage for EMRs and their indexes (excluding those indexes associated with content range conditions of a patient), and MapReduce for indexing EMRs and query processing for semi-structured data alone with RDBMS for structured data. We do not utilize Hbase, Hive, and Pig due to their lack of capability to handle structural information of XML. Comprehensive analysis is provided later in Section 15.7 as well as why we select Hadoop over other candidates, including Hive, Google's Bigtable, and some sophisticated XML index techniques. The system architecture of Xbase is illustrated in Figure 15.2, and the functionality of each component is as follows.

1. Connectors for applications: Xbase currently supports XQuery with online analytic process (OLAP), data mining, and high-level programming API sets for application development.
2. Metadata: It stores operational information for Xbase including the following four parts:
   a. KDB (Knowledge Database): This is used to store healthcare-domain-specific knowledge, such as diagnosis classification, medical terms, treatment procedure, medicine ingredient names, and doctors' expertise. This

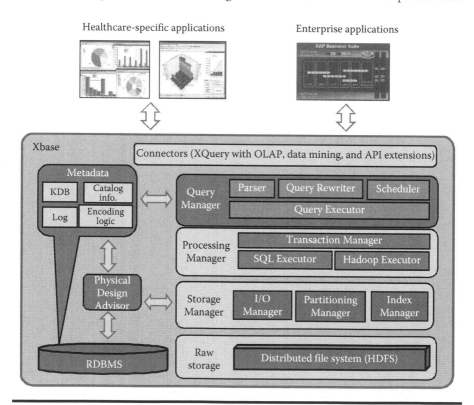

**Figure 15.2 System architecture of Xbase.**

KDB is needed for query relaxation, personalized result summarization, and access control as well as data cleansing and terminology homogenization during the EMR loading phase.

b. Catalog information: It stores metadata of indexes and EMR schema in Xbase. It also stores the statistics of EMRs, both content- and structure-wise, and query workloads. The statistics is used by the Physical Design Advisor when it recommends indexing strategies and by the Query Manager when it processes queries.

c. Encoding logic: Content and path information of EMRs is encoded into characters and numbers when they are stored and indexed instead of being in their initial forms. The purpose of such encoding is to reduce the footprint of EMRs and their indexes on storage and in the memory. The results and EMRs are converted into their original forms before they return to the querying applications. Encoding logic is derived by the Physical Design Advisor.

d. Log: It stores the log of workload execution, index usage, and history of indexing strategies recommended. This log is later used by Physical Design Advisor.

3. RDBMS: RDBMS is used to store, index, and retrieve metadata and patient data of EMRs. RDBMS is also used to index and retrieve content by range conditions of EMRs, which can be patient data, patient profile, and clinical data. Currently, MySQL is used in Xbase. In the current default deployment, a single instance of the stand-alone version of MySQL is deployed. Multiple instances of MySQL RDBMS or a cluster version of MySQL RDBMS may be deployed if RDBMS becomes a bottleneck.

4. Query Manager: This component is built specifically for Xbase and has three subcomponents as follows:

a. Parser: It converts the input queries to an Xbase internal form and passes the queries to the Query Rewriter.

b. Query Rewriter: It looks up metadata (i.e., KDB, catalog information, and encoding logic) and rewrites the queries into sub-queries for RDBMS and Hadoop, respectively, and marks query trees with proper indexes, if available.

c. Scheduler: It examines the serializability of all predicates of each query tree and generates an execution schedule in Xbase (in RDBMS and in Hadoop, respectively, and across these two components). Details of the scheduling logic are described in Section 15.5.

5. Processing Manager: Since queries are processed by both RDBMS and Hadoop, the Processing Manager is responsible for dispatching sub-queries to RDBMS and Hadoop as well as for coordination, including passing intermediate result sets across RDBMS and Hadoop and merging results. The SQL Executor and the Hadoop Executor correspond to the query processor in RDBMS and the workers in Hadoop, respectively. Since a transaction on a single EMR is

actually carried out across multiple components in RDBMS and Hadoop, the Transaction Manager is responsible for ensuring that the transaction on the EMR is committed only when all sub-transactions are committed.

6. Storage Manager: This component is a part of the standard distribution from Hadoop without enhancement. It has three subcomponents, namely, I/O Manager, Partitioning Manager, and Index Manager. The Storage Manager of Hadoop is in charge of the actual placement of physical indexes and EMRs. We store EMRs and their indexes into Hadoop via its APIs, and the actual nodes where the EMRs and indexes are stored and how replicas are synchronized is determined by Hadoop. In the current implementation, we use the default value, 3, as the total number of replicas automatically created when a physical block is stored in Hadoop. Replicas are created for load balance and fault tolerance. How we map our logical design to the physical deployment in Hadoop and how we map our query processing to the MapReduce framework are described in Sections 15.4 and 15.5 in detail.

7. Raw storage: We use the standard distribution of HDFS to store EMRs and structure-related indexes.

8. Physical Design Advisor: It takes application statistic information and recommended indexing strategies for both RDBMS and Hadoop parts. The Physical Design Advisor has two main components (not shown in the figure) as follows:

   • Placement Manager: It is responsible to prepare and store the content (including keys, data guide, raw clinical data, Bloom filter indexes, etc) that will be actually stored as a "physical block" on HDFS under Hadoop. The content structure of a physical block in Xbase over Hadoop is described in Section 15.5.3.

   • Indexing Manager: It is responsible for creating indexes for all semi-structured data and then passing the indexes to the Placement Manager to place them on Hadoop. Details of the Indexing Manager are presented in Section 15.4.

# 15.4 Indexing

Xbase is a record-oriented system that manages healthcare information with record IDs. Each patient, EMR, and clinical record have IDs; thus, Xbase manages all XML documents with a key and its value. Each document has a global unified ID as the key. All the other data is regarded as the value. In this section, we describe how we apply four types of indexes to content and structural information.

## 15.4.1 Content and Structures of EMR

An example of the tree-structured EMR is illustrated in Figure 15.3. The tree value of EMR contains patient data, patient profile, and clinical data from the left to the

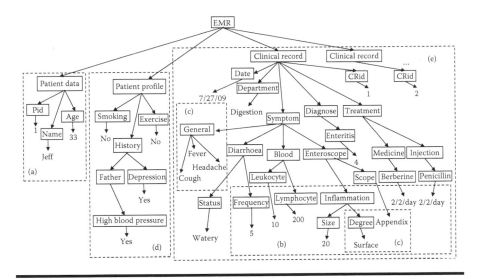

**Figure 15.3   Tree-structured EMR.**

right. In our current implementation, the patient data is structured, which is stored as relational data, and the patient profile and clinical data are semi-structured data, stored as XML data. The EMR consists of two types of information—content and structure, as follows:

1. Content:
   - *Fine-structured content (FC)*, as shown in Figure 15.3a: In an EMR, only patient data, such as Pid, patient age, name, and address, is *FC* and can be stored in RDBMS to utilize its indexing and query processing capabilities.
   - *Numerical value content (NC)*, as shown in Figure 15.3b: *NC* has numerical values. Range queries usually are issued over *NC*. *NC*, separated from path structures, can be stored in RDBMS to utilize B+tree indexes for efficient query processing.
   - *Set value content (SC)*, as shown in Figure 15.3c: Each *SC* contains a set of values following the same tag. An example of SC is symptom. Usually, the query over *SC* also contains a set of values. For fast query processing, the index structure for set operation should be applied over *SC*. In our system, we use Bloom-filter-based index [4].
   - *Frequently accessed path content (PC)*: In Figure 15.3d, some paths, for example, /patient profile/smoking and /patient profile/exercise, are frequently accessed together. Given that each path can also be considered as a value, Bloom filter indexes, instead of data guide indexes [10], are applied to a set of paths to facilitate efficient query processing.

2. Structure (*S*), as shown in Figure 15.3e: *S* represents the structure of each clinical record. Through the path in *S* we can find the content of the data including *SC* and *NC*. XML path index techniques, such as in [10,15,16,19,30], can be applied here.

Note that the design decision of applying Bloom filter indexes or data guide indexes for XML structures are based on the analysis of the Physical Design Advisor. The Physical Design Advisor first examines the occurrence frequency of a path in all records. It recommends indexing the path using FC-Indexes if it occurs in all records, using Bloom filter indexes if it occurs in the majority of records, and using data guide indexes if it occurs in a small portion of records. In this chapter, we do not discuss the details of the recommendation process due to space limitations.

## 15.4.2 Types of Indexes

In order to directly apply indexing schemes to native XML structures and content, we deployed four types of indexes in Xbase as follows:

1. *Fine-structured data content index (FC-Index):* With Pid as the primary key, FC is stored in relational tables. Traditional RDBMS indexes can be utilized for retrieving a proper ID set according to the query's predicates. We call the index structure of this part *FC-Index*. An example of FC-Index is shown in Figure 15.4a. The metadata contains FC's prefix path and its corresponding address. FC-Index structure is built over all the patient records without partitioning.
2. *Numerical value content index for range query (R-Index):* Xbase builds several special B+ tree indexes for range queries over *NC*. One metadata table holds the pairs of each path and its corresponding R-Index address. For each address, a relational table is built to store all pairs of Pids or CRids and their content. An example of FC-Index is shown in Figure 15.4b. R-Index is built over all the patient records.
3. *Set value content index with Bloom filter (BF-Index):* In the patient records, some attributes are described by tens, even hundreds, of data values. For example, a query including 20 symptoms can be issued over all the patient records, and there are more than 200 symptoms for each disease. Because the data value is a string (numerical values in *SC* and path value, for example, emr/patient profile can also be considered as strings) in essence, large-scale string matching is not trivial. We use the Bloom filter [4] signature and the Bloom filter tree index structure (*BF-Index*) to speed up the set query filtering process.

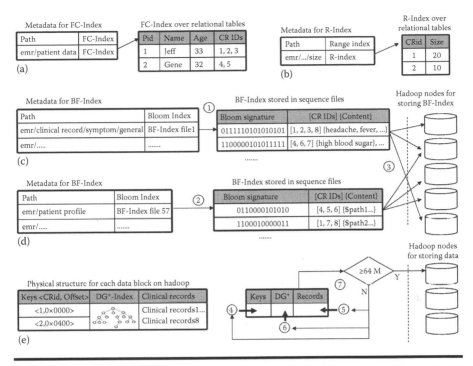

**Figure 15.4 Indexes for Figure 15.3. (a) FC data. (b) NC data. (c) SC data. (d) PC data. (e) S data.**

The Bloom filter signature is a bit vector that represents a set of objects and is often used as an approximate filter for supporting membership query. Its advantages like very quick comparison, easy maintenance, and none false negatives lead to its wide adoption in various applications [7,11]. A Bloom-filter-based signature consists of a vector of $m$ bits and $k$ independent hash functions ranging from 1 to $m$. According to the formula $p = (1 - e^{-kn/m})^k$ [4], $n$ is the distinct number of elements. We can observe that the size $m$ of the vector varies with the false positives rate. A Bloom filter applies to set values that do not consider the order. However, since we are assuming a single schema for XML, the order does not matter.

The signature of a value set is built through (1) hashing each data to $k$ values $f_{i1}, f_{i2} \ldots f_{ik}$, by $k$ hash functions $h_1, h_2, \ldots h_k$; and (2) setting the corresponding positions of these hash values to 1 on the $m$-bit vector. (For example, if a particular hash value equals to 4, we should set the fourth position of the vector to 1.) Based on the individual data signatures, a set signature can be computed over them with an "OR" bit operation. As soon as a query with a value set condition comes, its signature, $s_q$, is constructed at first, and compared with the data set signature, $s_d$. If $s_q \wedge s_d = s_q$, query $q$ may be potentially contained in the data. Otherwise, $q$ can be pruned safely. Benefited from the bit operation, all computations among signatures are extremely efficient.

BF-Index is built over the $SC$ part and some path value set $PC$ of all the patient records. As shown in Figure 15.4c, one metadata table holds all paths that have set content. Each path is associated with a BF-Index file name, as shown in the relationships ① and ② in Figure 15.4c and d. The BF-Index file is organized as key–value pairs and stored as a sequence file on Hadoop. The value includes a set of CRids and the raw data content in those IDs to be indexed, while the key is the Bloom filter signature for the raw data content. ① points to the BF-Index file $PC$ set data. For example, if a record $CR_1$ contains the paths with the prefix `emr/patient profile`, $P = \{$`emr/patient profile/smoking, emr/patient profile/ exercise, emr/patient profile/history` ...$\}$, the Bloom filter signature, which is the key, is built over the tree paths set $P$. The value includes the CRids whose $PC$ signature is the same with $CR_1$ and the content is the tree paths. While ② indicates $SC$ data, through testing the query signature with the data signature, large number of unqualified records will be pruned. However, the resultant CRids passing the Bloom filter are still not accurate, although we can adjust the false positives to be very small. Therefore, we also store the data contents in order to ensure the corrections. For example, if the clinical records 1, 2, 3, and 8 all have `emr/clinical Record/symptom/{fever, cough and headache}` whose BF signature is 0111110101010101, then, in the BF-Index file, there is a pair <0111110101010101, [1, 2, 3, 8] {fever, cough, headache}>. When building the BF-Index structure, Hadoop would partition the BF-Index file of each path into small file blocks and store them on different Hadoop index nodes, as shown in the process of ③ in Figure 15.4c.

4. *Structure index based on DataGuide (DG⁺-Index):* For the structure predicates of the query, Xbase uses the DG⁺-Index structure, which is shown in Figure 15.5. DG⁺-Index is designed based on the DataGuide index technique [10], which is a typical XML structural index for path expressions. To enhance the pruning power, DG⁺-Index also stores the CRid set on each internal indexing node indicating the clinical records that include the prefix path from the root to the current node. For example, in Figure 15.5, there is a CRid set {1, 2, 8} attached on the node "medicine." Therefore, the path `clinical Record/ treatment/medicine` is only contained in the clinical records 1, 2, and 8. Given a DG⁺-Index and a CRid, Xbase can also find the paths that are contained in that clinical record.

As illustrated in Figure 15.4d, each index is stored in a DG⁺-Index file on HDFS and the file is divided into blocks by HDFS. We further divide each block into three parts: the key part, the DG⁺-Index part, and the data part. The key part contains the CRids and the offset of the clinical records that are stored in the data

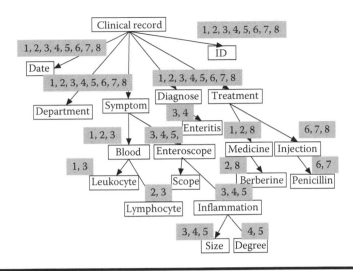

**Figure 15.5 Index for Figure 15.3e.**

part. The DG⁺-Index part contains the index structure for all the clinical records in the data part, while the data part stores the actual clinical records assigned to this block. Given a CRid, we can decide whether a clinical record is located in that data block or not. Given a path, the DG⁺-Index part is accessed and the related CRid is obtained or NULL is returned if no CRid can be found. With the CRid and the offset, we can further locate the clinical record in the block.

We store the clinical records that belong to the same patient on the some node in the index building phase. Before inserting a clinical record, the index manager would check the potential size of the current index after the insertion. If the size is bigger than the size of the block (we use 64M as an example block size), then the index file is flushed to Hadoop data nodes as a block appending to the DG⁺-Index file, which is shown in process ⑦ in Figure 15.4d. Otherwise, the clinical record and its key are inserted, as illustrated in processes ⑥ ④, and the DG⁺-Index is also updated, as shown in process ⑤ in Figure 15.4d.

Query processing for XML path information with DG⁺-Index requires tree traversal from the top down to the nodes where no match of prefix path can be found. It is considered a relatively costly step in query processing. In Xbase, we parallelize this step by partitioning the structural content into multiple nodes, and a DG⁺-Index is built for structural content stored in a single node; thus, the DG⁺-Index search is distributed and parallelized among all nodes.

The four types of indexes have different inputs and outputs, as illustrated in Figure 15.6. As FC-Index and R-Index are in RDBMS, they are built over both keys and values. Xbase can use clinical report IDs (CRids) to probe both of the indexes and get the corresponding values. Also, values can be used for probing the index to obtain their clinical report IDs.

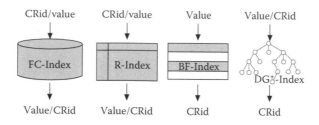

**Figure 15.6** Input/output of index structures.

For BF-Index, it only accepts a set of values. After the filtering process, CRids are returned. Among the four indexes, all the indexes can take advantages of serial-chain-style execution, except BF-Index. As we have introduced above, on each node of DG$^+$-Index, the clinical report IDs that contain their prefix paths are also indexed. Therefore, either paths or CRids can be used to probe DG$^+$-Index. The same set of CRids used as inputs for probing DG$^+$-Index need to be distributed over all nodes; each node can return qualified CRids as soon as there is no matching.

### 15.4.3 Building Index

For every piece of information in the patient records, the Xbase Indexing Manager will automatically determine which index structure should be used. For each path in the patient records, the Indexing Manager would determine which index structure should be selected for indexing. To build the index structures, there are two-phases as follows.

First, *rule generation*: The Xbase Indexing Manager first generates a set of rules according to the query workload and the knowledge of the structure characters from sampling the patient records. The rules for FC-Index are determined by the fine-structured data parts. The rules for R-Index are generated based on the characters of the *NC* data with frequently issued queries for a certain range. Given a workload threshold $\alpha$, those *NC* data whose query workload is bigger than $\alpha$ would be indexed by R-Index. The paths with set values should be included into the BF-Index. From the sampling, Xbase collects the information of different number of values *Dit* under a certain tag *T* over all the sample records, and average number of values *Avg* under the same tag *T* in each record. If *Dit* is bigger than $\beta$ and *Avg* is bigger $\gamma$, then the path over tag *T* should be indexed by BF-Index. Otherwise, DG$^+$-Index is better than BF-Index for reducing the overhead in the index structure. If a path cannot be included into any of the above rules, it would be indexed by the DG$^+$-Index structure. The parameters $\alpha$, $\beta$, and $\gamma$ vary with different system settings and application requirements. The index structures are different with different $\alpha$, $\beta$, and $\gamma$.

Second, *index building*: As shown in Figure 15.7, if a path can satisfy FC-Index rules, it should be indexed by FC-Index. Else, it is tested with R-Index rules. If it

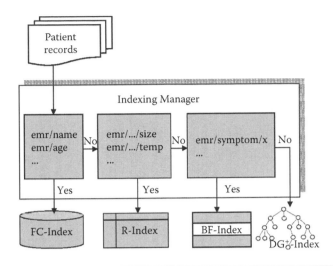

**Figure 15.7    Indexing Manager.**

cannot satisfy both FC-Index and R-Index, it should continue testing against the rules for BF-Index. If there are still no matches, DG⁺-Index will be selected for indexing that path.

# 15.5 Query Processing

Query processing in Xbase has several steps. When a query is submitted to Xbase, it is sent to the parser to be converted into an Xbase-specific internal format and then is passed to the Query Rewriter. A query with multiple conditions is divided into several sub-queries. Through the metadata of different index structures, the sub-queries can find their proper index addresses. Then, each subquery is rewritten into SQL or XQuery accordingly, depending on whether it runs at RDBMS or Hadoop. All the well-written sub-queries are then sent to the query plan generator for developing index-probing orders. After probing the index structure, each sub-query may obtain a set of CRids that satisfy the individual predicates. Then, the Result Consolidator will calculate the CRids for all the sub-queries. With the resultant CRids as the keys, the patient records will be retrieved and returned to the query. The details of each step are introduced in Sections 15.5.1 through 15.5.4.

## 15.5.1 Query Rewriting

Followed by the query parser, the Query Rewriter partitions each issued query into multiple sub-queries. For example, a query such as "Find the clinical records with *age between 20 and 40*, having *the enteroscope check with inflammation of appendix*

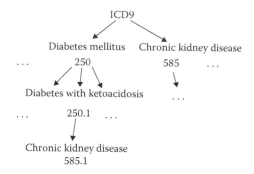

**Figure 15.8  ICD-9 example.**

*within 25 square mm and with the symptoms of headache, fever and cough"* will be rewritten into the following four sub-queries:

```
S₁:emr/symptom/enteroscope/scope=appendix
S₂:emr/symptom/enteroscope/inflammation/size<25
S₃:emr/symptom/headache, fever, cough
S₄:age >20 and <40
```

After probing the metadata tables, the sub-queries would find their own index types and index's addresses. Then, each sub-query will be translated into SQL and XQuery. In this simple example, we can find that $S_1$ is suitable for FC-Index or DG⁺-Index, $S_2$ for R-Index or DG⁺-Index, $S_3$ for BF-Index, and $S_4$ for FC-Index. A more complex example is as follows.

"Find the *top 2* frequently occurred diseases in all the clinical records which belong to *Diabetes mellitus* in ICD-9 family." The ICD-9 code stands for the International Classification of Diseases, 9th Revision [1]. In ICD-9, each disease has an unique code. The code of *Diabetes mellitus* is 250. An example is shown in Figure 15.8, where the path 250-250.1-585.1 indicates a detailed disease belonging to category 250. To answer the query, for each path in the ICD-9 code rooted at the sub-root 250, we need to calculate the number of patients whose clinical records include that path. Then, the top two paths are selected as the result. The query is rewritten as follows, and the queries (and sub-queries) are executed in the way described in Section 15.5.2:

```
<Result>
  for $x in doc (ICD9.xml)/root/250/*
      for $y in $x/*
        for $z in $y/*
      <condition path=$x/$y/$z>
        for $pid in doc(patients.xml/*
          for $x$y$z in $pid//*
        count $number
```

```
      order by $number
      count $count
      while $count < 2
        return <number>$number</number>
    </condition>
</Result>
```

## 15.5.2 *Plan Generation*

The query plan in Xbase is the order of index probing. Xbase's four index structures can be parallel-probed, as shown in Figure 15.9a. Using the example in Section 15.5.4, the sub-queries $S_1$, $S_2$, $S_3$, and $S_4$ can probe the four index structures at the same time, respectively. Each sub-query can get the results from one of the index structure. For example, the result of sub-query $S_4$ is outputted through FC-Index and the result of $S_1$ is obtained from probing DG⁺-Index. Alternatively, the four index structures can be probed in the serial-chain manner, such as in Figure 15.9b. Sub-query $S_3$ can probe BF-Index first and get the result (a set of Pids). Then, the result of $S_1$ together with the other sub-queries $S_2$ and $S_4$ can probe FC-Index and R Index in a parallel manner. In the last step, the results of $S_2$, $S_3$, and $S_4$ probe the last index, DG'-Index, with $S_1$ to obtain the final result.

Considering the example in Figure 15.9, suppose that the selectivity of sub-query $S_4$ is much bigger than that of $S_1$. If the parallel plan is adopted, after $S_1$ gets the result, Xbase should wait for $S_4$'s result before doing consolidation. However, if the serial-chain plan is chosen, $S_3$'s result, which are a small number of Pids, is used to probe FC-Index and check the predicate of $S_4$. In this way, the result can be generated faster if the selectivity of $S_3$ is small. The plan of whether to choose parallel or serial-chain index probing and how to serialize the sub-queries should be calculated according to the selectivity of the sub-queries.

Xbase's task scheduler has the responsibility for generating sub-queries' execution orders. Since DG⁺-Index has higher cost than the other three index structures,

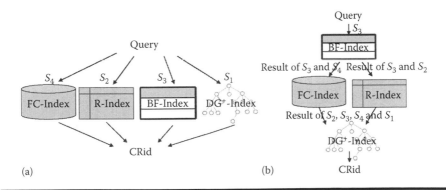

**Figure 15.9** **Parallel versus serial-chain execution. (a) Parallel index probing. (b) Serial-chain index probing.**

it is better to be probed in the end of the plan. BF-Index can only accept a value, and it is very fast due to bit operations during query probing. Therefore, Xbase prefers to put BF-Index at the front of the plan. For the other two index structures, FC-Index and R-Index, different parallel and serial plans can be selected by applying many of the traditional optimization rules in the RDBMS.

---

**Algorithm 15.1 Query Processing in Xbase**

---

**Input:** Query $Q$.
**Output:** Clinical Record ID (CRid).
 1: Parser $Q$ into internal format;
 2: Partition $Q$ into sub-queries $Q = \{S_1, S_2 \ldots S_m\}$ and find proper index structure for each query $I = \{I_1, I_2 \ldots I_m\}$;
 3: Rewrite each sub-query into Xpath Query or SQL;
 4: **for** each sub-query $S_i$ **do**
 5:    **if** $I_i \neq DG^+$-Index **then**
 6:       $P \leftarrow S_i$;
 7:    **end if**
 8: **end for**
 9: Task Scheduler $\leftarrow P$;//Sub-queries with $DG^+$-Index are scheduled at the end of serial chain
 10: Sort $Q$ according to the plan.
 11: **for** each sub-query $S_i$ **do**
 12:    **if** $I_i \infty \{\text{FC-Index, R-Index}\}$ **then**
 13:       Fetch result CRids from RDBMS through JDBC;
 14:    **else**
 15:       Create Map-Reduce job to get CRids;
 16:    **end if**
 17: **end for**
 18: Result CRid set $\leftarrow$ Join the result from different sub-queries;
 19: Data Retrieval from different Hadoop nodes.

---

## 15.5.3 Plan Execution

The query plan is then sent to Xbase's Processing Manager. For those sub-queries that require probing indexes, such as FC-Index or R-Index, the central relational DB is searched through the JDBC interface. For those sub-queries that need to probe indexes, like $DG^+$-Index or BF-Index, we create a MapReduce job (or distributed tasks). Through the map function, the partial results are obtained.

We deploy BF-Index and $DG^+$-Index on Hadoop to utilize its MapReduce computing framework. When a search on BF-Index is initiated, a MapReduce job is started where the mapper function is to check the compatibility between the given signature (generated based on the query) and each signature in the sequence file. If a signature is found to be compatible, the value (actual content of the clinical record) is further checked to see if it matches the query in order to eliminate false positives. The CRids of the matching clinical records are returned by the mapper function, and the reducer function collects all the CRids and sorts them. In the case of DG$^+$-Index, similarly, a MapReduce job is created for each probe on DG$^+$-Index. A hint CRid set (i.e., the partial result generated by previous subqueries) may be an additional input to the mapper function. The mapper function first checks the key part to see if this block is compatible with the given hint CRid set. If not, then the task is completed with an empty result. If it is compatible, a further search through the DG$^+$-Index is conducted to identify matching clinical records in the data part. The reducer function is the same as that in the probing BF-Index.

In Xbase's implementation, what we need is a distributed storage and processing framework, so that BF-Index and DG$^+$-Index can be distributed into multiple nodes. And the process code is also replicated and distributed to these nodes for processing local data. The final results are gathered into the Query Executor.

### 15.5.4 Result Consolidation and Data Retrieval

After probing the index structure, each sub-query should obtain a set of IDs as a temperate result. The result Consolidator will perform the "AND" or "OR" operation over these IDs to develop the final ID set and calculate the statistic information over the result set, such as "Find the percentage of" in our example query. For some of the queries, the original clinical records need to be retrieved. Based on the ID as the key, the requirement is propagated to data stores in the Data Retrieval step. In Xbase, the data are stored over Hadoop nodes. The query processing process is summarized in Algorithm 15.1.

# 15.6 Experimental Evaluations

We have conducted evaluations of two prototype EMR database systems: (1) Xbase, which is a hybrid implemented on both Hadoop and RDBMS, and (2) a proposed RDBMS-based solution as a strawman implementation to compare with Xbase. We start with the general setup for the experiments and then the evaluation results.

### 15.6.1 General Setup

#### 15.6.1.1 Hardware and Software Configurations

The experiments were conducted on a Hadoop cluster of 12 desktop-level computers. Each computer has an Intel Core 2 Duo 2.66 GHz CPU, 2G memory, 160G hard disk, and Ubuntu 9.04. The computers are connected via a 100 M fast ethernet switcher. The version 0.20.0 of Hadoop is used in our experiments, with the configuration of 1 name node, 1 job tracker, and 10 slave nodes (i.e., data nodes and task trackers). The replication factor is set to 3, while the maximum number of map and reduce tasks that will run simultaneously triggered by a task tracker is set to 2. As we use a single reduce task for each query job in our experiments, the number of reduce tasks per job is set to 1. The Hadoop cluster is used by Xbase only.

Additionally, an 8-core server (2 Intel Xeon X5460 processors, 4 cores in each CPU package, 12 MB L2 cache shared by 2 cores, 16 GB globally shared DRAM, and SUSE 10.0) with MySQL Cluster 5.1 installed is employed to store the relational data for Xbase and the strawman RDBMS implementation for the EMR application.

The prototype system is written in Java (JDK 1.6) and has two parts: index builder and query processor. The index builder scans source schema and XML documents (i.e., clinical records), and then creates corresponding index structures on the database and/or the Hadoop cluster. The source XML documents are also stored as part of the DG$^+$-Index on Hadoop. The query processor receives queries from the clients, composes query plans, and then executes them on the database (as SQL queries) and the Hadoop cluster (as MapReduce jobs).

In the experiments, we vary the following parameters: (1) the volume of data, (2) the complexity of the queries, and (3) the size of HDFS file blocks in Hadoop to measure their impacts on the query response time.

## 15.6.1.2 Data Sets, Query Patterns, and Solutions

Our data generator is based on XMLgen from XMark [2] with our own DTD designed for clinical records. We generate the clinical records with sizes varying from 5K to 625K records with a depth around 10 and the largest fanout around 50.

The distribution of the queries' predicates used in the experiments are summarized in Table 15.1. Three queries with predicates that utilize mixed types of indexes are denoted as Query 4, Query 8, and Query 16. Each of them contains different number of predicates requiring different sets of indexes. We also prepare two queries, one requiring paths with BF-Index while the other with DG$^+$-Index. We also list the numbers of MapReduce jobs required to initiate for each query. Please note that all predicates requiring DG$^+$-Indexes can be combined into a single MapReduce job as a single job can check multiple conditions at the same time. On the other hand, each predicate requiring BF-Indexes needs to invoke a MapReduce job separately, since BF-Indexes cannot be shared nor combined. Other predicates requiring no DG$^+$-Index nor BF-Index will be used on RDBMS, and thus do not need to invoke a MapReduce job.

To compare the query processing time, we develop a pure RDBMS-based EMR database system to compare with the Xbase solution. We implement the

**Table 15.1   Query Complexity**

|  | No. of Predicates | Predicates Requiring FC-Index | Predicates Requiring R-Index | Predicates Requiring DG⁺-Index | Predicates Requiring BF-Index | No. of MapReduce Jobs |
|---|---|---|---|---|---|---|
| Query 4 | 4 | 1 | 1 | 1 | 1 | 2 |
| Query 8 | 8 | 1 | 2 | 2 | 3 | 4 |
| Query 16 | 16 | 2 | 6 | 4 | 4 | 5 |
| Query-BF | 4 | 0 | 0 | 0 | 4 | 4 |
| Query-DG⁺ | 4 | 0 | 0 | 4 | 0 | 1 |

RDBMS-based strawman EMR database using MySQL Cluster 5.1 on an 8-core server. The schema is designed as one content table with three columns: #CR_id, #PATH, and #VALUE. For each XML-formatted clinical record, all the leaf nodes are extracted and stored in the content table together with its path and the clinical record identifier as triple tuples. An example of storing an XML clinical record in a relational table with the (#CR_id, #PATH, #VALUE) schema is illustrated in Figure 15.10. Table 15.2 lists the statistics of the relational tables in different data scales. As we can see, relational tables are not suitable for storing XML documents in terms of both space efficiency and query processing efficiency. The table shows to store 700,000 clinical records, which will result in more than 1 billion rows in the table. In the experiments presented in the later subsections, we show that such RDBMS-based implementation is far less efficient than Xbase, which is a hybrid system that consolidates the advantages of both RDBMS and Hadoop.

## 15.6.2  Effects of Data Scales

We first conducted experiments for different data volumes with a DG⁺-Index block size of 64M and BF-Index block size of 1M, which is denoted as the pair (64M, 1M). Figure 15.11 shows the average query processing time of the same queries on various volumes of data sets.

From Figure 15.11, we can see that the query processing time increases sublinearly with the increase of the data volume. This is because the number of blocks needed to be accessed grows with the increase of data volume, given the same block size. Therefore, the number of map tasks to be processed in one MapReduce job also increases. This impacts the performance of searching on DG⁺-Index and BF-Index. With the increase of query complexity, the number of MapReduce jobs to be submitted for one query also increases. To this end, the overall query processing time becomes larger.

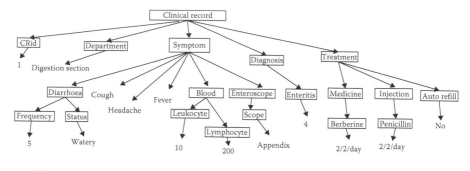

| CRid | Path | Value |
|---|---|---|
| 1 | Clinical record/department | Digestion section |
| 1 | Clinical record/symptom/diarrhoea/frequency | 5 |
| 1 | Clinical record/symptom/diarrhoea/status | Watery |
| 1 | Clinical record/symptom | Cough |
| 1 | Clinical record/symptom | Headache |
| 1 | Clinical record/symptom | Fever |
| 1 | Clinical record/symptom/blood/leukocyte | 10 |
| 1 | Clinical record/symptom/blood/lymphocyte | 200 |
| 1 | Clinical record/symptom/enteroscope/scope | Appendix |
| 1 | Clinical record/diagnosis/enteritis | 4 |
| 1 | Clinical record/treatment/medicine/berberine | 2/2/day |
| 1 | Clinical record/treatment/injection/penicillin | 2/3/day |
| 1 | Clinical record/treatment/auto refill | No |

**Figure 15.10   Example of RDBMS-based XML clinical record implementation.**

**Table 15.2   Data Statistics of Pure RDBMS Solution**

| Number of Records | Number of Rows |
|---|---|
| 5K | 7.5M |
| 25K | 37.5M |
| 125K | 187.5M |
| 625K | 937.5M |

Figure 15.12 shows the processing time of queries with mixed conditions on various volumes of data by the strawman RDBMS-based solution. Obviously, the increases of time consumption follow the trend of over-linear increases. And, with the increase of complexity of query conditions, the processing time of the strawman RDBMS-based solution increases over-linearly. It suggests that for a

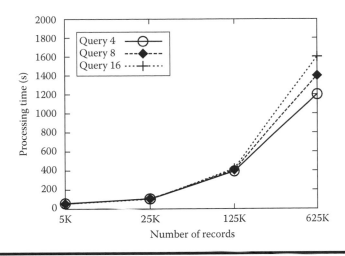

**Figure 15.11    Effects of Xbase solution under different data scales.**

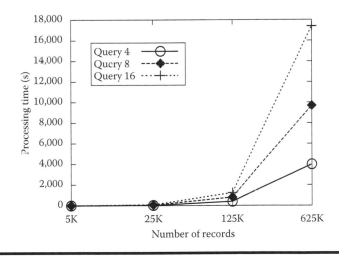

**Figure 15.12    Effects of pure RDBMS solution under different data scales.**

centralized database system, loading and query processing over large-scaled data involves high cost.

## 15.6.3 Effects of Query Complexity

To show the differences between Xbase and pure RDBMS solutions, we compare the processing time of Query 16 on various volumes of data. The results shown in Figures 15.13 through 15.15 indicate that under the small data scales, less than

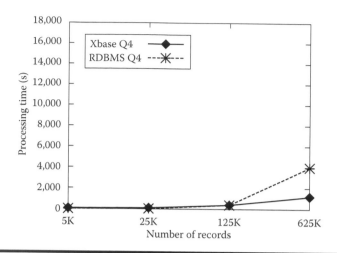

**Figure 15.13  Effects of Query 4 under different data scales.**

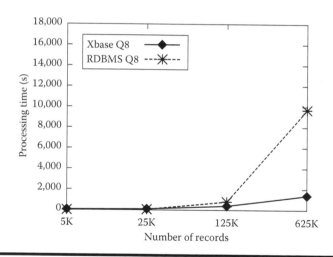

**Figure 15.14  Effects of Query 8 under different data scales.**

25K records, the Xbase and pure RDBMS solutions have similar query processing times. With the increase of size of data scale, the processing time of the pure RDBMS increases much faster than the Xbase solution. It is because that, traditionally, a centralized database system lacks the ability of scaling up. To process the queries over large-scaled data, even with a powerful server, the bottleneck of the system is in the I/O layer, data loading, and memory access. Since Xbase's XML processing capability is built on top of Hadoop, such a bottleneck can be solved by load distribution across a large number of smaller servers by the Hadoop infrastructure.

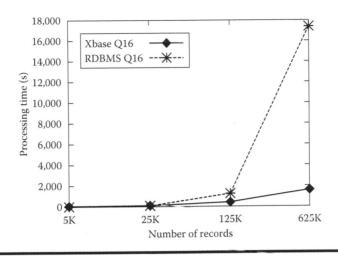

**Figure 15.15 Effects of Query 16 under different data scales.**

We also conducted experiments to evaluate queries with predicates requiring only BF-Indexes and DG⁺-Indexes, respectively. In these experiments, we set a relatively small size for the BF-Index file. This is because we expect a rather small size of key–value pairs for each Bloom filter. This is true if the parameters of the Bloom filter signature are selected appropriately. However, if the false-positives rate of such a signatures is high, the size of each key–value pair could be very large. In such a case, if the block size of the BF-Index file is smaller than the size of each key–value pair, the performance of probing BF-Index will be substantially impacted because the locality of the mapper task is violated and considerable amount of data have to be transferred among nodes.

Figure 15.16 gives the average query processing time of queries requiring only DG⁺-Index and BF-Index, respectively. The experiment shows that the DG⁺-Index-related condition check is much more expensive than the Bloom-filter-related condition check. The reason is that for BF-Index, after the coded query condition is sent to map function, most blocks are filtered by the Bloom filter mechanism. Thus, the total block search time consumed decreases. As for DG⁺-Index, it can be applied only to the path-related conditions, but not to the values of the leaf nodes along the paths. As a result, raw XML-formatted clinical records have to be loaded to check conditions related to leaf nodes' values. In the worst case, when most clinical records contain such paths, the bodies of most blocks have to be loaded and checked sequentially throughout the whole block. Thus, the processing time is high even when DG⁺-Index is applied. Additional improvement can be done by clustering structurally similar clinical records and placing them on the same blocks in order to reduce the processing time of path-related conditions.

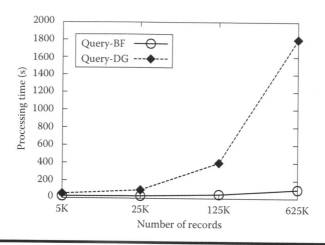

**Figure 15.16** **Effects of different data volumes.**

## 15.6.4 Effects of Hadoop-Specified Configurations

Given the fixed data volume, Figure 15.17 shows the query processing time when different block sizes are configured for index files on HDFS over 25K records. We can see from Figure 15.17 that with the increase of index file block size, the number of blocks per file and the number of tasks per MapReduce job decrease. Though each mapper task spends relatively more time to process a bigger block, since the

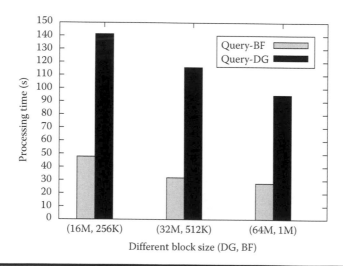

**Figure 15.17** **Effects of different block sizes.**

initialization of a mapper task also takes some time, the overall processing time per job drops from (16M, 256K), (32M, 512K), to (64M, 1M). Thus, the experiments suggest that a larger block size will lead to a comparatively lower overhead of Hadoop job invocation. However, a larger block size will only be beneficial if the number of mapper tasks per job is bigger than the number of available processing slots in the Hadoop cluster; otherwise, the computing resources of the system may be underutilized. To this end, selecting a block size that optimizes the system performance is quite complex and almost unfeasible given many parameters involved, such as the number of concurrent Hadoop workloads, the distribution of data skew, and the QoS of network transformation. A formal study of this subject would be left for future research work.

## 15.7 Related Work

XML is emerging as a de facto standard for information exchange among various applications on the World Wide Web. There has been a growing need for developing high-performance techniques to query large XML data repositories efficiently. One important problem in XML query processing is twig pattern matching, that is, finding in an XML data tree all matches that satisfy a specified twig (or path) query pattern. The survey in [12] classifies and compares major techniques for twig pattern matching. It considers two classes of major XML query processing techniques: the relational approach and the native approach. The relational approach directly utilizes existing relational database systems to store and query XML data, which enables the use of all important techniques that have been developed for relational databases. We build one prototype system of this kind (as shown in Figure 15.10) as a strawman implementation to compare with Xbase. In the native approach, specialized storage and query processing systems tailored for XML data are developed from scratch to further improve XML query performance.

As implied by existing work reviewed in [12], XML data querying and management are developing in the direction of integrating the relational approach with the native approach, which could result in higher query processing performance and also significantly reduce system reengineering costs. We call this a hybrid approach to XML database system. Xbase presented in this chapter can be considered such a hybrid system, while Xbase utilizes the Hadoop infrastructure to implement XML structural information repository and search capability.

Hive [27,28] is a data warehouse infrastructure built on top of Hadoop that provides tools to enable easy data summarization, ad hoc querying, and analysis of large datasets' data stored in Hadoop files. It provides a mechanism to put the structure on this data, and it also provides a simple query language called QL, which is based on SQL and which enables users familiar with SQL to query this data. At the same time, this language also allows traditional MapReduce programmers to be able to plug in their custom mappers and reducers to perform more sophisticated analysis, which may not be supported by the built-in capabilities of the language.

Bigtable [5] is a distributed storage system for managing structured data that is designed to scale to a very large size: petabytes of data across thousands of commodity servers. Many projects at Google store data in Bigtable, including web indexing, Google Earth, and Google Finance. These applications place very different demands on Bigtable, both in terms of data size (from URLs to web pages to satellite imagery) and latency requirements (from back-end bulk processing to real-time data serving). Despite these varied demands, Bigtable has successfully provided a flexible, high-performance solution for all of these Google products. In this chapter, we describe the simple data model provided by Bigtable, which gives clients dynamic control over data layout and format, and we also describe the design and implementation of Bigtable.

In order to store and retrieve XML documents efficiently, dozens of research and industrial works were carried out in the last two decades. Targeting the complexity of Xpath, many proposals on XML structural indexes express paths of an XML document as a set of equivalent node classes, which include DataGuide [10], 1-index [19], and *F&B* Index [15] and its disk-based extension [30]. Generally speaking, their basic idea is to match the path of query conditions with the precalculated skeleton of XML repository, and then, check the value by indexed nodes. The DG$^+$-Index proposed in this chapter is just an extension of them, based on the observations that long and complex paths tend to be uninteresting. Some work like A(k)-index [16], which is a family of indices by the extension of 1-index [19], exploits the similarity of short paths to reduce the size of the structure. Similar work includes D(k)-index [6] and M(k)-index [14]. Actually, the research works above can be involved into our framework without too much effort, which is because the DG$^+$-Index we proposed is the abstracted structure of them, which can be extended without any conflict with other index mechanisms.

Aiming to the variety of XML contents, several other related works focus on indexing values in XML [18], building indexes for XML range queries [17], and indexing XML fragments in RDBMS [21]. Though the other three index structures we proposed are extended from works above, one distinguished difference is that we build different index structures according to well-known data types, respectively, rather than general XML data. In the further, the XML data we aimed to is the application-specified EMR data.

New approaches were proposed in [22] and [13] to large-scale data analysis and a uniform data repository for mixed data types. These approaches tried to solve the similar problem addressed in this chapter; but our work is more healthcare specific and different system architectures are developed, especially our system on top of Hadoop enjoys distributed computing and fault tolerance provided by the Hadoop infrastructure itself.

## 15.8 Conclusion

XML is a more desirable format for modeling and storing clinical data in EMR applications for its extendibility; however, EMR systems are usually built on top of RDBMS or file systems. Few advanced database systems support native XML storage and retrieval capability; however, their capability supporting complex healthcare applications on a very large set of EMRs is very limited. We point out that complex healthcare applications demand usability, flexibility, reliability, performance, and extendibility.

We are developing a clouds-enabled information appliance, *Xbase*, supporting analytics on XML-based EMR databases. Here, we summarize how we design Xbase to meet these requirements.

- *Usability:* Xbase is designed and built specifically to support healthcare-specific style of query, search, and analytics, which involve a potentially large number of conditions, and query relaxation is built into the query processing scheme to incorporate terminologies in the KDB, such as diagnosis and treatment classification, doctors' areas of expertise, and access control list.
- *Flexibility:* Xbase supports data modeling and native physical storage for semi-structured data dealing with evolving data types and flexible schemas required in healthcare applications.
- *Reliability:* HDFS creates multiple replicas of data blocks and distributes them on compute nodes throughout a cluster to enable reliable, extremely rapid computations.
- *Performance:* In Xbase, query processing and indexing is applied directly to the native XML structure and content to ensure fast response time, while the Hadoop infrastructure provides automated load balance.
- *Extendibility:* Xbase is built natively on the emerging cloud computing infrastructure, Hadoop, to achieve almost unlimited distributed storage capability and computation capability. The extendibility of Xbase is enabled by and embodied in the Hadoop infrastructure.

## References

1. http://icd9cm.chrisendres.com
2. http://www.xml-benchmark.org
3. K. S. Beyer, R. Cochrane, M. Hvizdos, V. Josifovski, J. Kleewein, G. Lapis, G. M. Lohman et al. Db2 goes hybrid: Integrating native XML and XQuery with relational data and SQL. *IBM Systems Journal*, 45(2):271–298, 2006.
4. B. H. Bloom. Space/time trade-offs in hash coding with allowable errors. *Communications of the ACM*, 13(7):422–426, 1970.

5. F. Chang, J. Dean, S. Ghemawat, W. C. Hsieh, D. A. Wallach, M. Burrows, T. Chandra, A. Fikes, and R. E. Gruber. Bigtable: A distributed storage system for structured data. In *Proceedings of the Seventh Symposium on Operating System Design and Implementation*, Seattle, WA, 2006.

6. Q. Chen, A. Lim, and K. W. Ong. D(k)-index: An adaptive structural summary for graph-structured data. In *SIGMOD*, San Diego, CA, pp. 134–144, 2003.

7. Y. Chen. On the signature trees and balanced signature trees. In *ICDE*, Tokyo, Japan, pp. 742–753, 2005.

8. J. Dean and S. Ghemawat. MapReduce: Simplified data processing on large clusters. In *Proceedings of the Sixth Symposium on Operating System Design and Implementation*, San Fransisco, CA, 2004.

9. A. Gates, O. Natkovich, S. Chopra, P. Kamath, S. Narayanam, C. Olston, B. Reed, S. Srinivasan, and U. Srivastava. Building a highlevel dataflow system on top of mapreduce: The pig experience. *Proceedings of the VLDB Endowment*, 2(2):1414–1425, 2009.

10. R. Goldman and J. Widom. Dataguides: Enabling query formulation and optimization in semistructured databases. In *VLDB*, Athens, Greece, pp. 436–445, 1997.

11. X. Gong, Y. Yan, W. Qian, and A. Zhou. Bloom filter-based XML packets filtering for millions of path queries. In *ICDE*, Tokyo, Japan, pp. 890–901, 2005.

12. G. Gou and R. Chirkova. Efficiently querying large XML data repositories: A survey. *IEEE Transactions on Knowledge and Data Engineering*, 19(10):1381–1403, 2007.

13. M. N. Gubanov, L. Popa, C. T. H. Ho, H. Pirahesh, J.-Y. Chang, and S.-C. Chen. IBM UFO repository. *Proceedings of the VLDB Endowment*, 2(2):1598–1601, 2009.

14. H. He and J. Yang. Multiresolution indexing of XML for frequent queries. In *ICDE*, Boston, MA, pp. 683–694, 2004.

15. R. Kaushik, P. Bohannon, J. F. Naughton, and H. F. Korth. Covering indexes for branching path queries. In *SIGMOD Conference*, Madison, WI, pp. 133–144, 2002.

16. R. Kaushik, P. Shenoy, P. Bohannon, and E. Gudes. Exploiting local similarity for indexing paths in graph-structured data. In *ICDE*, San Jose, CA, pp. 129–140, 2002.

17. H.-G. Li, S. A. Aghili, D. Agrawal, and A. E. Abbadi. Flux: Fuzzy content and structure matching of XML range queries. In *WWW*, Edinburgh, U.K., pp. 1081–1082, 2006.

18. J. McHugh and J. Widom. Query optimization for XML. In *VLDB*, Edinburgh, U.K., pp. 315–326, 1999.

19. T. Milo and D. Suciu. Index structures for path expressions. In *ICDT*, Jerusalem, Israel, pp. 277–295, 1999.

20. C. Olston, B. Reed, U. Srivastava, R. Kumar, and A. Tomkins. Pig latin: A not-so-foreign language for data processing. In J. T.-L. Wang, editor, *SIGMOD Conference*, Vancouver, Canada, pp. 1099–1110. ACM, New York, 2008.

21. S. Pal, I. Cseri, G. Schaller, O. Seeliger, L. Giakoumakis, and V. V. Zolotov. Indexing XML data stored in a relational database. In *VLDB*, Toronto, Canada, pp. 1134–1145, 2004.

22. A. Pavlo, E. Paulson, A. Rasin, D. J. Abadi, D. J. DeWitt, S. Madden, and M. Stonebraker. A comparison of approaches to large-scale data analysis. In U. Çetintemel, S. B. Zdonik, D. Kossmann, and N. Tatbul, editors. *Proceedings of the ACM SIGMOD International Conference on Management of Data, SIGMOD 2009*, Providence, RI, June 29–July 2, 2009, pp. 165–178, 2009.

23. H. Plattner. A common database approach for oltp and olap using an in-memory column database. In U. Çetintemel, S. B. Zdonik, D. Kossmann, and N. Tatbul, editors. *Proceedings of the ACM SIGMOD International Conference on Management of Data, SIGMOD 2009*, Providence, RI, June 29–July 2, 2009, pp. 1–2, 2009.

24. The Apache Software Foundation. Information available at http://hadoop.apache.org

25. The Apache Software Foundation. Information available at http://hadoop.apache.org/hdfs

26. The Apache Software Foundation. Information available at http://hadoop.apache.org/hbase

27. The Apache Software Foundation. Information available at http://hadoop.apache.org/hive

28. A. Thusoo, J. S. Sarma, N. Jain, Z. Shao, P. Chakka, S. Anthony, H. Liu, P. Wyckoff, and R. Murthy. Hive - a warehousing solution over a map-reduce framework. *Proceedings of the VLDB Endowment*, 2(2):1626–1629, 2009.

29. Vertica Systems. Information available at http://www.vertica.com

30. W. Wang, H. Wang, H. Lu, H. Jiang, X. Lin, and J. Li. Efficient processing of XML path queries using the disk-based f&b index. In *VLDB*, Trondheim, Norway, pp. 145–156, 2005.

# Chapter 16

# Toward a QoS-Focused SaaS Evaluation Model

Xian Chen, Abhishek Srivastava, and Paul Sorenson

## Contents

# 16.1 Motivation

In the past decade, the growth of web service technologies and the emergence of service-oriented architectures (SOAs) have added tremendously to the increasing maturity of the Internet and the software industry. These advancements make it possible for software vendors to deliver effective software applications as web-based services using a new delivery model called *Software-as-a-Service* (*SaaS*). In simple terms, SaaS is a model of software deployment where an application is hosted as a service provided to customers across the Internet [1]. By eliminating the need to install and run the application on the customer's computer, SaaS alleviates the burden of software maintenance, ongoing operation, and client support for the customer. Conversely, customers relinquish control over software versions or changing requirements. Moreover, costs to use the service become a continuous expense, rather than a single expense at the time of purchase. SaaS applications are generally charged on a per-user basis and are shared by multiple independent customers [2]. Under SaaS, the service customer receives the benefits of the software, with clearly understandable costs, at a contractually defined service level [3].

While successful commercial SaaS applications like Salesforce.com and Google Apps are now deployed, tools and approaches to assist organizations in evaluating and planning for SaaS opportunities are not yet widely available. This chapter provides a model framework for evaluating SaaS applications based on quality-of-service (QoS) characteristics, and forms the basis for a toolset to assist the IT planning process.

# 16.2 Service System Quality Management

In studying SaaS evaluation, our focus on quality management is motivated by two basic assumptions about the nature of service system delivery:

1. Service systems operate most effectively when both the service customer and the service provider understand and actively engage in the co-creation of value [4].
2. Service system improvement is best achieved when the major service quality factors are mutually agreed upon, tracked, managed, analyzed, and acted upon by the service customer and the service provider.

The goal of service quality management is to provide lower cost, better products and services, and higher customer satisfaction. Traditionally, if a service provider understands what a customer wants from a service (typically defined with detailed specifications based on the customer requirements), manages the variables in the service delivery process that can lead to deviation from specifications, and delivers the service in accordance with the customer's stated requirements, the service system is properly managing with respect to service quality [5]. In practice, however, a dynamic approach must be used in managing service quality due to continuous changes in the cost of service delivery, customer requirements, and the emergence of new technologies. When existing customer expectations are not met, a new expectation benchmark must be set and service reevaluation undertaken. The need is growing for evaluation models to assess service quality on an ongoing basis and to improve/accelerate decision making related to the adoption of software services in general and SaaS applications in particular, given their rapidly increasing adoption [6].

Unfortunately, most current quality management approaches for SaaS services focus on the perspective of service providers, and thus do not fully take into consideration the collaborative nature of the two basic assumptions given at the beginning of this section. Approaches such as SERVQUAL [7], American Customer Satisfaction Indices (ACSI) [8], and Balanced Scorecard [9] incorporate the viewpoint of customers, but often not in combination with the provider's viewpoint. What is not present in the existing literature is an approach that adequately combines the perspectives of both provider and customer together with the nature of their ongoing business relationship. Therefore, at a general level, we are interested in addressing the following research problems: (1) the exploration of an integrated model that takes into account the shared nature of service quality in SaaS systems and (2) how to best track and improve the service quality effectively by applying the model.

## 16.3 SaaS Maturity Models

In the process of developing the foundation of our SaaS evaluation model, we explored a number of related models for assessing service system delivery and management. These are characterized as Service Delivery Models, and their approaches are summarized later in Section 16.7. These models are relevant and complementary to SaaS evaluation; however, their scope is broader than SaaS systems and is primarily concentrated on service delivery from the perspective of the service provider. In this section, we review the two main SaaS maturity models that have been proposed to date.

### 16.3.1 Microsoft SaaS Maturity Model

Microsoft introduced the first widely published SaaS maturity model in 2006 [8]. A four-level SaaS maturity model was proposed mainly to assess the maturity of single-packaged SaaS applications. According to the model description, SaaS applications can be classified by three key attributes of architectures: *configurability*, *multi-tenant efficiency*, and *scalability*. Each level in this model is distinguished from the previous one by the addition of one key attribute. A brief explanation of each level is as follows [10]:

■ *Level 1—Ad hoc/custom*: Each customer has a customized version of the application and runs its own instance of the application on the servers hosted by the provider. Migrating a traditional non-networked or client-server application to this level typically requires the least development effort and cuts down operating costs primarily by consolidating server hardware and administration.

■ *Level 2—Configurable*: The second maturity level provides greater application flexibility through configurable metadata that enable customers to use separate instances of the same application code. This allows the provider to meet the different needs of each customer through detailed configuration options, while simplifying maintenance and updating a common code base.

■ *Level 3—Configurable, multi-tenant efficient*: At the third maturity level, the provider adds multi-tenancy support to the second-level capabilities, enabling a single-application instance to service all customers. This approach allows better use of the provider's server resources without any apparent difference to the customer.

■ *Level 4—Scalable, configurable, multi-tenant efficient*: Better overall scalability for the provider's service delivery is the goal at the fourth level. This is typically achieved through a multitier architecture supporting a load-balanced farm of identical application instances, running on a variable number of servers. Effectively, a "cloud computing" [11,12] approach is adopted by the provider to support a set of application instances. The capacity of the provider's system can be increased or decreased dynamically to match the demand by adding or removing servers, without requiring changes to the application software.

## 16.3.2 Forrester SaaS Maturity Model

Forrester's model, the other major SaaS maturity model, provides guidance on strategy transformations to software vendors working with service providers who consider an SaaS business model. This model classifies the maturity of SaaS solutions on five levels, according to the way an SaaS system is delivered [13].

■ *Level 0—Outsourcing*: In outsourcing, a service provider operates one application or a suite of applications for a large customer organization. Typically, an outsourcing provider is obligated under contract to one customer and cannot directly leverage this customer's application for a second customer. Because of this restriction, outsourcing does not qualify as SaaS; thus, this level is not considered a formal maturity level. It is included as level 0 because SaaS providers often launch their business operations through outsourcing arrangements with a few preferred customers.

■ *Level 1—Manual ASP (application service provider) service*: The model at this level is mainly targeting midsize companies. An ASP hosts packaged applications (e.g., system analysis and program development [SAP] and PeopleSoft enterprise resource planning [ERPs]) for multiple customer organizations. Typically, the service provider allocates to each customer a dedicated server running that customer's instance of the application. This allows, as deemed necessary, the ability for a provider to customize the installation in the same way as self-hosted applications.

■ *Level 2—Industrial ASP service*: At this level, an ASP introduces advanced IT management software to provide an identical packaged application with customer-specific configuration options to many small-to-medium-sized customer organizations. A key element of the industrial ASP service is that the core elements of the software package are the same for all customers, and therefore a significant amount of the operating costs can be shared among multiple customers.

■ *Level 3—Single-app SaaS*: From this level on, SaaS capabilities become built into the business applications. These include web-based user interface access to all services and the ability to service a great number of customers with one scalable infrastructure. Single-application SaaS adoption focuses on small-to-medium-sized businesses. Like the industrial ASP service of level 2, the only way to customize the application is through configuration. Salesforce.com's customer relationship management (CRM) application initially entered the market at this level [13].

■ *Level 4—Business-domain SaaS*: At this level, the SaaS provider offers not only well-defined business applications but also a platform supporting additional business logic. This allows the single-app SaaS of level 3 to be augmented with third-party packaged SaaS solutions and optional customized extensions. The model can now satisfy some of the requirements of large enterprises by migrating a whole business domain like "customer care" to an SaaS solution.

■ *Level 5—Dynamic business Apps-as-a-service*: At this level, Forrester's model claims that a new Dynamic Business Application imperative "design for people, build for change" is embraced. Advanced SaaS providers coming from level 4 will offer a comprehensive application as well as an integration platform on demand, and pre-populate the platform with business applications or business services. Customer-specific and even user-specific business applications on various levels can be composed dynamically. The resulting process agility should be attractive to everyone, including large-enterprise customers.

There are similarities and some distinct differences between the two SaaS maturity models from Microsoft and Forrester. Both models describe a set of greater capabilities needed by the SaaS provider to manage common software architectures and infrastructure as the levels of maturity increase. Microsoft's model focuses on the increased capabilities of an SaaS deployment through the re-architecting of single-application packages delivered on a common infrastructure. These capabilities are embodied in three key attributes: configurability, multi-tenant efficiency, and scalability. Forrester's model takes an evolutionary approach that provides prescriptive guidance to software vendors and service providers in the transformation of enterprise-wide software. If we restrict our attention to single-application deployment of SaaS, levels 1 through 3 have significant similarities in the two models. The major difference at level 4 is the support for software across an entire business domain in Forrester's model. Level 5 of Forrester's model appears to have no counterpart in Microsoft's model. A scan of the SaaS literature indicates that there is likely no SaaS implementation in existence today that would be rated at Forrester's level 5.

An important observation of these SaaS maturity models is that neither focuses on quality of service. Without the ability to assess quality-of-service delivery, the decision makers (i.e., the customers and the providers) will have a difficult time planning and managing service improvements. In addition, these models largely ignore the perspective of service customer, and only emphasize what the service provider can do. It is our strong belief, based on the two fundamental assumptions about service systems identified in Section 16.2, that it is necessary to incorporate the perspectives of both service provider and service customer in any SaaS evaluation model.

## 16.4 Quality in SaaS Business Relationship

In this section, we introduce the notion of quality as it applies to service delivery, and then discuss how quality is often expressed or realized as part of an ongoing SaaS business relationship.

### 16.4.1 Quality Definitions

The definition of "quality" has been addressed and debated for a long time in a number of academic and industrial publications [14–18]. Of these, we have chosen to focus on the one developed by David Garvin [16], in which he identified five major perspectives to the definition of quality: transcendental, product based, user based, manufacturing based, and value based. We have found that for software services it is difficult to separate product (the software system) from service (the deployment or actual "manufacturing" of the system as a service). For quality of service, we only consider the following four perspectives.

- *Conformance quality*: This is equivalent to many aspects of a combination of Garvin's product-based and manufacturing-based perspectives focusing on conformance to specifications. Typically, the focus is internal and on determining that performance matches original design specifications often expressed in service-level agreements (SLAs). Approaches that can be applied to manage conformance quality include (1) QoS specification languages [19], in which quality requirements, quality capabilities, and quality agreements are expressed; and (2) service-level standards, such as IT Service CMM (IT Service Capability Maturity Model) [18] and ITIL (Information Technology Infrastructure Library) [19].
- *Gap quality*: This is equivalent to Garvin's user-based perspective focusing on whether customer expectations are met or exceeded. This is the most pervasive definition of quality, particularly as applied to business management. Most approaches on gap quality use the Gaps Model of Service Quality [22], which measures the gaps explicitly by considering both customer perceptions and expectations. These approaches include SERVQUAL [7], ACSI [8], and TechQual+ [23].
- *Value quality*: This is equivalent to Garvin's value-based perspective focusing on the direct benefits (value) to the customer. It is a universal measure for widely different types of objects, and can be an appropriate guideline for continuous quality improvement. Approaches on value quality introduce more business-oriented measurements, such as productivity, Return on Investment (ROI), and risk estimate, and provide greater insight into business goals.
- *Excellence quality*: This is equivalent to Garvin's transcendent perspective focusing on recognition of excellence. It stresses the features and characteristics of quality, but it may change dramatically and rapidly. In IT services, excellence quality is marked by uncompromising standards and high performance, and can be used directly as promise and advertisement. Therefore, it is usually externally defined and hard to relate to quality improvement.

Because of the difficulty in using excellence quality to identify quality improvement opportunities, we focus only on the first three definitions of quality in our work [24,25].

## 16.4.2 Quality Management in an SaaS Business Relationship

Basic to any SaaS deployment are business relationships between the provider organization and the various customer organizations to which the provider delivers its services. Two of these relationships, presented from a provider organization's view, are shown in Figure 16.1. The relationships, labeled *conformance quality* and *gap quality*, are depicted as measures in the diagram. These are measures that should

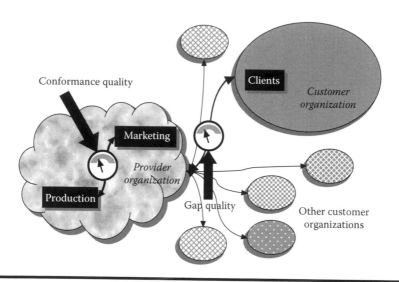

**Figure 16.1    Provider organization view of an SaaS business relationship.**

be managed by the SaaS provider as part of their business relationship with their customers. In most service arrangements, conformance quality is expressed as service levels agreed to with the client. With SaaS, service levels are often advertised in advance as part of the provider's marketing strategy and finalized under contract when a service sales agreement is reached with the customer. Therefore, in SaaS, the focus on conformance quality aspects, such as volume (transactions per minute), response time, and availability of service, is usually negotiated and agreed to up front between the production department (responsible for running service support) and the marketing and sales departments of the provider organization.

Providers are also involved in gap quality measurements with customer organizations. Typically, quality concerns related to ease of use, response to failures, and user training are determined by the provider using survey tools involving the customers. This form of user input identifies gaps between what the customers are experiencing in using a service and what they would like to be experiencing. This feedback is critical if a provider wishes to improve their service.

The view of SaaS business relationships from the customer's perspective is shown in Figure 16.2, in which two relationships are depicted. The first, named *functional needs*, expresses the user requirements for supporting their workplace activities in the customer organization. The business units of the customer organization usually consult with their users to determine if these service requirements can be met through a service offering by one or more SaaS providers.

The second relationship, labeled *value quality*, captures the value the customer organization places on deploying a service using an SaaS. Although there is no universally accepted definition of value quality, common approaches for measuring

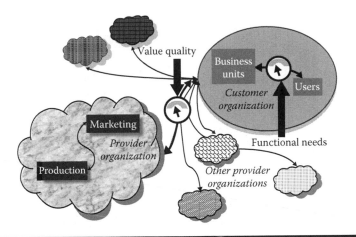

**Figure 16.2    Customer organization view of an SaaS business relationship.**

value quality include cost-benefit analysis [26], ROI analysis [27], risk management [28], or combinations of these approaches using a balance scorecard [9].

# 16.5  Co-Creation of Business Value in a Service Relationship

The discussion in Section 16.4 on value quality was from the perspective of the customer organization. But one of the fundamental definitions from the merging area of service science [4] is that a "… service system is a value co-production configuration of people, technology, other internal and external service systems and shared information." The question that arises is how is the notion of co-creation of value in an SaaS offering supported in value quality measures.

Let us explore this question by considering the possible co-value situations that can exist between a service provider and a service customer organization. These situations can be represented in Figure 16.3, where we express the customer and provider values, respectively, on simple *x–y* axes, each axis ranging in scale from a *low* to a *high* value. In general, the value measures for the provider and the customer are dependent on the nature of the service offering. For the purpose of this discussion, let us assume simplistically that the customer value is determined primarily by ROI analysis and the provider value is determined by the total profit (income after all expenses) from providing the service. In the diagram, we have characterized the five regions with names that reflect the relative maturity of the service offering [29]. When a service is first developed, it is typically done as a limited offering (or *research prototype*) based on research of market opportunities and the innovative application of new or advanced technologies or processes. From the

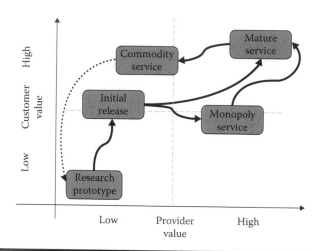

**Figure 16.3 Phases of service delivery based on co-value to the customer and the provider.**

perspective of value quality, the service provider sees low value (little or no profit) and the customer also sees low value, because the prototype service is limited in functionality with little commitment to sustainability because of the trial nature of its deployment.

Assuming that the service is well received for its initial functionality and responsiveness, and its user base increases, the value (as determined by ROI) will increase for the customer. During the early stages of growing the service from prototype to an *initial release* in the marketplace, the value to the provider (profit) remains low or at best increases slightly.

Once the service takes hold in a marketplace and large numbers of customers acquire the service, the value for the provider (profit) increases substantially in proportion to the number of customers. The value to the customer (ROI) is very dependent on the costs associated with the delivery of the service within a growing marketplace. If there is little or no competition for the provider, we move to a *monopoly service* situation typically generating higher costs and, therefore, lower relative value for the customer (ROI). Alternatively, the marketplace could quickly yield a healthy set of service providers that should lead to an increase in value for customers (ROI), because cost of service should not rise substantially if at all. This stage, labeled *mature service*, represents the situation when the co-value of the service business relationship for providers and customers is at its peak (we refer to it as a "win-win" value situation).

Note that it is rare for a software service marketplace to remain in a monopoly situation for an extended period, because the capital investment for new providers to develop competitive services is usually not extensive. Therefore, generally for SaaS, a monopoly service should quickly transition to a mature service situation.

A fifth stage that can occur is when service competition increases for the provider and marketplace adoption becomes so widespread that the service becomes commoditized. At this *commodity service* stage, the value to the provider (profit) can decrease significantly because of decreased profit margins on a per customer basis. The value to the customer can also decrease at this stage because the commoditized service is no longer a strategic advantage for customer organization, which may have its own set of competitors.

The transition from a commodity service to a research prototype is represented as a dotted line to show that often a new provider organization creates a new service innovation that impacts the commoditized marketplace. This new service will begin its own service maturation process that can displace the commodity service in that marketplace. An example of this is the rise of e-mail services in the last decade to replace much of the standard mail services that had been commoditized.

Of course, not all service offerings follow this form of "life cycle." Many new services do not make it past the prototype stage or linger in the initial release stage without garnering significant market presence. Some services, given the nature of their potential marketplace, may never be commoditized. Ideally, both service provider and service customer continue to seek ways of maintaining a "win-win" business relationship, where new or added co-value is continually being created for a service offering. At the core of the SaaS QoS model that we present in Section 16.6 are the characteristics of the business relationships between the service customer and the service provider.

## 16.6 Specifications of a QoS-Focused SaaS Evaluation Model

In this section, we present our initial version of an SaaS QoS evaluation model and illustrate its features using existing SaaS applications. This model prescribes the quality-of-service approaches for four service classes based on the business relationships between the service provider and the service customer: *Ad hoc*, *Defined*, *Managed*, and *Strategic*. The model is summarized in Table 16.1.

### 16.6.1 SaaS Maturity Levels

#### 16.6.1.1 Ad Hoc Service

An SaaS service is called *Ad hoc* if it is used by a customer on an as-needed basis in response to business requirements. The goal of the service customer is to ensure that

**Table 16.1  Maturity Levels of Business Relationship in SaaS Services**

| Maturity Level | Characteristics of Business Relationships | Service Customer Goals | Service Provider Goals | Quality Approaches |
|---|---|---|---|---|
| Level 1 | Ad hoc | Functionality needs achieved | Service delivery on an "as-needed" basis | Some quality measures may be in place |
| Level 2 | Defined | Functionality needs achieved with reliability and other desirable quality requirements guaranteed | Service delivery on a regular (defined) basis with defined capability | Conformance quality measures (SLAs defined and tracked) |
| Level 3 | Managed | Goals of Level 2 plus agreement on monitoring of service quality assurance | Service delivered with configurable capability; shared responsibility to monitor and manage service quality factors | Conformance plus gap quality measures |
| Level 4 | Strategic | Proper governance of service to ensure value goals defined and achieved using approaches such as cost-benefit analysis, ROI analysis, and risk management | Dynamic delivery with the shared goal of service improvement with customer | Conformance, gap, and value quality measures |

the service meets the critical needs of its users. Typically few, if any, QoS attributes are tracked by the provider on behalf of the customer. Examples of Ad hoc services are Amazon.com and Expedia.com when used widely in an organization to facilitate book and travel purchases, respectively.

## 16.6.1.2 Defined Service

An SaaS service is called *Defined* if it is described in a contract or an agreement that outlines service usage and guarantees the service-level capabilities typically through service level agreements (SLAs). The QoS concerns focus on measurable, performance-oriented factors, such as availability and responsiveness. A good example of a Defined service is Google Apps [30] Enterprise Edition, which has a defined SLA focusing on availability. Another example is SAP's Business ByDesign [31], which provides SaaS capabilities for ERP-level applications (integrated accounting, supply chain, HR, CRM, etc). SAP also provides an SLA focused on availability.

## 16.6.1.3 Managed Service

An SaaS service is called *Managed* if it is a Defined service with additional agreed-upon commitments by both the customer and the provider to share the responsibilities of managing the service. Examples of shared responsibilities include monitoring the service quality and refining the service to meet changing quality requirements. A good example of a Managed service is Salesforce.com's CRM service. They provide customization and integration capabilities that allow customers to set up their own unique CRM service and share customer-developed applications. Salesforce.com also supports tracking of service issues and commitments.

## 16.6.1.4 Strategic Service

An SaaS service is called *Strategic* if it is a Managed service in which both the customer and the provider are able to identify the common, agreed-upon business value of deploying the service. Typically, the decision to adopt a strategic service is based on business value analyses, such as cost-benefit analysis, ROI, and/or risk analysis. We have not found any good example of a Strategic service in today's SaaS solutions, since we do not see the application of business value analyses in SaaS services management.

Fundamental to our model is the increasing role that service quality measures play in the business relationship as this relationship moves from *Ad hoc* to *Strategic*. In an Ad Hoc service, there is little or no emphasis on QoS measures. A Defined service includes conformance quality measures, a Managed service adds gap quality to conformance quality measures, and a Strategic service includes value quality measures as well as conformance and gap quality measures. The goal of both SaaS providers and customers is to increase the depth of their business relationship as the service offering moves from Ad hoc to Strategic.

## 16.6.2 QoS-Value Graphs—An Instrument for the QoS-Focused SaaS Evaluation Model

For our model to be used effectively in the planning of IT services, it must be more than just descriptive. In particular, instruments must be available to support the definition, tracking, and analysis of the value quality for each QoS attribute that is agreed upon by the provider and the customer. Let us consider the following example scenario to illustrate how one such instrument, QoS-value graph, can assist in a key element of the model for the determination of co-value using QoS attributes.

Assume that an agreed-upon QoS attribute is the *average response time* for a set of five important service components of a service offering. We can represent in a QoS-value graph the relative value of different average response times for the customer and the provider. From this graph, the customer is prescribing that the response rates of less than 15 ms have highest values. The customer value decreases in a linear fashion for average response times between 15 and 30 ms, dropping to zero value for average response times greater than 30 ms. For the provider, the value related to response time performance is primarily determined by their capability to meet response time demands with their delivered service. The value curve in Figure 16.4 indicates that it is impossible for the provider to deliver an average response time of less than 10 ms for the current service offering. From 10 and 17 ms, the provider value increases rapidly, representing a technology space that could be achieved if significant costs were invested in improving the current service system. For greater than 17 ms, the provider value continues to increase in a linear fashion, representing decreasing response-time requirements for the SaaS provider.

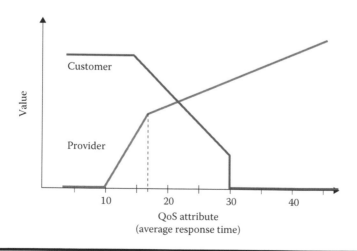

**Figure 16.4**  **QoS-value curve with QoS attribute of average response time.**

By using an instrument such as a QoS-value curve, the provider and the customer can share important information to assess co-value opportunities and arrive at an agreement over average response time commitments. In the case depicted in Figure 16.4, one could imagine the provider and the customer arriving at a decision to use 17 ms as the basis for an ongoing SLA.

These curves can be used across all QoS attributes that are deemed most important in any business relationship involving a Strategic service. As another example of the QoS-value curve instrument, consider the use of cost-benefit analysis, a value quality attribute, as part of a Strategic service partnership. Figure 16.5 represents the situation where the benefits to cost ratio is adopted as a QoS attribute that would be defined and tracked. Note that we have decided in this example to inverse the normal ratio of cost to benefits to benefits to cost, because it is easier to conceive of an increase in customer or provider value as the QoS attribute increases. For an SaaS service offering, the customer benefits are the funds saved by deploying a service, and the costs are primarily the funds as defined in the service contract with the SaaS provider. For the SaaS provider, the benefits would be primarily based on the funds received from the customer for delivering the service, and the costs would be the funds required to operate the service. The QoS-value curve shows that for the provider there is a narrow region (1.6–1.8) of the benefits to cost ratio in which the value increases significantly. This represents the situation in which the benefits outweigh the costs by a comfortable margin— enough to ensure that the service relationship yields real value for the provider.

For the customer, a benefits to cost ratio is of no value until it reaches slightly above 1. The customer value then increases somewhat until a ratio of 1.8, at which point it increases significantly in a linear fashion. Assuming that a strategic service relationship is sought and, therefore, co-value creation is an over-riding goal, the provider and the customer can share their QoS-value curves to assist

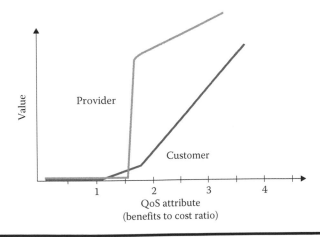

**Figure 16.5   QoS-value curve with QoS attribute of benefits to cost ratio.**

in determining what is a viable cost range for the service offering that allows the provider to make a reasonable profit and the customer to garner significant value from the service.

Additional tools and capabilities for our QoS-focused SaaS evaluation model are being planned, and these are outlined in the Section 16.8.

## 16.7  Related Work in Service Delivery and Management

In the past decade, there has been growing interest in the definition of maturity models and specifications of best practices in the general area of IT service management and delivery. This work is relevant and complementary, but does not apply directly to our narrower focus on SaaS evaluation presented in this chapter. For completeness, we include a summary of this work in this section.

Frank Niessink et al.'s IT Service CMM [20] is a service maturity model that enables IT service providers to assess and further improve their capabilities with respect to the IT service delivery. The structure of this model is similar to that of Carnegie Mellon University (CMU)/Software Engineering Institute's (SEI's) Software CMM with five maturity levels: *Initial, Repeatable, Defined, Managed*, and *Optimizing*; yet the contents are focused on key process areas needed for provisioning mature IT services. The model also introduces suitable and practical assessment approaches to determine and improve the maturity of the organization. However, this approach only aims at the implementation of service processes within IT organizations, and largely ignores the other important roles of the service customer.

The OGC's (Office of Government Commerce) ITIL [21] is a framework of best practices in information technology, primarily focusing on IT service strategy, design, transition, operation, and improvement. In the past decade, ITIL has been adopted worldwide as one of the most popular service-level standards in IT organizations. Instead of using ordered levels and process areas, ITIL organizes the processes as areas of best practices and describes the details of process implementation and activities. The emphasis in ITIL is on the delivery of IT services in-house by the Information Technology department. ITIL provides some general guidance to outsourcing strategies and externally delivered services.

The adoption of SOA solutions in IT requires more specific maturity models to assess the SOA implementation and identify the SOA business value. Sonic Software's SOA Maturity Model (SOA MM) [32] is one such model, defining maturity levels with key business impact within the organization. The model was extended to include five aspects by Inaganti and Sriram's Model [33]: Scope of SOA Adoption, SOA maturity levels, SOA expansion stages, return on SOA investment, and SOA cost-effectiveness and feasibility. Other SOA maturity models specialized in different areas of IT services include IBM's SOA integration model [34] and HP's SOA domain model [35].

## 16.8 Conclusion and Future Work

This chapter provides the basis for a QoS-focused SaaS evaluation model. The key contributions are the definition of a four-level SaaS system maturity model and the inclusion of a QoS-value graph instrument when using this model. The important aspects of this work include the recognition that SaaS evaluation must take into account the generation of co-value by both the provider and the customer, and that additional tools are needed to assist both the provider and the customer in assessing and improving the service quality on an ongoing basis.

Further research is needed into tools that can be adapted to SaaS service offerings, to automatically collect many of the QoS attributes that are agreed to as part of a provider/customer SaaS agreement. The evaluation model should also support regular reporting of QoS nonconformances and trends in service support (both positive and negative). Effort is also needed to integrate our work on SaaS evaluation with the evaluation of other service offering approaches, including in-house services and other forms of external services such as outsourcing. Finally, we are also investigating evaluation support for selecting the best (or currently most viable) SaaS offering among similar offerings by multiple providers. This work involves a weighted multi-QoS-attribute approach that could potentially allow the service selection decision to be delayed until just before the service is needed.

## Acknowledgments

Paul Sorenson would like to thank Norm Pass and Jim Spohrer of the IBM Almaden Research Center for several interesting discussions on co-value creation and service innovation that took place during a fall 2008 visit to Almaden. These discussions helped to form the basis of our QoS-value graph instrument. We also wish to acknowledge NSERC (National Science and Engineering Research Council) of Canada for funding support of this research.

## References

1. SaaS.com, Improving human productivity through software as a service, www.SaaS.com
2. B.J. Lheureux, R.P. Desisto, and M. Maoz, Evaluating software-as-a-service providers: Questions to ask potential SaaS providers, *Gartner RAS Core Research Note*, April 2006.
3. B. Waters, Software as a service: A look at the customer benefits, *Journal of Digital Asset Management*, 1(1), 32–39, January 2005.
4. J. Spohrer, P. Maglio, J. Bailey, and D. Gruhl, Steps towards a science of service systems, *Computer*, 40(1), 71–77, January 2007.
5. V.J. Peters, Total service quality management, *Managing Service Quality*, 9(1), 6–12, 1999.

6. M. Alvarez, Gartner predicts great growth in SaaS adoption, October 2008, www.ate-lier-us.com/e-business-and-it/article/gartner-predicts-great-growth-of-saas-adoption

7. A. Parasuraman, V.A. Zeihaml, and L.L. Berry, SERVQUAL: A multi-item scale for measuring consumer perception of service quality, *Journal of Retailing*, 64(1), 12–40, 1988.

8. C. Fornell, M.D. Johnson, E.W. Anderson, J. Cha, and B.E. Bryant, The American customer satisfaction index: Nature, purpose, and findings, *Journal of Marketing*, 60(4), 7–18, October 1997.

9. R.S. Kaplan and D.P. Norton, *The Balanced Scoreboard: Translating Strategy into Action*, Boston, MA: Harvard Business School Press, August 1996.

10. F. Chong and G. Carraro, Architecture strategies for catching the long tail, *Microsoft Corporation, Software as a Service Architectural Guidance Series*, April 2006, http://msdn.microsoft.com/en-us/library/aa479069.aspx

11. G. Gruman and E. Knorr, What cloud computing really means, *InfoWorld*, April 2008, http://www.infoworld.com/article/08/04/07/15FE-cloud-computing-reality_1.html

12. P. Gaw, What's the difference between cloud computing and SaaS? *Web 2.0 Journal*, July 2008, http://web2.sys-con.com/node/612033

13. S. Ried, J.R. Rymer, and R. Iqbal, Forrester's SaaS maturity model: Transforming vendor strategy while managing customer expectations, *Forrester*, August 2008.

14. P. Hernon and D.A. Nitecki, Service quality: A concept not fully explored, *Library Trends*, 49(4), 687–708, March 2001.

15. C.A. Reeves and D.A. Bednar, Defining quality: Alternatives and implications, *MIT Academy of Management Review*, 19(3), 419–445, Jul. 1994.

16. D.A. Garvin, What does "product quality" really mean? *Sloan Management Review*, Fall, 25–43, October 1984.

17. A. Parasuraman, V.A. Zeithaml, and L.L.Berry, A conceptual model of service quality and its implications for future research, *Journal of Marketing*, 49(4), 41–50, 1985.

18. B.W. Tuchman, The decline of quality, *New York Times Magazine*, 2, 38–41, 104, Nov. 1980.

19. G. Dobson, Quality of service in service-oriented architectures, 2004, http://digs.sourceforge.net/papers/qos.pdf

20. F. Niessink, V. Clerc, T. Tijdink, and H. van Vliet, IT Service CMM Version 1.0 Release candidate 1, 2005, http://www.itservicecmm.org/

21. Office of Government Commerce, *Service Delivery, IT Infrastructure Library*, The Stationery Office, 2001, http://www.itil-officialsite.com/home/home.asp

22. V.A. Zeithaml and A. Parasuraman, and L.L. Berry, *Delivering Quality Service: Balancing Customer Perceptions and Expectations*, New York: The Free Press, 1990.

23. T. Chester, F. Miller, and D.A. Trinkle. Service quality assessments with higher education TechQual+, *Educause Annual Conference*, Seattle, WA, 2007.

24. X. Chen and P.G. Sorenson, Towards TQM in IT services, *Proceedings of the 2007 Workshop on Automating Service Quality* (held in conjunction with *Automated Software Engineering*), Atlanta, GA, pp. 42–47, November 2007.

25. X. Chen and P.G. Sorenson, A QoS-based service acquisition model for IS services, *Proceedings of the Sixth Workshop on Software Quality* (workshop held in conjunction with *ICSE 2008*), Leipzig, Germany, pp. 41–46, May 2008.

26. Cost/benefit analysis: Evaluating quantitatively whether to follow a course of action, http://www.mindtools.com/pages/article/newTED_08.htm

27. CIO Council, The value of IT investments: It's not just return on investment, http://www.cio.gov/documents/TheValueof_IT_Investments.pdf
28. VOSE Software, Introduction to risk analysis, http://www.vosesoftware.com/
29. Marketing Teacher, The product life cycle, http://www.marketingteacher.com/Lessons/lesson_plc.htm
30. Google Corporation, Google apps service level agreement, 2009, http://www.google.com/apps/intl/en/terms/sla.html
31. SAP AG, SAP business bydesign: The most complete and adaptable on-demand business solutions, 2008, http://www.sap.com/solutions/sme/businessbydesign/overview/index.epx
32. Sonic Software Corporation, A new service-oriented architecture (SOA) maturity model, 2005, http://www.sonicsoftware.com/solutions/service_oriented_architecture/soa_maturity_model/index.ssp
33. S. Inaganti and S. Aravamudan, SOA maturity model, *BP Trends*, Apr. 2007.
34. A. Arsanjani and K. Holley, Increase flexibility with the service integration maturity model (SIMM): Maturity, adoption, and transformation to SOA, *IBM developerWorks*, September 2005, http://www.ibm.com/developerworks/webservices/library/ws-soa-simm/
35. HP SOA Maturity Model, 2007, https://roianalyst.alinean.com/calculators/hp/hpsoa/HP_SOA_Maturity_Assessment.html

## Chapter 17

# Risk Evaluation-based Selection Approach for Transactional Services Composition

Hai Liu, Kaijun Ren, Weimin Zhang, and Jinjun Chen

## Contents

## 17.1 Introduction

With the rapid development of the Internet and information technologies, web services has de facto become one of the most significant technologies in the domains of both academia and industry [1]. Web services is a modular, self-organized, and loosely coupled software that can be advertised and accessed programmatically across the Internet. It has changed the ways of traditional programming, such as object-oriented programming, which is based on the underlying layer, while the web services technology mainly focuses on the abstraction of the higher level. Therefore, compared to traditional programming, it is more convenient and faster for application designers to construct new softwares based on existing applications according to users' increasing requirements. Nowadays, more and more applications have been wrapped into web services, which are so-called SaaS (Software as a Service), introduced in the cloud area [1,19,20]. However, a single web service does not have to satisfy the requirements of users. Therefore, how to effectively integrate several web services into a composite one has been a challenge and is attracting more and more attention from the corresponding research area.

Web services composition (WSC) is a complex process involving several steps. One of the most significant steps is the process of web services selection for each task in WSC. Recently, lots of quality of service (QoS)-driven web services selection approaches [2–4] have been presented. Nevertheless, few of them consider the impact of failure risk in transactional WSC, especially in the scientific computing environment with transaction, where it possibly leads to losses such as wasted time and execution resources. To address this issue, we propose a risk-driven selection approach for transactional WSC, with which we can spend the same cost on the dimension of reliability, but reduce average losses for composition web services (CWS). Specifically, we first use a failure-causing tree based on failure atomicity to evaluate probable risk losses for each task in the transactional execution path. Then, a different relative impact is assigned to each task based on its risk losses, to specify reliability requirements. Finally, a modified QoS-driven web services selection method is presented. The experiment presented in this chapter proves the feasibility of our work.

The rest of this chapter is organized as follows. In Section 17.2, we give a detailed formal representation of our model on WSC with transactional properties. A specific scenario in the scientific computing domain is described. In Section 17.3, we introduce the method of risk evaluation for participant tasks based on our presented failure-causing tree and propose two algorithms, which are used to obtain the relative impact on each task. In Section 17.4, we bring forth a modified web services selection algorithm based on the common QoS-driven web services selection method presented as our former work. In Section 17.5, a simulating experiment has been performed to verify our solution, and then a performance comparison between our method and other related methods has been demonstrated. Section 17.6 provides the summary of related work. Finally, we conclude our idea and indicate the future direction in Section 17.7.

## 17.2 Formalized Model

In order that our work is well expressed, we first formalize the model of our solution to transactional WSC. According to the literature [5], the authors proposed that the process of WSC should be divided into two phases, which consist of application-level composition and concretion-level composition, respectively. The first phase mainly supports the abstract-level composition based on the types of web services, focusing on functional satisfaction for predefined user requirements. This generates the optimal workflow to satisfy users' functional requirements. The second phase assigns each task of the plan composed in the first phase with concrete instances of candidate web services based on nonfunctional properties. Accordingly, our work is based on the second-phase composition, assuming that it works after the first phase. This means that our work in this chapter has the precondition finished the first-phase composition. In our work, we formalize our model of WSC based on the assignment of specific instances of candidate web services that are based on nonfunctional properties. We also refer to the concepts proposed in the literature [2], where a path for a specific workflow or a kind of type-based composition is called for, and a plan for an executable path is named. For the sake of facility to represent our problem later, we distinguish between the concepts of task and instance of web service, where the latter will be assigned to the former so that the former can be executed in the plan. Actually, this concept of task is an abstract web service or a service class defined in the literature [2].

In the transactional aspect, we have the precondition that the transactional property of each task in CWS has been defined in advance by specific application designers. Therefore, the transactional property of the corresponding candidate web service should be in compliance with its assigned task.

---

**Definition 17.1** We define each task in a path as a seven tuple t = <tid,I,O,F,Q,e,tp>, where the notation tid represents the identifier of task t; notations I and O represent the input parameters set and the output parameters set on this task t, respectively; notation F denotes requirements of all functional properties of task t; and notation Q expresses requirements of nonfunctional properties, such as QoS parameters, involved cost, executing time, and availability. Meanwhile, notation e denotes the relative degree of impact in the entire path, which would be calculated based on our evaluation method presented in Section 17.3 for failure risk of task t in a specific path. This attribute is explained in Section 17.4. The last notation, tp, defines transactional properties specified by application designers according to the features of business application, where tp denotes the transactional properties TP = {r, c, nr, nc, rc, nrc, nrnc, rnc}. The description for each element in TP is given in Table 17.1.

**Table 17.1   Semantic Description for Each Transactional Property**

| Property | Semantic Description |
|---|---|
| r | It could be retried with another instance of candidate web services when the task t executing with the current assigned instance of web service causes a failure or an exception. |
| c | It denotes that task t can be compensated by a predefined process. |
| nr | It represents task t does not own the transactional property r. |
| nc | It represents task t does not own the transactional property c. |
| rc | The combination between property r and property c. |
| nrc | The combination between property nr and property c. |
| nrnc | The combination between property nr and property nc. |
| rnc | The combination between property r and property nc. |

In order to understand these transactional properties, we use a state transition diagram, as illustrated in Figure 17.1. There are five regular states for each task in a transactional CWS. Following is the process of these state transitions.

When one candidate instance of web service has been assigned to the task, the web service would be initiated. Correspondingly, the state of this task will change to start. After completing the initial process, the state will reach the active state, in which the task runs its assigned web service instance. Finally, the state of the task will reach the completed state. Certainly, there exist some uncommon states, such as abort/cancel and failed. The abort/cancel state is transferred from the start state or the active state. When a task with the transactional property 'r' is in the failed state, it can be transferred to the active state by replacing another alternative web service to retry, as demonstrated in Figure 17.1a. In the meanwhile, a task with the transactional property 'c' in the completed state can be transferred to the compensated state by compensating this task using the corresponding compensation operation, as shown in Figure 17.1b. In the nature of things, in case that a task with the transactional property 'cr,' which is the combination of the transactional property 'c' and the transactional property 'r,' is in the failed state or the completed state, its state can be changed to the active state or the compensated state according to Figure 17.1a and b, respectively, as shown in Figure 17.1c. Finally, Figure 17.1d illustrates the state transition for the task with the transactional property 'nrnc.' When it comes to the failed state, the active state cannot be reached because of the transactional property 'nr'; likewise, while it is in the completed state, it cannot be compensated because of its transactional property 'nc.'

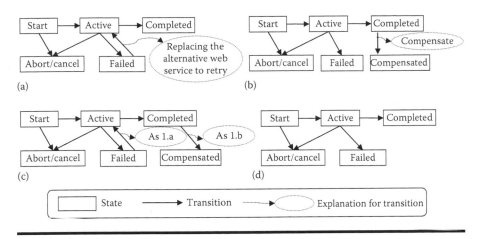

**Figure 17.1 State transition diagram for task with different kinds of transactional properties. (a) State transition for task with transactional property 'r.' (b) State transition for task with transactional property 'c.' (c) State transition for task with transactional property 'rc.' (d) State transition for task with transactional property 'nrnc.'**

**Definition 17.2** We define a quarter tuple s=<sid,tid,Q,R> for each instance of web service that is a member of the candidate services list for being assigned to a specific task, as defined in Definition 17.1. In this definition, notation sid represents the identifier of service s. Notation tid denotes the identifier of the task whose candidate services list includes service s. Notation Q represents a set of nonfunctional properties that should be advertised by the provider of service s. It is very similar with the notation Q defined in the task. Finally, notation R denotes the current reliability parameter of service s. This parameter can be advertised in the extended description language of the web service, such as the prevalent WSDL [21], by the provider.

**Definition 17.3** We assume that notation P denotes an execution path. In the meanwhile, according to the literature [6], P could be represented in the form of workflow patterns. In this chapter, three typical patterns are considered for our execution path, because the other workflow patterns can be reduced to these three patterns [4]. Now, we introduce some corresponding operators to denote these workflow patterns as follows:

1. Sequence pattern, which is represented by the notation ';'. For example, the execution path (t1;t2) means that task t2 should be invoked after task t1 is completed.
2. Parallel pattern, which is represented by the notation '|'. The execution path (t1|t2) means that task t1 and task t2 can execute simultaneously.

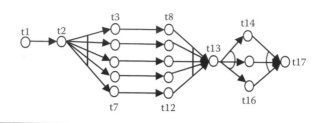

**Figure 17.2    Process of ensemble prediction formalized as (t1;t2;((t3;t8)|(t4;t9)| (t5;t10)|(t6;t11)|(t7;t12));t13;(t14 + t15 + t16)₁;t17).**

3. Alternative pattern, which is represented by the notation '+'. The execution path $(t1 + t2 + \cdots + tm)_n$ means that at least n tasks need selecting to execute parallelly from the task set $\{t1, t2, \ldots, tm\}$. On the condition $n$ equals to 1, we say that the alternative pattern becomes the single selection pattern.

Figure 17.2 shows a typical execution path that is our motivation application in the domain of scientific computing called the ensemble prediction business process. It is a new, interesting, and hot research technology in the area of numerical weather forecast, and includes several steps, which contain preprocess, perturbation generation, model forecasting for ensemble members, postprocessing, product generation and visualization, and so on [22]. In this figure, the whole of tasks t1 and t2 denotes the preprocess step; meanwhile, tasks t3–t7 that should be executed concurrently belong to the perturbation generation step. After the completion of the perturbation generation step, several initial samples will be produced, which are used as input data for tasks denoting the model forecasting step from t8 to t12. When all tasks in the model forecasting step have been performed successfully, task t13 representing the postprocessing step can be started. For the product generation step, there are several candidate ways represented by tasks t14–t16; however, only one candidate task can be selected for execution. Finally, when task t17 denoting the visualization step is performed completely, the entire execution path will be ended successfully.

In this application, each of the tasks has its own transactional properties for the inherent characteristics of this business process. Once a task encounters failures, in order to guarantee atomic consistency, forward recovery methods such as retrying operations, or backward recovery methods such as compensation operations are required to be executed. In this business process environment, the execution of each task needs a very long execution time and high execution cost. Therefore, the web services selection for each task needs to consider the impact of failure risk. Otherwise, it will waste huge cost in re-executing and recovering corresponding tasks in case several tasks cause exception or failure. In Section 17.3, a new evaluation method based on transactional CWS is presented.

## 17.3 Evaluation of Failure Risk Losses

### *17.3.1 Formation of Failure-Causing Tree*

The authors of literature [7] put forth the concept of failure risk; they proposed that failure risk was a characteristic considering the probability that some faults would occur and lead to an impact on the composite service. Distinguished from their work, our work just evaluates the losses caused by failure, so that we can obtain the relative degree of impact for each task in an execution path of transactional composition. We do not regard the probability that some fault will occur at a specific task or at a specific web service instance. Our method only needs to evaluate the causing losses in the event that a task encountered failures or exceptions. In order to evaluate failure-causing losses for all tasks in a specific execution path defined above, not only should we delve into the execution cost of each task in history, but we should also consider dependency among tasks in that specific execution path, especially in a transactional composition environment. Based on this idea, we first look into the dependency among tasks. In literature [17], the authors made Dependencies Management (DM) coordinate the execution of transactional workflow with Dependencies Rules (DR), which was composed of all kinds of formal dependencies rules. However, they did not detail these dependencies-related transactional aspects. Literature [17] also presented some dependencies between the services in transactional composition service (TCS) to guarantee failure atomicity requirement for transactional composition service. It gives four dependencies related to transactional properties in TCS. In this chapter, we mainly consider two dependencies, which are failure-causing dependency and compensation-causing dependency, respectively, on the basis of recovery policies of transactional CWS to obtain possible losses caused by the failure of individual tasks. In the following, we give the two dependencies based on our WSC environment defined in Section 17.2.

---

**Definition 17.4** Failure-causing dependency (from task ti to task tj): It can be denoted as $ti \xrightarrow{failure} tj$. This dependency represents that task tj would be canceled or compensated in case of failure of task ti. In other words, the failure of task *ti* will affect task *tj* in order to preserve transactional correctness for the whole of the process. How to perform actions for task tj is decided by its state, and these actions will be in support of the evaluation algorithm presented in Section 17.3.2. There exist three cases. In order to express well, we define function P(e) in view of the possibility of event e arising. Function occur(e) represents that event e has been triggered. Char '*' denotes any transactional property 'nr' or 'r.'

Case 1:
Precondition:

$[P(occur (ti.state == failed) \wedge tj.state == completed) \in (0,1)] \wedge (tj.tp ==' * c') \wedge (ti \xrightarrow{failure} tj).$

Event: occur (ti.state == failed).
Actions for task tj: Abort (tj) ∨ Compensate (tj).

Case 2:
Precondition:

[P occur (ti.state == failed) ∧ tj.state == completed) == 0] ∧ (tj.tp == ′∗∗′) ∧ ti $\xrightarrow{\text{failure}}$ tj

Event: occur (ti.state == failed).
Action: Abort (tj).

Case 3:
Precondition:

[P (occur (ti.state == failed) ∧ tj.state == completed) == 1] ∧ (tj.tp == ′∗c′) ∧ ti $\xrightarrow{\text{failure}}$ tj.

Event: occur (ti.state == failed).
Action: Compensate (tj).

Going back to Figure 17.2, there is one failure-causing dependency from task t8 to task t3. Namely, there is a condition t8 $\xrightarrow{\text{failure}}$ t3. Since task t8 and task t3 exist in a sequence pattern, the condition [P (occur (t8.state == failed) ∧ t3. state == completed) == 1] ∧ (t8.tp == ′∗c′) is true. Finally, according to case 3, task t3 will be compensated when task t8 causes failure. In the same way, there exists the condition t3 $\xrightarrow{\text{failure}}$ t4, and the value of Boolean expression P(occur (t3.state == failed) ∧ t4.state == completed) ∈ (0,1)] ∧ (t4.tp == ′∗c′) is also true. Obviously, according to case 1, we have the conclusion that task t4 may be aborted or compensated when task t3 causes failure.

---

**Definition 17.5** Compensation-causing dependency (from task ti to task tj): There is a compensation-causing dependency from task ti to task tj if the compensation of task ti causes task tj's compensation. This kind of dependency is caused indirectly by failure of one task in an execution path. We denote by ti $\xrightarrow{\text{compensation}}$ tj the compensation-causing dependency from task ti to task tj, which means task tj needs to be compensated after task ti is compensated.

There is a big difference between the two dependencies defined above. In the failure-causing dependency ti $\xrightarrow{\text{failure}}$ tj, the state of task ti must not be the completed state, and it may arise from two cases, which are its own failure and the situation that it is aborted by another task, respectively. In the compensation-causing dependency ti $\xrightarrow{\text{compensation}}$ tj, however, the precondition that the states of both task ti and task tj should be in the completed state must be satisfied.

---

**Theorem 17.1** Compensation-causing dependency has transitivity: It means supposing ti $\xrightarrow{\text{compensation}}$ tj and tj $\xrightarrow{\text{compensation}}$ tk to be true, we can obtain that ti $\xrightarrow{\text{compensation}}$ tj is true.

**Proof:** Let the compensation-causing dependencies $ti \xrightarrow{\text{compensation}} tj$ and $tj \xrightarrow{\text{compensation}} tk$ be true. If task ti has been compensated, then it exists in which task tj needs to be compensated according to the dependency of compensation causing $ti \xrightarrow{\text{compensation}} tj$; now it exists in task tj that will be compensated. Therefore, we can understand that task tk needs to be compensated in terms of the compensation-causing dependency $tj \xrightarrow{\text{compensation}} tk$; thus, it means that the condition of compensation of task ti can lead to the conclusion that task tk needs to be compensated. In other words, we can get the result of which compensation-causing dependency $ti \xrightarrow{\text{compensation}} tk$ is true.

---

**Definition 17.6** Failure-causing tree (let the root of the tree be task t): This kind of tree is very similar to a fault tree. It consists of nodes and links, where nodes contain two types, which are operator and task, respectively, while links also contain two kinds, which are links based on dependencies defined above. In the failure-causing tree of task t, the links connected immediately with task t or with operators that are connected directly with task t represent failure-causing dependency, and the others denote compensation-causing dependency. Following are several rules used for the formation of this kind of tree:

> *Rule 1:* If task t is retriable, as we know, in case of caused failure, it can be recovered by the mechanics of forward recovery, such as by restarting this task with other similar-function web services. Therefore, it need not compensate any other completed tasks. There is only one node representing the self of task t in its failure-causing tree.
>
> *Rule 2:* If there is a parallel pattern or a condition pattern in the original execution path, and the failure-causing tree of task t includes those nodes representing tasks in a parallel pattern or in a condition pattern and contains one node representing a task before these tasks, we should append these nodes representing the task to every offset representing a parallel pattern or a condition pattern in the failure-causing tree.
>
> *Rule 3:* Otherwise, all nodes in the failure-causing tree should conform to the tasks' structure corresponding to the original execution path.

Figure 17.3 shows an example on several dependencies correlating to the business transaction requirement in the execution path of ensemble prediction, and a typical failure-causing tree with the root node of task t13. Figure 17.3a illustrates failure-causing dependency and compensation-causing dependency, which are represented by two different kinds of dotted arrows, respectively. Due to limited space, we only outline the dependencies corresponding to task t13, while the others are not shown. It can be known from this figure that there are five failure-causing dependencies between task t13 and from task t8 to task 12. It

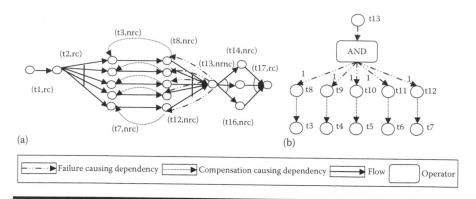

(a)            (b)

**Figure 17.3 An example of failure-causing tree. (a) Several dependencies in the execution path of ensemble prediction. (b) Failure-causing tree of task t13.**

also shows that there are five pairs of compensation-causing dependencies. Figure 17.3b illustrates a failure-causing tree according to dependencies showed by Figure 17.3a, where task t13, and task t8 to task t12 are connected with the operator AND, which represents that they have a parallel relationship in the failure-causing tree; the label on the side of each failure-causing dependency denotes possibility, as given in Definition 17.4. From this diagram, we can see P(occur (t13.state == failed) ∧ ti.state == completed) = 1, i∈ {8, 9, 10, 11, 12}, since there is a sequence pattern between task ti and task t13 in the original execution path. Meanwhile, the existing operator NULL that has been omitted between task t8 and t3 represents that they have a sequence relationship in the failure-causing tree. (*Note*: There are three kinds of operators corresponding to the workflow pattern defined above, which are SEQ, AND, and OR)

---

**Theorem 17.2** All of the completed nodes except for the root node in the failure-causing tree need to be compensated when the root node encounters failure.

**Proof:** According to Theorem 17.1, and Definitions 17.4 and 17.5, we can prove it directly.

## 17.3.2 Losses Evaluation of Failure Risk for Tasks

We postulate that these two dependencies have been established during the first level of WSC. So we can evaluate losses of each task with the help of these dependencies and historical execution information of individual tasks. In the following, we show our losses evaluation algorithms based on the failure-causing tree for each task in a specific execution path.

According to Theorem 17.2, we can infer that the losses caused by the failure of a specific task should involve two parts, which are compensation cost part and execution cost part along the failure-causing tree. We consider the cost metric as two dimensions that are execution time dimension and execution cost dimension, respectively. We define the following formula to evaluate the cost-taken of a specific execution path or sub-path:

$$
\begin{cases}
U_c^p = u * f_t(T_{time}^p) + v * f_e(E_e^p) \\
u + v = 1
\end{cases}
\tag{17.1}
$$

In this formula, functions $f_t(T_{time}^p)$ and $f_e(E_e^p)$ represent two different utility functions based on the parameter of time dimension and the parameter of execution cost dimension for path p, respectively. These two functions can be defined to unify metrics based on users' preferences. For example, we can transform the time metric and the execution cost metric into the universal metric such as money. Variables u and v are weight values specified by the user. Therefore, in order to evaluate the losses of a failure task, we should evaluate the total execution time and execution cost spent by tasks according to its failure-causing tree. However, there are different computing ways between execution time and execution cost due to different structures existing in the failure-causing tree, which makes us evaluate them based on its inherent structure separately. In the following, we show the respective ways to evaluate these two parameters based on three different structures corresponding to the operators in the failure-causing tree. Without loss of generality, we postulate that task t is the root node of the failure-causing tree, and let variables $T_{time}^p$ and $E_c^p$ represent the total losses of time and execution cost in a sub-tree p of the failure-causing tree. From the computing methods perspective, sub-trees with the same structure in the failure-causing tree may have different computing ways for different kinds of dependencies. In order to use a uniform evaluation method based on the structure of the failure-causing tree covering both kinds of dependencies, we lend the function P(e) as defined above to represent the possibility of event e arising. We can obtain P(e) as follows:

$$
P(e) = \begin{cases}
P(e); & \text{if dependencies belong to} \\
& \text{failure-causing dependency} \\
1; & \text{if dependencies belong to} \\
& \text{compensation-causing dependency}
\end{cases}
\tag{17.2}
$$

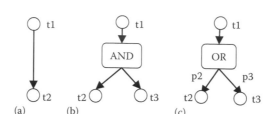

**Figure 17.4    Several probable sub-trees in a failure-causing tree. (a) A sub-tree with operator NULL. (b) A sub-tree with operator AND. (c) A sub-tree with operator OR.**

*Case 1:* If there is an operator SEQ between t1 and t2 in a path as illustrated in Figure 17.4a, we can evaluate their total time and cost consumed as follows:

$$
\begin{cases}
T_{time}^{p} = T_{time}^{pt1} + (T_{exectime}^{t2} + T_{cptime}^{t2}) * P(e_2) \\
\qquad + T_{exectime}^{\prime t2} * (1 - P(e_2)) \\
E_e^{p} = E_e^{pt1} + (E_{execCost}^{t2} + E_{cpCost}^{t2}) * P(e_2) \\
\qquad + E_{execCost}^{\prime t2} * (1 - P(e_2))
\end{cases}
\tag{17.3}
$$

*Case 2:* If there is an operator AND between t1 and t2–t3 as illustrated in Figure 17.4b, we can evaluate their total time and cost consumed as follows:

$$
\begin{cases}
T_{time}^{p} = T_{time}^{pt1} + \underset{i \in \{2,3\}}{Max}((T_{execTime}^{t_i} + T_{cpTime}^{t_i}) * P(e_i) \\
\qquad + T_{execTime}^{\prime t_i} * (1 - P(e_i))) \\
E_e^{p} = E_e^{pt1} + (E_{execCost}^{t2} + E_{cpCost}^{t2}) * P(e_2) \\
\qquad + E_{execCost}^{\prime t2} * (1 - P(e_2)) \\
\qquad + (E_{cpCost}^{t3} + E_{cpCost}^{t3}) * P(e_3) \\
\qquad + E_{execCost}^{\prime t3} * (1 - P(e_3))
\end{cases}
\tag{17.4}
$$

*Case 3:* If there is an operator OR between t1 and t2–t3 as showed in Figure 17.4c, where t2 and t3 have execution probabilities p2 and p3, respectively, we can evaluate their total time and cost consumed as follows:

$$
\begin{cases}
T_{time}^P = T_{time}^{pt1} + p2 * ((T_{exectime}^{t2} + T_{cptime}^{t2}) * P(e_2) \\
\qquad + T'^{t2}_{exectime} * (1 - P(e_2))) \\
\qquad + p3 * ((T_{exectime}^{t3} + T_{cptime}^{t2}) * P(e_3) \\
\qquad + T'^{t3}_{exectime} * (1 - P(e_3))) \\
E_e^P = E_e^{pt1} + p2 * ((E_{execCost}^{t2} + E_{cpCost}^{t2}) * P(e_2) \\
\qquad + E'^{t2}_{execCost} * (1 - P(e_2))) \\
\qquad + p3 * ((E_{execCost}^{t3} + E_{cpCost}^{t3}) * P(e_3) \\
\qquad + E'^{t3}_{execCost} * (1 - P(e_3)))
\end{cases}
\tag{17.5}
$$

*Case 4:* If there is only one node in the failure-causing tree, it means that task t just needs an executing forward recovery mechanism, such as retrying this task when it encounters a failure. Therefore, we can evaluate its total time and cost consumed as follows:

$$
\begin{cases}
T_{time}^P = Rty_{time}(t) \\
E_e^P = Rty_{cost}(t)
\end{cases}
\tag{17.6}
$$

For the evaluation methods defined above, we use a superincumbent and recursive approach to compute cost and time for each kind of sub-tree. Two new variables, $T_{time}^{pt1}$ and $E_e^{pt1}$, are introduced to represent evaluation time and evaluation cost for the sub-tree pt1, which is generated from the corresponding failure causing tree with algorithm of deep first searching (DFS) ended in task t1. $T_{execTime}^{t_i}$ and $T_{cpTime}^{t_i}$ denote the execution and compensation times of task $t_i$. Meanwhile, $E_{execCost}^{t_i}$ and $E_{cpCost}^{t_i}$ represent the execution and compensation costs of task $t_i$. Variables $T_{execTime}^{\prime t_i}$ and $E_{execCost}^{\prime t_i}$ are used to represent possible execution time and cost spent when task $t_i$ running is aborted by failure causing dependency. Variables $Rty_{time}(t)$ and $Rty_{cost}(t)$ denote the execution time and cost taken by retrying an operation that may be replaced by another candidate web service instance. All the variants proposed above can be predicted by the history execution information of individual tasks. We use the method of mean value on history information [2] or other history-based methods. For instance, presuming that task t has been executed five times in history, each of which has spent a cost of 50, 65, 70, 65, and 80, respectively, we can come to a conclusion with the following expression:

$$
T_{cpTime}^t = \frac{50 + 65 + 70 + 65 + 80}{5} = 66.
$$

Algorithm 17.1: Evaluating losses-taken for Task t (ELT)
Input: Head node T (t); // A failure causing tree of a task t
Output: Real Losses$_c^{FT(t)}$;
Begin:
1    if T (t).child!= $\varnothing$ ;
2      then do
3         ER(T(t),Time,Cost);
4         CaculateOvlapNodes(T(t),OvlapNodeSet);
5         EvaCosideringOvlapNodes(tempTime,tempCost,OvlapNodeSet, Losses$_{time}^{FT(t)}$,E$_e^{Tr(t)}$);
6      else do

7       $\begin{cases} T_{time}^{FT(t)} = Rty_{time}(t) \\ E_e^{FT(t)} = Rty_{cost}(t) \end{cases}$ ;

8    end if
9       Losses$_c^{FT(t)} = u * f_t(T_{time}^{FT(t)}) + v * f_e(E_e^{FT(t)})$;
10   return (Losses$_c^{FT(t)}$);
End

**Figure 17.5   Algorithm 17.1 for evaluating losses.**

We show our method of evaluating losses-taken for a specific task of the failure-causing tree in Algorithm 17.1, as shown in Figure 17.5, where step 3 is a function to compute the total execution time and cost with the failure-causing tree T(t). However, there are some overlapped nodes generated in the failure-causing tree T(t) existing due to several patterns before them in the original execution path such as parallel pattern, since these nodes need to be appended to every offset for the formation of the failure-causing tree T(t). Meanwhile, step 4 attains the set of overlapped nodes; step 5 obtains the eventual result of both execution time and cost considering overlapped nodes; step 7 represents the condition of the existing one node in the failure-causing tree. Finally, the algorithm obtains the losses for the task t with Formula (17.1) in step 9.

As mentioned by Algorithm 17.1, we can get the loss-taken for a specific task according to its related failure-causing tree. However, its precondition is that the execution path can be recovered by the backward or forward method. We also need to consider the situation that it exists in a task-assigned web service class with no compensated property. For this situation, in order to ensure failure consistency for executing in the execution path, for tasks after these tasks with no compensated property, we need to keep them with a retriable property or assign them the highest level of impact in the execution path so that we can select a higher, reliable web service to execute. For instance, we can set the reliability requirement for these kinds of tasks near to1.

Algorithm 17.2, as shown in Figure 17.6, gives the approach for attaining the failure impact of the entire tasks in a specific execution path P formalized as in Section 17.2. Step 1 finds the first task with no compensated transactional property. Step 2 initializes a set used for marking such tasks with the non-retriable property; therefore, steps 3–7 find these tasks with the non-retriable property after task t to

Algorithm 17.2: Calculating Impact for each Task (CIT)
Input: P;//An execution path with transactional properties generated at the first level composition),
which could be formalized as defined in section two.
Output: impact[t1..tn]: the impact for each task's failure risk
Begin
1   t=findFirstNCTask(P);//find t.TP not in {nc,rnc,nrnc}
2   P1={};//initialize set P1
3   while (t.next!=null ) do
4     t'=t.next;
5     if (t'.TP=nr*) //'*' represents c or nc or null.
6     Add(t',P1); add task t' to Set P1.
7   End do
8   for each task ti in P1
9     impact[ti]=μ;//specified by user;
10  for each task ti in (P-P1)
12    Losses[ti]=ELT(T(ti));//get the losses-taken of task t.
13    impact[t1..tN]=scale(losses[t1..tN]);
14    return impact[t1..tn]
End

**Figure 17.6   Algorithm 17.2 for calculating impact.**

store in set P1. Because these tasks found in steps 3–7 must not encounter any failures for ensuring correctness, we should set the failure impact value for these tasks higher than others, and the value is μ at step 9, which is input by the user. For other tasks in the execution path P, we first evaluate losses for these tasks using Algorithm 17.1, and then uniformly scale losses evaluated for these tasks in the domain [0,1] in steps 10–13. Finally, we return the array of failure impacts for all tasks in the execution path P. Currently, we have evaluated the failure impacts for all tasks in a specific execution path. In Section 17.4, a modified QoS-driven web services selection algorithm would be given based on the failure impact.

# 17.4  Selection Algorithm

Now we propose our web services selection approach that is very similar to the selection methods based on QoS constraints [2,8]. Our approach differs from these methods in that we specify firstly the requirement on the reliability dimension that is one dimension of QoS dimensions according to the failure impact of each task. Certainly, in the field of QoS-driven WSC, the higher the reliability requirement, the more efficient the performance. However, let us consider the situation with the same total cost constrained by the user. We need to constrain different requirements of reliability for a task base on its failure impact evaluated above, so that we can reduce average losses for the related execution path as well as save costs for users. Hence, what we first need to do is to decide the requirement of reliability dimension for each task in the execution path. In the following, we will give our optimization solution model with linear programming [9].

Let set constant $e_i$ represent the equivalent weight between cost dimension and cost-taken for reliability dimension from the user's prospect, which can be statistically calculated in terms of QoS information of candidates for task i. In other words, it will increase the cost-taken $e_i$ units for task i when we want to enhance the requirement of reliability by one unit for task i. Let set variant $r_i$ represent the reliability requirement for task i, on which standard task i will select the web service, and these kinds of variants will be computed by our linear programming later. The array impact[i] is calculated by our Algorithms 17.1 and 17.2 defined above. The constant $R_{user}$ and $C_r$ represent two values that are the lowest requirement of reliability for composition service and the cost constraint spent on reliability dimension specified by the user, respectively. The function $Reliability_{path}(r_1, r_2, ..., r_n)$ calculated based on the control construct of the execution path, by Jorge Cardoso et al. in literature [10], denotes the method of computing reliability dimension for a composition service that contains task $t_1$, task $t_2$, ..., and task $t_n$. In order to ensure the minimizing losses and to keep the same cost spent on reliability dimension, we will use the following minimum objective function:

$$\text{Impact}_{path} = \sum_{i=1}^{n} (1 - r_i) * \text{impact}[i] \tag{17.7}$$

For the purpose of keeping the same cost and to guarantee the lowest reliability requirement from the global prospect, the following constraints should be satisfied:

$$\sum_{i=1}^{n} (r_i * e_i) \le C_r \tag{17.8}$$

$$\text{Reliability}_{path}(r_1, r_2, ..., r_n) \ge R_{user} \tag{17.9}$$

$$\begin{cases} 0 < r_i, R_{user} \le 1 \\ e_i > 0, \quad i = 1, 2, ..., n \\ C_r > 0 \end{cases} \tag{17.10}$$

In terms of defining variants, functions, and constraints above, we can compute the values $r_1, r_2, ..., r_n$.

Based on the steps above, we can modify the web services selection algorithm such as Multi-dimension Multi-choice 0–1 Knapsack Problem (MMKP) that has been proved an np-hard problem[11,12] solved in our former work in literature [8], while one kind of constraint that the requirement on reliability dimension for each task i is $r_i$ should be added to [8] so as to assist the selection of candidate web services for each task in a specific execution path.

## 17.5 Experiments and Evaluation

To prove the feasibility for our method in this chapter, we perform the simulative experiment using our Algorithms 17.1 and 17.2 and the selection algorithm proposed in Section 17.4. We use the execution path of CWS, as illustrated in Figure 17.1 in Section 17.2. We assume that the compensation cost or retrying cost of each task is evaluated based on history information. We also presume that the communication cost is far less than the cost of compensation and execution in our application of ensemble prediction. So we can ignore the impact of communication between tasks. Our experiments were carried out on a Intel® machine with 1.86 GHz and 1.5 GB RAM running Microsoft Windows XP. We used lp_solve_5.5.0 to solve the integer planning model. All implementations were done in Java.

Table 17.2 shows the relative cost and impact obtained by Algorithms 17.1 and 17.2 for each task. In this table, symbol $\alpha$ represents the lowest impact factor specified by users or designers. The blank cell represents that the cost related to the task is very large comparing to other tasks. The last row of this table represents the impact for each task in CWS. Finally, we perform the simulative experiment to measure the average losses caused by the failure of tasks for CWS. For each task, we respectively limit the candidate web services providers from 5 to 12, whose reliability parameters advertised can be implemented by a random function defined in JAVA. For the sake of simplification, we postulate that each variable $e_i$ for task i has the same value. The lowest requirement of initial reliability for CWS is 0.5. Meanwhile, the domain of $r_i$ is divided into discrete values, which are constrained in the set $\{0.1,0.2,0.3,0.4,0.5,0.6,0.7,0.8,0.9,1\}$, and then they are amplified ten times so as to become integers. For the moment, we can make use of the Integer Programming–based method to get the requirement value of $r_i$ for each task i; then the method in literature [8] is applied to get the optimal execution plan.

The result of this experiment, as demonstrated in Figure 17.7, with the increasing number of execution times of CWS, is that the average losses with our method are always lower than the method [8] of QoS-based web services selection without considering the impact of failure risk. We also can see from this figure, with the number of execution times growing larger, that the gap of average losses between these two methods becomes more stable.

## 17.6 Related Work

In this section, we overview the major techniques related to our approach. To the best of our knowledge, few literatures discuss the full similar topic as our work to predict the relative impact based on the evaluation of risk cost for each task

**Table 17.2 Several Kinds of Costs for Each Task in the Execution Path of Ensemble Prediction**

| Cost | Task | | | | | | | | | | | | | | | | |
|---|---|---|---|---|---|---|---|---|---|---|---|---|---|---|---|---|---|
| | t1 | t2 | t3 | t4 | t5 | t6 | t7 | t8 | t9 | t10 | t11 | t12 | t13 | t14 | t15 | t16 | t17 |
| Retry | 20 | 15 | | | | | | | | | | | | | | | 30 |
| Compensation | 30 | 40 | 20 | 20 | 20 | 20 | 20 | 30 | 30 | 30 | 30 | 30 | | 25 | 25 | 25 | 15 |
| Execution | 30 | 40 | 35 | 35 | 35 | 35 | 35 | 40 | 40 | 40 | 40 | 40 | 50 | 20 | 20 | 20 | 10 |
| Loss-taken | 20 | 15 | 80 | 80 | 80 | 80 | 80 | 355 | 355 | 355 | 355 | 355 | 705 | | | | 30 |
| Impact (%) | 0.7 | α | 9.48 | 9.48 | 9.48 | 9.48 | 9.48 | 49.64 | 49.64 | 49.64 | 49.64 | 49.64 | 100 | 100 | 100 | 100 | 2.19 |

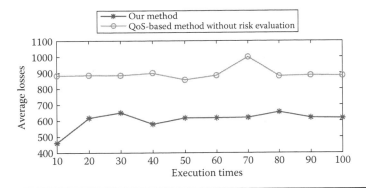

**Figure 17.7  Results for different selection methods.**

in CWS with transactional properties, which provides a policy in support of web services selection for CWS. Wu and Yang [13] studied an approach to predict QoS parameters for the composition of web services with transaction, and a specification model was defined to specify the execution processes of CWS according to the exception handling policies of transactions. This algorithm can reduce the error rate. However, our work involves a few differences. First, what we discuss is on evaluating failure risk losses for individual tasks, while their work focuses on the entire execution process. Second, our work is based on the selection of individual web services, while their work is based on the selection of execution processes.

Currently, there are several works proposed to evaluate the risk cost for the execution process of WSC. Kokash et al. [7,14] explored a method for evaluating the risk cost for WSC according to the probability of each candidate service. With evaluating the risk cost for all combinations of WSC, they selected optimal plans that lead to the least probable risk losses. Obviously, they can get optimal plans from the risk losses perspective by considering the risk probability for each candidate web service. However, the complexity of their method will increase greatly as the number of combinations for WSC becomes large, and its complexity rises by the exponent function. Meanwhile, it is very hard to calculate the accurate risk cost for CWS because of the uncertainty of each single web service hosted on the Internet. And our method to evaluate the risk cost for CWS is not based on a single web service. Since our method is based on Algorithms 17.1 and 17.2 and the selection algorithm from literature [8], our complexity is the largest among these three algorithms, which is the selection algorithm from literature [8]. Obviously, the complexity for our method is polynomial. What we use is only the historical execution information for each task participating in the WSC evaluated. Therefore, our complexity is lower than their complexity. At the same time, our method can be in support of the web services selection for each task in the specific composition service. Kokash in the literature [14] also proposed a means of service selection based on failure risk evaluation of composition to improve composition reliability.

The main distinctions of our work from his work consist of the following two points. First, our method for evaluating the failure risk cost is in terms of our proposed failure-causing tree that is in the context of transactional service composition. Second, our method for evaluating the failure risk cost does not consider the probability of individual service anticipating in the composition service, so that we need not consider all combinations for the composition service. Asnar et al. [15] refined the Goal-Risk framework introducing the notion of trust for assessing risks on the basis of the organizational setting of the system. The assessment process was enhanced to analyze risks along trust relations among actors. This method of evaluating risks is qualitative, and it does not provide a quantitative risk analysis, while our method provides a technique of quantitative failure risk assessment for each participating task in the composition service.

More recently, a lot of work has emerged on WSC with transactional support. El Haddad et al. [16] studied a QoS-driven web services selection approach in combination with the transactional property. In terms of the transactional behavior characteristic of the composition service, they defined two risk levels that are risk0 and risk1. Therein the risk0 level guarantees the successful execution of the system, whose completed results can be compensated by the user, while the risk1 level does not guarantee the system's successful execution. But if it achieves the results, the system cannot be compensated by the users. The selection algorithm proposed in that literature need check the requirement of the transactional behavior of composition services first, and then execute based on QoS-driven web service selection approach proposed by Zeng and Benatallah in [2]. It is distinguishable from our work in that we focus on the evaluation of risk cost for each task in the composition service in order to assign each task to the corresponding reliability requirement, and we have predefined transactional properties for each task according to specific business requirements. In the literature [17], the authors proposed a transactional approach for reliable WSCs by ensuring the failure atomicity required by the designers. A set of transactional rules had been defined to assist designers to compose a valid composite web service with regard to the specified accepted termination state (ATS). Its failure atomicity theory paves the way for our proposed formation rules of the failure-causing tree, which supports the evaluation of risk cost. In the literature [18], the authors explored WSC with transactional support. They orchestrated web services based on rules including both transactional behaviors and composition patterns.

## 17.7 Conclusions

Current QoS-driven service selection methods for WSC ignore the failure risk impact of each task, and few works focus on WSC with transactional properties. In this chapter, we have presented a risk-driven services selection method for WSC with transactional properties. In our method, a failure-causing tree has been proposed based on failure atomicity of CWS to evaluate risk losses for each task and attain the relative impact of each task in the transactional execution path of CWS. Then, a linear programming method based on the impact of each task in the execution path can be used to decide the requirement of reliability dimension for each task to support the selection of concrete web services. Actually, our method reaches the result proved by our experiment that can reduce average losses caused by failures of tasks in scientific computing applications, such as the ensemble prediction application. In future, we will apply our methods to the practical application of the Chinese Ensemble Prediction Application Grid to prove our conclusion further.

# References

1. L. J. Zhang and H. Cai, *Services Computing*. Springer Verlag and Tsinghua University Press, Beijing, China, 2007.
2. L. Zeng and B. Benatallah, QoS-Aware middleware for web services composition, *IEEE Transactions on Software Engineering*, 30(5), 311–327, 2004.
3. T. Yu and K. Lin, Service selection algorithms for composing complex services with multiple QoS constraints, in *ICSOC*, Amsterdam, the Netherlands. Springer, Heidelberg, Germany, pp. 130–143, 2005.
4. D. Ardagna and B. Pernici, Global and local QoS constraints guarantee in web service selection, in *ICWS*, Orlando, FL, IEEE Computer Society, Washington, DC, pp. 805–806, 2005.
5. V. Agarwal, G. Chafle, K. Dasgupta, A. Kumar, S. Mittal, and B. Srivastava, Synthy: A system for end to end composition of web services, *Journal of Web Semantics*, 3(4), 311–339, 2005.
6. W. van der Aalst, A. H. M. ter Hofstede, B. Kiepuszewski, and A. P. Barros, Workflow pattern, *Distributed and Parallel Databases*, 14(3), 5–51, 2003.
7. N. Kokash and V. D'Andrea, Evaluating quality of web services—A risk-driven approach, in *BIS 2007*, Poznań, Poland, 2007.
8. K. Ren, N. Xiao, J. Chen, and J. Song, A reverse order-based QoS constraint correction approach for optimizing execution path for service composition, in *16th International Conference on Cooperative Information Systems (Coopis 2008)*, Monterrey, Mexico, 2008.
9. H. Karloff, *Linear Programming*. Birkhauser, Berlin, Germany, 1991.
10. J. Cardoso, A. Sheth, J. Miller, J. Arnold, and K. Kochut, Quality of Service for workflows and web service processes, *Journal of Web Semantics*, 1(3), 281–308, 2004.
11. D. Ardagna and B. Pernici, Adaptive service composition in flexible processes, *IEEE Transaction on Software Engineering*, 33(6), 369–383, 2007.
12. X. Gu and K. Nahrstedt, On composing stream applications in environments, *IEEE Transactions on Parallel and Distributed Systems*, 17(8), 824–837, 2006.
13. J. Wu, F. Yang, QoS prediction for composite web services with transactions, in *ICSOC Workshops*, Chicago, IL, 2006.
14. N. Kokash, A service selection model to improve composition reliability, in *International Workshop on AI for Service Composition*, University of Trento, Trento, Italy, pp. 9–14, 2006.
15. Y. Asnar, P. Giorgini, F. Massacci, and N. Zannone, From trust to dependability through risk analysis, in *ARES 2007*, Vienna, Austria.

16. J. El Haddad, M. Manouvrier, G. Ramirez, and M. Rukoz, QoS-driven selection of web services for transactional composition, in *ICWS*, Salt Lake City, UT, pp. 653–660, 2007.
17. S. Bhiri, O. Perrin, and C. Godart, Ensuring required failure atomicity of composite web services, in *Proceedings of 14th International Conference on WWW 2005*, Chiba, Japan, 2005.
18. L. Li, C. Liu, and J. Wang, Deriving transactional properties of composite web services, in *ICWS*, Salt Lake City, UT, 2007.
19. L. M. Vaquero, L. Rodero-Merino, J. Caceres, and M. Linder, A break in the clouds: Towards a cloud definition, *ACM SIGCOMM Computer Communication Review*, 39(1), 50–55, 2009.
20. M. Armburst, A. Fox, R. Griffith, A. D. Joseph et al., Above the clouds: A Berkeley view of cloud computing, 2009.
21. G. Alonso, F. Casati, H. Kuno, and V. Machiraju, *Concepts, Architectures and Applications*, Springer Verlag, Berlin, Germany, 2004.
22. C. Liu, W. Zhang, Z. Luo, and Y. Zhong, A scientific-workflow-based execution environment for ensemble prediction, in *Proceedings of the 3rd International Conference on Grid and Pervasive Computing Workshops*, Kunming, China, May 2008.

# Index